DECLINE AND FALL

ALSO BY CHRIS MULLIN

Novels
A Very British Coup
The Last Man Out of Saigon
The Year of the Fire Monkey

Non-fiction
A View from the Foothills: The Diaries of Chris Mullin
Error of Judgement: The Truth about the Birmingham Bombings

DECLINE AND FALL

Diaries 2005–2010

Chris Mullin

edited by Ruth Winstone

PROFILE BOOKS

First published in Great Britain in 2010 by
PROFILE BOOKS LTD
3a Exmouth House
Pine Street
London EC1R 0JH
www.profilebooks.com

1 3 5 7 9 10 8 6 4 2

Text design by Sue Lamble
Typeset in Stone Serif by MacGuru Ltd
info@macguru.org.uk

Printed and bound in Great Britain by
Clays, Bungay, Suffolk

A CIP catalogue record for this book is available from the British Library.

ISBN 978 1 84668 399 2
eISBN 978 1 84765 290 4

The paper this book is printed on is certified by the © 1996 Forest Stewardship Council A.C. (FSC). It is ancient-forest friendly. The printer holds FSC chain of custody SGS-COC-2061

FSC
Mixed Sources
Product group from well-managed
forests and other controlled sources
Cert no. SGS-COC-2061
www.fsc.org
© 1996 Forest Stewardship Council

With love to Ngoc, Sarah and Emma;
in memory of Leslie and Teresa Mullin
and with gratitude to the people of Sunderland

CONTENTS

Acknowledgements

There are many people to whom I owe thanks. My constituents in Sunderland South for having allowed me the honour of representing them these past twenty-three years. The Sunderland South Labour Party for having allowed me to be their candidate through five general elections. My friends and erstwhile colleagues in Parliament, especially those I have unfairly traduced, for their unfailing good humour and for continuing to confide in me even though – indeed perhaps because – I am a diarist.

Above all, I owe thanks to Andrew Franklin and his team at Profile – Sarah Caro, Penny Daniel and Ruth Killick – for their energy, enthusiasm and professionalism. Finally, I must once again thank Ruth Winstone for cutting the manuscript down to size and for offering much useful advice.

Introduction

This is the second of what I hope will be a three-volume history of the rise and fall of New Labour. Like Alan Clark, I am publishing my diaries out of sequence. The first volume, *A View from the Foothills*, covered the period from July 1999, from the moment I was assumed into government, to 9 May 2005, when I was unceremoniously dismissed.

This volume describes the five years that followed. These years also marked a decline in my own political fortunes and the growing realisation that my useful life in politics was over. By now I no longer occupied any of the little vantage points from which I had observed – and from time to time played a part in – the political process. The only committee of any significance on which I sat was Standards and Privileges and since the deliberations of that committee, interesting though they were, are necessarily confidential the reader will not find them documented here.

Three main themes dominate the final years. First, the fall, for that is what it was, of the most successful leader in Labour history, paying the price for having linked us umbilically to the worst American president of my lifetime, with consequences that we all know about. Second, a largely but not entirely self-inflicted crisis of confidence in the entire political class, triggered by the Great Expenses Meltdown. Finally, the long, slow wobble to death of an exhausted government under a leader whose shortcomings were known, and indeed widely remarked upon, from the outset. The final act was played out against the background of a crisis of capitalism of such magnitude that for a while the entire global economy teetered on the edge of ruin. In between these great events, many small dramas and intrigues, public and personal, receive a passing mention in these pages.

In fairness, let it be said that it is doubtful that any leader could have won a fourth term, given the intensity of the storms that raged and the fact that after 13 years any government was vulnerable to the argument that it is time for a change. Let it also be recorded that it was decisive action by Gordon Brown and his Chancellor, Alistair Darling, in the autumn of 2008, by taking a controlling interest in several major banks, that prevented not merely a national but a global financial meltdown – a fact widely acknowledged abroad, but for some reason almost a secret in this country. That was the biggest political challenge of the twenty-first century, bar none, and he got it right. It may be that historians will be kinder to Gordon Brown than contemporary commentators – and indeed diarists.

Almost without exception, the most successful political diarists are people who have occupied the lower foothills. Perhaps because they have had time to look around and observe details that those who dwell in the stratosphere often fail to notice. And also because, not being significant players, we the humble inhabitants of the foothills do not have to waste time on self-justification. I like to think that I am in this category, though that is for others to judge.

Some who read my first volume have chosen to interpret it as evidence that all ministerial life is pointless. I do not accept this. There is a huge variation in the junior ministerial jobs. Much depends on whether you have a Secretary of State who is willing to delegate. My two years at the Foreign Office, under the management of Jack Straw, were among the happiest of my political life.

There is also a danger that readers of this volume may conclude that, because it charts the last days of an administration in decline, the New Labour era was an unmitigated failure. I do not accept this either. I have only to look at the lives of my least prosperous constituents to see that most have benefited significantly from 13 years of Labour government. It is all too easy to forget that, by the end of the Thatcher decade, male unemployment in Sunderland stood at well over 20 per cent; today it is less than half that. Contrary to what is sometimes alleged, we did redistribute some wealth, although perhaps we kept rather too quiet about it for fear of upsetting the meaner elements of the middle classes. We invested significantly in health, education and other public services, with results that are plain for anyone with eyes to see. In 1997 you could wait up to two years for a hip operation at City Hospital Sunderland; at the time of writing the waiting time is 18 weeks and falling. At Sandhill View, a secondary school in my constituency, in the early nineties fewer than 10 per cent of pupils were achieving the standard five GCSEs at grades A to C; today that figure is nearly 80 per cent. There are many other examples I could cite. No one can tell me that Labour governments don't make a difference.

This, then, is the sequel to *A View from the Foothills*. It starts exactly where the earlier volume left off – on the day after my dismissal from government.

Chris Mullin
July 2010

CHAPTER ONE

May–December
2005

Tuesday, 10 May
Sunderland

Up before six, unable to sleep. Veering between disappointment and anger. A hammer blow to my fragile self-esteem. For two years I have been kidding myself that I'd been doing something useful … Just before nine, the Number 10 switchboard rang with message to ring Jack Straw, but I was in no hurry to return his call and anyway Emma was in the middle of one of her massive nose bleeds.

To the office, where Pat and I sorted through boxes of redundant election literature for recycling. At about eleven Jack rang again. This time coming straight through. I didn't attempt to hide my feelings. 'Don't be bitter,' he said. No, indeed. Forward not back, as they say in New Labour. 'We are still mates, aren't we?' I assured him that we were, but try as I may I cannot suppress the feeling that he had a hand in this, if only by not offering sufficient resistance. My successor is Dave Triesman (who a few years back was eased out of the General Secretaryship of the Labour Party and into the Lords) thereby becoming the *sixth* Africa minister in eight years. Pure madness. We say we take Africa seriously, but we don't.

'Eccentric to say the least,' said Jack. 'Not the reshuffle I would have done.'

In the afternoon I caught the train to London. On the station at Sunderland a man from South Shields shook my hand warmly, saying he had just re-read *Error of Judgement*. He added, 'I voted for Labour, but not for Blair. That man is detested.' He repeated the word several times. 'The sooner he goes, the better.'

How quickly the waters close. This morning I rang the FCO to discuss the return of my personal effects. 'Lord Triesman's office,' answered a cheery voice.

'Can I speak to Bharat?'

'He's gone to collect the Minister, in the car.'

Car, eh? That's going to cost them an extra £60,000.

Wednesday, 11 May

To a jam-packed meeting of the Parliamentary Labour Party in Committee Room 14. A large press pack hovering in the corridor outside. The Man gave another of his bravura performances, which, with notable exceptions, was received with rapture. The trouble is we are in new territory now. Bravura performances are not enough any more. The euphoria was quickly punctured. Peter Kilfoyle was first up, talking of the need for sober reflection in the light of the fact that four million votes had gone missing since 1997. He won a few brave hear-hears. Then Geraldine Smith said that the leadership question needed to be resolved sooner rather than later. Michael Meacher called for 'a more collegiate, less presidential style'. Bob Marshall-Andrews talked of 'a rising tide of disaffection' and 'gross abuse of powers of patronage'. Then Glenda Jackson, looking miserable and angry as always (goodness knows what she won her Oscar for; certainly not charm), said, 'I didn't fight the Lib Dems and the Tories during the election. I had to fight you.' This provoked cries of 'disgraceful' and was followed by an unhelpful contribution from Claire Curtis-Thomas, who told the dissidents 'to go and find another party' (the last thing we need). There was no shortage of people to speak up for The Man or at least to warn against a war of attrition (not quite the same thing). Frank Field, who has suddenly come over all loyal, warned against an immediate change of leadership, talking of the election result being a contract with the electorate. Frank Dobson harked back to the vanished four million. Many people, he said, were telling him they would not vote Labour again while Tony Blair remained leader. 'We are standing on a very shallow beach. If we regard the recent election result as an endorsement of our policies on health and education etc., we are in danger of remaining on nine and a half million votes while the Tories don't.' Robin Cook, who was waving his arm furiously, failed to catch Ann Clwyd's eye.

The Man responded robustly. He stressed the need to remain on the centre ground, pointing out, fairly, that some – but not all – of his critics had been agin him for years. He conceded, however, that the end was in sight. 'I know you need to have a stable and orderly transition. Please allow us to bring that about so that we win a fourth election.' His best line: a glancing reference to Roy Hattersley, in whose Treasury team he had served in the eighties and who is now calling for his head; and then: 'I was loyal throughout three defeats. All I ask is a bit of loyalty throughout three victories.' Huge cheering. He departed to a standing ovation in which a small, but significant, minority, seated around Frank Dobson and Robin Cook, did not participate.

Thursday, 12 May

Hilary Benn was the first person I ran into this morning. The reshuffle, he said, was a shambles. No one even bothered to tell Gareth Thomaś, his Under-Secretary, that he was still in the job. Hilary had to ring Number 10 to find out. Later I heard that someone ran their eye down the list of new ministers at the crassly re-christened Department of Industry, Productivity and Energy and noticed there were no women, so out of the blue it was decided to add Meg Munn (to do goodness knows what), but since the ministerial allocation was used up, there is no money to pay her. The same happened with Michael Wills at the Home Office a while ago. Whatever else he's good at, personnel management isn't The Man's strong suit.

Lunch in the cafeteria with my erstwhile Assistant Private Secretary, Caron Rohsler, who came in with some of my personal effects and a card inside which everyone in the office had inscribed friendly messages.

Sunday, 15 May

To Chillingham for lunch with Humphry and Katherine Wakefield. About 20 guests, including Sir Richard Storey, the Baker-Cresswells, a delicate young Percy, a cousin of the Duke (who looked and sounded as though he had stepped straight from the set of *Brideshead Revisited*), and Nancy Lambton, a relative of the notorious Tony. She was formerly Professor of Persian at the School of Oriental and African Studies, 93 years old and bright as a button. Afterwards I peeped into the walled garden, silent and derelict as always, and reflected briefly on what might have been.

Back to Alnwick along the back road. The Till valley stunning in the evening sunshine.

Monday, 16 May

At the Members' Entrance this morning I was talking to Mike O'Brien, now Solicitor General, when a small, bald man who I didn't recognise from Adam tumbled out of a taxi and began chatting. Suddenly it dawned on me that he was not just a Member, but a newly appointed minister. I racked my brain, but try as I may I couldn't put a name to him.

'Who was that?' I asked after he had gone.

'Liam Byrne, he won the Hodge Hill by-election. He's just been appointed to the Department of Health.' One of the infinite supply of special advisers who have been shoe-horned into safe seats and who, before you can say 'New Labour', are wafted into government over the heads of we poor inadequates who have laboured for years in the salt mines. Is it just me or is there something not quite right about this?

At the meeting of the parliamentary party this evening I asked Geoff Hoon for an assurance that Parliament would have an opportunity to discuss plans for a new generation of nuclear weapons before any irrevocable decisions were made. Needless to say I didn't get one. Unless I am mistaken he looked a bit uncomfortable. I sense I have hit upon a rich furrow. I will plough further.

Tuesday, 17 May

The State Opening. A record 45 new bills. Ludicrous. A lot of vague talk about 'respect' and other concepts that can't easily be legislated for. I stayed for the opening speeches in the debate and then set off to a conference on Africa at Wilton Park in Sussex.

Wednesday, 18 May
Wilton Park

Up before six, I followed a path through the garden and (in glorious sunshine) out onto a footpath which led up through ancient woodland and onto the South Downs Way. A lone deer leapt out of a hedge and stood staring for a full minute before going into reverse gear. From the top, fine views across unspoiled countryside to the sea. I walked up to and around the Chanctonbury Ring and was back at the house in time for breakfast. There is much to be said for this conference lark.

Thursday, 19 May

Slept well for the first time in ten days and awoke feeling refreshed. To the House. I was wondering what I would do all day but in the event there wasn't a minute to spare. I went in for Geoff Hoon's first business statement as Leader of the House, at which he announced an outrageous 81-day summer recess. Why should we let the government award itself a three-month holiday from scrutiny? I protested vigorously, receiving the usual bland reply. Mine was the only intervention on our side, a point much remarked upon by the Tories. If MPs are not interested in Parliament, why should anyone else be? I went to the library and looked up the Modernisation Committee report which introduced September sittings. Sure enough, the deal was that sittings were to be aligned with school holidays 'in return for' (to quote Robin Cook) a two-week sitting in September. Well, it hasn't take long for the powers-that-be to renege on their part of the bargain.

Monday, 23 May
Sunderland

Awoke at 4.30am; unable to get back to sleep so I went downstairs and took a sleeping pill; something I have never done before, except on long-haul flights. After that I slept soundly until just after eight and awoke feeling groggy.

I notice the former special advisers tend to stick together in the Tea Room; some have already developed the short attention spans one associates with the upwardly mobile. Before the year is out they'll all be in government. There's a sort of first- and standard-class developing. Not for those in the first-class carriage the disappointments of opposition; most have never, nor will they ever (in public at least), ask a question that betrays even a hint of scepticism about the official version of events. All bright and personable, I'm sure, but oughtn't they be required to remain on the backbenches long enough to make a ripple or two before zooming away into the stratosphere?

Alternatively, perhaps we should adopt the American system, where the government consists of Friends of The Man and where scrutiny is an entirely separate function. That at least would spare us the inconvenience, resentment and inevitable abuse of patronage occasioned by the need to find seats in either the Lords or Commons for those on the inside track.

At six I went across to Number 10 for my farewell audience with The Man. A mite apprehensive. He was, as ever, all sweetness and light, but I emerged 15 minutes later none the wiser as to why I had been got rid of. He asked what I wanted to do. I mentioned a place on either the International Development or Foreign Affairs select committee and he looked meaningfully at his PPS, Keith Hill, as if to say, 'See what you can do' (not that the composition of select committees should be any of his business). Then, to my amazement, he said, 'Would you like to be my Africa envoy?' He went on, 'There will be a lot of running around to do after the G8 summit. All sorts of people want to see me and I don't have time to see all of them. An envoy carries more weight than a junior minister.' He mentioned Lord Levy and Brian Wilson.

'What about Dave Triesman? Surely that's his job.'

He then said something amazing. 'There's no longer an Africa minister as such. Dave has to do everything in the Lords. He won't be able to travel as much as you did.'

'You jammy bugger,' said Keith, putting his arm over my shoulder when we were outside in the corridor. Later, he told me that he had reported the conversation to Sally Morgan and she had responded, 'Whaaat?' Meaning presumably that The Man consulted no one before making his offer – if indeed that is what it was. I very much doubt whether anything will come of it. I am not holding my breath.

Tuesday, 24 May

Ran into Alan Howarth (former MP for Newport, now a Noble Lord) on Millbank, who offered sympathy at my untimely demise. 'The caprice of autocrats in our democratic system ... how very African.'

In the evening to a reception at Marlborough House, where I was showered with commiserations by a number of old Africa hands. Then to a BBC party in the atrium at 4 Millbank, where I had a long talk about Iraq with John Simpson. He visits every two months or so and says it's getting worse ('A civil war between the Sunni and the Shia has begun'). He thinks the Americans will retreat into seven or eight huge fortified compounds and that we will be stuck there for years. Like me, he was against the war at the outset, but thought they'd get away with it. I bent his ear about America's secret gulag and he expressed interest, leaving me his email address. I will follow this up.

Wednesday, 25 May

A coffee with one of the special advisers who is just back from visiting Washington with Jack, who had meetings with Condi, Cheney, Rumsfeld and Bush. He says Rumsfeld and Cheney are 'delusional' re Iraq. Condi, contrary to rumour, is not a cipher and does appear to have a mind of her own. The Americans are not interested in Africa. There is no way they are going to sign up to our G8 agenda on aid, finance or climate change.

Thursday, 26 May

To Heybridge to see Mum. She has another damn infection; only a question of time before there is another fall. We chatted cheerfully for almost four hours, during the course of which she remarked, very matter of factly (no trace of self-pity), 'It won't be for much longer.'

Friday, 27 May
Sunderland

A pile of *Echo*s awaited. This week's lead headlines:

> Saturday: 'BALLY: MAN IN COURT (stabbing accused charged with murder)'
> Monday: 'TUNNEL OF FEAR – yobs turn subway into tunnel of fear'
> Tuesday: '200 STITCHES – woman's eye repaired after glassing attack'
> Wednesday: 'BULLDOZED – treasured piece of heritage reduced to rubble'
> Thursday: 'ENOUGH: police pledge on drunken louts who bring terror to City's streets'
> Friday: 'THE FACE OF PUB VIOLENCE (the shocking picture that shows why it's time to get tough)'

Saturday, 28 May
The Holmes, Roxburghshire

Loaded up the car and headed for The Holmes. A world apart. Everything in its place. Peacocks, geese, a dozen varieties of chicken, numerous donkeys, horses and a couple of llamas who had a three-day-old baby, already skipping unsteadily around the big field in the wake of her mother. And of course, presiding over the entire menagerie, white-haired Mrs Dale, vigorous as ever.

Monday, 30 May

To the House of the Binns, home (since 1612) of the Dalyells, only to find that it isn't due to open for another couple of days. Disappointed, we climbed up to the folly behind the house and spent an hour enjoying the spectacular views over the Firth of Forth and were just about to leave when a woman, who from a distance I at first took to be Kathleen, emerged from The Big Hoose. In the event she was a cleaning lady who was with difficulty persuaded to concede that Tam might be in residence and showed me round to the back, where I rang the doorbell, which was answered by Kathleen. She had just returned from collecting Tam from the airport and they were about to set out again for Stirling. Much to my embarrassment she invited us in, sat us down at the kitchen table, gave us tea and cherry cake, roused Tam from his afternoon snooze and then insisted on giving us a tour of the house, which is a gem. Tam, who isn't in the best of health, didn't look well and I worried throughout that we might be responsible for his premature demise. Next time, I will give plenty of notice.

Tuesday, 31 May
The Holmes, Roxburghshire

Raining lightly. I walked along the river and up through the woods to Bemersyde for my annual general meeting with Dawyck Haig. Alert and sprightly as ever, he insisted on the usual glass of sherry and we sat in his magnificent drawing room discussing the state of the Tory party and the future of the EU Constitution (the French having just delivered a resounding 'Non') and the doings of his neighbours. Then he showed me out across the garden, to a back gate leading into a field and connecting with the footpath that leads back to Dryburgh, via the Wallace monument.

Wednesday, 1 June

Rain all day. The Eildons invisible. We took the girls for a riding lesson near Selkirk and then drove to see Robert Owen's mills at New Lanark, beautifully restored and displayed and so moving to think what that great man inspired. How would he wish to be remembered? As a socialist, an enlightened capitalist or a mixture of both? Whatever, his message is as relevant today as it was 200 years ago. Namely, that it is possible to make a healthy profit without grinding the noses of your workers into the dirt. Globalisers, please note.

Saturday, 4 June
Sunderland

We meandered home via Scott's View, Dundock Wood, the Hirsel and tea at Bamburgh with Charles and Barbara Baker-Cresswell. The weather held until just after three, when we were caught in torrential rain. So heavy that we had to pull over at Paxton until the worst had passed. Among the letters awaiting my return, a handwritten note from the Ethiopian Prime Minister, Meles Zenawi: 'I am deeply saddened to learn that you have been replaced as Africa minister. I had stayed up late at night to listen to your victory speech ... and I had hoped and assumed that your tenure ... would be much longer.'

Monday, 6 June

Janet Anderson remarked to me in passing today that The Man attaches no importance to the junior jobs. 'He regards them as sweeties to be handed out to keep the children happy.'

Tuesday, 7 June

Huge relief at the decision to dispense with the EU referendum, although Jack made the announcement with an entirely straight face. With one leap we are freed from the prospect of months of trench warfare trying to ram through an enabling Bill, followed by inevitable humiliation at the ballot box. At the meeting of the parliamentary party last night someone remarked, 'Whoever persuaded the Prime Minister to opt for a referendum was either a far-sighted genius or a complete fool.'

In the evening to a party at the Department for International

Development for the launch of their annual report. Hilary Benn presided, but disappeared upstairs to make an urgent call to Meles Zenawi about the election crisis in Ethiopia (the opposition won an unexpectedly large share of the vote, sparking angry demonstrations and a violent over-reaction from the police). Suma Chakrabati, the permanent secretary, remarked that it wasn't sensible to dispense with the Africa minister: 'Hilary is having to make the call because there is no one at the Foreign Office available to do so.'

Wednesday, 8 June

Norine MacDonald and her colleagues, Emmanuel Reinert and Fabrice Pothier, came to tell me about a programme they are running in Afghanistan. Norine is more or less based there now. The plan is to wean the Americans and the UN agencies off poppy eradication and instead persuade them to license opium and use it as a source of heroin for medical use. At present the American Drug Enforcement Agency is in charge and, as usual, they are only able think in terms of 'a drug war'. So far, according to Norine, they have eradicated about 50 hectares at a cost of eight lives and 150 million dollars. She says that, if they carry on with forced eradication, there will be serious instability. The reality is there are no alternative livelihoods available for most people. She wants me to try and interest HMG in her scheme to grow opium for medicinal purposes.

Lunch with Dave Triesman, the lucky man who now occupies 'my' grand office overlooking the Durbar Court. A delightful, warm, decent fellow; almost apologetic about what happened, even though he isn't in any way implicated. He and Jack have been friends since their student days, which is why, I suppose, Jack offered no resistance.

Later, Hilary Benn recounted last night's half-hour phone call with my friend Meles Zenawi, who was talking ominously of arresting the opposition leaders for 'treason'. It seems that the ruling party has lost control of all the cities, including Addis. The results still haven't been officially announced even though it is nearly a month since the election and there are the inevitable opposition claims of fraud.

Hilary, needless to say, urged restraint and is going to Addis next week to underline the message. Oh dear, it looks as if another of our favourite Africans is on the wobble.

Tuesday, 14 June

To Sunderland and back to give evidence at our appeal against the decision of the Boundary Commission to dismantle Sunderland South. My appearance before the inquiry took all of 15 minutes. A five-minute statement, followed by ten minutes of questioning by the barrister representing the Tories. On paper we ought to have a strong case. The Commission's terms of reference stipulate minimum disruption and their proposals will cause maximum disruption. They are also supposed to pay heed to existing communities and what they are proposing is to weld together two entirely different communities, separated by the huge canyon of the A19. However, the Commission also has an over-riding duty to even out the numbers and, as Greg Cook (who led for our side) pointed out afterwards, our alternative proposal would create the second largest constituency in the country (after the Isle of Wight). So, my guess is that we will lose and I will be saddled with a seat that the Tories could win next time. An inglorious end to my 23 years in Parliament. I sense I am on a downward trajectory.

Wednesday, 15 June

Another little reshuffle story: Charlotte Atkins, who was aviation minister for a mere seven months, didn't even receive a call to tell her that she was out. The Number 10 apparatchiks simply forgot that she existed. She was remarkably relaxed when I ran into her in the library and said that in any case she has since received a profuse apology from The Man, but doesn't that say it all? What is the point of making someone a minister for only seven months, unless they make a disastrous hash of it, which Charlotte didn't. She said, 'I was just beginning to ask questions about night flights.' Exactly the point I got to. No wonder the mighty vested interests at the heart of the aviation industry don't take us seriously; what have they to fear?

An amusing exchange with Jim Murphy, formerly PPS in the Foreign Office, now an odd-job man at the bottom end of JP's empire. Among other things, he is in charge of addressing 'the perception gap' (another phrase for my New Labour lexicon) i.e. the fact that many of our constituents don't believe a word we say. I suggested a couple of simple measures which might make a difference: (1) no 81-day summer recess, (2) junior ministers should stop riding around in official cars at £60,000 a time (Jim is also in charge of the government car service). To which I might have added: no more dodgy dossiers and no more swearing blind in your election manifesto that you will not introduce top-up fees ... and then promptly doing just that. It's not rocket science.

Thursday, 16 June

To Heybridge to see Mum. Frail as ever, but remarkably cheerful considering her plight. We talked mainly about the old days. Her first day at work in 1935, aged 15. Uncle Cyril delivered her to the front entrance of Electra House on the Thames Embankment in his gleaming new car, the only one in Ripley Road. The doorman, assuming she must be important, ushered her upstairs in the executive lift, tea was offered ... Only to be withdrawn when it was discovered that she was starting work as a messenger in the typing pool, at which point she was curtly informed that, in future, she should enter by the staff entrance, round the corner in Arundel Street.

Sunday, 19 June

Father's Day. The girls presented me with home-made cards. Emma's consists of a picture of a flashy car ('hint, hint'), interspersed with symbols of the things I care about (a spade, a bluebell, a sign pointing to a walled garden). Sarah's depicts me reclining in a swimming pool while she is dangling before me grapes on a fishing rod and Emma is offering a tray with a cool drink. Ngoc, meanwhile, is in the corner chatting on her mobile. Truly, I am a lucky man.

Tuesday, 21 June

A pleasant lunch with Bruce Grocott at which we reflected on the excesses of New Labour and the folly of Iraq. ('What made him do it when no one, but no one, was pressing?') According to Bruce, The Man is conditioned by his experience in Hackney in the eighties to believe that the Labour Party is always wrong when, on this occasion at least, the instincts of the dear old Labour Party happened to be spot on.

The Aye Lobby, 10.15pm

A brief exchange with Alan Milburn, who says The Man is in excellent spirits and will hang on for three years 'at least'. If so, how will Gordon and his playmates react? Actually, it is probably in Gordon's interests to take over a year or so before an election is due, as Major did in '92, so that he can be represented as a new broom. 'That's the rational response,' says Alan, 'but with Gordon the rational always vies with the irrational. One thing is certain: history will not look kindly on anyone who wields the assassin's knife.' He added, 'There is a lot of complacency about. If David Davis becomes leader – as looks likely – the Tories could get their act together and give us a run for our money.' Does Alan still hanker after the top job? I suspect he may. After all – as I pointed out and as Alan readily agreed – his upbringing is remarkably similar to that of David Davis.

Wednesday, 22 June

To the Athenaeum for lunch with Jonathan Steele of the *Guardian*. Like just about everyone else I talk to who has first-hand experience of Iraq, Jonathan says the violence is getting worse; in his view the only hope of restoring stability is a phased withdrawal of US troops. Later, on the terrace at the House, I had a long talk with Ann Clwyd, who has spent the day with Jack in Brussels, at an Iraq donor conference. To my surprise, she agreed with Jonathan that a phased withdrawal may help to reduce the violence and says one is already being planned. However, she says it can't even be hinted at until the

December elections are out of the way and the trials of Saddam and his cronies are over. On the latter, she says the Iraqis are determined to execute at least the top ten Ba'athists, but she is worried at the lack of protection being offered to witnesses and even to the judges and prosecutors and their families, all of whom are at risk

Thursday, 23 June

Temperature in the nineties for the third day running.

Clive Stafford Smith, a lawyer representing some of those interned at Guantanamo, came in, together with Stephen Grey, a journalist who used to work for the *Sunday Times*. They want me to press the government to take back those who were British residents, but not citizens, before their arrest; otherwise they are likely to be sent back to their countries of origin, which could result in death or torture. We also talked about the secret gulag into which alleged terrorists, some kidnapped in broad daylight from the streets of Europe, are disappearing. Apparently, they are being franchised out to torturers in Syria, Libya, Morocco, Egypt. I am keen to be helpful, but nervous about being too upfront given (a) that some of these people undoubtedly are terrorists and (b) the hysteria that was organised against me when I took up similar cases in the past.

Monday, 27 June

Charles Clarke made a statement about the continuing deportations of failed asylum seekers to Zimbabwe. A spectacular bout of hypocrisy from the Tories, and their leader-in-waiting David Davis, demanding that all removals to Zimbabwe cease forthwith. Who, watching this extraordinary display, would guess that this is a party that has just fought an election campaign in which the return of every last failed asylum seeker was a major plank? Davis was particularly shameless. Later, I came across him at the BBC and said that from now on I was proposing to refer to him as Shameless of Haltemprice.

The front page headline in today's *Daily Mail* is headed, apropos Zimbabwe asylum seekers, 'FOR PITY'S SAKE LET THEM STAY'. It makes one's stomach turn.

Tuesday, 28 June

Lunch with John Simpson. I like him. A mega-star making an effort to be modest. He asked about my days at the BBC and seemed genuinely interested in my opinions. John says the Americans cannot win in Iraq and that the only question is the manner of their exit. He thinks they should hand over to the UN – but who is to say that the UN won't come under attack, too? Then to the chamber to hear Charles Clarke introduce the ID cards Bill. Never have I seen a minister more intervened upon, but to everyone he responded calmly and courteously. Deep unease about ID cards. Not so much the civil liberties implications as about whether or not the technology will work and what it will cost. A whiff of doom about the whole enterprise. No way will it go through the Lords, except by force. If there were a free vote, it wouldn't get through the Commons either.

This evening, my long-awaited, much rearranged audience with Jack. A glass of wine in his room at the House while a spectacular electric thunderstorm raged outside. 'There was no animus, Chris. You just fell off the end. I know you think I could have saved you, but I couldn't.'

I recounted my 'Africa envoy' conversation, making clear that I didn't believe that anything would come of it. Jack wanted to know The Man's exact words. He seemed to take it more seriously than I, but is well aware of The Main Person's tendency to scatter vague promises like confetti. 'Tony's like a man who says, "I love you" to seven, eight, nine, ten women and they all go away feeling happy until they start to compare notes.' That nicely sums up The Man. For the record, Jack thinks he won't go until '07 at the earliest.

Wednesday, 29 June

My first caller this morning was Andrew Gilligan, a man with whom one must sup with a very long spoon. He's making a follow-up to his earlier programme on extraordinary rendition for Channel Four and is looking for evidence of British government complicity ('We haven't got any yet, but we're hopeful of finding some by the time the programme goes out').

Dinner in the Strangers' Dining Room with John Gilbert. He expressed disappointment that I have no interest in coming to the Lords. 'Whatever happens you must find something to do. Otherwise slowly, inexorably, imperceptibly you will go into terminal decline.'

I asked why we needed a new generation of nuclear weapons (a subject about which I pressed The Man at Questions today). John, needless to say, is strongly in favour.

'Why?'

'One word, dear boy: France. There's not the slightest chance of our getting rid of nuclear weapons while France has them.'

I hadn't realised our case was so weak.

Thursday, 30 June

Sat through most of the Africa debate. Hilary made a brilliant opening and Andrew Mitchell for the Tories was good, too. I had intended to speak, but when Hilary left after three hours I lost the will to go on and asked the Deputy Speaker to take my name off the list. Result: most of the day wasted. I should have gone to see Mum instead.

My meteoric downfall continues apace. According to Ann Cryer, who sits on the parliamentary committee, my name doesn't even feature on the list of proposed members for either the foreign affairs or international development committees. All that now remains is for the Boundary Commission to take away my seat and my humiliation will be complete. If I didn't have a family to support, I would get out …

Friday, 1 July
Sunderland

To Penshaw, where, along with a thousand or so others, I helped to form a circle around the monument – Sunderland's contribution to making poverty history. A light aeroplane came over and photographed us. To my surprise and mild irritation George Galloway was there, trailed by a BBC television crew. A set-up? Are we about to become extras in a broadcast on behalf of the Respect party?

'What's George doing here?' I inquired of one of the organisers.

'Oh, we wanted a fair spread across the political spectrum,' he replied shiftily.

'Why, in that case, didn't you invite the Ulster Unionists and the Welsh Nationalists as well?'

No reply, beyond a smirk.

Sure enough, come the speeches, George launched into a scathing attack on the G8 and all its works. Classic, rabble-rousing, easy politics. The sort of stuff George does brilliantly, although it didn't go down quite as well as I expected. A number of people walked away.

Monday, 4 July

Some fun at Defence questions. I teamed up with several Tory Friends of the Bomb in an attempt to persuade John Reid to come clean about plans for a new generation of nuclear weapons. Michael Gove, a recently elected young Tory fogey, started the ball rolling and I came in from our side, after which the exchange acquired a life of its own and Reid became slightly ratty. I have raised the subject half a dozen times so far and I'm determined to keep at it until the powers-that-be come clean. One doesn't have to be a CNDer to entertain the possibility that there are better things to do with £10 billion or whatever they are proposing to spend on a successor to Trident. I bet a fair swathe of the military top brass take that view, too.

Wednesday, 6 July

To the Gay Hussar for lunch. I boarded a 24 bus, but before it had gone far it became ensnared in traffic so I got off and walked. As I reached Trafalgar Square a great cheer went up, strips of coloured paper began to shower down from the sky and the bells of St Martin-in-the-Fields began to toll: London has been chosen for the 2012 Olympics.

Later, I ran into The Man's Man, Keith Hill, who was in even better humour than usual. 'This will do wonders for The Man's street cred,' I said.

'Indeed. You know what they're saying?'

'Tell me'

'Four more years.' He held up the fingers of his right hand and disappeared down the corridor, cackling.

Thursday, 7 July

Olympic euphoria was short-lived. Bombs have gone off all over London, on Underground trains at Aldgate, King's Cross and Edgware Road and on the top deck of a bus at Tavistock Square.

I arrived at Hampstead Underground just after nine to find a jam-packed train, doors open, sitting in the station. At this stage there was no inkling of what had happened. Then a London Underground employee in a blue blazer came and announced that the station was being evacuated due to 'a power surge'. Several people ranted. In particular a well-dressed man who said he was from Greece (as if the Greeks have anything to teach us about the smooth-running of public services) and a red-headed yob who demanded to know how he was going to get to work in Knightsbridge. The Underground man, an Asian, kept his cool admirably.

Outside, still no clue as to what was happening, I walked down the hill and boarded a 24 bus which meandered for about a mile before being turned back at the far end of Camden High Street. Someone said something about a bomb. I got off and started walking. Gradually the traffic dried up. Euston Road was sealed. Police were letting through only ambulances and other emergency vehicles in the direction of King's Cross. Wailing sirens everywhere. I crossed into Tottenham Court Road. People were clustered round shop windows displaying television sets which were showing scenes of chaos just a few hundred yards away. Looking left into Bloomsbury, the side streets were taped off. At Trafalgar Square I came across Sir George Young on his bicycle. 'My visit to the Cheadle by-election has been called off,' he said, feigning disappointment.

By the time I reached the House it was clear that we had a catastrophe on our hands. For a while, proceedings carried on as usual. The whips put the word around that we should string out Business questions for as long as possible in order to give Charles Clarke a chance to put his statement together, but eventually the Speaker suspended the sitting. In due course Charles appeared and delivered a short, sombre statement, thin on detail since the full facts were not yet known. No one pressed him and there was no grand-standing. It was announced that The Man was on his way back from the G8 at Gleneagles to chair COBRA (the Cabinet committee in charge of emergencies). Then back to normal business – a debate on defence. I had intended to harass John Reid on nuclear weapons, but in the circumstances decided not to. The highlight was a coruscating speech from George Galloway, the gist of which was that we had brought all the bombings on ourselves as a result of our association with the American adventures in Iraq and Afghanistan. Vintage George, delivered unfalteringly, without a piece of paper in sight. And to avoid giving ammunition to his many enemies he went out of his way repeatedly to condemn the bombings. He was heard in uncomfortable silence by all save one foolish new Tory who was contemptuously brushed aside. The problem with George's thesis, of course, is that 9/11 preceded the occupations of Afghanistan and Iraq. Even so, it would take a brave man to assert that we would have been attacked today had we not gone into Iraq. Later, George Bush was on television, prattling about evil men who kill innocent people and I couldn't help thinking of that picture of a distraught father grieving over the half-dozen – or was it eight – little bodies of his children after one of Bush's bombs went astray over Kabul.

All day long we went about our business accompanied by the distant wail of sirens. By evening St Pancras, but not King's Cross, was reported open. There was no Underground and only a handful of buses so I set out on foot, towing my little bag behind me, through Embankment Gardens and up through the Inns of Court. At the top of Chancery Lane, a loud bang. Everyone froze – the silence audible – and then we relaxed as it became clear that it was a controlled explosion. A policeman waved us quickly across Holborn, which was sealed to traffic; so was the Euston Road. I reached St Pancras at about a quarter to seven to find it, too, was closed, but I hung around with a crowd of other pedestrians and after a while we were allowed through. From St Pancras I caught a (nearly empty) train to Doncaster by way of Sheffield, arriving at about eleven. Only half a dozen people waiting. The digital signboard indicated no more trains, but the station staff assured us they were expecting one about midnight and in due course a train appeared. Reached Durham at 1.30am and took a taxi home. The taxi driver was reporting 50 dead and hundreds of casualties. 'The chin-wag is that it was the French,' he said with apparent sincerity. 'I wouldn't put anything past that Chirac.'

Sunday, 10 July
Helions Bumpstead, Essex

Mum's 85th birthday. Probably her last. Liz laid on a magnificent spread. All four of us children and all but one grandchild showed up. As usual the girls produced their own cards. Emma's showing Granny as Queen, a flag flying at full mast over her palace; Sarah's showed Mum on top of Ben Nevis, which in a moment of madness she walked up 30 years ago, despite her crippled feet. Mum frail, but generally competent, although as the afternoon wore on she did lapse into occasional nonsense; by evening she was looking tired, but happy. Great heat – temperature in the thirties; it wasn't until the shadow passed over Liz's garden in the early evening that we were able to sit outside.

Monday, 11 July

To London – with trepidation since the organisers of last week's outrages are still thought to be at large. At King's Cross the entrance to the Underground was sealed; a sign directed passengers to Euston. On road signs and railings around the station home-made posters of the 'missing' put up by desperate relatives. One a picture of a bright-faced, dark-haired young woman called Miriam, no doubt the apple of her parents' eye, 'last heard of being evacuated from King's Cross ...'

At four The Man made a statement which was greeted by a huge bout of me-too-ism from all sides. Even Michael Howard was lavish in his praise. After an hour one almost longed for a George Galloway to get up and puncture the complacency.

At the meeting of the parliamentary party the names of the new select committee members were read out by Hilary. As expected, mine was not among them. Despite the improvements prompted by last year's uprising, the selection process remains deeply unsatisfactory; the executive still has the biggest say as to who will scrutinise it.

This evening in the Tea Room, John Prescott remarked that our Olympic bid is seriously underfunded. 'I warned them that if we got it, we'd have to find a lot more money.' He said that the sports minister, Richard Caborn, had asked ministers in several countries that had recently hosted the Olympics what they would have done differently and they all said they should have got the budget right to start with.

Tuesday, 12 July

A young man called Abdul came to help resolve a glitch in my printer. He said that all the IT on the parliamentary estate is soon to be upgraded. I asked what will happen to the old stuff. His reply was shocking: 'It will be thrown away.'

'Recycled, surely?'

'No. It's not worth sending to the Third World and the parts aren't worth re-using. It will go into landfill. The same happens with old mobile phones. There are two for every adult in Europe.'

In-fucking-sanity. We will be cursed by future generations.

The police appear to have identified three of the four perpetrators of last week's bombings. All British citizens, born and bred in Leeds; two of them young. The implications are not hard to grasp – the virus of Islamist terror has taken root in British soil.

Wednesday, 13 July

Another blazing-hot day.

With Sheila Williams to Hampstead to see dear old Michael Foot. We found him seated at the table in his basement, French doors opened onto a secluded, sunny garden. One-eyed, lopsided, wild-haired, but absolutely sound of mind. Books, old and new (letters and cuttings protruding), piled on tables, sideboard, floor, everywhere. No effort to disguise his disenchantment with the regime – a half-page newspaper photograph of Gordon Brown was taped to the mantelpiece behind him. He greets me like a long lost friend. Odd that he should take such a shine to me after the battles of the eighties. I owe Sheila for putting him right. He commiserates over my loss of office. 'You were just about the only member of the government who I haven't heard say something stupid.' Half an hour is spent bemoaning the *Daily Mail* ('the forger's gazette'), which recently serialised a salacious biography of Jill. Sheila urges him not to respond, but he is clearly tempted. Later Ian Aitken rings with the same advice, but Michael keeps returning to the subject, clearly upset. He also complains about a book on H. G. Wells which makes the great man out to be bitter and curmudgeonly in his final years. 'Nonsense. I knew him very well. He wasn't like that at all.'

What a wonderful arrangement this is. Michael, 92 next week, is determined to die in his own home, surrounded by his books, papers and mementoes. A succession of carers look after him, working ten-day shifts. Molly, who once worked in the Cabinet Office, is on duty today. Sheila showed me his library upstairs, full of rare first editions. And Jill's study, also piled high (even the fireplace is book-lined). Incredibly, Michael still sleeps on the third floor and climbs up and down by himself every day; no sign of a stairlift.

If only we could have done this for Mum. I curse myself for not trying harder.

Monday, 18 July

Ted Heath has died. In later years at least he was a sad, grumpy old bugger, but unlike many of his contemporaries right about some big issues – fascism in the thirties and in the seventies British membership of the EU. In later life he had a blind spot about China though, prompted perhaps by large amounts of dosh from his Chinese business interests. Latterly, according to one of the Special Branch men who accompanied me to Pakistan, he whiled away the evenings drinking alone in country pubs around Salisbury, with only his minder for company.

Tuesday, 19 July

A call from Number 10 to discuss how I might be useful in Africa. Well, well. What prompted this? A word from Jack perhaps. I remain sceptical, but you never know.

A minister whispered in the Tea Room that 11 soldiers, one a colonel, are to be court-martialled in connection with the abuse – and in two cases killing – of prisoners in Iraq. Several have been charged with 'war crimes', which seems a bit over the top. Needless to say the military top brass are mightily upset and John Reid is not best pleased either. The *Mail* and the *Telegraph* are already gearing up for a big offensive. 'It's going to be horrendous,' he said. He added that the courts martial process was deeply flawed. Apparently the three soldiers convicted of abusing prisoners last year have quietly had their sentences reduced by their commanding officer and upon release they are to be taken back into the army. All this without any announcement, despite the enormous publicity that attended the original sentencing.

Wednesday, 20 July

A robust exchange of emails with the Deputy Serjeant at Arms over the treatment of the House of Commons cleaners who are on strike over their disgraceful terms and conditions – they are paid little more than the minimum wage and receive only 12 days' holiday a year. They are almost all contract cleaners. There is also the little point that, in this age of jihad, it may not make sense to outsource the cleaning of Parliament to demoralised, alienated workers of mainly Third World origin. This is the one argument that might just cut some ice with the foolish gentry who run this place.

This morning, in Committee Room 8, I presided over a conference on drug policy in Afghanistan, sponsored by the Senlis Council.

It attracted very few Members, but a lot of interested officials and think-tankers. Their basic argument is that crop eradication and substitution isn't working and that we ought instead to switch to allowing limited, licensed opium growing for medical purposes. As several people pointed out, there are serious practical difficulties with this approach. Not least the problem of diversion – how do you prevent legally grown opium finding its way onto the black market? Before long you are back to the old arguments about legalisation and regulation versus prohibition. Sir Keith Morris, a former ambassador in Colombia, said afterwards that a former Cabinet Secretary had told him that he was now a legaliser and that half the 1997 Cabinet were, too.

John Biffen was in front of me in the queue at the cafeteria at lunchtime. 'For how long,' he inquired, 'are they going to go on pretending that the recent bombings had nothing to do with Iraq?'

Thursday, 21 July

M called in. He says he has it on good authority that three of the four London bombers – and not the one so far conceded – were known to the police in advance of the bombings. Their names apparently surfaced in something called 'Operation Crevice'.

More bombs – at Oval, Warren Street and Shepherd's Bush Underground and one on a bus in Hackney. Mercifully, they all failed to detonate, leaving the police with a wealth of clues, but travel in London is becoming scary.

Friday, 22 July

This morning the police chased a man into Stockwell tube station and shot him dead in front of terrified commuters. According to eye-witnesses he was more or less executed. Five bullets in the head. It turns out he was unarmed and is not suspected of having been one of yesterday's bombers.

Saturday, 23 July

Sarah appeared in our room at 3am, having been woken by screaming and smoke from the top of the street. It turned out that a car belonging to a young German woman staying at Number 1 had been torched by a passing barbarian. The fire brigade arrived quickly and doused the blaze before it could spread to the nearby house. By the time we got up the car had been removed, leaving only burnt vegetation, a patch of blackened tarmac and a pool of glass which I later cleared.

Prompted by yesterday's bloodletting, the nastier tabloids are demanding more summary executions. 'SHOOT ALL BOMBERS', screams this morning's *Express*. The trouble is that yesterday's victim was not a bomber and it is beginning to look as if he may have been wholly innocent. Not that such namby-pamby considerations will be of any interest to most *Express* readers, let alone their odious proprietor. In fairness, it must be said the Great British Public are remaining remarkably calm, despite attempts by our unscrupulous tabloids to organise hysteria.

Sarah has gone to France with the school. Having waved her off, I went with Emma to pick strawberries and raspberries at Plawsworth, in preparation for tomorrow's party. Our exchanges included the following (apropos her long-running campaign to replace our M reg Volvo with a vehicle with air conditioning and a CD player):

'Dad, you're like Jesus.'

'Oh?'

'Everyone expected Jesus to come on a chariot. And they expect their MP to drive a new car. Instead you've got an old one.'

A crisis. Bruce our cat has disappeared. She was last seen on Friday and by this evening had been absent for an unprecedented 24 hours. We are haunted by visions that she may be trapped and starving in a neighbour's outhouse. Or kidnapped and tortured by a gang of feral youths. Or perhaps she just felt unloved having been on the receiving end of one telling-off too many for leaving a trail of fluff around the house. Ngoc, the author of most of the tellings-off, is feeling particularly remorseful. Come back, Bruce, all is forgiven.

Sunday, 24 July

The man executed at Stockwell turns out to have been a wholly innocent Brazilian electrician, which only goes to show you can't be too
careful when it comes to hunting terrorists.

Still no sign of Bruce. Emma printed out a poster which she and her
friend Patricia pinned to trees in the terrace. Later we distributed
copies through all the front doors in the vicinity. By evening there
were several reported sightings, but still no Bruce. Then, just as we
were retiring for the night, a slightly bedraggled cat appeared at the
back door and with much purring and miaowing resumed her seat on
the chair in the upstairs living room. Great relief all round. I was
dreading having to break the news to Sarah, on her return from
France, that Bruce had gone.

Tuesday, 26 July
Sunderland

En route from my office to home, the following exchange with one of
the new breed of privatised traffic wardens, a big bone-headed man in
a bright yellow safety jacket, bristling with technology.
     'Afternoon, Councillor Mullin.'
     'I'm an MP, not a councillor.'
     'So you're an MP now? Well done.'
     'I have never been a councillor. I have been in Parliament for
nearly 20 years …'
     'So what do I call you now you're an MP?'
     'Chris.'

A huge famine in Niger. A third of the country is dying. It's been going
on for some time, but of course no one – not least the government of
Niger – noticed until the television cameras arrived. On the BBC news
this evening, heart-rending interviews with an extended family of
nomads who hadn't eaten for a fortnight. Three children and three
adults already dead; emaciated grandma lying under a tree, close to
death; livestock dead around them. One of the surviving children was

stuffing handfuls of the rotting carcass into his mouth. We have the technology to beam these people instantly into our living rooms, but not to feed them ... And after all this talk of saving Africa.

Thursday, 28 July
Sunderland

Rain all day. By evening my beautiful purple phlox is bent double, a little pile of spent blossom on the lawn underneath.

Among today's visitors a delegation of Unison officials warning of a looming – and entirely self-inflicted – crisis over something called 'single status'. In a nutshell, having used the Equal Pay Act to bludgeon the local authority into regrading its entire workforce and paying out the best part of £10 million by way of compensation to female employees for many years' loss of earnings and 'hurt feelings', Unison now discover they have an uprising on their hands from their male members, bin-men and the like, who are facing cuts in salary of up to one-third. It seems only just to have dawned on Unison's finest that there would be losers as well as winners in the course of creating a workers' paradise. Their proposed solution? Four years' 'protection'. In other words the down-graded should continue to be paid at their old rate in the hope that their losses will gradually be eroded by inflation and increments. The cost? Another £8 million and since, by common consent, the local authority doesn't have £8 million they propose that I and other MPs ask Gordon Brown to write out a cheque. Oh, and this must all be sorted by 1 October if the council is to avoid another round of litigation. I explained, as gently as I could, that this was cuckoo land. There is no way Gordon is going to write out a cheque. In which case, they said, they would have 'no choice' but to pursue industrial action. I asked if they remembered what happened last time they organised a strike by bin-men. They looked blank.

'Eighteen years of Tory government.'

Ah yes, that did ring a vague bell.

Needless to say, this seems to be a northern problem. Unison has never been very brave when it comes to taking on Tory councils further south. 'Is this an issue in Surrey or Sussex?' I inquired.

'No,' they chorused.
'How come?'
'They outsourced most of their services years ago.'
Quite so.

Friday, 29 July

The evening news reported the arrest of the three remaining perpetrators of last week's failed outrages – two in west London, one in Rome. Huge relief, but who knows what comes next?

Sunday, 31 July

Sarah is back from the Ardeche, unfazed by the 27-hour coach journey, full of stories about camping, caving, canoeing and 'gorgeous' instructors. Dear Lord, please allow us to get through GCSE year without boys ...

Wednesday, 3 August

Gamekeeper's Cottage, Northchapel, West Sussex

Today's *Sun* is nastier than usual: 'LAWLESS BRITAIN', screams the splash headline over a catalogue of the country's alleged ills – bombers, gypsies, illegal immigrants, paedophiles ... you name it. And then the sly punchline: 'meanwhile our MPs are on holiday'. When it comes to preaching hatred our odious tabloids could teach the mullahs a trick or two.

Thursday, 4 August

Gamekeeper's Cottage

Today's tabloid headlines (glimpsed in the local supermarket) include: 'Fury over BBC's bias towards Muslims' (*Express*); Joan Collins: 'Why I despair as I watch my country destroying itself from within' (*Mail*). The *Sun*, meanwhile, is 'putting the Great back in Britain' (one can almost hear the clip of jackboots). Only the *Star* has its feet firmly on the ground: 'Sienna pregnant by "love cheat" Jude.'

We went plum picking.

Friday, 5 August
Gamekeeper's Cottage

'What a useless creature I have become,' remarked Granny as I helped her down the step into the living room. 'To think, I used to work for Help the Aged.' But she's not at all useless. She has perfect hearing and eyesight and she's good company, especially when talking of the past. And the longer she's with us the more alert she is becoming. This evening she read the *Guardian* from cover to cover. I would have trouble remembering what day it was if I was condemned to sit staring at the wall all day in the company of people most of whom are more infirm than she is. What's remarkable is that she has held up so well. Over and over, I have tried to persuade her to come to Sunderland. If not to live with us, then to a nursing home nearby, but she will have none of it, not wanting to be a 'burden'.

We spent the afternoon in the beautiful gardens at Parham.

Sunday, 7 August
Gamekeeper's Cottage

Robin Cook is dead. Yesterday afternoon, at the top of a Scottish mountain. Lucky man to go in a blinding flash like that. And at the peak of his reputation. The tributes all speak of his brilliance, but to be brilliant is not enough. There are plenty of brilliant people screwing up the world. Sound judgement and integrity are also required and, as he demonstrated so spectacularly, he had both. His weakness was that he relied too heavily on his razor-sharp wit and made little effort to cultivate a following. He wasn't much liked at the Foreign Office. Someone (I can't recall who) said he was hopeless at taking decisions and should have been an academic, but I don't buy that. Frank Dobson is quoted as saying that he added lustre to the trade of politics. And so he did.

Tuesday, 9 August

Gamekeeper's Cottage

'How old is Robin Cook's wife,' asked Ngoc on our way back from a walk in Petworth Park this afternoon.

'Forty-eight,' I replied, 'and he was 59.'

'Eleven years – a big gap.'

'The same as between me and Orlando Bloom,' said Sarah wistfully.

Wednesday, 10 August

Gamekeeper's Cottage

Ngoc drew my attention to the following passage in Andrew Marr's introduction to his book *My Trade*: 'Despite having a first class degree and reading an unfeasibly large number of books, it began to dawn on me that I couldn't actually do anything. I can't sing, act, tell jokes, play any musical instrument, hit, kick or catch a ball, run for more than a few yards without panting, speak another language or assemble things without them falling apart immediately ... journalism seemed the only option.'

'That's you,' she said.

And so it is, minus the first class degree.

Tuesday, 16 August

Montréal du Gers

We are enjoying the hospitality of Ray and Luise Fitzwalter in this land of sunflowers, vines and medieval hill-top villages.

After dark, a huge storm over the Pyrenees. Ray and I stood in the garden for over an hour watching the yellow flashes and occasional but massive forks of lightning. At first it was too far away for the thunder to be audible, but as the storm grew nearer there was a distant rumble, reminiscent of the guns at Sala Pak Oum. It went on late into the night, our bedroom illuminated by the lightning flashes.

Friday, 19 August

Awoke to grey skies, à la Sunderland. In the afternoon, drizzle. This is not how it is supposed to be in the south of France.

Mo Mowlam is dead. A bright star who flashed across the firmament and was gone.

Wednesday, 24 August

In a back-copy of the *Guardian*, a warts and all obituary of Mo Mowlam by Julia Langdon, concluding that Mo was her own worst enemy. Not quite fair. Her achievements in Ireland were real enough and she brought a touch of colour to the otherwise bland world of New Labour.

Friday, 26 August

We drove to Clermont-Ferrand where we caught a train to Paris and from there to Waterloo on Eurostar. Emma extracted a promise from Sarah that she would give up eating meat, except free-range chicken, as soon as we reached British soil. She kept reminding Sarah throughout the journey and as the train emerged from the tunnel in Kent she remarked triumphantly, 'Sarah's a vegetarian now.'

Thursday, 1 September

A huge catastrophe in America in the wake of Hurricane Katrina. New Orleans and much of the surrounding coastline is under water, thousands dead and tens of thousands (mainly poor blacks) trapped in 90-degree heat without food or water. The fault-lines in American society exposed as never before. When the order was given to evacuate, the middle classes loaded up their SUVs and drove away, leaving the urban poor to bear the brunt. Unlike the passive Third World refugees who normally fill our screens many of the American poor are aggressive and seriously overweight. It may just be me, but I find it harder to sympathise with a 20-stone woman bawling that she hasn't eaten for five days than I do with a family of starving peasants in

Niger. As for Bush, he's completely impotent. All those crapulous slogans about waging war on terrorism and fighting for freedom aren't much use to him now.

Wednesday, 7 September

I am reading a fascinating book, *Against All Enemies*, by Richard Clarke, a former national security adviser to three presidents. This is his account of life in the Bush White House on the morning after 9/11: 'I had expected to go back to a round of meetings examining what the next attacks could be, what our vulnerabilities were, what we could do about them. Instead I walked into a series of discussions about Iraq. At first I was incredulous that we were talking about something other than getting al-Qaeda. Then I realized with almost a sharp physical pain that Rumsfeld and Wolfowitz were going to try to take advantage of this national tragedy to promote their agenda about Iraq. Since the beginning of the administration, indeed well before, they had been pressing for a war with Iraq ...'

A few days after 9/11 he quotes Rumsfeld as 'complaining that there were no decent targets for bombing in Afghanistan and that we should consider bombing Iraq, which, he said, had better targets. At first I thought Rumsfeld was joking. But he was serious ...'

Nowhere is there any suggestion that we exercised the slightest influence in Washington. Indeed, The Man is only mentioned by name on page 273. It reads: 'When prime ministers wonder in future if they should risk domestic opposition to support us they will reflect on Tony Blair in the UK and how he lost popularity and credibility by allying himself so closely with the US administration and its claims.' Amen to that.

Thursday, 8 September

To my surprise, and slightly to my disgust, I still find myself moping over the loss of office. Not office *per se*, but the particular job that I had. Every time I hear Dave Triesman on the radio I find myself thinking, 'That should have been me.' I must have caught the bug that

Kenneth Baker referred to when I was first anointed, but which passed me by first time around. Pathetic really, after only two years. What must it be like after ten years – and at the top? Presumably, it all depends on the manner of your exit. If your tenure comes to a natural conclusion – courtesy of the electorate or by your own hand – you feel you've done your best and move on. But when it comes out of the blue and with the inevitable implication that you weren't quite up to it, that's what hurts. The feeling is compounded by the absence of any useful alternative and the resulting loss of self-confidence. It's the lack of anything useful to do and the prospect that it might be like this for the rest of my days – the beckoning void – that is unsettling. In the past, I always knew where I was going. There was always something to aim for – an issue, a cause – but now I am lost.

Friday, 16 September

To Front Street, Sowerby, where I unveiled a plaque to Joan Maynard. On the way there I stopped at Thornton le Street and left a couple of pink roses, cut from our garden, on her grave.

Wednesday, 21 September

To Victoria Tower Gardens to be interviewed for a *Newsnight* profile of David Cameron, one of the Tory leadership contenders. The questions were all about his role in the select committee drugs inquiry supporting the very modest proposals for focusing on harm reduction rather than simply prohibition. I declined to play, insisting that Cameron was a useful, sensible, constructive member of the team (which he was) and pointing out that, in any case, the Tories on the committee split three ways. In the end, having asked the same question in about five different ways, Michael Crick gave up.

Monday, 26 September
Labour Party Conference, Brighton

The usual mixture of seediness and Regency elegance. *Big Issue* sellers on every second corner. The media, having nothing better to do, are trying to organise a leadership crisis. Gordon's speech is being pored over for evidence of treason. Tomorrow it will be The Man's turn. It was the same last year and by my reckoning we've got at least another two years of this. It may be my imagination, but attendance this year seems thinner. In the public gallery curtains have been drawn to hide banks of empty seats. And no wonder. For much of the time there is not even a pretence of debate, just a succession of ministers bragging about New Labour triumphs. This afternoon Tessa Jowell presided over a great Olympic love-in. Apparently we are all to be provided with 'a multi-media tool kit' to help us enter into the spirit of the occasion. Ugh.

Tuesday, 27 September
Brighton

Didn't go in for The Man's speech. Instead I high-tailed back to my lodging, intending to watch the big event on TV. Unfortunately I nodded off, missing most of it. Judging by what I did hear, it was full of the usual guff – onward and upwards, modernise, be bold etc. If we were going to be really bold, we could dispense with Trident, but I suspect that's one piece of modernisation we won't be contemplating.

Earlier I came across Tony Benn holding court in the cafeteria. On fine form, denouncing New Labour and all its works at five fringe meetings a day. We had our picture taken together with Jack Jones, who is in his nineties. Later it was reported that Tony had collapsed and been rushed to hospital. His son Stephen, who I came across outside the Grand Hotel later this evening, said he seems completely recovered, although the hospital was keeping him in overnight for observation.

Wednesday, 28 September

The Lycee, Kennington (my London flat)

A PR catastrophe at Brighton. Walter Wolfgang, an old nuclear dis-armer who has haunted Labour conferences for as long as I can remember, was forcibly evicted from the public gallery for heckling mildly during Jack's big speech. Clips of two burly stewards frog-marching a frail 82-year-old out of the hall dominate tonight's news bulletins. To cap it all, he turns out to be a refugee from Nazism. What greater gift for New Labour's many enemies?

Thursday, 29 September

House of Commons

The papers are full of Walter Wolfgang. Pictures on just about every front page of a steward hoisting him from his seat by the scruff of the neck. 'This is how Labour deals with dissent' is the theme. Nonsense, of course, but the symbolism is irresistible. Everyone's at it – from the Campaign Group to the *Daily Mail*. The top brass, including The Man himself, have been apologising all day, but too late. The damage is done.

Lunch on the terrace, where I came across David Davis, fresh from his leadership campaign launch. We chatted for about ten minutes. He's utterly confident of victory, saying he had more support among MPs than all the other candidates combined.

The *Evening Standard* has been swabbing toilets in the Grand and the Metropole Hotels at Brighton and claims to have found wide-spread evidence of cocaine use, the implication being that this is yet another sign of New Labour decadence. Maybe, but given that those places are swarming with journalists and lobbyists – outnumbering politicians by about five to one – there are other possibilities. As for swabbing toilets, are there no depths that the Rothermere press will not plumb?

Friday, 30 September

Sunderland

All hell has broken lose. The *Sun* ('after months of painstaking detective work') has discovered the whereabouts of the so-called Lotto Rapist who, having served 18 years in prison, has been living in my constituency under police protection and an assumed name. The Home Office minister, Paul Goggins, tipped me off about him months ago, but until now the hacks couldn't find him. Mass hysteria is being organised on the grounds that (a) the likes of him shouldn't be allowed to win the lottery and (b) the neighbours have a 'right to know' his identity, presumably so his house could be torched and he lynched by a mob of shaven-headed *Sun* readers. Fiona Mactaggart, the prisons minister, rang this evening to say that she was looking at changing the law to allow victims of rapists who come into sudden riches to sue out of time. Officials are advising against, needless to say.

Sunday, 9 October

Silly David Blunkett has been set up again. This time by a posh estate agent whom he met in Annabel's. Annabel's for heaven's sake. What on earth was he doing there in the first place? According to today's papers, it has been a scam from the start. Someone in a position to know remarked to me two weeks ago that David's detectives suspected it was a set-up, but that it wasn't their job to save him from himself.

Monday, 10 October

Our first day back. Geoff Hoon paid tribute in the House to Robin Cook's 'far-reaching reforms'. I used that as my cue to query our disgraceful 80-day summer recess. People shuffled uncomfortably and there was bit of mumbling and I can see it's not doing me any good with the Speaker (he looked around desperately for someone else to call, but there was no one so he had no choice). I am almost on my own on this – in Parliament. Outside, it's a different story. The whole thing's a disgrace. I intend to go on rubbing their noses in it.

Then to Committee Room 14 to hear The Man address the

parliamentary party. Better than his conference speech. Brimming with energy and self-confidence; not a note in sight; still less any suggestion that he is contemplating retirement. His main point: the Tories are being forced to fight on our territory, we must pin them down on the inconsistency of their new position, i.e. wanting to invest in public services, but not wanting to pay for them. He also promised to get tough with the Lib Dems: 'We must force them to decide what kind of a party they are. I intend to do that.' A change of line here. Thus far his position has been that the Tories, not the Lib Dems, are our real enemy. 'I know I've got back time to make up,' he said, to some amusement.

Dave Clelland asked why the government was encouraging private medicine: 'I'm all for choice, but we said we were going to make the NHS so efficient that the private sector will be irrelevant. Now we are encouraging it. Why?' The Man gave no quarter: 'It's the only basis on which we are going to expand.' He added, 'We have expanded the public sector by 600,000 people, so when I hear some of our trade union colleagues say, "You are destroying the public sector", I go, "Huh?"'

Tuesday, 11 October
A chat with Angela Eagle in the Tea Room. She says the apparatchiks are up to their old tricks again. She caught them opening the NEC ballot papers – or at least the outer envelope – two weeks before polls closed so they could be 'verified'. The purpose, according to Angela, is to see who hasn't voted and then to gently remind those who can be relied upon to toe the official line. It used to happen with Shadow Cabinet elections in the bad old days, until Alice Mahon became a teller and put a stop to it. Angela says she had to have a stand-up row with the General Secretary to put an end to this latest jiggery pokery. In the event she was elected by only a single vote and says she's sure she wouldn't have been had the ballots been 'verified'.

Wednesday, 12 October

I had Question Nine to the PM today but only eight were reached. I was proposing to inquire why, if it is now so essential that the police be given three months to interrogate terrorist suspects, they only asked for 14 days last time around? The subject was raised, however, and The Man insisted that he found the case 'absolutely compelling'. Just as he did with WMD, I thought.

Monday, 17 October

To Church House to hear the Archbishop of Cape Town propose that a group of 'wise men' be set up to monitor progress on the G8's commitment to Africa. My heart sank. Yet another lot of African big-wigs having to be ferried Club Class back and forth across the continent courtesy of the G8 taxpayer, and met at airports by fleets of top of the range BMWs, all the while denouncing us for our shortcomings while remaining resolutely silent on their own.

Then to the meeting of the parliamentary party in Committee Room 14 to hear Patricia Hewitt being given a going-over for her department's plans for shaking up Primary Care Trusts only three years after the last great upheaval. Needless to say, no one seems to have been consulted. Her plans were variously described as 'Maoist', 'hugely destabilising' and 'drawn up on the back of an envelope'. No one had a good word to say. Patricia, in reply, was soothing and apologetic, but conceded little, insisting that there were far too many chief executives, finance officers etc. and scope for considerable savings. I dare say she's right, but why is this necessary after only three years?

Tuesday, 18 October

Walked in from Kennington via Courtney Street. A gaggle of photographers outside Ken Clarke's house, waiting for him to show his face. Later we heard that he had been eliminated in the first round of the Tory leadership election. From our point of view, a pity. From theirs, sensible. He would have split the party from top to bottom. It's beginning to look as though David Cameron is going to come out on top, which could give us a problem in due course.

Wednesday, 19 October
The Library

Jean Corston remarked, 'Cameron is going to make Gordon look old and wooden. We could lose.'

'Who would you prefer?'

'Hilary Benn.'

'So would I. Spread the word.'

Dinner with Ruth Runciman, who wants me to join the board of the Prison Reform Trust. I am not sure I am liberal enough, given what goes on in Sunderland. After Ruth had gone, I rang Ngoc, who reported that last night criminal youths slashed every tyre on every car in the street.

Thursday, 20 October

The second round of the Tories' leadership election. Cameron is now comfortably ahead. Have they recovered the will to win at last? Bruce Grocott, who I came across in the otherwise empty Tea Room this evening, was sanguine. 'Being leader of the Opposition is the toughest job in politics. John Smith, who had been Shadow Chancellor for years before becoming leader, told me he was totally unprepared for the unrelenting demands of leadership. Cameron is completely untested. He'll have to weather all sorts of little crises between now and the election. Such as whether or not to send his children to public school ....' Bruce added ruefully, 'It's about time the tide turned against this cult of youth. If it's possible to become leader of the Opposition after about three weeks on the front bench, then the rest of us have wasted the whole of our professional lives.'

Three wee problems with Bruce's analysis: (1) leading the Tory party in opposition, with half the press on-side, is a mite less stressful than being Labour leader; (2) I see every sign that Cameron is up to it; (3) the Cameron offspring are very young and no decision will need to be taken about their schooling between now and the election.

Monday, 24 October

The *Independent* has published my piece saying that I shan't be supporting the Terrorism Bill as long as it contains the 90-days-without-trial clause. It won't do me any good but I am beyond caring.

Hilary Armstrong remarked, apropos my campaign to shorten the summer recess, 'We all think you are mad.' Never mind, I take comfort from the fact that outside the Westminster village an entirely different view prevails. Nick Soames said of the rise of Cameron, 'It means, of course, that you won't be able to have Brown. That'll cause a huge row in the Labour Party. Can't wait. Ho ho.'

This evening, dinner in a private room at Shepherds with President Museveni of Uganda. I had been due to sit next to him, but some unseen hand rearranged the place names so I ended up between Bob Blizzard and Bill Cash's wife, Biddy. Museveni was in benign mode, performing his usual party tricks about the height of Ben Nevis, asserting that Uganda was a net donor to the West and that the war in the north would have been over long ago, if only the donors hadn't tied his hand over military spending. There was no opportunity to challenge him about his proposed life presidency or the fact that a large part of his army appears to be made up of ghosts.

Tuesday, 25 October

To the PM's room for a meeting with Home Secretary Charles Clarke about the Terrorism Bill. About 35 people attended. Charles was anxious to persuade us to support the Bill on second reading tomorrow and argue about the details later. Happily, I shall be en route to Tanzania by the time the vote is called so I shall be spared the dilemma. It seems clear Charles is up for a compromise over the 90 days, but his problem is that The Main Person is not. We'd probably be doing Charles a favour if we organised a nice big protest vote. He had read my article and inquired when I was coming back. 'In time for report stage,' I said with a big smile.

My literary agent, Pat Kavanagh, came in for dinner.

Wednesday, 26 October

A big turnout for the debate on the Terrorism Bill. A huge number of interventions, ranging from the sceptical to the downright hostile. No one except Bill Cash spoke in favour. Charles took it all in his stride, responding calmly and considerately. My, how he has changed from the thuggish Kinnock-minder of the 1980s. I was called at about five and made clear I wouldn't be going along with 90 days under any circumstances. Then I made a dash for the airport and was airborne by 8pm.

As I was leaving, a call from my assistant, Graham March, to say that the Angolan family we have been trying to help have been taken away pending removal. They have two small children and face destitution unless I can find someone to help them. I instructed Graham to ring Tony McNulty's office and ask him to hold fire until I get back next week, but I am not holding my breath.

Thursday, 3 November

Touched down from Dar es Salaam at about 5.30am feeling surprisingly chipper, having managed to sleep most of the way, courtesy of a couple of beers and a sleeping tablet. Yesterday, it seems, was eventful. Not only was Blunkett sacked (again), but the Terrorism Bill has imploded. Bob Marshall-Andrews's attempt to amend the 'glorification' clause failed by just one vote (had I been there, it would have been a draw); better still, faced with an amendment by David Winnick (which also bears my name), Charles Clarke has had to withdraw the 90-days-detention clause and is to come back with a compromise next week. On top of all that, there has been an unseemly wrangle over the proposed ban on smoking in public places which John Reid has managed to water down even though he represents a Scottish constituency where a total ban on smoking in public buildings is about to be introduced. The general view seems to be that The Man is in trouble. His friends are melting away and his critics are growing bolder by the hour. 'Blair's power drains away' is the headline across the front page of the *Telegraph*. For once it may not be wishful thinking.

Some extraordinary stories around the Blunkett departure. It seems he was called to Number 10 twice. After the first visit he emerged thumbs up and smiling, but within a few minutes he was called back and told he would have to go. What had in fact happened was that, after David's first visit, The Man was presented with yet more evidence of David's misdemeanours and realised that he couldn't sustain the position when he faced Michael Howard at Questions later in the morning.

Home on the 19.00 with Alan Milburn. While we were on the train The Man rang Alan on his mobile, twice. He disappeared to the other end of the carriage and they talked for about 20 minutes. Fragments drifted back. 'Don't get too exasperated,' I heard Alan say. During the second call there was a lot of laughter. The Man, according to Alan, is in defiant mode. 'If anyone thinks he's going to let everything we've achieved unravel, they'd better think again. Monday's parliamentary party meeting will be interesting.'

'Tell him not to overdo it.'

'I did.'

Ngoc met me at Durham. 'Do you understand the government's education plans? They must be mad. That Ruth Kelly talks in slogans.'

Also a note from Pat Kavanagh: 'The next time I am in your company I will ask you to explain the government's new education policy. If I understand them right, they seem to me utterly wrong-headed.'

Friday, 4 November

Sunderland

At tonight's meeting of the management committee, much complaining about The Man's plans for an education free-for-all. Councillor Pat Smith, who chairs the education committee, said, 'Ten years ago I went to a conference in Newcastle where Theresa May told us to do all the things we are now about to do. I don't know whether I'm Labour or Tory any more.'

Monday, 7 November

To a crowded meeting of the parliamentary party, to hear The Man tell us why it is absolutely vital that we all get behind his plan to detain suspected terrorists for up to 90 days. Far from seeking compromise, he seems to be raising the stakes, turning it into a mini vote of confidence. Yesterday he was on the telly accusing his critics of 'woeful complacency', even as Charles Clarke was talking compromise. It is beginning to look as if Charles has been leapt upon from a great height. A minister, who shall remain nameless, recounted how this morning his officials rang the Home Office to find out what the line was, only to be told, 'We don't know.' Anyway, the situation soon clarified. It's 90 days or bust. The Man was on sparkling, amazing form. I haven't seen him so good since he talked us (or most of us) into invading Iraq. The mood was revivalist. Billy Graham couldn't have done better. One after another people spoke up to say they had seen the light and were now more than ever convinced of the One True Path. Of the critics there was no sign. Apart from Paul Flynn, who said to loyalist groans that he thought The Man should go sooner rather than later. Paul apart, the mood was adulatory, the applause thunderous. Can it be that this man is so articulate, and we so gullible, that he can talk us into anything, however foolish? Oddly, his argument was almost entirely about wrong-footing the Tories. Silly me, I thought all this was to do with fighting terrorism.

Well, it's had the opposite effect on me. I am not voting for this nonsense under any circumstances, even though it means jettisoning any thoughts of a comeback.

Tuesday, 8 November

6pm, Committee Room 12

Gareth Peirce came to urge us to stand firm on the Terrorism Bill. The meeting was sparsely attended but he offered two nuggets. First, that two of the 7 July bombers were under surveillance – photographic and audio – well before the bombings. Which confirms what M told me soon after the event and contradicts the original police version. Second, that the suspect who did a runner in the so-called ricin plot, one of the cases highlighted by Assistant Commissioner Hayman, had been released after only two days in custody, thereby making nonsense of the claim that had the police been able to hold him longer, they might have snared a major terrorist. This detail is omitted from Hayman's letter, one of the key documents in the police case for greater powers. I shall look for an opportunity to get that on the record.

Wednesday, 9 November

11.30am: the big day. A huge lobbying operation underway. Gordon is on his way back from Israel, after only an hour on the ground. Jack is coming back from Moscow. Several messages for me to ring Hilary Armstrong and one to 'call Number 10'. I ignored the Number 10 message, but called in to see Hilary, who was at her most emollient. 'Chris, I need your help.' I politely explained that I was unable to oblige. That I wasn't revelling in being a rebel. That, on the contrary, I was deeply depressed by the prospect. In any case my name is on the Winnick amendment and there is no way I can leave him swinging in the wind. 'In that case, I think The Boss will want to talk to you.' Yes, I am sure he will. It's an exact repeat of the Iraq vote. There is a pecking order of pressure. First, the junior whip. Then Hilary. Then The Man. Or JP or Gordon, as appropriate. In vain I protest to Hilary that I ought not to waste The Man's time. After all, he's entertaining the Chinese president, the Polish prime minister and goodness knows who else, on top of which he has to answer Questions in 20 minutes. I am just getting up to leave, when Hilary's factotum puts his head round the door and says, 'The Prime Minister is on the line for Mr Mullin *now* ...' Oh Lord. I have been set up. Hilary suddenly vanishes and I find myself alone at her desk, clutching her telephone, talking to Himself.

His tone is, as ever, friendly; not at all assertive; unhurried despite having to face Michael Howard across the dispatch box just 18 minutes from now. 'Chris, I need you to vote with the government.'

'I'd love to Tony, believe me, but I spent much of the eighties and early nineties rescuing people who had fallen foul of the so-called terrorism experts and I don't want to go through all that again.'

'There are safeguards. A High Court judge.'

'Some High Court judges are very gullible.'

'That's not my experience.'

For once it is I who bring the conversation to a close, pointing out (as if he doesn't know) that he has Questions in a few minutes.

'We must talk again,' he said.

Not if I can help it, I said to myself.

Two other points from the conversation with Hilary: (1) she had the audacity to assert that the reason we are sticking to 90 days was because our backbenches are demanding it; (2) that, contrary to reports, Gordon had not been summoned back from Israel. He (and Jack) had been paired so their absence would have made no difference. Gordon was coming back of his own accord, presumably because he wants the world to know that The Man's survival depends on him. Indeed, there is evidence that his unseen hand is already at work. I ran into Joan Ruddock, who is strongly opposed to 90 days, but who has now come over all wobbly. Why? 'Because Gordon has come back.' Obviously she still has hopes of preferment.

Unfortunately for Gordon, the situation is too far gone for him to make any difference to the outcome.

12 noon, the Chamber

Michael Howard on superb form, relentlessly exposing the chasm between Charles Clarke and The Man. Our side, subdued (so much for Hilary's assertion that they are gung-ho for 90 days). From the other side cries of 'Why don't you publish a dossier, Tony?'

Until now I assumed the regime would triumph, especially after The Man's bravura performance on Monday. The signs are, however, that, far from caving in to pressure, most people are holding firm and The Man's strategy of dividing the Tories isn't working either. Also, it appears that Ian Paisley and his merry men will be voting against the government, too. Not least because the master strategists have chosen this day to publish a Bill granting immunity from prosecution to IRA 'on-the-runs'. Nice one, lads.

1.30pm–4.30pm, the Chamber

Charles doing his best, but clearly damaged. Unable to explain why until Monday he was talking compromise and why suddenly the shutters came down. Everyone knows why, of course, but he can't say. He's also hobbled by the presence at his side of Hazel Blears, a shiny-faced New Labour automaton, who is gung-ho for everything Number 10 comes out with. God forbid that she ends up in his job, but it can't be ruled out.

A veritable blizzard of interventions, some from loyalists, but mainly hostile. Charles deals courteously with everyone, friend and foe alike, apparently unruffled. Until he starts praying in aid the ricin case. At which point, egged on by Clare Short and Kate Hoey, I get up and point out the inconvenient detail that the police forgot to mention – namely that they released the suspect after only two days and, therefore, this example is of no relevance to the case for 90 days. It may be my imagination, but things went a bit quiet at that point. Charles replied almost under his breath.

David Davis was lacklustre although he did make one good point – how dare New Labour accuse the Tories of being soft on terrorism when they had lost Airey Neave, Ian Gow and Tony Berry to terrorist bombs? David Winnick, on the other hand, was brilliant. Truly, his finest hour. I forgive him all his many sins.

4.56pm

Ayes to the right, 291. Noes to the left, 322. New Labour's first ever defeat. The Rubicon has been crossed.

Later, the Tea Room

'Your intervention was devastating,' said Mike O'Brien, our Solicitor General, who was sitting next to Charles on the front bench throughout. He reported the following, *sotto voce*, exchange between himself and the Home Secretary while I was on my feet:

'Is that true?'

'Yes, it is.'

'Does it damage our case?'

'It does.'

'Oh fuck.'

Thursday, 10 November

'TRAITORS,' screams this morning's *Sun* in letters two inches high. 'MPs betray public,' says the strap-line. On an inside page pictures of Osama Bin Laden, Al Zarqawi and Clare Short. Mercifully, I seem to have escaped a monstering, although a full list of 'traitors' is to be found on the *Sun* website. One amusing snippet: the 7 July victim whose bloodied image was plastered across the *Sun*'s front page on Tuesday turns out to be a Cardiff professor who is wholly opposed to 90-day detention and outraged by having his picture so shamelessly misused. No chance of *Sun* readers being told about that.

To the Education Department, where Ruth Kelly spent 40 minutes taking me through her – or rather Number 10's – plans for the latest shake-up of secondary education. The meeting was at her request. The opening round of a big push to ensure that it doesn't all end in tears. As she explains them, the proposed reforms don't sound so wicked. No school will be compelled to opt out of local authority control; the Bill will be merely an enabling measure. It's about giving working class parents the same 'choice' that the middle classes already enjoy by virtue of their social mobility and their sharp elbows. Maybe, but I still worry about a free-for-all leading to more, rather than fewer, sink schools. For the time being I am keeping an open mind. I don't want to be part of another uprising, but at this distance I won't rule it out, otherwise no one will listen.

Geoff Hoon announced the recess dates for the next year and, sure enough, he has dropped September sittings, thereby reneging on Robin Cook's much vaunted 'deal'. A few of us protested, but I have no doubt we are a minority. Odd, we fight hard enough to get into this place, but having clawed our way in we can't wait to go home.

Friday, 11 November

To the Immigration Detention Centre at Yarlswood near Bedford in an attempt to rescue the Angolan family from Hendon who face destitution if they are sent back.

I hired a young Angolan woman to interpret and we interviewed the family for a couple of hours. The woman seemed deeply depressed and just stared ahead blankly. The man, though fairly buoyant, is still in denial. He doesn't believe it's going to happen. I think it will. When I said that to him he began to shake. Meanwhile the little boys played happily in the background, oblivious to the fate that awaits them.

I was about to depart when a woman security officer wandered in and said casually to the husband, 'Go to your room and pack. You've been released.' Only temporarily, as it turned out. But of course they had no home to go to. Their house in Cairo Street is boarded up and a call to the Chief Immigration Officer at North Shields quickly established that there wasn't a chance in hell of getting it unboarded by this evening. Instead they were expected to make their way into and across London and report to a hostel at Heathrow, where they were to wait until Monday and then find their way back to Sunderland. Never mind that they hardly speak English, that they are utterly unfamiliar with the terrain, that it is rush hour on Friday and that they are carrying all their worldly goods and two small boys.

'This is madness,' I protest.

'It happens all the time,' replies my relentlessly cheerful minder.

After some discussion we agree that I will take the family to King's Cross and put them on a train to Newcastle, where they will be picked up by friends who will accommodate them for the weekend.

Only when I see their baggage do I realise what I have let myself in for. It is 8pm by the time we reach London and even then there is the difficult task of transporting the family and their bags the 600 yards from the Thameslink to the mainline station. I buy them all a sandwich, load them onto the 21.00 train to Newcastle and wave them goodbye. Then I race back to Parliament, collect my bags and get back to King's Cross just in time to catch the last train to the north. Home at 2am.

Monday, 14 November

Unless I am mistaken the mood is turning ugly. At the parliamentary party meeting this evening there were calls for retribution against some of last week's rebels. Clare Short in particular, for referring to last week's meeting as 'a Nuremberg rally' and Bob Marshall-Andrews for allegedly colluding with the Tory whips. Last night I caught a glimpse of Tessa Jowell on television talking of 'betrayal'. And this evening someone drew my attention to an article on the *Guardian* website by Kitty Ussher, a young upwardly mobile New Labour zealot elected a mere five months ago, saying that those of us who voted against 90 days will have blood on our hands in the event of another atrocity. How dare she? What does she know of Guildford, Woolwich, Birmingham, Judith Ward, the Maguires? The trouble with these shiny New Labour types is that they think history started in May 1997.

A call from a Ugandan of my acquaintance to say that Museveni has arrested the opposition leader and charged him with treason; the man had recently returned home after several years in exile and there is an election pending. Another of our favourite Africans sets off down the slippery slope. We have the same problem in Ethiopia, where my friend Meles Zenawi has locked up the opposition and is charging them with treason. If this goes on we will have no choice but to withdraw support. What's the use of increasing aid, if there is nowhere to spend it?

A chat with Alan Milburn in the Tea Room. He says it is vital that The Man is allowed to see through his programme. 'If there is a long lingering death, it won't just be Tony who is damaged; it will destroy the Labour Party.'

In that case, I say, The Man is going to have take us all into his confidence. No more proclamations from on high. No repeat of last week's folly.

On that last point, Alan doesn't accept that 90 days was folly. On the contrary, he says, the issue may have to be revisited in the next year or two. As regards proclamations from on high, he agrees and says he's told The Man so. 'I told him not to oversell the education reforms. Apart from the fact that the education white paper is unreadable, the proposals aren't all that Tony claims.'

Wednesday, 16 November

A new horror from Iraq. American troops have discovered 170 starving, terrified prisoners in cells underneath an Interior Ministry building; some have been hideously tortured. And that's not all. After weeks of denials – the latest only yesterday – the Pentagon has been forced to own up to using napalm in Falluja. Where will all this end?

Thursday, 17 November

The Garden Room, Clarence House

Gwyneth Dunwoody regal, radiant, dressed entirely in red save for a long string of pearls, occupies a chair by the mantelpiece. A dozen of us lesser Members are arranged tightly on a pair of luxurious sofas. HRH immaculate, pin-striped, double-breasted, a maroon white-spotted handkerchief protruding from his breast pocket, a large gold signet ring, his only jewellery, on the small finger of his left hand. We are about the same age, he slightly younger, but his brow is furrowed, his face deeply lined, his complexion a teeny bit florid. The burden of office? The frustration of being forever in waiting? Or is it angst about the state of the country, the planet? Let no one doubt, he cares about these matters and has thought more deeply about them than most of us.

Alongside HRH, slumped (that is the right word) the Hon. Nicholas Soames, normally the life and soul of any party, except that today he is on his best behaviour, expertly chairing our little gathering, introducing each of us, referring to HRH as 'Sir' even though they have been friends for 20 years or more.

We have stepped back in time. We are in the cluttered Edwardian sitting room of a great house. The date is any time in the last 100 years. A huge tapestry depicting a turbaned Arab potentate dominates the rear wall. Opposite, to the right of the mantelpiece, an exquisite Chinese cabinet full of tiny drawers. A grand piano, covered with framed family photographs, mainly black-and-white; one depicting Princess Margaret as a young woman to the fore. Autumn sunshine, filtered by the plane trees, streams in through the long windows. A servant dispenses refreshment. The room, indeed the entire lower floor, is exactly as it was when the Queen Mother was in residence. One half expects to see the old lady come hobbling in on her sticks or perhaps just to catch a glimpse of her disappearing around a corner.

HRH addresses us. He speaks without notes, with passion and self-deprecating humour, holding our attention for a full 20 minutes. His theme, the work of his various charities. Their range is vast, but always he comes back to the same point. How to widen the horizons of the young, especially the disaffected, the unlucky and even the malign. I confess I am impressed. This is a man who, if he chose, could fritter away his life on idleness and self-indulgence, as others who have borne the title Prince of Wales have done, and yet he has chosen to take an interest, a detailed interest, in the human condition. What influence he has he uses, sometimes to great effect, even at the risk of treading on official toes. It isn't just talk. His mentality is can-do – and he has a track record of achievement clearly visible for anyone who cares to look. To be sure he has faults. Don't we all? But let he who has done more cast the first stone.

A discussion ensues. Everyone contributes. HRH making the odd note with a thin gold pen. Some of our number use the occasion to invite him to their constituencies, which is not really the point of the exercise. Dari Taylor describes her childhood in the Rhondda. Others address the bigger picture. Alan Simpson turns the discussion to sustainable living, another of HRH's passions. It is apparent that the Prince has taken a shine to Alan. There is talk of a Great Exhibition. Alan says to him, 'Don't take this wrongly, but there is a role for someone to be the Jamie Oliver of the environment.' Adding sadly, ' I don't think the lead will come from Parliament.'

The meeting lasts nearly two hours. When it ends HRH presses an ornate button on the table beside him and the door opens, but he doesn't disappear. On the contrary, he lingers. On the way out I persuade the butler to give me a tour of the dining room. The walls are crammed. A veritable art gallery. A Sickert of George V at the races; an unusual Monet depicting a stark granite mountainside; various portraits of the Queen Mother, a large one of her as a young woman hangs over the fireplace; a series of bleak paintings of Windsor, commissioned at the outbreak of war because the King and Queen feared that the castle would be destroyed and wanted to preserve the memory.

Out into the garden and away across the park. A crisp, clear autumn day. Sunshine on golden leaves. A homeless woman sits scribbling on a park bench, her possessions piled around her. What is she writing? A letter to the Prince of Wales perhaps?

Friday, 18 November

Sunderland

To the Women's Centre in Green Terrace. An excellent enterprise which for 20 years has been enticing otherwise excluded women back into the world of education and work. Single mothers, asylum seekers, women who, without the lifeline of education, face a life ensnared in benefit culture. Fernanda, the Angolan woman who I helped to rescue from Yarlswood last week, is there learning English. Exactly in line with government policy one might think. It was. Until recently. But now the line from On High has changed. The focus is now relentlessly on the young. As a result the City of Sunderland College has slashed its funding. An application to the lottery has been rejected, on the grounds that it is not the business of the lottery to make up a shortfall in government funding. Result: the centre faces annihilation. It's the same all over town. All traditional sources of finance – Single Regeneration Budget, European Social Fund – are drying up simultaneously. If nothing changes, we face a wholesale collapse of the voluntary sector. The women who run the centre want my help, but what can I do? I will write a stern letter to the lottery and provide a 'To Whom It May Concern' letter to enclose with future funding applications, but we all know it's not enough.

Monday, 21 November

The Strangers' Cafeteria, House of Commons

Joined at lunch by a Yorkshire MP, a mild-mannered fellow, incensed by The Man's latest foray into education. 'We're opening the door for selection. Whatever safeguards we put in place, whatever assurances we give will be absolutely worthless once the Tories are in power.' And then: 'I think we will lose the next election. The Tories will come to some sort of understanding with the Lib Dems and we'll find that we've opened the door to the market in health and education. And when we protest they will reply, "But this is your policy; you started it." We'll be vulnerable for years. Our benches will be full of ex-ministers who won't have the stomach for the fight.' As he talked his anger mounted and most of it was directed at The Man. A straw in the wind.

Tuesday, 22 November

The Adjournment Restaurant, Portcullis House.

Lunch with Bruce Grocott, who shares the general dismay at The Man's latest education wheeze. We talked of reshuffles. Bruce, who has attended many, says that when it comes to the lower ranks they are totally arbitrary. Who is in, who is out depends less on ability than on the way the dice fall. Very few Cabinet ministers put themselves out to save junior colleagues who are at risk of the chop, although Jack is one who does. Which makes my downfall all the more mysterious.

A summons to see Deputy Chief Whip, Bob Ainsworth. Ostensibly to receive a bollocking for voting against the government last week, but in practice to sound me out about the future. The whips are terrified that the impending uprising over education will prove fatal both to The Man and to our prospects. Bob is a good man. Decent, down to earth, no bluster. He said, 'Your standing in this place has gone right down. It used to be that high' – he raised his hand – 'and now it's down here' – he lowered his hand. 'Why? Because no sooner are you out of government than you start voting against the whip.'

'I prefer to look at it another way,' I replied. 'I've never devoted much time to sucking up to my superiors in the hope of preferment, and the fact that I have been preferred anyway is a source of resentment among those who *have* sucked up.' That, plus the fact that many of my friends have retired or been dispatched to The Other Place.

'Where do you stand on the education reforms?'

I was non-committal. 'I've no desire to become a serial rebel, but I shall listen carefully to what my local authority has to say. Anyway, I'm not your problem.' I cited yesterday's conversation with the anonymous Yorkshireman.

'If Tony's defeated he will have to go. There will be chaos and we'll lose the election,' said Bob.

'Then he'd better start listening.'

I may be wrong, but I had the impression that was Bob's opinion, too.

Monday, 28 November

Victoria Line Tube, between King's Cross and Green Park

I am sitting opposite a moon-faced Arab woman dressed exactly as the failed suicide bomber arrested in Jordan the other day – in a headscarf and a long gown that reaches to her ankles. She is fiddling interminably with the contents of a British Home Stores plastic bag under which is concealed some sort of thin strap. Am I the only one who has noticed? She sees me watching. She stops, throwing occasional anxious glances in my direction. After a while I notice that the thin strap leads to her handbag, but I am not entirely reassured. A relief to disembark at Green Park and watch the train disappear into the tunnel, one ear half-cocked for the explosion which, mercifully, never comes.

Committee Room 14

Gordon Brown addressed the parliamentary party; attendance surprisingly thin. He spoke well, with passion and occasional flashes of humour but, as ever, something is lacking. There is no light in those eyes and he looks dreadfully out of condition – exhausted, flabby, stomach starting to spill over his belt. Oddly enough, his faithful acolyte, Ed Balls, is developing the same haunted, driven look as his master. Is there something in the water at the Treasury?

Tuesday, 29 November

This evening, an appearance on *Newsnight* to discuss 'extraordinary rendition', the American habit of kidnapping terrorists and franchising them out to foreign torturers. People are beginning to ask how much HMG knows about all this. Not a lot is my guess, but there is such a thing as wilful ignorance.

Wednesday, 30 November
The Lycee, Kennington

A BBC television crew came to interview me about Tony Benn. They are preparing an hour-long obituary programme, prompted by his recent collapse and the discovery that they have nothing substantial on the stocks. They focused mainly on the battles of the late seventies and early eighties, having already interviewed Denis Healey, Neil Kinnock and Shirley Williams. My role, therefore, was to be a witness for the defence. I steered clear of Tony's later retreat into impossibilism. With any luck it will be many years before it sees the light of day. When I looked up my notes from that era I did find one lovely line. His description of Kinnock: 'A vacuum surrounded by charisma.'

Friday, 2 December
Sunderland

At this evening's meeting of the management committee, an ear-bashing re my vote on the Terrorism Bill. The Silksworth women are on the warpath and a councillor, who I have long suspected of treason, muttered, 'If you can vote with your conscience, I'll vote with mine when the time comes.' Even Dave Allen started up, asking why MPs weren't subject to the same discipline as councillors, until I reminded him that he had been one of those insisting that I vote against the government on Iraq, at which point he went quiet. A couple of people whispered 'Well done' as they went out, but they had kept their mouths shut throughout.

Monday, 5 December

To the chamber for Gordon's pre-Budget statement. A note of humility might have been in order, given that his growth forecast was way out of line with reality, but Gordon doesn't do humility. Instead, cheered on by the troops, he unleashed a blizzard of facts and figures (all conveniently in billions rather than percentages) with a view to overwhelming anyone who dared question his stewardship. Young George Osborne, who, as Gordon was at pains to remind us, is the seventh Shadow Chancellor to face him across the dispatch box, was almost swept away in the torrent. I can't believe that Osborne will last any longer than his predecessors. He looks permanently pink and facetious, as though life is one big public school prank.

Then to an upper committee room for the first meeting of the all-party group on extraordinary rendition, which, for a committee that has never met and has no formal status, is attracting an enormous amount of attention. Andrew Tyrie, whose brainchild it is, was in the chair and Menzies Campbell and I are his deputies. Happily our meeting coincided with a carefully worded statement by Condoleezza Rice which, at first glance, appeared to be an indignant denial of the suggestion that the US was handing prisoners over to foreign torturers. We took evidence from Stephen Grey, a journalist who has been tracking the movements of the mysterious CIA planes which have been using UK airports, and James Crawford, a professor of international law. The key question, which keeps coming up, is the extent to which the UK is implicated. There is no evidence that we are involved but we do seem to have been displaying a disappointing lack of curiosity. When asked to comment, Jack looks distinctly sheepish.

Tuesday, 6 December

Most of this morning's papers suggest that Gordon was trounced by Osborne yesterday. Only goes to show how wrong one can be. Or perhaps I was attending a different event.

At three o'clock I turned on the television to witness the anointing of David Cameron. I must say the Tories have conducted themselves well during their ballot. Little or no unpleasantness, a civilised exchange of views involving a wide audience. It can only be good for them and for British politics as a whole. All the signs are that they have recovered the will to win. Cameron comes across as fluent, fresh, open-minded. We underestimate him at our peril.

Wednesday, 7 December

A big turn-out for David Cameron's first PMQs. The galleries were packed as well as the chamber. He was all right, but not brilliant. At one point he departed from his script to have a go at Hilary Armstrong, who was behaving badly on the front bench. The Man was very gentle with him, which was sensible in the circumstances.

Thursday, 8 December

A hilarious moment at Treasury questions (which I unfortunately did not witness). George Osborne was complaining about Gordon's overestimate of the growth rate, whereupon Dennis Skinner rose and said, 'Is my Right Honourable friend aware that in the seventies and eighties we'd have thanked our lucky stars in the coalfield areas for growth of 1.75 per cent?' Then, after a suitable pause, he added, 'The only things growing then were the lines of coke in front of Boy George and the rest of them.' Uproar. The Speaker called on Dennis to withdraw, which he declined ('It must be true, it was in the *News of the World*'), scurrying out of the chamber before the Speaker could evict him. I came across Dennis holding court in the Tea Room. 'I warned him, I warned those public school boys that I'd do them.' Apparently Osborne and his mates had been taunting Dennis about his age.

Monday, 12 December

To London. From the train, fine views of Lumley Castle and Burn Hall, illuminated by winter sunshine. Nearer London a distant glimpse of the vast black cloud arising from the huge fire at an oil depot at Hemel Hempstead. Across the aisle, a woman with a small blond boy. It wasn't until we were past Doncaster that I realised she was Sarah Brown. She looked exhausted and preoccupied so I made no attempt to strike up a conversation until we were pulling into King's Cross. I'm glad I did because she had recognised me and was friendly once we established contact.

Wednesday, 14 December

A call from Nick Raynsford. Would I like to take part in the uprising over the Education White Paper? Ever so respectable. Estelle Morris is leading the charge and David Blunkett is lurking somewhere in the background, acting the honest broker. Nick emailed a ten-page paper, intended as a constructive alternative to the White Paper, and I agreed to sign up, but steered clear of the press conference. I hope the government has the sense to listen, otherwise another crisis looms.

Tuesday, 20 December

An opinion poll in the *Guardian* puts the Tories ahead of us for only the second time in 12 years. If asked to choose between David Cameron and Gordon Brown the gap widens. Might just be a blip, but I somehow doubt it. I think we're in trouble.

On the train home I finished reading *A Spin Doctor's Diary* by Lance Price, a surprisingly readable first-hand account of New Labour's total obsession with news management. Price speaks highly of The Man but of Gordon he says, 'He does come across as a pretty ghastly human being sometimes, but his friends seem to like him.' One can't help wondering if Gordon is really the man to see off Cameron. I guess it is too late. We're going to end up with Gordon come what may.

Thursday, 22 December
Sunderland

To Sandhill View School, a New Labour success if ever there was. Twelve years ago it was a sink school with falling rolls and less than 10 per cent of pupils graduating with five or more GCSEs at grades A to C. Today on precisely the same catchment, more than half the children are achieving those grades. To what do we attribute this miracle? First, a brand-new school with state of the art facilities (a Private Finance Initiative, by the way). Second, a switch to vocational training for less academic students. Third, some first-rate dedicated teachers. One veteran teacher spoke of the difficulty of motivating boys. 'Mothers around here have low expectations of their sons. It is assumed that daughters will be responsible for everything – earning, bringing up children, housekeeping.'

Saturday, 24 December

I called at Hill's Bookshop, which is closing after 140 years. The manager says it's hopeless trying to compete with the chains. Some of the big supermarkets are demanding discounts of over 70 per cent and 'three for two' deals on new books are destroying the independent sector. A new hardback in some of the big chains has a shelf-life of just two weeks, after which if they fail to sell, they go back to the publishers to be pulped. Madness.

Tuesday, 27 December–Friday, 30 December
Helions Bumpstead, Essex

Three days with Liz and Mum. Weather for the most part icy. Despite snow and sleet long walks each day with Liz's dog, Rosie. Mum bright, but frail and increasingly bent. Up and down to the toilet every half-hour. 'I never thought I'd end up like this,' she said as I helped her to the bathroom for the umpteenth time. Of Brewster House she remarked, 'I thought it was only temporary. I never expected it to be a life sentence.' And when, just before Liz took her back to Brewster House, we took a photograph she said quietly, 'The last picture of

Granny.' Despite all, no real sign of self-pity. Mostly she was chatty and cheerful, playing cards and Scrabble with the children. Underneath, however, I detect a deep melancholy. Especially as regards the sale of Manor Drive. Had she been willing to cooperate and had we tried harder to persuade her, there is no reason why she shouldn't still be there today.

Saturday, 31 December
The Lycee, Kennington
The end of 2005. Not a good year.

CHAPTER TWO

2006

Wednesday, 4 January

To Newcastle for a tour of the new Crown Prosecution Service HQ. One interesting snippet. A senior prosecutor confirmed what I have long suspected – that GCHQ does tap domestic traffic. No doubt that helps to explain why the Security Service is so reluctant to make intercept evidence admissible in court.

Thursday, 5 January

I am reading the wartime diaries of Jock Colville, Churchill's private secretary. Aside from Colville's general brilliance and the maturity of his judgement (he was only 25 when the war started), several things strike me:

(1) The extent to which, even as late as 1940, the country was run by aristocrats; virtually everyone Colville knows is a toff and he is always bunking off for weekends at country houses and dining at posh clubs in St James's.

(2) How laid-back it all seemed, at least in the early days of the war; the diary is full of entries such as 'Rode at Richmond before breakfast ...' 'Back to work at 3.30pm after dining at home ...' Even on the morning of the Norway debate, which brought down the government, the Prime Minister's Assistant (as he then was) Private Secretary is to be found 'riding at Richmond under cloudless skies ...' And this is from the entry for 15 May 1940, the day of a

Cabinet reshuffle: 'Most of the afternoon was spent offering under-secretaryships to various politicians and it was my difficult job to explain on the telephone to Kenneth Lindsay, the Duke of Devonshire, Lord Denham and Captain McEwen that their services were no longer required.' Imagine the row these days if a minister, instead of being called personally by the Prime Minister, were telephoned by some 25-year-old under-strapper to be told that he was being 'let go'.

(3) How absolutely useless the French were. If Colville is to be believed, their military by and large refused to engage the Germans, only threatening a fight when we demanded they surrender their fleet, rather than handing it over intact to the Germans.

(4) How ruthless the Americans were as regards the terms they extracted from us in return for aid (at one point Colville compares the American demand for bases with Russia's blackmailing of Finland).

(5) How often our Secret Services were wrong about German morale and other vital matters (cf Iraq et al).

Friday, 6 January
Sunderland

Uproar on all fronts at this evening's meeting of my local party's management committee. Complaints about the local government settlement (Sunderland had one of the lowest); the proposed introduction of competition in postal services (well ahead of our European competitors, whose markets remain firmly closed); the underfunding of our election commitment to provide free bus fares for pensioners; and the upcoming reform of incapacity benefit. The greatest anger, however, was reserved for New Labour's plans for trust schools, which everyone interprets as the re-introduction of selection. All very depressing. Is it that Labour Party members are an out of touch sect who have continually to be press-ganged into the twenty-first century by their far-sighted young leaders or could it possibly be that on some, at least, of these issues New Labour has lost the plot?

Sunday, 8 January

Sarah and I were watching a drama about Churchill when Ngoc came in and said that Tony Banks was dead. I can't believe it. I just can't take it in. Apparently he suffered a massive brain haemorrhage in Florida yesterday.

Monday, 9 January

Sunderland

Awake in the early hours thinking about Banksie. At 4.30am I gave up trying to sleep, went downstairs and spent a couple of hours leafing through the last two volumes of the Benn diaries, looking up the references to him. Later, from the train, I rang the *Guardian*, offering to do an obituary. They had already run one by Julia Langdon in their later editions, but agreed to take 300 words.

House of Commons

Everyone has a fond memory of Tony Banks. Jean Corston recounted her last exchange with him, a few days before Christmas. She asked how he was finding life in the Lords? 'Wonderful,' he replied. 'I've gone from being a boring old fart to a young Turk in a single leap.' My favourite was an occasion about ten years ago when Norman Tebbit was called to speak. In the silence that preceded his opening words Banksie, in that cheeky-chappy voice of his, was heard to say, 'What's he doing out? It's not dark yet.'

No one seems to have a contact number for Sally, who is still marooned in Florida. I dropped her a note which I hope she will find as soon as she gets home.

A note from the whips' office to say that I have been nominated for the Standards and Privileges Committee.

Tuesday, 10 January

Prompted by my experience with the Angolan family, I had a 90-minute debate on the iniquity of removing children to dysfunctional countries. I had hoped that Tony McNulty, the immigration minister, would respond, but of course he sent one of the under-secretaries. I tried to keep within the realms of the possible, rather than being tempted down the path of 'stop removing all children', which is where many of the immigration lobbyists wanted me to go, but I'm not hopeful that anything will come of it.

The Boundary Commission is due to pronounce on Sunderland tomorrow. The word is that they are sticking to their original conclusion, which means that Sunderland South – or Central, as it will become – will be marginal next time round.

Wednesday, 11 January
The Lycee, Kennington

Awakened at 4am by terrible, murderous screeching. Put my head outside the door to find two foxes who had apparently been fighting, though neither seemed the worse for wear. A few minutes later a third fox put his head round the corner, but made off when he saw me. All this, only 50 yards from the national headquarters of the Countryside Alliance.

A call from Tam Dalyell. He wants me to take an interest in the Libyan convicted of the Lockerbie bombing, who, Tam believes, is innocent. In passing he mentioned that he had just been talking to an undertaker who said that his grandfather had been in the same line of business and used to receive letters from a man who signed himself, 'Yours eventually'.

Thursday, 12 January

Lunch with Robert Fellowes and Juliet Lyon, who want me to join the board of the Prison Reform Trust. It was Ruth Runciman's idea. I don't think I am tolerant enough after 30 years of inner city living, but I may give it a go. To my amazement Lord Fellowes, a former Private Secretary to the Queen who lives in a leafy area of Norfolk, said that he had been burgled half a dozen times, 'which I suppose is about average for someone of 63'. Actually, I think it is way above average, especially for citizens of his pedigree. Most people have never been burgled at all.

Home on the 20.00. The train was an hour and a half late, owing to a body on the line at Biggleswade. There was another yesterday near Grantham. 'It often happens at this time of the year,' said one of the stewards. 'It's when the credit card bills for Christmas arrive.'

Friday, 13 January

Sally Banks rang this evening. She sounded calm but said, 'I know I have a difficult road ahead.' We agreed that I will call on her when I get back from Liberia next week.

Sunday, 15 January

To Liberia to represent HMG at the inauguration of Ellen Johnson Sirleaf, Africa's first woman president. Jason from the Foreign Office collected me at 5am and we set off by taxi for Heathrow. The weekend newspapers are busy organising a row over John Prescott not having paid council tax on his grace and favour apartment at Admiralty House. Comparisons are being drawn with an elderly widow who was arrested for refusing to pay. Entirely spurious, of course, since no one had informed Prescott that he was liable and, as soon as he was informed, he paid up. But the poison is seeping – the taxi driver was on about it on the way to the airport until I pointed out the facts. One other snippet: Bill Clinton has suggested that The Man would make an excellent General Secretary of the UN (there is a vacancy at the end of this year). I am sure he would, but I can't see the idea going down with the General Assembly. The interesting point is that Clinton wouldn't have floated the idea without The Man's approval, which suggests a search for an early-exit strategy is underway.

We flew all day. Excellent views of the snow-capped Atlas mountains and the Sahara. Arrived in Monrovia early evening to be met by Our Man, David Lelliott, with whom I am staying.

Monday, 16 January

Monrovia

Not quite the style to which I am accustomed (last time I stayed with the American Ambassador). No view of the ocean, no fawning servants. Instead, from David's living room, a view over a wall topped with razor wire into the American compound and a row of sinister black Land Cruisers with shaded windows which later this morning will form part of the convoy bringing Laura Bush and Condi Rice into town. The security is awesome. About a hundred secret service men have been flown in and more or less taken over the organisation of the inauguration from the Liberians (who until Saturday did not even have a seating plan). Yesterday a C5 Galaxy arrived full of gleaming armoured Land Cruisers and an ambulance (also armoured). Condi and the First Lady will only be on Liberian soil for five hours, two of which will be spent driving to and from the airport.

Breakfast with Chris Gabelle on the terrace of his lovely house at the Hard Rock compound. Then through the streets of this ruined city to the gold-domed Capitol, where we took our seats (white plastic garden chairs) in good time for the ceremony. I am in the third row, behind the Chinese foreign minister and EU Commissioner Louis Michel. Old friends abound: Nana Akufo Addo (foreign minister of Ghana), Said Jinnet (the African Union's peace and security commissioner), Mohammed Chambas (ECOWAS General Secretary), Mrs Nkosi (Nigerian finance minister). The most difficult question: 'What are you doing now?'

Heads of state occupy the front row. Eleven are expected, including Presidents Mbeke and Obasanjo. In the best African tradition they dribble in at intervals throughout the morning, many arriving after the ceremony has commenced, the last (the President of Niger) when it is nearly over. 'This is Africa,' sighs Jinnet. Condi Rice, Laura Bush and the First Daughter, Barbara, arrive on time and to loud cheers. The Bush girl wearing a body-hugging, turquoise dress and wobbling self-consciously on the highest of high heels. Condi, by contrast, *très élegante*, demure almost, in a beige skirt, light orange jacket and a simple straw hat; never has so much raw power been concealed behind so innocent a facade.

The ceremony commences. A singer, a large woman in white, leads a rousing rendition of the national anthem, 'All hail Liberia ...' A bishop recites a prayer, after which proceedings were briefly interrupted by the arrival of the presidents of Senegal and Sierra Leone. Each head of state is welcomed by name, rising in his place to acknowledge the applause of the crowd, which, in some cases, is distinctly muted. Then it is the turn of the other delegations, including 'The Personal Representative of the Government of the United Kingdom'. The master of ceremonies reads a list of previous Liberian presidents, some of whom came to a very sticky end, the last but one of whom has been indicted for war crimes.

The Speaker, a comical figure in top hat and tails (allegedly a villain of some magnitude), convenes the recently elected lower house. Nervous laughter while he checks the quorum, 'to see whether we can do business'. No one would have been surprised had he found that they couldn't. A resolution is moved and duly agreed, transferring power from the transitional government to President-Elect Ellen Johnson Sirleaf, magnificently attired in a long cream gown topped by a matching headdress. 'Are we prepared to dissolve ourselves?' the Speaker inquires of the Representatives. He has to ask twice before eliciting a loud 'Yes.' The Representatives are a rum bunch. They include several mega-villains and half a dozen are said to be barely literate. One of the women is said to hire out girls.

The Chief Justice, a little man in a black gown with scarlet trimmings and a monsignor's hat with a red bobble, steps forward to swear in the new president. A big cheer from the crowd when she swears to discharge her responsibilities, 'So help me God.'

The arrival of the President of Mali is announced.

Then it is the turn of the vice-president, an elderly bewildered-looking gentleman. More disruption while the President of Niger arrives (is there a competition to see who can arrive last?), ambling onto the podium, entirely unashamed, pausing to shake hands with each of his fellow heads of state.

Finally, The Speech. And what a speech. Delivered with confidence and beautiful clarity. Hitting all the right buttons, promising 'a fundamental break with the past ... Forgiving, but not forgetting ... An end to physical destruction and moral degradation ...' Liberia, she says, is not a poor country, but a rich country that has been grievously mismanaged. She talks of creating a meritocracy. Of lean, efficient state agencies. Of honesty, hard work and visible progress – all concepts that until now have been anathema. When she promises 'to take on forcibly and effectively the debilitating cancer of corruption', a great cheer goes up. When she declares that all office holders will be required to declare their assets and that she will be the first to comply, the cheering is prolonged. And when she turns to the Speaker, challenging him to declare his assets too, the cheers turn to whooping and cries of 'Yeah'. He, at least, has the grace to smile, which is more than can be said for the Representatives, whose demeanour is distinctly surly. She concludes by pledging that 'no inch of Liberian soil will be used to conspire against neighbouring countries. The days of the imperial presidency are over. The best days are coming.'

Does she mean it? Undoubtedly. Will it happen? Who knows? The odds against are formidable. This is a country in ruins. Without running water, mains electricity or any other functioning public service. Where good men and true are in distinctly short supply. If anyone can succeed, Ellen Johnson Sirleaf can. If she does, she will become a role model for Africa. A truly uplifting occasion. A privilege to have been present.

Tuesday, 17 January

Breakfast on the terrace of the US Embassy club, overlooking the ocean and the helicopter landing pad. Then to UNMIL headquarters for a meeting of the West Africa contact group. I sat next to the American Assistant Secretary of State, Jendayi Frazer, a stocky, no-nonsense black woman. Several of the Africans seemed anxious to repeat the mistakes of the past, calling for an early end to sanctions and a bigger army. After lunch we adjourned to the Executive Mansion for a meeting with the President. To each of our questions she gave straight, clear answers. Listening to her it is easy to forget the gargantuan task she faces. This is a woman of 67 years who could, if she chose, be leading a comfortable retirement in Europe or America. Here she sits, alone in this monstrous pile of concrete. Is she to be pitied or admired?

In the afternoon, we spent two hours in the company of the local Oxfam rep walking around West Point, a teeming slum not ten minutes' drive from the city centre. The squalor is indescribable. Flies, filth, defecating children. Yet, in the midst of it all, little people in immaculate green tunics and yellow socks on their way home from school. Truly, the human spirit is uncrushable.

Wednesday, 18 January

Breakfast at the Hard Rock compound followed by an hour with the US Ambassador, Dan Booth, then back to the mansion for a private audience with the President. She was running late but gave us nearly an hour.

Then lunch in a beachside restaurant with Geoff Rudd, the EU representative, followed by a meeting with Alan Doss, who is in charge of the UN operation and effectively the most powerful man in the country. Finally to the airport, where we held our final meeting in the VIP lounge with Harry Greaves, one of the new president's advisers. Just before eight we took off for Brussels. So good to be back in action, even if only for a few days.

Friday, 20 January

The tabloids are gunning for Ruth Kelly. '150 PAEDOS IN YOUR SCHOOLS', rages this morning's *Sun*. No wonder we are becoming a nation of paranoids and hypochondriacs.

Much of the day completing my Liberia report. At lunch John Austin quoted Archbishop Tutu: 'When the first white men came to Africa we had the land and they had the Bible. They said, "Close your eyes and pray." When we opened them, we had the Bible and the white man had the land.'

A bottle-nosed dolphin has become stuck in the Thames. The first ever recorded in the river. The poor creature has got as far as the Albert Bridge. A large crowd has turned out to watch and desperate efforts are being made to turn it around before it becomes stranded.

Saturday, 21 January

To Wanstead for Tony Banks's funeral. Standing room only. Several members of the Cabinet – JP, Margaret Beckett, Tessa Jowell and at least a dozen other MPs, plus Bruce Grocott, Alastair Campbell, David Mellor and Tony Benn, a clutch of lobby correspondents and several of Tony's friends from the world of football. A simple ceremony with lots of laughs. Banksie arrived in an environmentally sound wicker coffin crowned with white lilies. There were four speeches, of which David Mellor's was the best, we all sang 'Jerusalem', there was a moment of reflection and then Banskie disappeared to the sound of Mozart's Clarinet Concerto.

Afterwards, at the reception in Newham Town Hall, I asked Alastair when he hoped to publish his diaries. He said he had been intending to wait until Tony retired, but now realised that he wouldn't be able to publish while Gordon was in office either, because there is a great deal of chapter and verse about the differences between him and Tony. He added that, throughout his time at Number 10, he had been required to defend a lie – namely, that all was well between Gordon and Tony when it wasn't; keeping the diary had been a release. Obviously it's going to be sensational.

Tuesday, 24 January

To my first meeting of the Standards and Privileges Committee, ably chaired by that most civilised of Tories, George Young. Then for a cup of tea with Hilary Benn, to report on Liberia. On the way out of the Tea Room I ran into Tristan Garel-Jones, who said, with only the slightest twinkle in his eye, 'We're grateful to you lot for all you've done during the last ten years. You've given us a good conservative prime minister, but now the ruling classes are back so you can fuck off.'

John Hutton made his long-awaited announcement on his plans to reduce the numbers on Incapacity Benefit. It was generally well received on our side, reflecting a feeling that our vast benefit culture is long overdue for a challenge – a view shared by many of my working class constituents, who deeply resent the scams they see going on around them. Later, during a division, John whispered that he knew of an amateur football team, currently topping a local league, in which eight of the eleven players recently fielded were on Incapacity Benefit.

Wednesday, 25 January

Much satisfied chortling in the Tea Room over George Galloway's prolonged and spectacular self-destruction, which reached its climax last night when he was evicted from the Big Brother house. The consensus is that George is finished politically. However, he does seem to have won his libel case against the *Daily Telegraph*. Personally, I think that's the best of both worlds. The *Telegraph*'s case was not that what they had reported was the truth, but that they could say what they liked because it was in the public interest. We all have an interest in seeing that line of argument defeated.

Martin and Mori Woollacott came to dinner. Martin takes the view that there is no need to panic over the possibility that the Iranians are building nuclear weapons because they know full well that to use them would invite their instant annihilation. I hope he's right. The weakness of Martin's argument is, of course, that Iran's present management believe in paradise for the righteous, which may not make them entirely rational.

Thursday, 26 January

To a meeting on Africa in Acton organised by the local Labour Party. About 30 people showed up, half of them Somalis. For the most part, we had a sensible dialogue until one of the Somalis started ranting and when one of the others told him to behave he turned and slugged him in the face. Eventually the police were called, he was taken away and the meeting resumed.

Tuesday, 31 January

To the Methodist Central Hall to hear an address by Kofi Annan, commemorating the anniversary of the United Nations, which was founded in the very same hall 60 years ago this month. He spoke beautifully, in that soft, modest tone of his, and yet he was robust. Afterwards I ran into Michael Williams, who now works at the UN, and asked if there was any chance that The Man might succeed Kofi when his term ends in December? The answer was a firm 'No'. Firstly, because there is an understanding that the job never goes to a member of the permanent five. Second, because under the inevitable UN system of Buggins' Turn the job has to go to an Asian.

Wednesday, 1 February

A historic day. George Bush, in his State of the Union address, conceded that America is 'addicted' to oil.

A chat with Jim Cousins re The Future. He shares my view that a Gordon leadership is potentially disastrous and that Hilary Benn is our best hope.

Thursday, 2 February

Shell have announced a £13 billion profit for last year, the largest ever recorded by a British company and at a time when energy prices are going through the roof. Dennis Skinner thinks Gordon should impose a windfall tax. I came across him bending the ear of Ann Keen (Gordon's Parliamentary Private Secretary) in the Members' Lobby this afternoon.

Monday, 6 February

Hosted a meeting in an upstairs committee room for a party of Afghan farmers, for whom I helped the Senlis Council obtain visas. They were hard, lean men whose sunken cheeks and unsmiling eyes reflected harsh lives. They had between eight and eleven children apiece, save for one who had lost all his to war and famine. The purpose of the meeting, a last-minute affair, was to tell us what it was like being on the receiving end of the 'war on drugs'. Everyone in Afghanistan, they said, grew opium. It wasn't possible to survive without doing so. Two said their crops had been aerially sprayed and that the sprayers made no distinction between wheat, fruit, vegetables and poppies. Result: hunger. One said that children in his village had died after eating poisoned fruit. Someone asked how much of the billions in foreign aid had reached them and their families: a kilo and a half of fertiliser, they said.

To my pleasant surprise Home Secretary Charles Clarke remarked at this evening's meeting of the parliamentary party that he had read my speech on the removal of children to countries like the Congo and Angola, he was thinking about it and would come back to me.

Tuesday, 7 February

Jack Straw joined me at lunch in the Tea Room and I took the opportunity to bend his ear about the handful of British residents stranded in Guantanamo. He used to argue that they were none of our business, but now seems receptive to doing something. 'I know you think I'm a hard bastard,' he said.

'I don't,' said I. 'I just think you need a prod from time to time.'

Wednesday, 8 February

A message from UK Visas saying that one of the Senlis Council's Afghan farmers has done a runner. Apparently he went to the toilet as the party were departing Heathrow yesterday and hasn't been seen since. A blow to my credibility since the visas were only granted reluctantly, on my recommendation. The first time I have ever been proved wrong in all my dealings with the immigration and visa departments.

At close of business this evening we all filed into the chamber to have our photo taken to mark the centenary of the founding of the Parliamentary Labour Party. The Man, the entire Cabinet and just about every Labour Member turned out. A few Tories stayed to watch.

It was dressed up as an Adjournment debate in the name of Ann Clwyd, whose seat was once represented by Keir Hardie. Ann made a speech extolling our achievements over the last hundred years, the mention of Ramsay MacDonald's name provoking some good-natured cheers from the Tories and jeers from our side. Then the photographer, in the gallery above the Opposition benches, marshalled us for the historic photo and we ended with a chorus of the 'Red Flag'.

Friday, 10 February

Against all odds, the Lib Dems have won the Dunfermline by-election. Bad news for us and for Gordon in particular since Dunfermline is his home ground.

A group of A-level students from the college came to my surgery this evening to lobby against plans to abolish their cheap travel cards in order to fund free bus travel for pensioners. It will cost them another £30 a month and many of them are harder up than the pensioners. Needless to say they are mightily upset and, if this goes ahead, we can kiss goodbye to any prospect of winning their votes at the next election. Among the customers at my surgery this evening was a pensioner who had come to say he didn't want free bus travel if it could only be delivered at the expense of young people and cuts in services. Other pensioners are quoted in the *Echo* expressing similar sentiments. Once again, it seems New Labour has devised a formula for upsetting everyone, victims and beneficiaries alike.

Sunday, 12 February

A big push is on to present Gordon as a prime minister in waiting. He's taken to spouting populist claptrap about 'Britishness' and calling for a 'Veterans' Day' public holiday. Today he made a speech promising to be tough on terrorists, even hinting that we might need to revisit the pre-trial 90 days' detention, the folly that was so resoundingly rejected a few weeks ago. If this is all he has to offer, the cupboard is well and truly bare.

Monday, 13 February

ID cards went through this evening with little sign of the promised uprising. Personally I think it was a fuss about nothing very much. The main case against is that they will be very expensive.

Tuesday, 14 February

Along with several others, I went to see Margaret Beckett to discuss global warming and related matters. 'The scientific argument is won,' she said, 'but the economic argument isn't'. On nuclear power she said, 'The Prime Minister says, in public and in private, that he has an open mind, but there is no doubt that some of those around him don't.' She added, 'There is no question that last year, after the election, a blatant attempt was made to bounce the government into taking an immediate decision. The danger is that, once we opt for nuclear power, the pressure to develop sustainable alternatives will disappear.' Kitty Ussher, a former special adviser at the DTI, recounted the struggle ministers had with pro-nuclear civil servants in the run-up to the 2003 Energy White Paper. It's a straight replay of what happened in the seventies when both the departments of Energy and Trade and Industry were deeply in bed with the nuclear lobby. I later talked to Malcolm Wicks, the energy minister, who insisted that all concerned had open minds, but I reminded him that some of us were old enough to remember what happened last time around.

'Were you part of that small elite who were invited to participate in a weekend school at an Oxford college when we were preparing for office in 1996?' inquired Nick Raynsford, apropos our difficulties over the proposed trust schools. I wasn't, but Nick was. He said, 'We were treated to a brilliant lecture by a *Financial Times* journalist called Andrew Adonis on great policy disasters, with particular reference to the Poll Tax, which we were told had been pushed through by a small group around the prime minister, without any evidence of public support and against the grain of policy advice.' Nick went on, 'I recently reminded Andrew of it.'

'I trust the colour drained from his face.'

'He didn't want to see the analogy.'

This evening by a majority of more than 200 we voted through a ban on smoking in public places, the government having wisely, if belatedly, opted for a free vote. A landmark decision. The Health Secretary, Patricia Hewitt, who I had always understood to be on the side of the angels, behaved very oddly. This morning she was on the radio implying that she intended to support a compromise that would have exempted working men's clubs and other private institutions, but by nightfall she was back in the complete ban lobby.

Wednesday, 15 February

A chat with Keith Hill and Bob Ainsworth regarding yesterday's smoking vote. It appears there was more to it than met the eye, Patricia Hewitt having been persuaded at the last moment, and against all medical advice, to support exemption for private clubs. The Man, who apparently was not bothered either way, promptly declared that he would back his Secretary of State, thereby raising the ghastly spectre of the prime minister being in the losing lobby and dissipating the enormous goodwill that might be expected to accrue from having, for once, done The Right Thing. This necessitated some deft footwork by Keith and the whips to persuade Patricia (who usually has an unerring instinct for the winning side) to re-defect and thereby ensure that The Man ended up among the righteous. Keith, as it happens, favoured the exemption but, in the interests of the greater good, nobly steered The Man into the Aye Lobby and then went off to vote the other way.

A long talk with Alan Milburn, who shares my view that Gordon may not be a winner. He hinted that this is The Man's view, too. However, Alan also reckons that in the short term there is no one to beat Gordon or even to raise the signatures required to trigger a contest, which means that we may be locked into a position which will inevitably end in defeat. Alan thinks (or rather hopes) that the longer Tony stays the more apparent Gordon's shortcomings will become.

Friday, 17 February

Home, to find a winter gas bill of £534 (compared to £350 for this time last year) and a promise of more to come – British Gas have announced another 23 per cent increase. Much talk that the European energy companies are operating some sort of cartel, but maybe the global energy crisis is coming sooner than expected. Also, a report today that the Greenland icecap is melting faster than anyone has previously anticipated.

Monday, 27 February

Gulu, northern Uganda

To the north to find out about the war against the Lord's Resistance Army. Ben Shepherd, my Foreign Office minder, and I flew up early this morning in a small Cessna. Fine views of the Nile and Lake Kyoga. Everywhere clusters of round thatched Acholi huts, abandoned to the Great Terror. We spent the day visiting – the archbishop, the paramount chief, a reception centre for rescued children. The children spoke in whispers, avoiding eye contact. Only the younger boy, who had escaped from the LRA after two months, had any light in his face. Later, we visited a night shelter accommodating some of the hundreds of children who trek in from the villages and camps around the town to avoid being taken by the LRA.

Main impressions: exhaustion, quiet desperation. Most Acholi, even the archbishop, speak in a slow whisper, pausing frequently to rub their eyes. This nightmare has been going on for 20 years; they feel abandoned by their government and, despite all the aid, by the international community. Also, ambiguity. The LRA fighters, for all their unspeakable brutality are, after all, kidnapped children – *their* children. Much talk of the need to negotiate, but what is there to negotiate about? The more I listened the more I felt that, as with Savimbi in Angola, one bullet – in the head of Joseph Kony – is all it would take to bring this madness to an end. But who is to administer the *coup de grâce*?

Tuesday, 28 February

Gulu

A curious town, this. The focal point of Gulu is the Acholi Inn, owned by a Ugandan intelligence officer who has had a good war and who (according to those who know him) is in no hurry to see it come to an end. He is currently playing host to two big LRA defectors, Sam Kollo and Colonel Kamdulu. Kollo was rescued by helicopter after sending an SOS, saying that Kony was about to have him killed, but so far as can be determined he has said nothing of any significance to anyone since he arrived and there is a suspicion that he may be a plant. On most evenings Kollo and Kamdulu are to be found drinking in the garden of the Acholi Inn, alongside the very Ugandan army officers who until lately were trying to kill them, members of all the local political parties, and an assortment of UN officials and aid workers. The army apparently pays their bills. Meanwhile, in camps not five miles away, their erstwhile victims, in their tens of thousands, are crammed into encampments, too terrified to return to their homes in the bush for fear of what terrors the darkness holds. A bizarre scene; one which requires an Alan Bennett or a David Hare to do it justice. The only parallel I can think of is the bar of the Hotel Constellation in Vientiane, but in Laos, venal or incompetent though they may have been, neither side kidnapped children or chopped up civilians in cold blood.

This morning we drove to a camp for displaced people about 12 miles out of town along a red, dusty road. The Acholi usually live not in villages but in family groups, a cluster of round, thatched tulkuls. Now, as a result of this nightmare, they are crammed into crowded encampments close to the road; the same round thatched houses, but only feet apart with only the crudest sanitary arrangements and children defecating openly. In the dry season fires break out and, when the rains come, cholera. Nearly two million people, 90 per cent of the rural population across three provinces, live like this. We talked to the chief, an elderly man in a technicolor shirt depicting stations on the New York underground. He was polite but weary, complaining of high blood pressure and diabetes. He had lived like this for ten years. Many white people had come to ask him questions, he said, but nothing ever seemed to change. 'We are grateful to you for feeding us, but why can't you help us to defeat Kony? In the 1940s we fought for the King, why can't the Queen help us now?'

Tuesday, 7 March

At the behest of a little animal charity which has been put on to me by Tony Benn, I tabled an early-day motion calling on the Ministry of Defence to stop importing bearskins for use by the Guards regiments. This prompted a call from John Gilbert, who said that he had taken this up when he had been at the MOD, resulting in a letter of protest from the heir to the throne. It had gone unanswered because John was unwilling to agree a suitably reassuring reply. The official position is that the MOD is examining alternatives, but of course they are dragging their feet. Good to know that John is sound on bearskins – if not nuclear weapons.

Wednesday, 8 March

Lunch at the Commonwealth Club with the acting Ugandan High Commissioner, a very bright woman who used to work for Museveni, who lamented the absence of an Africa minister in the Commons. 'Does the government care about Africa?' she inquired.

Thursday, 9 March

A light week, not a single Division. I whiled away several hours in the library reading Traudl Junge's absorbing account of the final days in the Führerbunker, *Until the Final Hour*, and wept over the fate of the six little Goebbels children.

Friday, 10 March

Emma has been learning about the Ten Commandments, but they have not had the desired effect. 'I think God is very selfish,' she remarked to Ngoc after school the other day.

'Oh?'

'Because he says, "Don't listen to anyone except me".'

Yesterday she came home and pronounced firmly, 'I don't believe in God.' So that's God and Santa Claus disposed of in the space of 12 months.

Monday, 13 March

To the meeting of the parliamentary party to hear a final plea from Ruth Kelly for us all to get behind the Education Bill. She spoke well, but then she has had plenty of opportunity to hone her arguments. Never has a White Paper been more intensively consulted upon, albeit in retrospect. There is a curious ritual at meetings of the parliamentary party in times of crisis. No such occasion is complete without a heartfelt plea for loyalty from George Howarth. He is usually followed by Barry Sheerman, who concedes that he may once have entertained a scintilla of doubt, but now reveals that he is 1,000 per cent behind whatever the government is proposing. Finally, JP is wheeled in to rally the troops with his own unique brand of rhetoric, which on this occasion, as on others, skirted perilously close to several minefields (more than once I saw eyebrows raised on the top table), but managed to end up in just about the right place. Afterwards, I was subjected to a good-natured ear-bashing by David Miliband apropos my question to the Prime Minister the other day about Foundation schools. By an extraordinary coincidence, another opportunity for mischief has presented itself: I have been drawn second in the ballot for PM's Questions on Wednesday immediately before the House is due to consider the Bill.

Morale very low. Colin Burgon, once a teacher, believes the Education Bill will widen rather than narrow the attainment gap. He also complained about the lifestyle of some of the New Labour elite – Mandelson, Blunkett, Jowell and her husband, and the increasingly shameless correlation between big donations and peerages. 'We're all contaminated,' he said to Ed Miliband, Helen Goodman and myself as we sat in the Members' Lobby awaiting the outcome of the division.

No one spoke. 'I can tell by your silence that you all think I'm loopy,' said Colin gloomily, walking away. But we didn't actually. 'The reason for my silence was that I agree,' said Ed Miliband after Colin had gone. He added, 'The trouble is that we are all held hostage by what *he* decides.'

Tuesday, 14 March

Awoke to a horrifying discussion about asylum on the *Today* programme. Edward Leigh (chairman of the Public Accounts Committee), who obviously hadn't a clue what he was talking about, was allowed *carte blanche* to resurrect the asylum bogie. Later, John Humphrys, sounding more like Richard Littlejohn, ranted away at the immigration minister, Tony McNulty (who is already ruthless enough without being pushed into greater excesses), demanding to know why we were not sending home more. No one mentioned that many of the worst offending countries – Iran, for example – won't accept back their citizens or that there is no government in Somalia to negotiate with (indeed there's a famine underway there at the moment). We're already sending back people to death and destitution in such places as Angola and the Congo, what more do they want? Later, I bent Edward Leigh's ear on the subject. He was a bit sheepish and more or less admitted that he didn't know much about the subject.

Wednesday, 15 March

For the second week running my name came up at PM's Questions. I asked one suggested by Nick Raynsford and for the second week running was duly rewarded with a non-answer. More than ever The Man dwells in the stratosphere, floating above us, only visiting our little world for an hour or two each week. He has long ago worked out when he will leave and nothing that happens between now and then is going to make much difference.

At least that what's I thought until early this evening, when Angela Eagle whispered that there was a big new crisis brewing. It appears there is a secret list of mega-donors, most of whom have featured on honours lists and who have loaned the party vast sums on terms which remain opaque. It seems that no one told the party treasurer, Jack Dromey, and tonight he has gone public, demanding an inquiry. According to Angela, when the subject was raised at the parliamentary committee this afternoon the blood drained from The Man's face and his replies became monosyllabic, a sure sign that this is a big one.

Earlier I had a quiet chat with Bob Ainsworth (Deputy Chief Whip), who was surprisingly frank. 'What are we going to do about him? He's becoming outrageous. Like Louis XIV – *l'état, c'est moi*. Sooner or later there will be a coup attempt.' A couple of hours later Jack Dromey launched his Exocet.

Thursday, 16 March

The loans crisis has blasted our difficulties over the Education Bill off the front pages. It looks like a scam designed to get us round the disclosure laws on party funding that we are so proud of having introduced. Apparently, a similar scheme was put to Dave Triesman when he was General Secretary and he vetoed it. Likewise Charles Clarke when he was chairman. So they just waited until someone more pliable came along. It's clear The Man is in this up to his neck. Indeed he admitted as much at his press conference this morning, at which he appeared uncharacteristically chastened. The sums involved are much larger than has so far been disclosed – at least £10 million. Goodness knows how the party was ever supposed to pay it back. Technically it's legal, but it stinks to high heaven. The Tories on the whole are keeping their heads down, as well they might since they've been into this sort of thing much longer than we have.

'We've lost our moral and political compass,' remarked Colin Burgon, whose gloom increases with every passing day.

Sunday, 19 March

Sunderland

A couple of deeply demoralising hours canvassing for a council by-election in Millfield. Only a handful of those who claimed to be Labour supporters offered any indication that they will actually vote. Even those with postal votes seemed to lack the energy to fill them in. Not necessarily a symptom of our present difficulties, at least no one referred to them, merely of overwhelming, mind-numbing indifference, a feature of the times in which we live. Only catastrophe or the threat of it will wake us from our slumber.

Monday, 20 March

Perhaps it's my imagination, but I get the feeling that the loans-for-peerages crisis has peaked, at least for the time being, although the stain will linger for years to come and may yet hasten The Fall. Today the party published the names of our 12 lenders who made loans and Charlie Falconer announced an inquiry into party funding, to be conducted by a retired mandarin, which will ease the pressure for the time being. The hacks, of course, are doing their best to keep it going. A naive young woman from *Newsnight* called and asked if I'd like to 'discuss the impact' on The Man, a theme that's been done to death already. She lost interest when I suggested that the more interesting question is how are democratic politics in Britain to survive, given (a) that the two main parties are effectively bankrupt and (b) the public are against all the available options: joining, donating and state funding? Time to resurrect Mike O'Brien's idea that every taxpayer should be given the option of making a modest tax-free donation to the political party of his or her choice.

Wednesday, 22 March

The media are still hammering away at 'Blair's millionaires' (whose identities have been voluntarily disclosed) while simultaneously displaying a remarkable lack of curiosity about the Tory donors whose identities the Tories are resolutely refusing to reveal. The suspicion is that some of them are foreigners. Dennis Skinner is said to have given Jack Dromey a bollocking at yesterday's meeting of the National Executive Committee for taking his complaint 'outside the family'.

PMQs was curiously subdued. Cameron steered well clear of the tricky issue of party funding and from our side came only risible lollipop questions. In the end Alan Haselhurst punished us by calling a succession of Opposition questions, instead of following the usual practice of alternating. The Speaker's secretary told me afterwards that the teenage bother boys in Number 10 were on to him at once, demanding an explanation. How dare they?

Thursday, 23 March

Steve Byers says The Man thinks that Jack Dromey's outburst was a coup attempt. Unlikely, but an interesting insight into his state of mind. Steve also says, as though it were common knowledge, that Jack Straw will be Gordon's deputy. I've long suspected that was what Jack was aiming for, but hadn't realised it's a done deal. You have to hand it to Jack, he has managed to slide from one camp to the other without creating so much as a ripple on the surface of the pond.

Saturday, 25 March

Sarah went for a walk in the park this afternoon WITH A BOY. 'Don't worry, Dad,' she said as she was leaving. 'He's not exactly Mr Darcy.'

Monday, 27 March

My visitors this afternoon included the chief executive of Groundwork, an environmental agency which was part of my many responsibilities when I was at Environment. I asked how many ministers he'd had to account to since we were elected. 'We're on our tenth,' he replied. 'And from the government's point of view it's wholly counterproductive.'

At this evening's meeting of the parliamentary party, which was addressed by Gordon, Dennis Skinner hijacked the proceedings with a long rant, apropos the 'loans for peerages' row, about the inadvisability of hanging out our dirty washing in public. 'I hear the word "transparency" trotted out every ten minutes. I wasn't born into a world where we all said, "Let's be transparent." It was "Whose side are you on?"' He warned our select committee members against too much inquiring. 'This is not the moment to get us into a deeper mire than we are in. This is the time to come to the aid of the party.' Applause was modest. There were grim faces at the top table. The trouble is that the world into which Dennis was born is not the one in which we live today. JP said that the National Executive was determined to regain control of party finances. A couple of people pleaded for a smooth transition and were heard in embarrassed silence. Then David Winnick said something about not being in favour of selling peerages (as if anyone is), which set Dennis off again. There was agitation on the top table. I could hear JP murmuring, 'Come on, Dennis', but no one dared shut him up. It was a full 20 minutes before Gordon's turn came.

Tuesday, 28 March

The Tea Room

I was sitting with Bob Ainsworth lamenting the money we had lavished on the salaries of doctors and consultants (which is partly responsible for the current NHS funding crisis) when we were joined by Alan Milburn, architect of the present pay structure. He was unrepentant. 'The real story,' says Alan, 'is that in many places hospitals have been so successful at reducing waiting lists that they have run out of work. They need to start reducing staff. There is nothing wrong with a few unemployed doctors and nurses. Until now we have been dealing with a monopoly provider. We need a labour market in the NHS, just like there already is in other areas of the economy.'

Alan also thinks we need to scrap tax credits and instead reduce taxes for the poorest. 'Tax credits are based on the belief that the state can micro-manage people's lives – and it can't.'

'A fundamental philosophical difference between yourself and Gordon,' said I.

'It is,' said Alan.

This evening, in a crowded room at 1 Parliament Street, Andrew Tyrie and I took evidence from the wife and brother of two British residents trapped in Guantanamo. They have been treated disgracefully. Arrested in Gambia, ghosted to a secret prison in Afghanistan, where they were grievously mistreated, and from there to Cuba. Until now Jack has refused to authorise any representations on their behalf on the grounds that they are not our responsibility, but lately there have been signs of movement, prompted by the revelation that one of them appears to have been co-operating with the security service, which promptly washed its hands of him as soon as he was no longer useful. The poor woman has been left on her own to bring up five children aged between three and eight. Unlike their father, they are all British citizens. She said the oldest boy asked the other day, 'Mum, why don't I give Dad my passport, then he can come home?' Mr El Rawi, whose brother is the other captive, remarked afterwards, 'I grew up hating Iraq for what it did to my father. I don't want these children to grow up hating Britain for what it is doing to their father.'

Wednesday, 29 March

To the Home Office to see Charles Clarke re my concerns over the removal of children to dysfunctional countries. He was very affable, coming out in person to collect me from the waiting area. I begin to suspect that beneath that man-in-a-hurry, all-business exterior a decent heart beats. As ever, he moved swiftly to the point: 'What's your solution?'

'First, stop removing families with children to places like the Congo, Angola, Sudan. No need to call it an amnesty. Just stop doing it. Second, if you must remove them, then make an arrangement for them to be met and re-integrated at the other end.' Charles promised to reflect and report back after Easter.

Thursday, 30 March

To Brewster House to see Mum, who is in reasonable spirits, all things considered. She suffers from two unshakeable delusions: (1) that Dad died only a few days ago and (2) that she has recently been back to Manor Drive. That apart, she is entirely *compos mentis*. As we sat in the conservatory among the gaga she remarked astutely, 'It must make you shudder to think that in 20 years' time you might end up like this.'

Friday, 31 March

At this evening's surgery, a family of Sri Lankan asylum seekers. Father, mother, three lovely daughters, all at Sarah's school. The father's story is that his sister married a Tamil, whom he subsequently employed in his wholesale grocery business, thereby bringing down upon his family the wrath of the security apparatus. He has lost two brothers, one arrested and not heard of since, one murdered (they produced photos of his funeral); his house was shot up and his business burned. The poor man is traumatised and clearly believes he will be killed if he is sent back – and who is to say he won't? Even the judge who turned down his asylum claim pleaded for him to be allowed to stay, but the Home Office is having none of it. Tony McNulty, the immigration minister, won't even talk to me about the case. What am I to do?

These intractable asylum cases occupy more and more of my time. My current caseload includes two Congolese, a woman from Sierra Leone with a 16-month-old child and a family of Angolans. They all face either destitution or torture (and in some cases death) if returned and yet, increasingly, I have to look them in the eyes and say there is nothing I can do to save them.

Saturday, 1 April

Awoke before six, still worrying about the Sri Lankan family, to say nothing of one of the Congolese whose benefits have been cut off and who is only surviving on handouts from other asylum seekers. Unable to sleep, I went downstairs and, for light relief, read Nikita Khrush-chev's account of the Great Terror.

Wednesday, 5 April

The singer Gene Pitney has been found dead in a hotel room, a few hours after giving a concert in Cardiff. What a way to go. Not for him the long, slow decline into frailty and incontinence. He just closed his eyes and went to sleep with the applause of the crowd still ringing in his ears.

Friday, 7 April

A letter from David Graham, chairman of the local hospital trust, saying it is £4 million in deficit, despite being one of the best managed in the country. Just under a million is accounted for by increased heating bills, which is fair enough, but £1.8 million is, he says, down to the underfunding of centrally agreed pay awards. In other words the trail leads back to Gordon.

Sunday, 9 April

I am becoming short-tempered. The smallest difficulty can render me apoplectic and sometimes distraught. The symptoms were always there, even in adolescence, but lately they seem to be returning with a vengeance. Madness? The onset of Alzheimer's? Who knows? The cause, I begin to suspect, is a growing sense of failure. A feeling that I let down Dad during his long, terrible final illness and that now I am letting down Mum, albeit she is difficult to help. That, plus the fact that I no longer have anything useful to do in politics. Yet every day I count my blessings: good health, lovely children, money in the bank. I read the other day about a cotton farmer in India who committed suicide over a debt of £390 – the cost of Sarah's school trip to France – which he had no hope of repaying. He had a 16-year-old daughter, too. What would he have given to change places with me?

Easter Monday, 17 April

That foolish woman Margaret Hodge has caused a great fuss with a statement that eight out of ten of her Barking constituents are contemplating voting for the BNP in the local elections. Result, acres of airtime devoted to earnest discussions on the unlikely prospect of a BNP electoral triumph, endless vox pops with whingeing, disaffected inhabitants of the East End benefit culture who are allowed to claim – unchallenged – 'Labour's done nothing for us' and that everything is being spent on migrants. On *Today* this morning a chillingly plausible BNP spokesman (introduced as 'Dr' somebody or other) was given a prime-time opportunity to state his case. All courtesy of Margaret Hodge.

Wednesday, 19 April

The Man was shamelessly brilliant at Question time, insisting that it was a matter for rejoicing that we had the highest-paid doctors in the world. The truth is, of course, that we've allowed ourselves to be completely conned by the British Medical Association into paying over the odds for work most doctors were already doing.

I came across Margaret Hodge in the library corridor and gave her a piece of my mind. She appears to be in denial.

Friday, 21 April

A new row over Cherie Blair's latest extravagance. Apparently she charged the Labour Party £7,500 for having Andre, her hairdresser, attend upon her throughout last year's election campaign. Yet more fuel, if any were needed, for the notion that the New Labour elite live on another planet from the rest of us. One can't imagine Norma Major or Mary Wilson needing a personal hairdresser or a life-style guru let alone a £3.6 million house. Whatever one thinks of Gordon, there will be none of this nonsense when he and Sarah move into Number 10.

Charlie Falconer rang this afternoon to discuss party funding. We had a long chat about the overall state of play. He remarked that, despite everything, the Tories don't seem to be making much headway. Maybe, but the sad truth is that the punters loathe us all in equal measure and with every new faux pas the pit gets deeper.

Monday, 24 April

Angela Eagle says she has been told by Andrew Tyrie, the Tory MP who is charged with drawing up his party's policy on funding, that a Tory government will certainly ban all donations from trade unions. She also says there is talk of a Blair Foundation, à la Bill Clinton, so that when he goes all the corporate cash will go with him and the party will be left high and dry. *Après New Labour le déluge.*

Tuesday, 25 April

A new disaster looms. The Home Office this afternoon has admitted that for at least the last seven years it has failed to implement any deportation orders against foreign criminals on completion of their sentences. Murderers, rapists, paedophiles, you name it, they have all been simply released back onto the streets. Worse, it seems that the ministers were alerted months ago, but nothing was done. Illegal migrants and paedophiles, a toxic mix. The tabloids will go bananas.

Wednesday, 26 April

As if we aren't in enough trouble, it appears that John Prescott has been screwing his diary secretary. This morning's *Mirror* splashes five pages of pictures of the happy couple and by lunchtime everyone was on the case. Then, to crown all, Patricia Hewitt was shouted down at the annual conference of the Royal College of Nursing, supposedly the responsible wing of the medical profession. Meanwhile a hunt is underway for the missing foreign criminals. It's only a question of time until one is found to have killed or raped someone, then Charles Clarke's position will be untenable. He was in the Tea Room this afternoon, looking very subdued.

Today is being dubbed 'Labour's Black Wednesday'.

Thursday, 27 April

A chat with Dennis Skinner. He reckons that our recent difficulties are as nothing compared with the late seventies.

Not everyone is as sanguine. Nick Raynsford took me aside in the Noe Lobby this afternoon. 'This can't go on,' he said. 'We've no support anywhere. Even *The Times* has abandoned us. There will soon be nothing left. If we do as badly as expected, someone will move against him.'

I pointed out that taking over now would not necessarily be in Gordon's interests. The hacks would have three years to destroy him, instead of one.

To which Nick replied, 'At least with Gordon and Sarah there will be no trouble with expensive hair-dos or holidays with Berlusconi.'

Sunday, 30 April

Awoke to the inevitable news that Prescott's lover has sold ('for a six-figure sum') her version of events to the *Mail on Sunday*, which has splashed the sordid details across no fewer than nine pages. JP meanwhile clings tenaciously to office, as does Charles Clarke, though I can't see how either can survive. Four days to go until the local elections, when meltdown looms. How are we supposed to ask people to vote for us in this climate? Ngoc remarked yesterday, 'If I wasn't your wife, I wouldn't vote Labour next week.'

Monday, 1 May

It's clear that Charles is a gonner, probably by the end of the day, certainly by Thursday. Who will replace him? There are no obvious candidates. The Man is increasingly friendless as all around him succumb. He could go for a shiny New Labour lightweight, such as Hazel Blears, but she will cut no ice with the public.

Tuesday, 2 May

Coffee with an old friend who has spent a year working for Lord Levy, fundraiser extraordinaire. 'I became aware of a Labour Party I didn't know existed,' he says. 'A cluster of mega-rich, unideological, Blair-worshippers who are lunched and dined in grand hotels, granted favoured access and whose opinions are listened to with rapt attention. They have much more influence than the other Labour Party.'

And what about our little 'loans for peerages' difficulty? He had overheard one or two conversations and Levy always went out of his way to make clear that there was no promise of an honour, adding slyly, 'but I will just make two points: (1) a donation does not rule out an honour and (2) contributions to good causes can lead to honours. If you wish, I can send you details of one or two good causes that might qualify.'

Came across Doug Henderson in the library. 'The question is no longer, "When will Gordon take over?"' he said. 'It is, "Can even Gordon save us?"'

Wednesday, 3 May

Awakened at 5.30am by one of those night flights that I failed to ban when I was laughingly known as the aviation minister. Read a chapter of Khrushchev's memoirs on his relationship with Mao and then walked to Westminster in glorious sunshine, arriving just as Big Ben struck eight.

Simon Jenkins in the *Guardian* is talking of 'systemic failure' ('and the system is Blair's'). He's not wrong. All this hyperactivity, the ill-thought-out, underfunded initiatives, the compulsive target-setting is getting us into trouble on every front and most of it originates from Number 10. The trouble is Gordon is a control freak, too. If anything, worse than The Man. He's not the solution, but part of the problem. We need a clean break with the past, but we are not likely to get it. Perhaps we are hard-wired for self-destruction?

I went in for PMQs and stayed for Charles Clarke's statement on the failure to deport foreign rapists etc., and emerged mildly cheered.

David Davis performed poorly, shades of Kinnock and Westland. For a moment I found myself thinking that perhaps we don't need a reshuffle after all. Maybe we should just tough it out rather than surrender to the baying mob.

Prescott is much in evidence, looking and sounding surprisingly bullish. He was lunching with Geoff Hoon and his loyal assistant, Joan, at a nearby table in the cafeteria and sounding much like his normal self. How dare he?

Thursday, 4 May
Sunderland

Local election day. The only visible political activity is the BNP man driving around the town in a van festooned with Union Jacks and loudspeakers endlessly blaring 'Land of Hope and Glory'. A columnist in tonight's *Echo* complains about the invisibility of the candidates in his ward. Only one of the parties – and it wasn't us – has put a leaflet through his door. 'If the candidates can't be bothered,' he asks, 'why should we?' Quite.

Friday, 5 May

A small earthquake, but not the predicted meltdown. In Sunderland we lost only a single seat, but even here unmistakable signs of a Tory recovery. They, not the Lib Dems, are the principal beneficiaries of the pounding we have taken in the last few weeks. Also, the BNP did well among the lumpen, capturing 11 seats in Barking, almost enough for a little fascist statelet.

Frank Dobson was on the radio this morning, very sore at the loss of Camden, saying that the party was a hollow husk and calling for The Ultimate Sacrifice. He was followed by Gordon Brown, whose mantra for the day was that we had to do more listening (whatever else Gordon is good at, listening sure ain't one of his strong suits). By lunchtime came news of a big shake-up: Charles Clarke is out, replaced by the ubiquitous John Reid, but the surprise is that Margaret Beckett has replaced Jack Straw (who becomes Leader of the House, a considerable demotion); his canoodling with Gordon has obviously not gone unnoticed.

Saturday, 6 May

Drastic though it was, the reshuffle has not doused the flames. The hacks are affecting knowledge of a letter said to be circulating among Labour backbenchers demanding The Man's early departure. BBC journalists, who are as bad as the tabloids when it comes to fantasy politics, are ringing round asking if we've signed and, if we haven't, would we? They called twice yesterday, but I refused to play. So far as I can see, no such letter exists. Perhaps it has been dreamed up at a *World This Weekend* editorial conference.* By Monday, however, it may well have become self-fulfilling.

Monday, 8 May

6 p.m., Committee Room 14

To a jam-packed meeting of the parliamentary party for what the media are billing as yet another showdown between The Man and his critics. A large party of hacks lurking at the door, kept at bay by two policemen. Entire Cabinet on parade, minus Margaret Beckett, the new Foreign Secretary, who's in New York discussing what to do about Iran; grim faces at the top table; Jack, Gordon studiously inscrutable; Charles Clarke, now reduced to the ranks, studiously jovial.

Enter The Man, tired, tense, glazed, but surprisingly tanned, as though he has spent the weekend in the garden, after Friday's butchery. As usual on these occasions, not a note in sight. He talks of difficult times; of deciding whether we get through or go under. 'To set a public timetable,' he says, 'would be as foolish as it is possible to imagine.' Then the key phrases: 'Ample and proper time', 'a stable and orderly transition'. A reference to 'what is called in the press my "legacy"'. Pause for effect, and then: 'My legacy is a fourth victory.'

---

*It turned out to have been drafted by Neal Lawson of Compass, an obscure think tank; there was no evidence that any MP had anything to do with it.

Applause. A glowing reference to Jack, 'the most respected parliamentarian in the place ...' Oddly, little or no applause, either because no one believes The Man is sincere or because Jack's fan club (of which, despite recent disappointments, I remain a member) is smaller than I had imagined. Contrary to rumour, we are assured that Jack's removal had nothing to do with differences over either Iran or Europe. So what was it, then?

A final assurance: 'I hope you understand, I do have the interest of the Labour Party at heart.' Should we believe him? On balance, yes. Applause is generous, but far from unanimous. A significant minority, by no means all Usual Suspects, sit with arms conspicuously folded; others tapping noiselessly. The messages from the floor are distinctly mixed. Only David Blunkett and Gerald Kaufman are unequivocally loyal (Gerald quoting a wonderful line from Stephen Sondheim, who had once been asked by an actor, 'Who do I have to sleep with to get out of this show?' To which the great impresario replied, 'The same person as you slept with to get into it.') There was a lot of talk of the need for clarity and timetables, but no one has a clear plan. The blunt truth is that everyone knows we are in a deep pit, but no one knows how to get out. Apart from The Friends of Gordon (even now a fairly small club), there is a growing realisation that he may not, after all, be the answer to our prayers. Thus far such treasonous sentiments are only whispered, but you don't have to scratch the surface very hard to find them.

Later, the Tea Room

Supper with Alan Milburn and a veteran of the civil wars in Scotland who has observed Gordon at close quarters and is under no illusions ('paranoid' and 'manic' was his considered opinion of Our Leader in Waiting).

Alan seems mildly cheered by the party meeting and thinks that the worst may be over for the time being. 'They've peered into the precipice and they don't like what they see.' He thinks that Gordon is unstoppable, but that he will cost us seats. Alan is also surprisingly critical of The Man, recounting that when last year he was invited to rejoin the government for the duration of the election campaign, he (Alan) was so distrustful that, much to The Man's irritation, he put his conditions in writing. How interesting that even The Man's friends don't entirely trust him. Alan says, 'Tony is not as loyal to his friends as Gordon is to his. A serial sacker. He just doesn't care about junior ministers. It's bad government and bad politics.'

Tuesday, 9 May

Sally Banks came in and we strolled through the royal parks, stopping for lunch at the restaurant by the lake in Hyde Park and for tea in the orangery at Kensington Palace Gardens. Sally says she had sounded out Tony Benn on the possibility that Hilary is leadership material. He had dismissed the idea, on the grounds that Hilary is not ruthless enough.

Wednesday, 10 May

The Man took quite a battering at Questions. I decided to be boring and asked about an arms trade treaty; and for once, primed by Keith Hill, he gave me a serious answer.

Afterwards, a word with Jack Straw, who is putting a brave face on his sudden removal from the Foreign Office. In some ways, he says, it was a welcome release after nine years in the front line. He has no idea why he was removed, but thinks that, if the Americans had complained about him, Condi would have told him. His use of the word 'nuts' in relation to a possible invasion of Iran had been deliberate. 'The one thing I learned from Iraq was that once the process starts rolling it's very difficult to stop.'

He asked my view on The Big Question. 'Gordon must be given at least a year,' I said.

'He'll need more than that,' said Jack.

Thursday, 11 May

It's becoming clear that Monday's meeting has resolved nothing. Gordon is said to be pressing for The Man to name a date, in front of witnesses, and for the first time in years we are trailing the Tories in the polls. Yet the same polls say that, if Gordon was in charge, we would be even further behind. As for Prescott, who clings tenaciously to his Cabinet salary and grace and favour houses, his position is utterly untenable – he is a figure of fun. With every day that passes the edifice is crumbling. No one I speak to thinks this can go on much longer; but no one on the other hand can see a way out. I never dreamed it would end like this. I used to think The Man would go while he was still at the height of his powers, taking us all by surprise. Instead we are being treated to a long, slow wobble to death. The other day, leafing through Alan Clark's account of the fall of Thatcher, I came across the following: 'I don't think she realises what a jam she's in. It's the Bunker syndrome. Everyone around you is clicking their heels. The saluting sentries have highly polished boots and beautifully creased uniforms. But out there at the front it's all disintegrating. The soldiers are starving in tatters and makeshift bandages. Whole units are mutinous and in flight.'

The more one learns about the reshuffle, the barmier it seems. The building is full of the disappointed, the bewildered and the downright angry. Geoff Hoon apparently emerged thinking he was still in the Cabinet, went off for a celebratory lunch before learning that he would be allowed to attend by invitation only. Cathy Ashton in the Lords was told she would have to speak for two entire departments because there was no money left to pay for another minister – and she has refused. People who have spent a year getting their feet under the table, mastering huge new briefs, suddenly find themselves whisked off to new departments where they must start all over again. David Miliband from Local Government to Environment; John Reid to his seventh Cabinet post in seven years; Liam Byrne, who was last week sorting out the reorganisation of the health service – a subject with which he was well qualified to deal – suddenly finds himself dealing with the Report stage of the Police Bill; Ian Pearson, a fish out of water at the Foreign Office, is now (as he cheerfully admits) a fish out of water at Environment, where he has replaced Elliot Morley, who had total mastery of the brief and, suddenly and inexplicably, finds himself out on his ear. And God knows how many aviation ministers there have been – no wonder the industry always get its way. How is it possible to establish any kind of working relationship or achieve anything useful if no one stays anywhere for more than a year? And why should officials take seriously ministers who they know are (a) wholly ignorant of their subject and (b) aren't likely to be there a year hence? It's barmy, barmy, barmy.

Members' Tea Room

'I may have some good news on pensions,' whispered John Hutton as I ordered my baked beans. 'What would the party most like us to do?'

'Restore the link.'

'Yes.'

'When?'

'From 2012 – a pledge in the next manifesto.'

'Is it affordable?'

'Eminently.'

'Is The Man up for it?'

'He's very keen.'

'And Gordon?'

'Not so happy.'

'Why?'

'Because he didn't think of it first and he's afraid Tony will get the credit. Unusually, for once, TB is where the party is and Gordon is opposed.'

Friday, 12 May

Sunderland

Just three customers at this evening's surgery. Two Iraqi brothers, long ago naturalised, who want visas for their sister and her four children. Her husband was gunned down in front of her and they are living in terror in Baghdad, where a thousand people were randomly murdered last month. They are decent, respectable, hard-working people. I have been dealing with them for years – first to get their mother into this country and then helping to rescue a brother who spent two years on the run in Jordan after refusing to serve in Saddam's army. I explained as gently as I could that there is not the slightest chance of his sister and her family being admitted, but they won't take no for an answer. 'They won't cost the British taxpayer a penny … It would just be for a couple years …' and so on.

The other one was a well-spoken, middle class, middle-aged woman whose life had gone pear-shaped. She had known better times: a husband, two children, a job and her own home, but now everything was in ruins. Husband gone, house sold, she has lost her job and is several thousands in debt. For eight months she has been battling with the hard hearts in the Benefits Agency, who have declined to help on the grounds she cannot satisfactorily account for the proceeds from her share of the sale of the family house. She claims to have given them reams of documents, which they keep losing and then demanding more. Now she is on the point of being evicted because she can't pay her rent. The poor woman was deranged, babbling, unable to focus on the simplest question and yet, self-evidently, she has known better times. She spread her vast paperwork across the table, shuffling through it aimlessly. 'I know you can't help me,' she kept saying, 'nobody can.' And I kept thinking, 'There but for the grace of God …'

Monday, 15 May

The Man has launched yet another fatuous initiative. This one, called 'Let's Talk', involved him being filmed listening earnestly to a supposedly random selection of citizens, many of whom seemed to be research assistants, press-ganged at the last moment to provide camera fodder.

Tuesday, 16 May

Dorney Wood, Buckinghamshire

The country residence of the Deputy Prime Minister, no less. Much in the news of late, as he clings to it so tenaciously – and no wonder. A late-Victorian mansion of relatively modest dimensions (five receptions, eight bedrooms, as opposed to the 20-odd reported in the media), set in several acres of exquisite gardens, the rear facade clothed in a luminous blue wisteria. I am here courtesy of the parliamentary gardening club. Janet Fookes, Lady Masham (wheelchair-bound), Adrian Palmer (laird of Manderston) and David Clark from the Lords; from our end of the building Messrs John Spellar, Brian Donohoe and myself.

We were treated first to a tour of Burnham Beeches followed by a splendid buffet lunch at Dorney Wood, left to the nation by Lord Courtauld-Thomson and complete with butler, cook, gardener etc.; part of the unseen reservoir of prime ministerial patronage which helps ensure the loyalty of senior subordinates. Contrary to reports, it is funded not by the taxpayer but by a private trust, and the lucky beneficiary must pay out of his own pocket for hospitality. JP is apparently in residence for between 30 and 60 days a year. I scanned the guest book. Visitors include the Queen, The Man, various of JP's friends and family (young Prescott cheekily signing himself 'Two Jags jnr'), but no sign of the notorious Tracey.

Wednesday, 17 May

The Tories, despite all that talk about being kinder and gentler, are playing the asylum card again for all it is worth. At Questions Cameron baited The Man over the admission by a senior Home Office official that he didn't have 'the faintest idea' how many illegal immigrants are in the country. Of course he doesn't. How could he? The Tories abolished exit controls ten years ago. And, what's more, they were right to do so, since exit controls only told you who had left, not where they were. But the Tories and their friends in the media are having none of it. An avalanche of synthetic indignation has been unleashed.

Thursday, 18 May

I was sitting reading the *Daily Telegraph* at a table in Portcullis House when Angela Eagle and Martin Salter passed by, Angela remarking cheerfully re the longevity of The Man, 'We managed to shave off a year last week, but if things go well again, which I don't think they will, he'll take it back off us.' Angela and Martin are among The Disappointed. He because his talents have not been recognised; she because she was unceremoniously dumped after two or three years in office. Although they would both no doubt indignantly protest that they have no thoughts for anything but the common weal, I suspect they believe that The Coming of Gordon will be to their advantage. I, happily, suffer from no such illusion.

William Hague was on the train. We had a pleasant chat. My, how he has grown in confidence and stature. As we were talking, a man leaned over and whispered that he was the best leader the Tories have had. 'They didn't say that at the time,' he laughed.

Tuesday, 23 May

To Lancaster House for a lunch hosted by Dave Triesman in honour of a ministerial delegation from South Africa headed by the uptight foreign minister, Dr Zuma, who was marginally more congenial than the last time we met. I was seated next to defence minister Lekota, who reckons that the reason for the impasse in Zimbabwe is that Mugabe is terrified that, if he stands down, he will be dragged off to the The Hague to account for his crimes. 'He has seen what happened to Milosevic, Pinochet and Charles Taylor and he is worried it may happen to him.' Afterwards I talked to our High Commissioner, Paul Boateng, who reckons we are approaching endgame in Zimbabwe, although he points out that the better elements in ZANU PF (are there any?) will have to play a part in any post-Mugabe settlement.

Wednesday, 24 May

The Library

'A consequence of the Prime Minister believing that we have achieved nothing in health, education or on migration,' remarked John Denham apropos a poll giving the Tories a four-point lead. He continued, 'If there is one thing Blair and Cameron agree on it is that we have achieved nothing. I can't see any plausible way in which we are going to get out of our present difficulty.'

Thursday, 25 May

To the City for a board meeting of the Prison Reform Trust. Everyone in despair at the current feeding frenzy, which is making impossible rational discussion of penal or asylum policy. It's not helped by John Reid going around saying the Home Office is dysfunctional. Meanwhile the prisons are full to bursting. At the present rate of sentencing it will only be a matter of weeks before a new crisis looms. Later I did an interview with Radio 4 re the asylum frenzy saying that we had all gone barmy. Glad to get that off my chest.

Sunday, 4 June

The silly season has started early with the hacks doing their utmost to provoke a contest for Prescott's job in the hope that it will trigger several months' more turmoil. The BBC even trailed JP to America, where he is making a speech on the environment, in the hoping of tricking him into saying something silly. For once, he got the better of them. 'Have you come all the way from the UK,' he asked a hapless BBC hackette, 'to ask a daft question like that?'

Monday, 5 June

A Mori poll in the *Sun* puts us ten points behind the Tories, mainly due to the fact that the middle classes appear to be abandoning the Lib Dems and returning to their natural habitat.

Norine MacDonald, hotfoot from Helmand province, stopped by

to say that southern Afghanistan is going pear-shaped. We are turning from liberators into oppressors and the Taliban are turning from oppressors into freedom fighters. 'We have to see life from the point of view of the Afghans,' says Norine. 'Democracy is of no relevance. All it has meant so far is the Americans bombing civilians and bull-dozing their crops. Why can't the international community stand up to the Americans?' Why indeed.

Later, dinner with Jean Corston in the Adjournment. She recounted how upset The Man was when, having announced that he would not fight another election, she had pointed out to him that there was no way he could hope to serve a full third term and that he would have until the autumn of 2008 at the latest. It didn't seem to have occurred to him that he would have to give his successor at least a year to bed in.

Tuesday, 7 June

Highgrove

Tuscan urns, white wisteria, water dribbling from a moss-encrusted fountain, security cameras concealed discreetly in foliage. The ulti-mate garden. A combination of unlimited resources and exquisite taste. We are being shown around by an upright, cut-glass, white-haired Home Counties lady in a straw hat and pale green frock. Our party consists of half a dozen Members and their spouses, Tories all save for Alan Simpson, his partner, Pascal, their five-month-old daugh-ter, and myself. Strictly no photography, although no one mentions this until the tour is underway. Pascal is first to be pounced upon. She was ordered to delete her digital picture; likewise I am apprehended snapping a secluded alcove. 'I hope you are not going to make me tear the film from my camera,' I joked, but the stern Sloane who cornered me is definitely tempted. Even the mighty Nicholas Soames is repri-manded when he pulls a camera from his pocket in the arboretum.

Lounge suits are the order of the day but Soames, defying conven-tion, is wearing posh casual: sports jacket, straw hat, shepherd's crook and sinister dark glasses. He is reading the copy of *A Very British Coup* that I autographed for him two weeks ago. 'Fantastic, f-a-n-tastic, but you don't really believe that's how it is, do you?'

Our tour lasts an hour and a half. The garden is series of rooms – terrace garden, sundial garden, azalea walk, potager, stumpery, arboretum ... Stunning vistas – thyme walk, a four-acre wild flower field; and from the house, a fine view of the tall, sharp spire of Tetbury church, two miles away. The scent of philadelphus hangs in the air. Everything in perfect order, nicely understated. Everywhere little memorials, busts of friends, of the Prince himself and in a glade among the trees a delicate sculpture of the murdered daughters of the Tsar; there is even a little memorial to a dead dog. Only one glaring omission: Diana. Of her, no mention.

'We must hurry. The Prince has left the house,' says our guide as we round the far end of the topiary. How does she know? Telepathy? A secret earpiece? A clue: the French window is now wide open; when we passed earlier it was ajar ... Hastily we repair to the terrace of the Orchard Room, where another dozen Members, spouses and HRH himself await. We loiter in little groups. Alan and Pascal's baby, which until now has been as good as gold, starts screaming. HRH, protection officer and private secretary hovering discreetly, moves among us, talking seriously, intelligently, knowledgeably, never lost for words. I can't help admiring the guy. Much may have been given him, but he has put a lot back. He has done something with his life; he has made a difference. Alan Simpson (no soft touch he) agrees. As Liz Forgan says, however, Charles would be a hopeless king 'because he wants to *do* things' and, in a constitutional monarchy, kings have to be seen and not heard.

Soames and I are photographed, arm in arm, clenched fists raised, outside the Orchard Room, out of sight of the stern Sloane enforcer. 'Gordon Brown will destroy you,' whispers Soames amiably. 'Cameron will murder him.'

'Why?'

'First, because the public don't want a Jock. Second, because Cameron doesn't give a fuck. He's relaxed, laid-back, but Gordon wants it desperately.'

'Who would you go for, in our shoes?'

'Alan Johnson.'

Can't say we haven't been warned.

Tuesday, 13 June

Lunch in the Members' Dining Room with Bruce Grocott, who reckons that it is 'ridiculously self-indulgent' to talk of Anyone But Gordon and that there will be no contest. The deputy leadership, he says, must go to someone who isn't a candidate for the top job – i.e. not Alan Johnson or Hilary Benn, but maybe Jack. Re The Man and Iraq, Bruce says, 'I am not aware that he was under pressure from anyone – in the Cabinet, the Foreign Office, the parliamentary party or anyone – to ally us with the Americans. It was all his own work.'

Thursday, 15 June

To Seven Kings to see Mum's sister, Maureen, who was 90 on Monday. I called on Uncle Peter first and we walked round together. What a delightful fellow Peter is. 'I'll probably live long enough,' he said, 'to be the only person on the planet who has never used a mobile phone, never been in an aeroplane and doesn't have a television.' He quoted Bob Hope: 'Give me *terra firma*. The more *firma*, the less *terra*.'

Monday, 19 June

John Spellar joined me at lunch in the cafeteria. Like so many others he is talking regime change. 'I don't see how he can go on much longer. Does he wish to be remembered as the man who won three elections and who then had to be airlifted off the roof of Number 10 as the barbarians stormed the gate?'

Wednesday, 21 June

I walked in this morning, toying with the idea of saying the unthinkable: that Gordon is unelectable and that we should consider the alternatives. Of course, the messenger will be shot on the spot. Not even the likely beneficiaries will dare to express their gratitude. So it has to be said by someone with no prospects and who is not seen as being too closely associated with the present incumbent. I am ideally suited. A last service to the party before oblivion? Several nagging doubts, however: do I feel strongly enough to risk self-immolation? When it comes to unpalatable decisions regarding failed or failing leaders the dear old Labour Party never bites the bullet. Why wager all on a gesture that is likely to be futile?

Sunday, 25 June
Sunderland

Three days since we last caught a glimpse of the sun – and this is supposed to be summer. In the south it is ten degrees warmer and in Germany the World Cup is being played in temperatures of 30 centigrade and more. At the time of writing (3 p.m.) rain has been falling for almost 24 hours, decimating the garden. The pink climbing rose in the back, which was a mass of blooms, has broken free of the wall and is lying in a sodden heap. Ngoc has a persistent cough and cold and I have been afflicted by food poisoning. Has the time come to abandon dreams of retirement to a garden in Northumberland and instead contemplate joining Ray and Luise in the south of France? No sooner had this thought crossed my mind than an article appeared in the travel section of yesterday's *Telegraph* saying that Gascony is the new Tuscany and that the British middle classes are flocking there. Damn. As with the mythical walled garden, by the time our turn comes we will have been outpriced.

Monday, 26 June

To London on the usual train. King's Cross station was closed by a fire and so we had to be evacuated at Peterborough, amid scenes of bedlam. Fortunately, Alistair Darling was on board. He rang his office and before we knew it a taxi had been commandeered and we were on our way to London. All a bit cloak and dagger. We extricated ourselves sharpish from the station and disappeared around a corner out of sight of the crowd. Alistair, until recently Transport Secretary, feared that the mood could turn ugly had he been recognised so the taxis were booked in the name of a Mr A.D.

Greg Cook, the party's number cruncher, addressed the parliamentary party this evening re the outcome of the local government elections. His message: don't panic, no meltdown; just a bit of mid-term unpopularity.

Tuesday, 27 June

Charles Clarke has set the cat among the pigeons with a series of interviews complaining that the government is 'becalmed' and 'lacks direction'. Most of his ire is directed at John Reid in retaliation for Reid's rubbishing of Charles's record at the Home Office, but The Man comes in for some stick, too, and inevitably that is what has attracted most attention. Asked on the radio this morning whether The Man should carry on, Charles replied slyly, 'If he can recover his sense of purpose and direction, yes.' What can he be up to?

This evening, an hour on the terrace with Keith Hill and Terry Rooney, Keith making no secret of the consternation at Number 10 over Charles Clarke's outburst. Much speculation as to his motive. Can it really have been a call to arms, given that Charles is no friend of Gordon? Or was he provoked by Reid? The consensus seems to be that this is not quite a Geoffrey Howe moment and that The Man isn't going anywhere for the time being, at least until he's past the ten-year mark.

We turned to the other big question: can we win with Gordon? Keith and Terry think we can, saying that our present poor showing in the polls is not terminal and pointing out that, a year before the '87 and '92 elections, we had been miles ahead in the polls and were still trounced at the election. The '92 result can be read both ways, however. John Major was a new broom, Gordon on the other hand is very definitely *ancien régime*. As Keith said, there are no significant political differences between Gordon and The Man; it's all personal. According to Keith, relations have improved. Gordon and The Man are meeting frequently. There *is* a strategy. The Man's plan is that difficult, unpopular decisions should be taken on what remains of his watch so that Gordon can ride in on a blaze of glory and lead us to victory.

We fell to trying to identify The Friends of Gordon. General agreement that it is a remarkably small club. Although we are all (more or less) reconciled to the inevitability of Gordon's ascent, those who rejoice in the prospect are thin on the ground. After listing a handful of True Believers (Douglas Alexander, Ed Balls, Nick Brown) we were struggling. I mentioned Alistair Darling, widely tipped as Gordon's Chancellor, but Keith says they are not particularly close. Gordon has to find about 90 members for his government. Where is he going to get them without relying heavily on the existing pool?

Later, after Terry had gone, Keith and I discussed Afghanistan, which is showing all the signs of becoming a quagmire. I mentioned the Senlis Council's plan for growing opium under licence for medicinal use, à la India and Turkey. In passing, Keith, who sits in on Cabinet meetings, remarked how 'unchallenging' they are. Discussion is minimal and there is little rigorous questioning. A few months back John Reid (then Defence Secretary) had given a presentation on Afghanistan, but there was scarcely any discussion ('although,' says Keith, 'a number of questions occurred to me'). Bruce Grocott used to say much the same. Keith added that, despite rumours to the contrary, the atmosphere at Cabinet meetings was fairly informal. No one was discouraged from contributing and it wasn't unknown for ministers to cut across The Man without incurring displeasure. So what is it that keeps them so tame? Perhaps, I suggested, it is The Man's habit of reaching decisions via small working groups, involving a handful of relevant ministers and outside experts, and then imposing them top down, with the result that the Cabinet isn't so much taking decisions as being informed of decisions already taken. Keith did not demur.

Wednesday, 28 June
'You're mad, completely mad ...' said Simon Burns, a Tory, addressing Shaun Woodward, Dave Watts and myself in the Tea Room. He glanced about cautiously to make sure that none of his own side were within earshot, '... to be getting rid of a leader who has won you three successive general elections with good majorities ...'

Later, a chance cappuccino in the atrium at Portcullis House with that most brilliant and agreeable of colleagues, Nick Raynsford, who like me, and for the same reasons, finds himself at a loose end. Nick has a plan for Gordon: be as different as possible from Cameron (and Blair). Play to your strengths. Make clear from the outset that you intend to concentrate on stability and delivery rather than presentation and candy floss. No more day trips to Africa or photo opportunities with Angelina Jolie. No more phoney nonsense about 'Britishness'. A halt to the plethora of initiatives. An end to the destablising and demoralising annual ministerial reshuffles. Instead ministers will be expected to remain for the duration unless they screw up or are ambushed by events. And how about a moratorium on new legislation save that which is absolutely necessary for the functioning of government? Alas, there is little in Gordon's track record to suggest he is capable of rising to the occasion. He is, as we know to our cost, a compulsive spinner who can't resist playing with the pieces. All the same, a nice idea.

Tuesday, 4 July

'The forces of darkness are not happy about our exchange on the summer recess last week,' whispered Jack Straw as we passed through the Noe Lobby this afternoon. 'I may need your help.' A reference to my suggestion that a 76-day summer recess was a disgrace and to Jack's sympathetic reply. I have no doubt we will lose a vote on the issue, but I am determined to force one.

Monday, 10 July

Mum's 86th birthday. Liz and I took her to lunch at the General's Arms in Little Baddow. Afterwards, Mum in her wheelchair, we strolled along the promenade at Maldon. She appears to be in good spirits, but occasionally lets slip a clue as to her real state of mind. As I pushed her downhill, 'Why don't you let go? That would solve the problem.' A passing remark, said with apparent good humour, but deep down I suspect she's serious. She wants to die. So, in her situation, would I.

Wednesday, 12 July

A drink on the terrace with Clive Soley, who seems to be liaising informally between The Man and Gordon re the succession. He is seeing The Man tomorrow and Gordon next week. They are both in listening mode, he says (as well they might be given the mess we are in). The immediate issue, on which Clive seeks my opinion, is what to do about JP? 'Confiscate his mobile and send him on a very long holiday,' I suggested. 'On no account leave him in charge when The Man takes his holiday.' Clive's preferred solution is that JP should be replaced as Deputy PM by Margaret Beckett, but remain as deputy leader of the party. I say, fine, if Margaret can stay as Foreign Secretary, but if it means moving her we should go for Jack.

Next question: how do we get through the conference in September without the wheels coming off? Clive's solution is for The Man to announce that this will be his last conference and that he will stand down in September next year. Whatever happens, he says, it is not in Gordon's interests to take over now since any bounce he might get from not being The Man would have well and truly worn off by the time of the election. Fingers crossed that Gordon has grasped this simple point.

Today's bad news is that The Man's fundraiser extraordinaire, Lord Levy, has been arrested. How much worse can it get?

Thursday, 13 July

To the Robing Room of the House of Lords, where incongruously, beneath full-length portraits of a youthful Victoria and Albert, we celebrated the life of Tony Banks. A packed meeting, masterfully compered by Don Brind. Even Dennis Skinner, who rarely ventures down this end of the building, showed up. Afterwards, on the Lords' terrace, we toasted Banksie in champagne and almost immediately came the sound of knocking from the direction of the Cholmondley Room. Good old Banksie, he's up there somewhere.

Sunday, 16 July

The Israelis have invaded Lebanon, triggering a vast new bout of ruin and misery and bringing down upon their heads a fusillade of Hizbollah rockets. The Americans seem content to let them get on with it while the rest of the world watches in impotent silence. Iran is making warlike noises. A huge new conflagration beckons.

Monday, 17 July

A heatwave, temperature in the middle 30s.

At this evening's party meeting, a rousing speech from the relentlessly cheerful Hazel Blears calling for a summer of frenetic activity to counter the newly re-invigorated Tories, but of what possible use is a blitz of glossy New Labour press releases in the face of the daily drip, drip of media poison and 'gotcha' journalism? Better if we took the summer off and let them get on with it. As someone later remarked, Hazel seems to be living in a parallel universe.

Keith Hill, who I came across in the cloakroom, says there is no question of JP being left 'in charge' this summer. 'A number of ministers have been persuaded to change their holiday plans,' he said with a twinkle in his eye. 'If someone needs to be put up to speak for the government, I think you will find that JP is a long way down the list.'

Tuesday, 18 July

Angela Eagle, hotfoot from a meeting of the National Executive Committee, says the party is facing financial meltdown. The treasurer budgeted for an income this year of £4 million, but has in fact raised only £700,000 and, in the present climate with the police knocking on the door of our donors, no one is going to be willing to help. Overall the party has a deficit of £14.5 million. The Tories have a slightly larger one but, as we all know, their supporters have deep pockets and the scent of power is likely to keep money flowing into their coffers. 'What a legacy,' says Angela. 'Membership halved, four million votes disappeared and an almost bankrupt party. No chief executive would be allowed to get away with that.' In fairness Angela did, when pressed, concede that the collapse of politics was a problem across much of the developed world and not unique to this country, so our current difficulties cannot simply be blamed on The Man. She added, 'The public has almost made up its mind about us, as they did with John Major's government after the autumn of '92. Another six months and it will be too late.'

The Man reported back from the G8 summit in St Petersburg. Most of his statement was taken up with the situation in the Middle East; disgracefully he uttered not a single critical word of the Israelis despite the mayhem they have caused.

Thursday, 20 July

To the Home Office for a much postponed meeting with Lin Homer, the head of the Immigration and Nationality Department. It seems that my pleas to show mercy towards asylum seekers with children may be bearing fruit after all. John Reid, she said, had chosen his words with care. Ministers are planning an amnesty – though they won't be calling it that – for families with children who have been trapped in the system for years. The extent will depend on the political reaction and the quid pro quo will be a harder line for those, families included, whose cases are processed quickly. An announcement will be made next week.

Horrifying scenes from Beiruit, where Israel is bombing the suburbs to rubble. Half a million people are said to have been displaced. Carloads of refugees are being targeted by Israeli jets. These are war crimes, but thus far our ministers have shamefully confined themselves to mealie-mouthed expressions of regret.

Friday, 21 July

Several requests for interviews or articles following my intervention on Margaret Beckett in yesterday's debate on the crisis in Lebanon. I hesitated. Knowing that no good can come of expressing opinions about such matters. In the end I recorded a short clip for *The World at One*, describing Israel's assault on Lebanon as a war crime. Within minutes the emails and other interview requests started coming in. Do I really want to get sucked into the Middle East? For the rest of the day I lay low.

Saturday, 22 July

'Mum, do you think that Sarah will ever have a boyfriend?' Emma inquired as Ngoc was taking her to school the other morning.

'Of course, but there's no hurry. She can wait until she goes to university.'

'*University?* That's much too late.'

'No it's not. She needs to concentrate on her studies.'

'I will have a boyfriend before I do my GCSEs.'

'What sort of boyfriend are you looking for?'

Obviously this was a matter to which the small person has already given considerable thought because she replied straight away, 'Kind, brainy and good fun, but not too posh.'

Friday, 28 July

The Residence, Kinshasa

Everyone on tenterhooks. Supporters of John Pierre Bemba went on the rampage yesterday, raping, looting and killing three policemen. Plus they burned down the HQ of the quango that is supposed to be ensuring fair access for all sides to the state-run media. Then to crown all, the French decided to mount a little show of strength, flying two of their military jets low over the city at exactly the moment when a fire started in John Paul Bemba's compound, igniting some of the considerable stock of ammunition he has stored there, killing several children and inevitably spreading rumours that the French had bombed Bemba. That was yesterday. Today has so far been fairly quiet – the only report of violence being an exchange of gunfire between Kabila's and Bemba's bodyguards when their convoys inadvertently crossed, another policeman killed.

The Deputy Head of Mission gives a briefing on personal security. The Congo is a very dangerous place, he says. We are enjoined to keep our vehicle door locked at all times. 'And if you are involved in an accident, even with a pedestrian, do *not* get out of the car; drive on and report it later.' Eric Joyce and I agree that we find that hard to accept, but then as the DHM pointed out, it is not unknown for white men unwise enough to disregard such advice to be lynched.

Tuesday, 1 August

A warehouse in Kinshasa. The scene which greets us is one of utter chaos. Ballot boxes stuffed with votes dumped unceremoniously in the open air, mixed with boxes of unused ballot papers, some burst apart; hapless officials searching through the mess to recover the plastic envelopes containing meticulously compiled returns which diligent polling clerks laboured all night to complete; trucks loaded down with ballot boxes and paperwork arrive every hour, adding to the mess. If those who queued so patiently to cast their vote could see this they would weep; on second thoughts, this being the Congo, they would probably burn the place down.

Inside, clerks seated idly on orange plastic garden chairs, gossiping, staring dead-eyed into space; occasionally an envelope is opened, examined, set to one side. No one seems to know what to do. At the bank of gleaming computers along the rear wall the putative operators are also idle. Not a single result has yet been entered.

Wednesday, 2 August

The compilation centre now resembles a landfill site. Many tons of votes have accumulated and been stored under a lean-to at the side of the building. Most of the plastic envelopes containing the returns have been retrieved and opened and lie in discarded drifts, along with surplus ballot papers and other detritus. The computer operators are still idle, although there is slightly more activity at the tables in the hall. So far, we are told, just seven presidential results have been entered. No one has yet given any thought about the assembly results, which may well be unverifiable. Whoever devised this system should be shot.

This evening at the Residence, dinner for the papal nuncio and assorted local churchmen to discuss what is to be done about the growing problem of children denounced as witches and driven from their families. Solange Ghonda, the sister of a former foreign minister, lucidly outlined the problem. Twenty years ago, she said, it wasn't an issue. It began with the influx of Protestant evangelists and their local imitators. All over the Congo, and across West Africa, fake pastors had set themselves up, searching out and denouncing evil. Typically, when misfortune struck, a family would attribute it to an evil spirit and pay one of these bogus pastors to search out and destroy it. More often than not, they would find it lurking in a child who would then be beaten, tortured, even murdered; often they were driven from the family and ended up on the streets. Children as young as six or seven were forced to carry on their slender shoulders the belief that they were the source of the evil spirit that had brought misfortune upon their family. It is estimated that the number of children so denounced may be as high as a quarter of a million; every street in Kinshasa contains one of these bogus churches. One of the priests said they had attempted an audit and given up after finding 900 in one district alone. There are signs that the sickness may be spreading among west Africans in Europe; remember Victoria Climbie and the West African child whose remains were found in the Thames?

Tuesday, 8 August
Gamekeeper's Cottage, Northchapel, West Sussex

Glorious sunshine. A woodpecker tapping away in the oak tree. I rose early and sat in the garden reading William Hague's excellent biography of Pitt the Younger. Granny awoke late, red-faced from yesterday's sunshine and confused. 'Where am I?'

I explained.

'Oh, I thought I was in Broomfield Hospital.'

This afternoon we had a pleasant stroll in the park at Petworth, Granny in a wheelchair, which the children and I took turns in pushing.

'Chris, you must be tired.'

'Not in the least, Mum.'

'Don't strain your back.'

The same mantra repeated over and over, 30, 40, 50 times. In between she's perfectly sane, but her short-term memory is fading – and she knows it.

Wednesday, 9 August

Gamekeeper's Cottage

Awoke to grey drizzle which by lunch had, mercifully, given way to sunshine. We spent the afternoon in the garden at Parham. In between her usual exhortations that whoever is pushing the wheelchair should not strain his or her back, Granny has a new mantra: 'All the butterflies seem to be white this year.' True, they are, but once I had heard this observation repeated 50 times it did not seem so interesting.

Thursday, 10 August

Gamekeeper's Cottage

Awoke to news of some great new terrorist bomb plot, apparently involving liquid explosive concealed in soft drink bottles. Arrests, airport chaos, but as yet no smoking gun. The real thing or another cock-up? The broadcasters, having previously had their fingers burned, are referring pointedly to an 'alleged' bomb plot. In the absence of The Man, John Reid seems to be making most of the running. JP is being kept firmly under wraps, just as Keith Hill predicted. The hacks, however, have quickly cottoned on and are starting to run 'Where is JP?' stories.

Friday, 11 August

Gamekeeper's Cottage

'Bomb plot chaos' has eclipsed the carnage in Lebanon as the main story. Still no hard evidence. At least none that we know about. It appears that none of the alleged terrorists had even got around to buying an airline ticket, let alone filling his Coke bottle with liquid explosive. Still, you can't be too careful these days. This evening the nation was treated to a brief glimpse of JP, striding self-consciously down the corridor that leads from the Cabinet room to the Number 10 lobby, where he was allowed to read a brief, uninformative statement, but not to take questions. The object of exercise seemed to be to prove that JP was still alive, but it seemed to demonstrate the opposite. Could he have a double?

We passed a pleasant day at West Dean, picnicking in the sunshine, Granny still going on about butterflies.

Monday, 21 August

The lead in today's *Telegraph* gloatingly asserts that the Labour Party is on the verge of bankruptcy and struggling to pay next month's wage bill; distressingly plausible.

Tuesday, 22 August

A poll in the *Guardian* gives the Tories a nine-point lead; we are at our lowest ebb for 14 years. I suppose we shouldn't be surprised, given our recent battering.

Wednesday, 23 August

Today's bad news is a *Guardian* poll (a second instalment of yesterday's) that only 37 per cent of the electorate believe that ten years of economic stability and continuous growth have anything to do with Gordon Brown's stewardship of the economy; 52 per cent believe there is little or no connection. It gets worse. The majority believe, despite clear evidence to the contrary, that they are worse off under Labour and that more people live in poverty now than under the Tories. Why do we bother?

Thursday, 24 August

Sarah's GCSE results: seven A* and four As. Which only goes to prove what I have always known – that she is bright as well as beautiful.

Friday, 25 August

The papers are full of the usual August stories alleging the dumbing down of GCSEs. As if to prove the point, Sarah (the recent recipient of an A* for Geography) inquired this evening, 'Dad, where is Latin America?'

Wednesday, 30 August

The Man was interviewed on television last night, desperately trying to project an air of business as usual, looking washed out – despite having only just returned from three weeks in Barbados. Obviously determined not to be driven from office, but he knows he's in deep trouble.

Thursday, 31 August

A call from Keith Hill at Number 10, sounding as cheerful as always, despite the rumble of approaching artillery.

'What's The Man going to say at conference re The Big Question?' I inquired.

'What do you think he should say?'

'I think he just has to tough it out,' I said lamely, but even as the words were out of my mouth, I knew it wouldn't wash. My trouble is that I don't believe Gordon is the answer to our problems. If he was I'd say, 'Get on with it.'

Friday, 1 September

A message on the answerphone from a Katherine at *The World This Weekend*: 'We're doing a little survey ... just a couple of questions.' I know what the game is and I'm not playing. An alarming number of people are though. This evening's television news featured clips from Clive Betts, George Mudie and Julie Morgan, all calling for a sign from heaven.

Tuesday, 5 September

The madness is intensifying. This morning's *Mirror* splashed a ludicrous memo, purporting to have been written by one of the inner circle, outlining a plan for The Man's re-entry into the earth's atmosphere. Sample: 'He needs to go with the crowds still wanting more. He should be the star who won't even play the last encore.' (What planet are these people on?) By early evening the bulletins were dominated by reports of a letter said to have been signed by 17 of the hitherto ultra-loyal (including an as yet unnamed junior minister) demanding a timetable. Chris Bryant and Siôn Simon are said to be the instigators. Meanwhile messages are being frantically smuggled out of the bunker in the hope of appeasing the mob. David Miliband was on the radio this morning talking confidently of 'the conventional wisdom' that The Man would be gone within 12 months. And the early edition of tomorrow's *Sun* announces (presumably with official blessing) that all will be revealed on 31 May next year.

This evening, via the Number 10 switchboard, a call from Nita Clarke asking if I would add my name to a statement being organised by Karen Buck, calling for calm. I duly agreed.

Wednesday, 6 September

The signatories of Chris Bryant's missive are mainly bright, shiny, upwardly mobile New Labourites, including no fewer than seven parliamentary private secretaries. It's like a mass suicide pact by members of a religious cult. The junior minister is Tom Watson, who always struck me as decent and reliable, though never hero material. He has duly resigned or been sacked, resulting in an acrimonious exchange of letters. Panic is everywhere. New Labour is in meltdown. All, so far as I can see, self-inflicted. There is no serious pressure from outside the party for a date to be named; no great ideological differences between the contenders. The Man has said he's going anyway. The rest of the country looks on bemused. Have we all gone barmy?

Thursday, 7 September

The Man made an outing to a school in St John's Wood. Outside 11- and 12-year-olds in uniform mysteriously waving 'Blair must go' placards (which unscrupulous adult put them up to this?). He made a conciliatory little statement, apologising to the public for the recent turmoil (he does humble very well) and including a formula, presumably agreed with Gordon, suggesting that he will be going sooner rather than later, but conspicuously declining to name the day. Will this be enough to douse the flames? This evening that most sensible fellow, Tony Wright, was on the airwaves. 'What colleagues have to consider,' he said, 'is whether they really want to start a civil war, not over whether Tony Blair is going – he has said he is; not over which year he is going – we already know he's going next year; but over which *month* he should go.'

Saturday, 9 September

Just as the flames were dying down Charles Clarke has opened a new front with a head-on assault on Gordon Brown, questioning his fitness to lead. Real gloves-off stuff. Talk of 'psychological issues', 'control freakery', 'delusions'. My first reaction, dismay. Upon reflection, however, there is a strategy behind this apparent madness. Charles wants to stop Gordon and realises that time is running out. If he waits until the starting gun is fired, it will be too late. It may be too late already. There is a large grain of truth in what Charles said. We all know that, but until now (with the fleeting exception of Alastair Campbell) no one has dared say so out loud. Now it's all on the table instead of being whispered. Perhaps, after all, we shall be allowed an election instead of a coronation. A high-risk strategy, however, since if it fails (and the odds are that it will), we shall find ourselves saddled with a leader who is badly wounded and who may well be unelectable.

Sunday, 10 September

Gordon has responded to Charles Clarke's outburst with a states-manlike interview with Andrew Marr, designed to demonstrate that he is really a sane, lovable, tolerant man of the world. He talked loftily of forming a government of all the talents, even suggesting that it might (for goodness' sake) include Charles. Perhaps if I were to question Gordon's sanity, he might consider me for a place in his Cabinet.

Cleaned the street, cut the hedge and then Ngoc gave me a lift to Darlington, from where I caught a train to London.

Monday, 11 September

To Heybridge to see Mum. We sat outside in the little courtyard. She remarked several times that the weather was surprisingly good for December. That apart, she was on good form.

On return to the House, I ran into Keith Hill and we briefly dis-cussed the events of last week. Keith is firmly of the view, which pre-sumably reflects that of his master, that the events of last week were a coup attempt, citing by way of evidence Tom Watson's visit to Gordon in Scotland.

Today was the warmest September day since 1949 – almost 30 degrees in London.

Tuesday, 12 September

The Lycee, Kennington

Awakened at 3 a.m. by the sound of heavy rain; couldn't get back to sleep so I sat up finishing Christopher Meyer's book, *DC Confidential*. His comments about ministers are caddish, but accurate, and his account of the lead-up to Iraq fascinating. Meyer reckons, as he freely admits with the benefit of hindsight, that (a) The Man failed to make sufficient use of his leverage with the Americans; (b) had the weapons inspectors been given more time, a French veto was not inevitable and (c) the war could have been postponed until the autumn of 2003 or even until early the following year and the time gained might have been used to get Saddam to back down or to obtain greater consensus for an attack.

To the House, where I ran into John Spellar and Bruce Grocott in the lobby of 1 Parliament Street. Bruce said firmly, 'Gordon Brown will become leader and no one should do anything to undermine him.'

Wednesday, 13 September

A call from Steve Byers, who is taking soundings on behalf of The Man as to when he should go. I asked what the options were. Steve said an announcement in mid-February was a possibility, although Tony would naturally prefer to go on much longer. Gordon, of course, would like him gone by Christmas. According to Steve, The Man is well aware that, whatever happens, Iraq will be his monument. What was it he said to me in December 1994? 'It may all end in tears and disillusion …' So it has.

Friday, 15 September

Just as everything is quietening down up pops that most cautious of politicians, Geoff Hoon, to say that The Man should go sooner rather than later. If he can't carry the Geoff Hoons of this world, then he really is in trouble.

Wednesday, 20 September

A call from Michael Meacher. He wants to run for leader. Would I be willing to nominate him? He reckons to have about 30 names so far, though he has no plans to publish them. I replied that Hilary Benn was my preferred candidate, but I don't expect him to run, in which case I would be happy to consider Michael in the interests of ensuring a contest. Good old Michael. He has been in parliament 36 years and yet his energy and enthusiasm remain undiminished. If only I could say the same.

Monday, 25 September
Manchester, Labour Party Conference

Gordon's big speech. The stakes were high. He had to convince everyone that, despite everything, he is *papabili*, which he just about managed to do, ringing most of the right bells, referring by name to a dozen or so Cabinet colleagues (to the distress, no doubt, of those omitted); hinting at better things to come – greater powers for Parliament over patronage, war and peace etc. A glowing tribute to The Man, accompanied by a couple of unsynchronised nods in his direction. The word 'regret' even escaped his lips for past unpleasantness. A tiny shot across New Labour's bow ('politics is about service, not image'). Huge applause when he said he would relish a chance to take on Cameron's Tories, followed by a long, heartfelt standing ovation. For a glorious moment all doubts were swept aside; like it or not, the succession seemed assured; the audience, after all, comprised the bulk of the selectorate. Who will dare take on the mighty Gordon after this?

It took little more than an hour for the warm glow to dissipate. I was sitting outside, enjoying a cup of tea in the sunshine with Tony Benn when the rumour reached us that Cherie, on hearing Gordon speak of his pleasure in working with her beloved, had been overheard hissing, 'That's a lie.' There is only one witness, a reporter from Bloomberg, and Cherie needless to say is denying all, but no one believes her. The hacks are beside themselves with joy.

Tuesday, 26 September
Manchester

The headlines this morning:

> Cherie rains on Gordon's parade (*Mail*)
> Brown makes peace with one of the Blairs (*The Times*)
> Cherie in the Brown stuff (*Sun*)
> 'That's a lie,' the remark that wrecked Brown's day (*Guardian*)

Only the *Express* ('Romanian migrants in £8 flights to Britain') is away on a little fascist fantasy of its own.

Gordon must be incandescent.

This afternoon it was the turn of The Man. The incorrigible New Labour spinners had been hard at work, distributing handwritten placards, no slogan too fatuous ('We love you, Tony', 'Best PM ever' and so on). A series of brief, hysteria-inducing standing ovations triggered by I know not what. Then we were treated to a short film trailer listing 'his' ('our') greatest achievements. 'And I thought *I* was in show business,' whispered David Puttnam sitting just across the aisle. And suddenly, he was among us. The big question on everyone's mind: how would he deal with Cherie's Latest Blunder? We needn't have worried. A finely judged little joke about 'the bloke next door' and the record was expunged. Uplifting, unapologetic, always on the high ground, eyes fixed on the wide horizon, his every sentence applauded (even a reference to ID cards). For a fleeting moment the grim realities of Iraq and Afghanistan, the love affair with George W. Bush, were banished. We were up there with him in the stratosphere. He ended by affirming his undying support for the Labour Party 'wherever I am' – a touch of the New Testament here, was he about to be assumed into heaven? (Or onto the board of News International?) No matter. By common consent, his greatest performance ever. There were even unconfirmed rumours of a tear or two among the press corps. We are going to miss him when he's gone.

Wednesday, 27 September
Manchester

Sure enough, the hacks had no choice but to report it straight. The Man's finest hour etc. Everyone agrees. But with the dawn of a new day daylight seeps in on magic. The plain fact is that we are in deep shtuck. The party is all but bankrupt (and ironically more dependent than ever on the unions), membership is in freefall and we are locked into unwinnable wars in Iraq and Afghanistan – not to mention the wars with much of the public sector, which used to form the core of our support. This, too, is an unavoidable part of his legacy with which we who remain must grapple while he jets off to fame and fortune.

Thursday, 5 October

Sunderland

A call from a woman who claims that Maxine Carr, ex-partner of the Soham murderer Ian Huntley, has moved into a nearby house. She hadn't seen her, but a neighbour had. She has already been on to the *Echo*, the *Sun* and the Home Office and now she's getting up a petition. 'How can I be sure my children are safe?' I pointed out that there was no evidence whatever that Maxine Carr posed a threat to children. She had never been suspected of being involved in the Soham murders, merely of providing a false alibi for her boyfriend on the grounds that she believed him innocent. Needless to say this cut no ice. As far as my constituent was concerned, and we have our odious tabloids to thanks for this, Maxine Carr is the new Myra Hindley. 'She's being protected by the government,' the woman asserted. No, I replied, she's being protected by the courts; not the same thing, but the distinction, of course, was lost on her. She then started on about the effect on the value of her house and how she had scrimped and saved to get out of a council estate. I pointed out that, if she carried on making her mouth go, she was going to get someone – not necessarily Maxine Carr – killed. That seemed to sober her up a little. As soon as she was off the phone, I rang the editor of the *Echo*, who said that the press was injuncted on pain of the heaviest penalties not to publish the slightest hint of Maxine Carr's whereabouts and he undertook to remind his news desk of this. Then I rang Chief Superintendent Pryer, who said he would check with the Home Office. He rang back later to say that they would neither confirm nor deny, even to him, but he would send an officer to see my constituent with a view to calming her down. That was the last I heard.

What with Wearside Jack and the Lotto Rapist, we've had them all this year.

Wednesday, 11 October

The Man was comprehensively done over at Question time. Cameron started with NHS cuts, then moved on to our overflowing prisons, before demanding to know whether The Man would be 'happy' to be succeeded by Gordon. Instead of replying 'Yes' and swiftly retreating to *terra firma*, The Man simply dodged the question, not once, but twice, to huge Tory ridicule and embarrassed silence on our side. The Tories were cock-a-hoop. A long time since I have seen him so badly wrong-footed.

Saturday, 21 October

Clare Short has resigned the whip. I am sorry it has ended like this. Despite everything, she was one of our most successful ministers and no one can take that away from her.

Sunday, 22 October

Heybridge

To Brewster House to see Mum, cheerful as ever sitting among the gaga. 'I'll be like them,' she said, 'by the time I leave here.'

Monday, 23 October

House of Commons

To a meeting addressed by Bahram Salih, a deputy prime minister of Iraq. It was he who spoke so eloquently in favour of the war on the night that Robin Cook resigned. Calm, frank, fluent, civilised. I wouldn't have his job for all the tea in China. He came as close as anyone in authority to admitting that it was all a mistake: 'Many of us are guilty of expectations that did not prove right.'

Thursday, 26 October

'It takes a special talent to turn the NHS into a vote loser,' remarked Terry Rooney in the Tea Room. He was referring, of course, to Patricia Hewitt but, in truth, for all her patronising, she is merely the fall girl. Responsibility for our current difficulty has more to do with Treasury insistence that the huge deficits racked up by some trusts have to be put right within a single financial year. That plus New Labour's addiction to endless, demoralising reorganisation and the fact that we have allowed ourselves to be conned by the medical profession into massively increasing their salaries in return for little or no increase in productivity.

The midnight news is reporting that up to 60 Afghan civilians have been killed in a NATO bombing raid.

Monday, 30 October

From the station at Newcastle I rang the Speaker's office to request an emergency (private notice) question on the reported deaths of Afghan civilians in a bombing raid by 'NATO planes' (for which read American?) on a nomad encampment near Kandahar at the end of last week. Considering the enormity of the slaughter, it has received remarkably little attention. Needless to say my request wasn't granted, but I raised it at Defence questions this afternoon and received a vague reply from Des Browne, who seemed unfamiliar with the incident, despite having been in Afghanistan last week. The Tories meanwhile were blathering on about 'our brave boys' and no one else seemed interested. It is incredible how little concern there is for Afghan lives. Exactly how do we hope to win hearts and minds if this is how we carry on?

The big news is that Nicholas Stern unveiled his long-awaited report on global warming and, by common consent, it is a very serious piece of work. He predicts catastrophic storms, huge waves of refugees, a 20 per cent loss of Gross National Product – all within our lifetime unless we undergo a drastic change of lifestyle. Interestingly, he suggests that catastrophe could still be averted by an investment of a mere 1 per cent of GDP. This assumes, of course, that China, India and the USA decide to grasp the nettle and all the signs are that they won't, at least not until it is too late. The new-look Tories are making a great show of supporting Stern, even having the cheek to say that it is what they have argued all along and accusing the government of inaction. Their media friends, however, are still behaving true to form: 'Secret Green Tax Blitz' is the heading in yesterday's *Mail on Sunday* and the early editions of tonight's *Standard* are telling its readers that they will all have to pay an extra £2,000 a year. Inside there is a story quoting with approval the ludicrous Tory claim that the government's proposed council tax reforms will result in 'Londoners' (they don't care about anyone else) having to pay an extra £5,000. Presumably that's in addition to the new green taxes touted on page one. Laughable if it wasn't so serious. What hope of achieving anything in the face of this blizzard of lies?

Tuesday, 31 October

This evening a briefing by Greg Cook, the party's number cruncher. He flagged up one ominous little straw in the wind: unemployment, the economy and tax are no longer big issues for the public; they have been replaced by, guess what, immigration and asylum.

Wednesday, 1 November

A debate on September sittings and the introduction of a proposed 'Communications Allowance' to legitimise the abuse of the postage and office costs allowance that has grown up in recent years. I managed to erode my already slender base within the parliamentary party by arguing robustly for returning in September and against the proposed new allowance. As soon as I sat down Jack Straw passed me a note saying my remarks were 'uncharacteristically unfair to many of our colleagues in marginal seats (and others); and will be used against them'. I scribbled a defiant reply pointing out that my seat would be marginal next time round, too. 'You wait until Ashcroft's money starts pouring into your constituency,' he said. 'We're counting on you to put a stop to that,' I countered. He sighed, as though it's going to prove more difficult than he at first expected.

Thursday, 2 November

A number of papers, including several of the nastier tabloids, have picked up my remarks yesterday about 'vanity publishing', which won't have endeared me to colleagues. I was amiably ticked off by both Jacqui Smith and Bob Ainsworth. 'Just try standing for the parliamentary committee and see how you get on,' joked Bob. I'm not bothered. It's a five-minute wonder and will blow over.

Monday, 6 November

Jack Straw outlined his plans for Lords reform to the parliamentary party this evening, reminding us of the devastating fact that in 1945 only 16 of the 1,000 or so peers took the Labour whip. An entertaining discussion followed during the course of which it rapidly became clear that his plans for a part-elected, part-appointed upper house stand little or no chance of success. 'A dog's dinner,' someone said. Everyone has their own solution, most wholly impractical. If we are not careful we shall be bogged down for months. Why not simply focus on what everyone agrees about – disposing of the remaining hereditaries, introducing a little retirement scheme, cleaning up the appointments process – and forget the rest?

Tuesday, 7 November

To Committee Room 10 to hear Gordon Brown explain his plan for an international financial facility to fund a worldwide programme of immunisation. Basically, it involves enlightened First World governments borrowing huge sums on the bond market and undertaking to repay gradually from future aid commitments. Once the world is immunised there are plans to extend it to ensure a place in school for every child in the world. If it works it will be wonderful, but as with all New Labour plans to save the world it sounds too good to be true. Half a dozen governments plus Bill Gates and the Pope have signed up so far, but much will depend on the degree of co-operation in the developing world. Gordon spoke passionately and without notes for 20 minutes, demonstrating an impressive grasp of detail in matters well outside his brief. I couldn't entirely work out his motivation. Idealism or part of his campaign for the leadership? He kept thanking us for all we are doing when, in truth, we are almost irrelevant to the success or failure of the enterprise. Gordon may be obsessive, driven and somewhat lacking in the sense of humour department, but deep down he is a good and capable man.

Wednesday, 8 November

The House is prorogued. I spent most of the day in my little office in the eaves, tapping out a speech on junk journalism that I have to give at a conference at Sunderland University next week. In the evening I dined at Clapham with John and Sheila Williams. On hearing that Donald Rumsfeld had resigned, following a Democrat landslide in the Congressional elections, Sheila cracked open a bottle of champagne.

Thursday, 9 November

At last the tide is turning. The Republicans have lost control of both the Senate and the House of Representatives, which means that Bush isn't any longer going to have things all his own way, but it is still far from clear how we are going to extract ourselves from the Iraq quagmire.

Saturday, 11 November

A Bangladeshi family have been burned out in Hendon. They escaped, but their father-in-law, who lived nearby, believing his family were trapped inside, collapsed and died. By the time I got there the street was deserted and the house boarded up.

Monday, 13 November

Mum is dead. Dear stubborn, stoic Mum. Always good-humoured, forever thanking us for the little we did for her, anxious that she should not be putting anyone to trouble (little did she know the logistics involved in a 600-mile round trip to Heybridge). Just occasionally, when the pain from her twisted knee became unbearable, the mask slipped, but otherwise she was delightful company. Who could have predicted that she would end her days marooned among the gaga, hunchbacked, able to walk only with a frame, constantly in need of the toilet? Not so long ago, in her early eighties, she was delivering meals on wheels to people younger than her, and working behind the counter in the Oxfam shop, laundering the altar cloths at the local church, weeding the garden. She had a comfortable home, four prosperous children each with homes of their own and yet she ended up alone, cared for by strangers. To the end of my life, I will never shake off the feeling that we – I – let her down, even though she was so hard to help.

Tuesday, 14 November

Today I successfully managed to top up my mobile phone account via a cash machine. Another first in my battle with the twenty-first century.

Wednesday, 15 November

To Chelmsford on a glorious autumn day. Liz met me at the station and we proceeded to the undertaker's (the same one who did for Dad), where we went through the grisly details, coffin, flowers etc. Outrageously, the borough council wants to charge us double for interring Mum in the Writtle Road cemetery on the grounds that 'she lived outside the borough'. In fact she lived in Chelmsford for 64 years, only ending up in Heybridge on the recommendation of social workers.

To Brewster House, where we collected the death certificate. Mum's little room untouched. Pyjamas neatly folded on the bed, her evening biscuit on the bedside table, flowers still in bloom on the windowsill.

Then into Maldon to register the death and finally back to Chelmsford to check out a hotel for the funeral wake. I was back at the House by six.

Wednesday, 22 November

Sally Banks and I went on our quarterly outing – to Kensington to see the eccentric house of the Victorian artist Sir Frederick Leighton. Then through Holland Park to Notting Hill where, on impulse, we rang Tony Benn's doorbell; his daughter Melissa was there, too, and we had tea with them both and then took a taxi back to the Commons. Tony seems in excellent shape, still racing from one engagement to another but for how much longer? Mum was still vigorous at his age – and look how she ended up. One of Tony's little aphorisms I must note: 'Be nice to the people you meet on the way up because you may meet them again on the way down.'

Monday, 27 November

According to Angela Eagle, who is on the National Executive Committee, the bankers are telling the party that there can be no discretionary spending, everything must go to pay off debts. There are even doubts whether we can afford a leadership election.

What a legacy. We are going to end up more dependent on the unions than ever.

Tuesday, 28 November

Passed much of the day reading David Profumo's account of his father's downfall (I am a judge in the Channel Four political book award). A wonderful line from Harold Macmillan on being informed that Profumo had resigned: 'Well, at least it was a woman this time.' And Noël Coward's note of commiseration to Valerie Profumo: 'Do remember that nothing ever matters quite as much as one thinks it does.'

Wednesday, 29 November

A damning indictment of The Man by Martin Jacques in today's *Guardian*: 'It is to New Labour's eternal dishonour that a figure who has become so discredited has been allowed to continue in office for the sake of his vanity and legacy. In any proper system of accountability he would long ago have been ejected and impeached. But Labour, alas, seems to have lost its sense of dignity, rectitude and conviction since the death of John Smith.' Ouch.

Friday, 1 December
Church of Our Lady Immaculate, Chelmsford

Mum in her coffin before the altar, topped by a huge wreath of white lilies. A good turn-out. Most Foleys, all the Mullins, friends and neighbours, delegations from the WRVS, the Oxfam shop and Brewster House. About 80 in all.

The priest was good. No claptrap, no phoney sympathising. He just got on with the service and left the tributes to us. David, voice breaking, read half a dozen verses from the Book of Revelation. Amiria read a poem, 'Warning', by Jenny Joseph. I delivered the appreciation, getting off to a good, clear start, provoking one or two laughs, but by the end (at the mention of 'these last three sad years'), I too was struggling. Mild embarrassment when none of the Mullins presented themselves for communion. Fortunately there were a lot of devout Foleys ... I could see the priest looking to see whose lips were moving during the mass, but he didn't say anything, a true professional.

Then to Writtle Road cemetery, where we buried Mum at the back, in a patch of bare ground between the Britvic factory and the old A12. A brief prayer, a splash of holy water and it was over.

Monday, 4 December

The Man announced, to no one's surprise, that we intend to update Trident, at a cost of between £15 and £20 billion (excluding maintenance). The case for doing so is threadbare (even he admitted it was an 'on balance' decision) and has more to do with 'punching our weight' than military necessity. Some rumbling at this evening's meeting of the parliamentary party, but mainly from Usual Suspects. Margaret Beckett, once a CND supporter, went out of her way to say that she had now changed her mind. The government can afford to be relaxed about a rebellion because it knows it has the support of the Tories.

Tuesday, 5 December

To Committee Room 6 to hear the EU's Afghan envoy, Francis Ven-drell. He did his best to sound upbeat, but it is clear we are in deep trouble. High praise for the Brits under General Richards, but very critical of NATO in general and the Americans in particular: 'I am amazed at the way NATO operates. Despite having a unified command, each country needs to consult its own capital.' On the American com-mander who is about to take over command of ISAF: 'He was there in 2003 and he did not leave a very good impression.' On the situation in the north – allegedly one of our successes – 'I would be wary of saying there has been a success. The Germans have been too passive. The warlords remain entrenched. It was great mistake not to use force against them.' On crop eradication: 'We are under enormous pressure from the Americans who want to destroy by whatever means. Ironic, since 90 per cent of the heroin ends up in Europe.'

Lunch at Carlton Terrace with the President of Mozambique. James Arbuthnot, the Tory chair of the Defence Committee, remarked that since yesterday's announcement about Trident had more to do with politics and diplomacy than military necessity, perhaps the cost should come out of the Foreign Office rather than the Defence budget. Now there's a thought.

Ann Clwyd, the incumbent, has been narrowly defeated by Tony Lloyd for the chairmanship of the parliamentary party. Another little sign that the centre of gravity is shifting towards the incoming management.

Wednesday, 6 December

A message from Michael Meacher. Would I call him urgently? I didn't reply immediately since I knew what it was about, but he swiftly tracked me down. Michael is proposing to announce his leadership bid soon after Christmas and wants to use my name. Oh dear, this is so obviously a kamikaze exercise which will only increase my current isolation. I can't argue with his analysis – that Gordon needs to be pressed to set out his stall and this is the only opportunity. But must we really throw ourselves on the barbed wire for a cause that is inevitably doomed? How many names can he count on? About 30, he reckoned, but almost immediately revised that estimate downward to 'between 20 and 30'. Reluctantly, I agreed, whereupon he instantly produced a beige folder containing a statement of intent which he invited me to endorse, which I duly did. There were only six other signatures.

This evening with Ruth Winstone to Westminster Cathedral for the parliamentary choir's performance of Mendelsson's *Elijah*. As we walked up Victoria in rush-hour traffic a fox appeared from one of the roads beside the cathedral and, looking neither to right or left, ran straight across the busy road, disappearing in the direction of St James's Park.

Thursday, 7 December

Lunch in the Adjournment with Bruce Grocott. Inevitably we discussed The Man. Bruce said, 'I can give you a list of his strengths as long as your arm, but he is not the best judge of people.'

Tuesday, 12 December

Frantic behind the scenes scurrying prompted by rumours that Number 10 has done a deal with Hayden Phillips re the funding of political parties. Sir Hayden is reportedly demanding a £50,000 donation cap that would apply to unions as well as individuals. He has also come up with a madcap scheme for 'individualising' the political levy, giving each of the several million levy payers a chance to opt out annually. Fatal, were we ever daft enough to sign up to it. Quite apart from anything else, it would cost more to administer than we would gain. By evening the situation had calmed. Keith Hill says The Man was mortified at the suggestion that he would sign up to anything so ruinous and will make his position clear in the next few days. Keith added, however, 'this is a negotiation and we may have to compromise. There is a prize for us: stopping the Ashcroft money.'

Thursday, 14 December

Ann Clwyd, off to Iraq tomorrow, says that The Man believes her defeat as chair of the Parliamentary Labour Party was entirely due to her association with him and had apologised profoundly. To which she had gallantly – and accurately – responded that she was happy to be associated with him because she agreed with him on most things, particularly Iraq.

Friday, 15 December

Tonight's news reports that The Man has become 'the first serving prime minister in history' to be interviewed as part of a police inquiry. The hacks can't believe their luck. You could practically see saliva dribbling from the mouth of Nick Robinson, the BBC's clever but deeply cynical political correspondent.

Sunday, 17 December

Sunderland

To a carol service at Holy Trinity. Afterwards I was introduced to an elderly woman. She took one look at me and exclaimed, 'Ee, you'd think they could have found someone local for a safe seat like this.'

'I've lived here for 25 years,' I replied.

'That's not what I meant.'

'I know what you meant,' I said.

Monday, 18 December

The Times reports a survey of 1,500 under-tens, asking them to list their favourite 'thing'. The first three places were taken by 'celebrity', 'good looks' and 'being rich'. God came tenth.

Wednesday, 20 December

A hard frost which lingered for much of the day. Heathrow fogbound. The *Guardian* is leading with a poll putting the Tories on 40 per cent and us on 33. It's been like that for several weeks. The trend is unmistakable.

Friday, 22 December

Called on the Bangladeshi whose home was firebombed last month. Like most Sunderland Bangladeshis a peasant from Sylhet; he has lived here about 20 years. Pleasant, undemanding, remarkably sanguine considering that he has lost everything. He declined the offer of council accommodation on the grounds that he feels safer living among his fellow countrymen in the handful of streets that comprise Sunderland's Bengali quarter. His burned-out house is unlikely to be rebuilt until July at the earliest. In the meantime he and his family are camping with friends and neighbours. We sat in the cold, bare front room of the house in which he and his wife are currently lodged. Everything has gone: clothes, family photographs, passports, birth certificates – vital evidence of his children's British citizenship. Even the family's cooking pots are borrowed. The house was insured, but not the contents. He asked if financial help is available to help restock his house when the time comes to move back and I promised to make inquiries. In the meantime he is all but destitute.

Christmas Day

For the first time in years, Santa did not call at St Bede's Terrace, Emma no longer being a believer. The girls, however, still insisted that their presents be left outside their rooms in Christmas sacks. We drove to Malcolm and Helen's house in the wilderness above Haltwhistle. A hoar frost clinging to the trees and fences. Malcolm and I walked down the old railway track into Haltwhistle, arriving in the fading light, and Helen collected us.

Friday, 29 December

Awoke to the news that Saddam Hussein has been hanged.

CHAPTER THREE

2007

Monday, 8 January

Ruth Kelly is in trouble for sending one of her children to a private school ('HYPOCRITE,' scream the early editions of the *Standard*). This afternoon she issued a statement explaining that the child had serious special needs and that it was only for a couple of years, after which he would be returned to the state system, where her other kids are being educated. Hopefully, that should keep the vultures at bay. All the same, another fuss that we could do without.

At this evening's meeting of the parliamentary party the New Labour elite were hugging and kissing her as though she had suffered a bereavement.

Monday, 15 January

Another foolish feeding frenzy has developed around the failure by the Home Office to register the details of British citizens who have committed crimes abroad. No matter that the task is impossible, that the information received is in many cases incomplete, that ministers were not informed, that no system of any sort even existed until the last year of the Tories – the hacks want blood. We've got at least another two years of this before the electorate puts us out of our misery. John Reid must rue the day he labelled his department 'not fit for purpose'. He's dug himself a pit out of which it will be impossible to climb.

This evening, with half a dozen others, I was invited to Charlie

Falconer's room to be sounded out about a little U-turn he is contemplating on the Jury Trials (Fraud) Bill. Once our business was complete, he produced a bottle of Château Latour and proceeded
hilariously to regale us with an account of his recent appearance on
Question Time, where, by all accounts, he suffered a terrible roasting.
I do like Charlie. Can there ever have been a Lord Chancellor so
totally without airs? He would have been a success in either House,
save the little matter of his children's private schooling.

Later, in the Tea Room, a chat about our prospects with David
Miliband, who is beginning to suffer from the disease that afflicts so
many inhabitants of the stratosphere: an inability to concentrate
while others are talking. His eyes were darting all over and he was
bobbing up and down every couple of minutes. Alas, it can only get
worse as he accelerates away from our little lives.

Tuesday, 16 January

To an upper committee room for a meeting with the Iraqi vice-president, a Sunni. Somewhat ominously, he seemed to be pleading with
us to put pressure on his prime minister to take on the Shia death
squads and start releasing prisoners, of whom there are said to be tens
of thousands. Today's horror story: car bombs at Baghdad University,
carefully timed to catch students as they were emerging from a lecture;
one at the front, the other minutes later at the rear; at least 60 dead,
mainly young women.

Wednesday, 17 January

Nick Lyell, ten years a law officer in the Thatcher and Major governments, joined me at lunch in the cafeteria. He had the supreme satisfaction of doing jobs he enjoyed for long enough to make a difference.
He lamented the frenetic turn-over of ministers, which was a feature
of governments in which he served, as well as ours. 'All governments
have an epitaph,' he said. 'This government's will be its tendency to
micro-manage.'

He added, 'Of course, if you want to win the next election – and

I'm not saying you won't – you should vote for Jack Straw. A very good minister, in touch with the mood of the public; also a nice man and the public would see that.'

Friday, 19 January

Ruth Turner, a member of the inner circle, has been arrested. Just why the police needed to bang on her door at 6.30 a.m., when they could just as easily have telephoned and asked her to stop by the police station, is not clear. It is rumoured that Jonathan Powell will be next.

Monday, 22 January

'If anyone in Number 10 is charged,' remarked Angela Eagle a propos the alleged 'loans for peerages' hoo-ha, 'we're fucked'. She thinks The Man should go sooner rather than later before the damage becomes irreparable. The difficulty is that the polls suggest we'd do worse under Gordon, even though his hands are clean.

Tuesday, 23 January

Des Browne invited me to his room to talk about Trident. Could I be persuaded? Unlikely, I said, but I'd listen to the arguments. Anyway, why bother with the likes of me, given that the Tories are onside? 'Because it would be embarrassing if we had to rely on the Tories to get it through.' Des didn't try a hard sell – some vague talk about unspecified future threats, plus of course Iran and North Korea. I said I thought it was all about keeping up with the French and retaining our permanent seat on the Security Council. Interestingly, Des said that the Foreign Office had included that argument in the first draft of the government's position paper, but he had asked for it to be struck out.

Wednesday, 24 January

Awoke to a light dusting of snow, increasingly rare in London.

To a committee room off Westminster Hall for the annual meeting of the Extraordinary Rendition Group. Andrew Tyrie, Norman Lamb and Lord Hodgson attended. Tyrie is the main mover: dynamic, bright, sharp. We agreed, among other things, to focus on trying to rescue the ten British residents, particularly the two picked up in Gambia on the say-so of MI5. Word is that the government has asked for one of the 'Gambians', but the Americans are saying 'all or none'.

Then to the Victoria Tower, one of the few parts of the building I have never so far penetrated, for a tour of the parliamentary archive. The Commons archives were destroyed in the fire of 1834, but the Lords are intact – originals of every Act since 1497, shelf after shelf, handwritten on vellum, each with the sovereign's signature on the top left-hand corner, rolled, tagged and tied with a thin strip of cloth. Our party consisted of two peers, John Lee and Nora David, and myself. Nora David is an upright, snowy-haired, bright as a button 93-year-old; not even a walking stick or a hearing aid. 'I had to walk in this morning so I am feeling a little tired,' she remarked as we waited in the Royal Gallery.

'Where from?'

'The far end of Ebury Street.' About a mile and a half.

I thought of Mum, and all those sad old folk mouldering in Brewster House. Maybe there's something to be said for the House of Lords, after all.

Thursday, 25 January

Ran into Michael Jay, just back from the US, where he has been talking to Congressmen about climate change. He says the White House has been marginalised. 'I thought that Bush might change tack, seeing the result of the mid-term elections, but no ...'

Monday, 29 January

Confidence in the government is said to be at an all-time low – 21 per cent according to YouGov in today's *Telegraph*. The Man's approval rating is a dismal 26 per cent. For once the *Telegraph* captures the mood of the hour: 'It's like watching a particularly grisly horror film – the corpse should be still, yet still it stumbles on, blood draining from a thousand cuts.' I have to say, that's not how it appears in here. The Man is on good form, regularly getting the better of Young Dave, but such little victories count for nothing in this fevered world.

Tuesday, 30 January

John Reid looks remarkably chipper considering the storms that rage around him (mostly, it has to be said, of his own making). I found myself briefly alone with him in the Noe Lobby this evening and remarked on his cheerful demeanour, to which he responded, 'Like you, I have an inner calm.' He added that he had managed to wring some money, although not enough, out of Gordon for more prison places, but that he had been faced with the possibility that he might have to release thousands of prisoners simply because the jails are overflowing – and it still might come to that.

Wednesday, 31 January

JP was subdued and uncharacteristically coherent at Questions this morning. When he talks slowly and calmly the words come out in the right order, as they did today, though he got a bit excited towards the end. The actor Timothy Spall, who bears passing resemblance to him, was in the gallery observing his every move. Are we to expect *JP: The Movie*?

Thursday, 1 February

To the City for the board of the Prison Reform Trust. I asked Robert Fellowes, the Queen's private secretary at the time of Princess Diana's death, whether he had seen *The Queen*. He said he hadn't, but he had heard from those in the know that The Man's role had been greatly exaggerated. Alastair Campbell had suggested flying the flag and inserting the phrase 'and as a grandmother' into the broadcast, but that was about all. He added that he greatly admired Helen Mirren and hoped she won the Oscar.

On the way back to the House by tube, Ruth Runciman pointed to a newspaper headline: 'PM to be interviewed again over honours'. When will it end?

Monday, 5 February

To the meeting of the parliamentary party to hear Jack explain his latest thinking on Lords reform. Before that, however, we were treated to a long rant from Dennis Skinner re the honours inquiry, the gist of which was that the police can't be trusted, they were leaking like a sieve and trying to stretch out their investigation until the May elections in order to inflict maximum damage. He added, to cheers, that contenders for the deputy leadership should 'keep their traps shut'.

Re the Lords, Jack announced that he had changed his mind – having previously supported an all-appointed upper house. He now favours a 50/50 hybrid. Why? 'Because we are not where the public are on this. We will put ourselves in the position of defending the 1831 franchise.' He also announced that he was proposing that we adopt an alternative voting system in order to avoid a repeat of last time, when we made ourselves look foolish by voting down all options. At this there was a certain amount of hurrumphing from John Spellar and Dave Clelland, who favour little or no change. Jack assured them that no change would be an option, but he insisted that there must be a clear outcome one way or the other.

Tuesday, 6 February

Growing pissed-offness at the way the police are handling the so-called cash for peerages investigation; people on our side are whispering that it's some sort of coup attempt. Apropos of which Angela Eagle drew my attention to an unpleasant piece in the *Sunday Times* by Simon Jenkins which concludes as follows:

> At times I can understand countries whose officer class, sitting in their barracks over brandy and cigars, finally lose their cool and

send tanks onto the street to 'defend the nation' against corrupt
ministers and weak assemblies. Britain in 2007 has a leader who
refuses to go and a parliament that refuses to remove him. His
fate is in the hands, if not of the Brigade of Guards, then a
commissioner of police.

Jack announced his plans for Lords reform amid disgruntlement on
all sides. No one seems to think anything will come of it and one
wonders whether Jack does either. I suspect it may have more to do
with not being wrong-footed by the Tories, who, having resisted
reform of any sort for 100 years, are now posing as ultra-democrats.
The Man's heart obviously isn't in this. Asked at Questions today
whether he would be voting for any of the options, he pointedly
avoided answering.

This evening, to the Channel Four awards. Jeff Rooker was the
Peer of the Year, remarking to the discomfort of MPs present that,
having been a minister in both houses, he could confirm that the
quality of scrutiny in the upper house was far superior to that in the
Commons.

Most Inspiring Political Figure of the Year, chosen by viewers
rather than politicians, was Brian Haw – the eccentric who has been
camped in a tent in Parliament Square for the last three years. He
came to the rostrum in a hat covered in badges and a T-shirt inscribed
in large letters with the word BLIAR and delivered a lengthy, incoher-
ent rant. General Sir Richard Dannatt was the runner-up and he is not
even supposed be in the business of politics at all. Blair and Cameron
scored 8 and 6 per cent respectively. Clear evidence, if any were
needed, of the anti-politics virus that is taking root among the public.
Or at least among Channel Four viewers.

Friday, 16 February

To the soon-to-be-closed Pyrex factory. Another 240 manufacturing
jobs down the swanny. Closure will mark the end of glass-making in
Sunderland, a tradition which goes back several hundred years.

First, a meeting with management, who talked me through a
little slide show demonstrating the inevitability of closure. A familiar

story: a doubling of fuel costs, new factories in China and Kazakhstan, prices squeezed by the supermarkets. Result: several years of losses that show no sign of abating. All this plus the not insignificant fact that Pyrex is now owned by a French family company, Arc, who, faced with a choice of closing either their British plant or one of their two in France, have unsurprisingly chosen us. The suspicion is that they only bought it for the brand name.

Then to see the representatives of the workforce who are not at all reconciled to the inevitability of closure. Egged on by the full-time union officials (struggling to demonstrate their relevance), they have convinced themselves that it is the fault of the government on the grounds that it is cheaper to dismiss British workers than French ones and, if not the government, then the local council are to blame; they are said to be eyeing the site for redevelopment. There were demands for import controls, subsidised fuel prices and even that the taxpayers should fork out to keep the plant open indefinitely, à la West Midlands car industry circa 1975. To be fair, most of them knew they were clutching at straws. One has only to glance at the vast industrial graveyard all about us to realise that we are on the receiving end of a process that is remorseless. 'The government is faced with a choice,' I hear myself saying. 'Either we can stand on the beach and ask the tide to turn or we can try and equip our people to cope with the chill winds of the global market. We have opted for the latter.' Then, in a forlorn effort to inject some urgently needed optimism, I point out that the local economy is buoyant and that recent experience suggests that those who want to be re-employed will find new jobs within a year. Understandably, they are sceptical. Many have worked at Pyrex for upwards of 20 years and they will not easily adjust to life in a call centre. It's not for me, I say, to make the management's case. You must decide what course of action you want to take and I will help in any way I can. That is how we left it.

This evening to the Minster to see *Noye's Fludde* involving children from half a dozen different primary schools. A joy to behold. Two decades of Tory rule had virtually wiped out music in Sunderland and now, after a decade of renewed government funding, school music is thriving again. Who says Labour governments don't make a difference?

Monday, 19 February

This morning's *Times* runs a poll of doctors saying how they loathe the government, asserting that all the money we've poured into the NHS has made no difference, morale at an all-time low etc. and that most of them want to leave the NHS and work abroad. It makes my blood boil. We've stuffed their mouths with gold and this is our reward. In fairness, I should add that the respondents were self-selecting, but even so.

Jack Straw delivered a masterful little statement announcing that he'd changed his mind about using transferable voting to decide on Lords reform. Who else could have managed a U-turn with such good grace? Far from turning on him, everyone was congratulating him on his wisdom.

Tuesday, 20 February

An ICM poll in today's *Telegraph* gives Cameron a 13-point lead over Brown, which would give the Tories a comfortable overall majority and put us back where we were in the mid-eighties. The warning signs are everywhere.

Wednesday, 21 February

This evening, to the Members' Lobby to see the Speaker unveil the statue of Margaret Thatcher. She was there in a cream two-piece, looking puffy and impassive. So much so that we all wondered how much she was taking in, but when her turn came to reply she read out a humorous little speech which was warmly applauded by all sorts of improbable people. Ghosts from cabinets past hovered – Tebbit, Biffen, St John Stevas, Geoffrey Howe, John Major, Douglas Hurd. After the unveiling they all lined up and had their picture taken with her. Goodness knows what Ted Heath would have made of it all. His bust stands next to her at about knee level. He'd probably demand that it be turned to face the wall. As for the statue, it is a disappointment: wrong colour, wrong size and not a good likeness.

Saturday, 24 February

Emma and I cycled to Whitburn along the coast and back via Fulwell and Southwick. As we were crossing Wearmouth Bridge we became mixed up with the football crowd. 'There's that MP,' sneered one, adding, 'You're all useless. If I had my way, I'd gas the lot of you.' Gas, yes that was the word he used.

As I pulled away I could hear him shouting that the BNP were the only decent party.

Monday, 26 February

Peter Atkinson, the Tory from Hexham, was on the train. He remarked that, despite all, The Man was still popular in Middle England with ladies of a certain age who judged by appearance, not by the poison in the newspapers.

Ruth Kelly addressed the parliamentary party on housing. As ever, she comes across as technocratic and detached, competent but no real feeling. She used the phrase 'going forward' (the current favourite piece of business-speak among the New Labour elite) at least half a dozen times, but it wasn't clear we were going anywhere. As several people pointed out in the excellent little debate that followed, accelerating prices have put the possibility of home ownership beyond the reach of about half of the younger population, more in central London, and the situation is getting worse by the day. 'Right to Buy' had reduced local authority housing to the point where there isn't the slightest chance of rehousing someone on most local authority waiting lists, unless they have loads of children, or one ('preferably two') disabled. Often those who do qualify are asylum seekers, which just fuels resentment. Now a pernicious new phenomenon has arisen – the buy-to-let landlord. Karen Buck said that in her part of London, where the cheapest flat costs ten times the average income, the local authority is spending £70 million a year renting mainly ex-council houses from buy-to-let landlords. Speaker after speaker said that housing was the number one issue – and not just in the south. Clive Betts (Sheffield) said he dreaded dealing with homeless families at his surgery because he could offer no hope. The message was clear:

shared-equity schemes are not enough; if the market can't provide – and it clearly can't – local authorities are going to have to become landlords again. What goes round comes round.

10 p.m., The Noe Lobby

John Reid resplendent in tuxedo ('Fancies himself as Churchill,' somebody mutters), fulminating about the difficulty of getting officials to provide him with a decent speech for some dinner he's been addressing. Earlier he announced a batch of concessions to his foolish plans to part-privatise the probation service, having been advised by the whips that he's in danger of losing the Bill. I am one of those who signed Neil Gerrard's amendment. Now the whips are moving among us, trying to persuade us back on board. 'Some people have a different agenda,' whispers Bob Ainsworth. 'They want to damage Blair and the government.'

'If the government wants to avoid damage,' I said, 'it should stop picking unnecessary fights with our core supporters.'

Bob smiles. I know he agrees.

Tuesday, 27 February

Lunch in the Peers' Dining Room with John Gilbert, who reveals that a letter signed by 20 former Labour ministers in the Lords has gone to Gordon Brown saying they want nothing to do with Jack's plan for a partly elected upper house and that, unless he wants the issue to dominate the first year or two of his premiership, he should quietly junk it. The letter was apparently put into Gordon's hands on Boxing Day by Murray Elder. No response has been forthcoming, but I'm sure Gordon has got the message. As we were sitting there Patricia Scotland passed by with a High Court judge in tow. 'We regard you as the scourge of our profession,' he said, more or less amiably, adding carefully, 'You showed that, on some occasions, the emperor had no clothes.'

Wednesday, 28 February

To the City Inn in John Islip Street for the launch of the Milburn/ Clarke 'website'. A surreal event at which hacks outnumbered MPs by ten to one. Much lofty talk of 'the need for debate' and 'long-term perspectives', but everyone knows it's all about stopping Gordon. Only one problem: no sign of a credible candidate. Alan and Charles managed to keep a straight face throughout, as questions about the leadership rained down from the massed ranks of unbelievers. One or two tricky moments. Had they consulted Gordon? 'We briefed him on Monday.' Was he happy? 'He was concerned about one or two aspects of the timing.' I bet he was.

Then to the House where the whips have worked themselves up into a frenzy about plans to part-privatise the probation service. A hilarious scene last night when the clerks in the Public Bill Office informed Neil Gerrard that his amendment could not be voted on because government amendments would take precedence. Neil responded by advising his supporters to vote against the entire Bill, whereupon the whips, fearing they would lose the Bill, took it upon themselves to negotiate with the clerks on Neil's behalf. I saw him, ashen-faced, being taken under escort to the Public Bill Office. Neil is now assured of his vote but even so the whips were still in panic mode, muttering darkly about a conspiracy. Just before noon I received a call from someone at Number 10 saying the Prime Minister would like a chat, but I told them I was unavailable. Then John Reid, in shirtsleeves, cornered me in the library corridor and bent my ear amiably; later he even came into the chamber and beckoned me out to hand over a piece of paper supporting one of his assertions. In the event, about 50 Labour Members fell in behind Neil's amendment, but the Tories abstained, giving the government an easy victory. Even so, the whips were still putting it about that they were nine votes short of victory at Third Reading, which was palpable nonsense. In the end John Reid made a conciliatory speech, packed with concessions, and the Bill went through with a majority of 25. I abstained.

Monday, 5 March

This morning, before setting out for London, a cameo appearance on the *Today* programme, to discuss the mayhem being caused by a ruthless and parasitic (those were my very words) species of no-win, no-fee lawyers over the implementation by local authorities of the equal pay laws. In a nutshell, women who've already received up to £9,000 in compensation plus a substantial pay rise, are being encouraged to demand more. A twenty-first-century tale of greed and stupidity which, if carried to its logical conclusion, is going to enrich the lawyers (whose cut is 30 per cent), impoverish their clients (many of whose jobs will be outsourced) and collapse local services. A complex issue, easily capable of misrepresentation by those bent on mischief, and sure enough, by the time I arrived in London, a clutch of emails awaited accusing me of being opposed to equal pay for women. I responded robustly, but in truth I am a little nervous. Hundreds of my constituents are involved, just about all Labour voters.

To the meeting of the parliamentary party, where Margaret Beckett and Des Browne sought to convince us to vote for the upgrading of Trident. Margaret kept saying it had been in our manifesto and we were, therefore, committed to it, but as I pointed out, the manifesto only binds us for a parliament, not for eternity. Margaret also remarked that no one wanted to have to rely on the French or American bomb. To which Joan Ruddock responded, 'We are under the American nuclear umbrella, whether we like it or not.' Apart from Joan, Gavin Strang and one or two others, there wasn't much resistance. Parliamentary CND seems to have melted away at the first whiff of grapeshot – or should I say radiation?

A brief exchange with Jack Straw re the Hayden Phillips inquiry into party funding, which appears to be coming to some potentially ruinous conclusions regarding the trade unions. Jack said, 'I've told him in terms, with two note-takers present, that if he gets it wrong, I'll screw him. He's seeing Tony tomorrow. The trouble is he's getting mixed messages.' Which I took to mean that The Man is more inclined than Jack to go with whatever Phillips comes up with.

Wednesday, 7 March

Much excitement this evening when, after two days' debate, we voted by a substantial majority to 'democratise' the Lords. Fogies such as myself were against, on the grounds that an elected upper house will only undermine the authority of the Commons, but the new lads and lasses were having none of it, voting by a thumping majority for 100 per cent election. Even Jack Straw, a late convert to an elected upper house, had only been asking for 80 per cent. It soon became apparent that things were not quite as they seemed, since a number of those who were irrevocably opposed to election decided at the last minute to go for the 100 per cent option on the entirely cynical grounds that it has least chance of success. Jack, nevertheless, declared a huge victory and everyone went off to watch the football. Significantly, Gordon Brown voted in the 80 per cent lobby, although no one thinks he will want to devote much of his first year or two in office to slugging it out with the Lords. My guess is, he will stick something in the manifesto and only pursue it if we are re-elected. If not, it will be up to the Tories. I can't say that I am overjoyed at the prospect of an upper house filled with C-list candidates who have failed to get into our end of the building – or rejects from the Scottish, Welsh or European parliaments. The idea that a wholly elected house will be any more democratic that the present arrangements is likely to prove fanciful since the odds are that it will involve some sort of list system and inclusion on that is likely to require the *imprimatur* of the very same person who currently nominates people to the upper house – our beloved leader, no less.

By chance, after the voting, I found myself alone in the Tea Room with John Prescott. This was not the angry, exhausted JP of old, but an affable, relaxed, demob-happy JP. We covered the waterfront, the fallout from the Tracey affair, relations with the Americans and the Brown–Blair relationship. He outlined a hush-hush plan to push The Man into announcing his retirement date at the end of this month on the grounds that, were he to wait until after the May local elections, when we are likely to be massacred, it will look as if he's being forced from office. JP is content for The Man to stay until the end of June, but not much longer. Supposing, I said, The Man doesn't buy it and wants to go on until the conference in September? 'I've made clear that I'm not having that.' JP would simply announce his intention to stand down anyway, thereby forcing The Man's hand. He also has a plan to cool the deputy leadership campaign by calling for nominations and then telling the candidates to shut up until the elections are out of the way. Finally, he wants to do away with having the party chairman in the Cabinet, which costs the party the best part of £100,000 a year and, in his opinion, hasn't been of much use. If he's to do any of this, he'll have to get it past the National Executive on 20 March. Watch this space.

According to John, The Man (recognising that a Gordon succession is now inevitable) is trying to tie him down across a wide front, knowing that Gordon is hamstrung following his failed coup last summer. JP does not approve. Hence his plan to threaten the nuclear option.

On cash for peerages, he reckons the police can't find a smoking gun and are casting about for someone to blame.

Tuesday, 13 March

Pressure is mounting re tomorrow's vote on Trident. The government is worried that it will have to rely on the Tories to get it through and will, therefore, open up the old wounds about our alleged weakness on defence. Jack Straw buttonholed me in the Tea Room this evening. He deployed several arguments: (a) the need to avoid government embarrassment at dependence on Tories; (b) greater dependence on the Americans, if we didn't have Trident; (c) whatever we do the Iranians and other rogue states are unlikely to follow our example. Finally, flattery: 'You're a thoughtful chap, Chris.' Indeed I am. That's why I am voting against.

Lunch on the terrace for the first time this year, in view of three Greenpeace demonstrators who have lodged themselves atop a crane on a barge parked by the end of Westminster Bridge in protest against Trident.

Wednesday, 14 March

Despite the usual high-level arm twisting, 95 of our side went into the lobby against Trident, but the government won comfortably with Tory support. A small earthquake, not many killed. Nigel Griffiths resigned, after ten years in government, along with a couple of parliamentary private secretaries. In truth, however, The Man's authority is draining away and everyone knows it. Interestingly, Jack remarked to Andrew Mackinlay that 'events will move very fast after the local elections'. He emphasised the 'very'. Is the bullet about to be bitten?

Thursday, 15 March

Hayden Phillips's long-awaited report on the funding of political parties was published today, calling for all-year-round caps on both spending and donations. He seems to have bought the Tory line that this should apply to union donations too, which would be ruinous for us. The Tories are not, however, keen on all-year-round spending limits, which would put an end to their latest scam whereby huge sums are poured into marginal seats in the year or two before an election, avoiding the existing rules which apply only to the five or six weeks of an election campaign. We have to close this loophole, which they exploited to great effect last time around. Jack delivered a masterful statement firmly rebutting attempts by Theresa May to pretend that the union levy was the problem. As ever, Jack had done his homework, producing devastating quotes from Alistair McAlpine and Michael Ashcroft, and by the end La May, who had little or no support on her own benches, looked chastened. It's obvious that we aren't going to get any help from the Tories in cleaning up party funding, so we are going to have to try and reach agreement with the Lib Dems and the smaller parties.

Afterwards, in the Tea Room, Jack described the Phillips Report as 'shoddy, poorly researched and worthy only of a C had it been a student thesis'. He also confirmed what I heard the other day from someone in the Lords, that David Cameron has privately told the Tory peers that Lords reform is 'a third-term issue'. So the Tories new-found love of democracy in The Other Place is, after all, entirely bogus.

Monday, 19 March

To a packed meeting of the parliamentary party in Committee Room 14 to hear Gordon Brown deliver an upbeat assessment of our prospects. 'Have confidence' was his theme – and he plainly does. An impressive performance. To be sure, he said, people were fed up and wanted change, but this wasn't the seventies, when we found ourselves ideologically out of tune with the country. The damage is reparable. 'We are the party of aspiration ... of rising employment ... we can renew the New Labour coalition ... Tory plans will fall apart on close inspection.' He ended with a nice little story about Nixon which he had picked up during the recent visit of the President of Ghana. As vice-president, Nixon had attended the Ghanaian independence celebrations in the sixties. After the ceremony, he went around shaking hands, crassly inquiring of everyone he met, 'How does it feel to be free?' Eventually, he came across a man who replied, 'How would I know? I'm from Alabama.'

Tuesday, 20 March

The former Cabinet Secretary, Andrew Turnbull, is quoted at length in today's *Financial Times* denouncing Gordon for 'Stalinist ruthlessness' and alleging that he treats his Cabinet colleagues with 'more or less complete contempt'. Immensely damaging and, of course, it has the ring of truth, but that's not the point. What is a senior civil servant doing saying things like this about a serving minister, the next prime minister indeed. He is apparently claiming that he thought he was speaking off the record. He's either a fool or a knave.

Wednesday, 21 March

The budget. Gordon's last. A triumph. Gordon on top form, disposing of Andrew Turnbull with a neat little joke, shooting Tory foxes left, right and centre. David Cameron was left with nothing to say, although it will no doubt be portrayed differently in tomorrow's Tory papers.

To the Royal Court Theatre in Sloane Square for a party in honour of David Green, who is retiring after eight years in charge of the British Council. He delivered an excellent little speech, pointedly remarking that he had served under eight ministers in the space of as many years. Sat next to Michael Jay, who is mightily pissed off with Andrew Turnbull, who has, he says, set a bad example to civil servants of lesser rank and will seriously damage relations between ministers and officials. 'Ministers will say, "How can we trust them?" And who can blame them?'

Headline in the later editions of tonight's *Standard*: 'TAX CUT IS FINAL TRICK BY BROWN'.

Thursday, 22 March

To the board of the Prison Reform Trust where, as usual, the talk is of how to persuade the government to reduce the burgeoning prison population. Not without irony, since I spent much of yesterday trying to persuade the relevant authorities to revoke the bail of a criminal youth who is running wild in Grangetown, to the terror of his victims.

Saturday, 24 March

'It seems to be the settled will of the Labour party that Brown is to be its next leader,' writes Martin Kettle in today's *Guardian* in an article headed, 'Labour is beginning to look like it actually wants to lose'. He goes on, 'One is driven to asking the simple question, why? In personal terms the answer is undeniably impressive: the record, the roots, the grasp, the brilliance, the long wait and the pre-eminence. No one has a greater personal claim to be leader of the party than he. The deeper difficulty is political … I understood when Tory MPs assassinated Thatcher and put Major in her place … I do not understand why Labour MPs lack the same survival instinct and political seriousness today. But then I do not understand why people stay in abusive relationships or why squaddies in the Somme went over the top in such good heart. These things happen too.'

If we blow it, he suggests, Labour may be shot for a generation. I think so, too. Except that a generation may be an underestimate.

Sunday, 25 March

Jack Straw was on *The Andrew Marr Show* this morning, looking relaxed and happy, announcing that he will be Gordon's campaign manager, thereby completing his seamless transition from Blairista to Brownite, assuring himself of a prominent place in The New Order. What an operator.

Monday, 26 March

At this evening's meeting of the parliamentary party Phyllis Starkey pointed out that the Tories are already spending huge sums in marginal seats like hers and that, unless we get on with closing the loophole that permits unlimited spending between elections, it will soon be too late. John Spellar complained that the Tories were way ahead of us in selecting candidates. For the National Executive, Angela Eagle pointed out that the Tories were awash with funds whereas we'd had to lay off half our staff and were struggling with a huge deficit, on top of which no one was donating, thanks to the police investigation. As for closing the spending loophole, we need to get the Lib Dems on board if we are to get any kind of reform through the Lords.

A Friend in High Places came in for dinner. She says The Man is exhausted, continually dosing himself with tea to keep awake. My friend has sat in on two video conferences with George Bush. Her verdict? 'I just don't know where the idea comes from that in private Bush is brighter than he appears in public. He's unfocused, forgets names, uses words like "thingamy" and refers to the prime minister of Iraq as "that Maliki guy".' Apparently the video conferences are a weekly event, which means that somewhere buried deep in the archives a huge treasure trove awaits future historians.

Tuesday, 27 March

A chat with Alan Milburn in the Tea Room. It is still possible, he says, that David Miliband might run against Gordon. Does he know something I don't? He half winks, but when pressed retreats a little. 'I don't rule it out. I still believe the party has the will to win.'

'Does it?'

'Well, if that's gone, we've had it.'

For the first time in years, Gordon acknowledged me as we filed through the Aye Lobby in support of his budget this evening. 'How's Sunderland?' he asked. The correct answer, of course: 'Sunderland is booming, oh Great Leader and Wise Teacher, thanks to your brilliant management of our economy.' But as ever he had moved on before I had spluttered out half a sentence.

Wednesday, 28 March

Tonight we were required to march through the lobbies in support of casinos, the latest piece of New Labour foolishness. No one's heart was in it. 'I wouldn't be all that upset if we lost,' I remarked to a female colleague as we sat in the Aye Lobby. 'I hope we do,' she replied. Frank Field said mischievously, 'Increasingly I find that the only way I can stick with the government is to avoid going into the chamber to listen to the minister.'

In the event the government had its way with a much reduced majority and not a few absentees. The Lords, however, have thrown a spanner in the works and Tessa Jowell has gone away to 'reflect'.

Thursday, 29 March

To lunch with a journalist from *The Economist*. Talk was mostly of the coming revolution. He thinks that Jack will be Chancellor. Gordon and his henchpersons have a distressing tendency to bully, he says. If you write something they don't like, they stop speaking to you. If they accept an invitation to lunch, they are liable to turn up with a file of your recent writings, with passages of which they disapprove highlighted in green, and proceed to hector you as to where you have gone wrong.

Monday, 2 April

A row has broken out over the £5 billion a year that Gordon took – by removing tax credits on dividends – from the pension funds soon after we were elected, about which the Tories have been banging on ever since. The Treasury has been forced under the Freedom of Information Act (another of our liberal reforms comes back to bite us) to disclose the advice offered by officials at the time and although, like most official advice, it lists pros as well as cons, it seems on balance to have come down against. Opinions differ as to how significant it was (the dot-com collapse and contribution holidays taken by employers were many times more expensive). There is also the detail that the removal of tax credits was pioneered not by Gordon, but by Norman Lamont, although of course no one wants to know about any of that. To compound our difficulty Ed Balls has foolishly claimed, without the slightest evidence, that the move was supported by the CBI, which triggered indignant denials and only served to add fuel to the fire. All very damaging. The Tories are playing it for all it's worth and will carry on doing so right up to election day. If Gordon wasn't going to be our leader, we wouldn't be hearing any of this.

Tuesday, 3 April

We are being bombarded with identically worded emails from nurses protesting at the staging of their 2.6 per cent pay award. A put-up job by the Royal College of Nursing, which is always at its bravest when taking on a Labour government. Who would guess that most of these same nurses have just enjoyed an average pay increase of – not, as they would have it, a mere 1.9 per cent, but 4.9 per cent, as a result of the upgrading from which many of them have benefited; or that we have increased the starting salary for a nurse from just over £12,000 in 1997 to nearly £20,000 today; or that there has been a large increase in the number of nurses since we came to power. Little or none of this is acknowledged; instead each advance is simply pocketed as they move seamlessly on to their next demand. And not just nurses; the doctors are at it, too. Increasingly, like the natives of Borneo when first encountered, I find myself shooting back when shot at. I've just had a row with a doctor in East Herrington and I have declined to address the North East Pensioners' Convention, which is full of elderly militants who flatly decline to accept that anything has changed for the better since we were elected, even though the evidence is plain as a pikestaff. A high-risk strategy for someone in what is now a marginal seat, but I don't see why we should waste time appeasing the unappeasable.

Wednesday, 4 April

To Athol Street, Hendon, to visit a Bangladeshi woman whose home has come under attack from a local bigot. The lock of the house into which she is about to move has been super-glued, paint has been poured all over the doorstep, along with a frying pan full of fat. All this is in addition to a good deal of verbal abuse and threats of more to come. The victim, unusually, is willing to give the police a statement. A Bangladeshi family over the road have had their windows broken several times and are too scared to even set foot outside their front door, coming and going through the rear entrance.

I rang the police. They were already on the case. The perpetrator, a woman with a long record of misbehaviour, is in custody, cameras are about to be fitted and they are planning to take advantage of the perpetrator's absence to collect more evidence with a view to throwing the book at her. I rang the local Environment Department to see if they can clear up the mess on the doorstep before the Easter paralysis sets in. A friendly, efficient-sounding woman promised to do her best.

Thursday, 5 April

A call from the police inspector in charge of the Athol Street case: the officer he sent round last night (with the man in charge of installing the cameras) is complaining of 'racism'. Apparently two Bangladeshi youths, one of them the younger brother of the woman whose house was attacked, were making their mouths go to the effect that all police are racists etc. I rang the woman and said this was not a good idea.

She affected not to know what I was on about. Anyway, the good news is that council workmen have removed the paint from her door and doorstep. She didn't sound all that grateful.

Arrived home this evening to find on the front doorstep a post-card urging me to vote Respect in the local elections. They are putting up a local Bangladeshi, a stooge who this time last year was purporting to be a Lib Dem.

Good Friday, 6 April

John Humphrys was at his hectoring worst on this morning's *Today* programme. First, he harangued John Reid to the effect that crime has risen when, as Reid calmly pointed out, it has clearly gone down in most categories, with the notable exception of street crimes related to the theft of mobile phones (unsurprisingly, since hardly anyone possessed a mobile phone ten years ago). Then Humphrys, his every word reeking of *Daily Mail* outrage, turned his fire on a hapless admiral, asserting that the Iran hostage incident was really a national humiliation. The admiral, who clearly wasn't used to being on trial for his life, responded with considerable restraint. If it were up to me, I'd have been tempted to order a keel-hauling.

Thursday, 12 April

In a several months old edition of something called the *Parliamentary Monitor* I came across the following: 'When, perhaps quite soon now, the history of New Labour comes to be written one important theme will surely be this: how did a basically, if modestly, successful administration come to be regarded with such dislike?'

A very good question and one I find myself increasingly pondering. The article, which is the work of our old friend Andrew Gilligan, goes on: 'There have been no recessions, no riots, no three-day weeks, no devaluations, no massive spending cuts. Most people have prospered. Some public services have improved. Yet, as I write, Labour is polling at 29 per cent, a psephological sub-basement last explored under the leadership of Michael Foot.'

Needless to say Gilligan acquits his media colleagues of responsibility for this remarkable state of affairs. Instead he nominates Iraq, spin and an 'almost wilful failure to align expectations with reality. Endlessly talking of "transforming Britain" while all along planning a much more limited programme was bound to end in tears. The chronic overhype of the first term (£40 billion for the NHS, anyone?) means that even now when the government has real achievements to boast about, it is simply not believed.' It is painful to admit that a chancer like Gilligan could be right, but I fear that, to a large extent, he is. He might have added to his little list of reasons for our downfall, New Labour's love affair with rich men.

Monday, 16 April

To the House to see Des Browne fending off demands for his resignation over the unwise decision to permit the servicemen recently released by Iran to sell their stories to the media. He managed tolerably, helped by an appropriate display of humility.

Tuesday, 17 April

The Residence, Abuja

Touched down about 4 a.m. A couple of hours' light sleep, followed by breakfast with HE, Richard Gozney and his wife, Diana. I am here to bear witness, on behalf of HMG, to this weekend's presidential election. The omens are not auspicious. From all over Nigeria, reports of the mayhem and shameless skulduggery that accompanied last week's regional elections. At least 50 deaths, ballot boxes hijacked, underage voting, polling stations opening late or not at all, 'significant discrepancies' between local results and those eventually announced. The Delta states are off limits to foreigners on the grounds that they are too dangerous – 150 kidnappings in the last year. To compound the problems a last-minute Supreme Court ruling has ordered the reinstatement on the ballot paper of the allegedly venal vice-president, which means that 60 million ballot papers are having to be reprinted and distributed in the space of two or three days. All of

which poses a dilemma for the international community. Not to recognise the outcome would be a recipe for chaos in Africa's most popu-
lous country; on the other hand, dare we recognise an outcome that
is clearly fraudulent?

This evening, a reception for the Queen's birthday, briefly threatened by a storm; strong winds whipping up sand, bending trees,
threatening to uproot the drinks tent in the garden. Servants rushed
about clearing furniture from the house, in case the party had to be
relocated indoors. Happily, however, the storm passed. Among the
guests, Richard Dowden, a British journalist, who spent last weekend
in Ekiti and said he didn't see a vote cast all day, although he was shot
at twice and witnessed thugs thumb-printing ballot papers. He also
saw a mob attacking the home of an official of the ruling party and
emerging with ten stuffed ballot boxes. 'What upsets me,' remarked
the Canadian Ambassador, 'is that it is so in-your-face.'

Saturday, 21 April

Kaduna

Election day. A shambles. The ballot papers arrived late, lacked serial
numbers and made no mention of the candidates' names, only their
party symbols. Richard Gozney and I drove around for four hours
before we saw a vote being cast. Once the polls did open, however,
most of those who wanted to – at least on our round – succeeded in
casting their vote. This evening, after dark, we visited the collation
centre for the north of the city to find a large, angry crowd and no
sign of the presiding officer. The only light came from torches, which
added to the air of menace. Three of the 42 ballot boxes had been
stolen by unidentified hoodlums.

Sunday, 22 April

Kaduna

To the headquarters of the city council in search of the absent presiding officer. She turns out to have been kidnapped, held overnight and
then released, minus her results papers. Outside an angry mob was

gathering, fearful that they were about to be cheated. The harassed official in charge, who had been up all night, promised to start the count after he had his breakfast, but no one believed him. Situation very tense. The last bout of intercommunal violence here left a thousand dead. In the event, the official was as good as his word. We returned to find him calmly seated at his desk in the council chamber, as district polling officers stepped forward one by one to report their results. Beside him, scrupulously noting the figures, the young woman who had been kidnapped. In our country she would have taken a month off, sought counselling and lodged a claim for compensation.

Abuja

Mid-afternoon. A meeting of ambassadors at the German residence to hear a report from the chief EU observer. Not encouraging. From all over the country, reports of ballots boxes stolen, stuffed or otherwise tampered with. Everywhere polling opened late; in some places not at all. Many states have declared improbably high victories for the ruling party. 'Not credible' was the EU verdict. The irony is that just about everyone believes that the best man has 'won'.

Monday, 23 April

The Residence, Abuja

Awoke this morning with nothing in the diary save a vague promise of breakfast with the national secretary of the ruling party, Ojo Maduekwe, who had clearly forgotten we were coming when Richard Gozney and I pulled up at his house just before eight. By lunchtime, however, we had been received by both President Obasanjo and President-Elect Yar' Adua. That is how things happen in Nigeria. Nothing is predictable, but it usually comes right in the end.

One phone call from Ojo and the meeting with Yar' Adua was arranged. We were directed to a governor's lodge, a vulgar mansion on a street of vulgar mansions, bade wait and in due course (without the slightest fanfare) Yar' Adua appeared. A modest, soft-spoken man of saintly demeanour and fragile health. By what accident has a man of such transparent integrity triumphed in the cesspool of Nigerian politics? How can such a man survive? Does he have any concept of the mighty vested interests he will have to take on and defeat if he is to govern effectively? If it all goes wrong, his successor will be the inaptly named vice-president, Goodluck Johnson, whose democratic credentials are a mite less shiny.

We then called on Nasir El-Rufai, a dynamic young minister who is likely to feature prominently in the new government. Also, one of a handful of people with a direct line to the president. No sooner had we indicated that we would like to see the president than he pulled out his state of the art mobile and tapped in a number. 'Abdul. Is the president there? He's in a meeting. Would you ask him to call me back?'

Within minutes Obasanjo himself was on the line. 'Mr President, I have Mr Mullin and the British High Commissioner with me. They would like to see you. Good, I'll bring them round now.'

With that we piled into the flag car and were whisked through the multiple rings of security, into the presidential compound in the shadow of Aso Rock, along cloisters crowded with courtiers, cameramen and supplicants, pausing only for El-Rufai to have his photo taken with the Nigerian national football team, straight into The Presence. Obasanjo was alone in his vast, domed office; the decor red and gold. Our main purpose was to warn him that he was in for a battering from the international community for the manner in which the election had been conducted and that he should not get too upset because it was richly deserved. Not that he needed our advice. He had already worked this out for himself. Contrition was the order of the day. He knew that the election had been over-rigged – at one point, he said, he had been shown a poll suggesting that the ruling party would win an utterly incredible 35 out of 36 states and had sent word to his henchmen to cool it (in the event they only took 29).

For all his faults, one can't help having a grudging respect for Obasanjo. He has been reared in a hard school. He may be ruthless, occasionally brutal, perhaps even a little corrupt, but at the end of the day it is he who has laid the basis for Nigeria to climb out of the deep, dark pit into which it has sunk. None of the technocrats would have lasted five minutes without his backing. Now he is about to hand over power to a hand-picked civilian who, if he survives, can be relied upon to carry on where Obasanjo left off. Only once before in Nigeria's fraught post-colonial history has power passed to a civilian government and that, too, was Obasanjo's doing. He may be an uncouth old rogue, but you can't take that away from him.

By early afternoon we were back at the residence, mission complete. I tapped out my report for The Man and spent half an hour reading in the garden. This evening there was a farewell dinner for a departing British military adviser and his wife. Among the guests, the general manager of the Abuja Hilton, who told a hilarious story of a recent visit from Gaddafi, who had arrived with 200 female bodyguards, and proceeded to hold court from a tent pitched in a ground-floor conference room. The bill – a cool $200,000 – was paid in cash by a moustachioed gangster in dark glasses.

At dinner a gloomy French diplomat remarked, 'I give Yar' Adua six months.'

Wednesday, 25 April

The Lycee, Kennington

Last night I dreamed that Mum was alive and home again. There she was in her red cardigan, *sans* walking frame. 'I am so happy you are back,' I said. She beamed back at me and was gone.

Thursday, 26 April

To Michael Meacher's office in Portcullis House, where he produced a pile of signed statements by 24 colleagues promising to nominate him. His purpose is to demonstrate to John McDonnell – who he reckons has no more than about 15 promises – that he, Michael, is the only one who stands a chance of reaching the magic threshold and that John should, therefore, withdraw in his favour. Needless to say John is having none of this. Instead he has organised a write-in by campaign groupies around the country urging Michael's supporters to switch to him. So far I have received half a dozen emails and this

afternoon in the Commons I was waylaid by a couple of union officials who are camped in the Central Lobby, bending the ear of anyone
prepared to listen about the merits of a McDonnell candidacy. The
truth is, of course, that neither of them is going to make it. Gordon is
already reported to have accumulated over 200 promises.

Sunday, 29 April

St Bede's Terrace, Sunderland

Emma has suddenly got serious about her education. A reaction
perhaps to doing badly in a recent maths test. I came down this
morning to find her seated at the kitchen table with what she called
'my schedule' on which she had written out a programme – 'maths',
'reading', 'bath' and so on – to which she adhered for most of the day.

Monday, 30 April

A long talk with Alan Milburn in the Tea Room this evening. He, like
everyone else, now seems reconciled to the inevitability of Gordon,
although he believes Miliband could have won had he been persuaded
to stand. Why are we all falling in behind Gordon even though we
know in our hearts that it makes a fourth victory less likely? It is not,
as some commentators allege, that we have been consumed by a collective fit of madness. Merely that no one can see the point of having
a contested election when the outcome is preordained. Also, we know
that defeating Gordon would require a huge and damaging earthquake which could prove fatal anyway. And so we soldier on, marching without enthusiasm towards the sound of gunfire, hoping for the
best, but fearing the worst.

Wednesday, 2 May

To the Home Office to discuss asylum with Liam Byrne. The latest
round in my campaign to prevent the removal of families with children to dysfunctional countries like the Congo. I suggested he ought
quietly to let those who have been here for several years stay. He

listened sympathetically, but I am not sure anything will change unless he is ordered by the courts. Hearts have hardened as a result of the battering we have received in recent years. I floated the idea that we should stop facilitating arranged marriages, a huge loophole in the immigration rules. To my pleasant surprise Liam is moving in that direction. It is proposed to raise the age at which spouses may be imported from 18 to 21 – a proposal that met stiff resistance when I first suggested it three years ago – and to require spouses to speak passable English.

A bizarre suggestion from Steve Byers, who I briefly encountered in the Tea Room. It's being suggested, he said (by whom he did not say), that even those of us who are sceptics should nominate Gordon in a great show of unity and put out a little statement as we do so. We didn't get as far as discussing what this statement should contain, but presumably it would seek to distance the signatories from the common herd of Brownistas. Sounds completely potty and I told him so. My guess is that all those who have been most opposed to Brown will end up nominating him, leaving mugs like me swinging in the wind.

Steve added that Charles Clarke was willing to run, if nominated, but he thought that would be divisive in view of Charles's behaviour last year. Indeed it would.

Tuesday, 8 May

This evening, for the first time, I was approached by one of Gordon's agents, Nick Brown. 'We've got you in our "unknown" column,' he said. I replied that I was planning to nominate Michael though I bore Gordon no malice. Nick didn't seem bothered by this, remarking only that Gordon was anxious not to have to tour the country sharing a platform with John McDonnell.

As Nick and I were talking, alone in the Aye Lobby, Alan Milburn passed through and gave me a quizzical look. I could see he thinks I'm playing some sort of double game, but he's wrong. I am a man with no prospects.

Wednesday, 9 May

To the City for a meeting of the Prison Reform Trust. The deputy director, Geoff Dobson, recounted a recent telephone call from an anonymous police officer who described seeing a prison van parked in Horseferry Road, rocking alarmingly from side to side. Upon inquiry he was told by the escort that they were awaiting instructions as to which prison they should deliver their human cargo. They had been waiting some hours, all the local prisons being full, it was a hot day and meanwhile the inhabitants of the van were becoming agitated. Hence the frantic rocking. He had heard later that they had finally been accommodated in court cells because no prison vacancies could be found. Evidence, if any were needed, of the knife edge on which the entire prison service is living. I later relayed this to Charlie Falconer, who has this very day inherited responsibility for prisons in the new Justice Department, but he merely remarked that he had recently visited half a dozen prisons and they seemed to be coping.

This afternoon I was lobbied by Bob Ainsworth, who has hopes of becoming Chief Whip under the new order and asked me to put the word about. I said I would do what I could but pointed out that, as he had not long ago reminded me, I am these days a person of little or no influence and, therefore, in no position to assist his advancement.

Thursday, 10 May

To the University of Birmingham for a conference to mark the tenth anniversary of the Criminal Cases Review Commission. A number of faces familiar from campaigns past – including Sir Igor Judge, who represented the Crown to such devastating effect at the 1988 Birmingham appeal and who is now in charge of the Court of Appeal; charming, amiable ('May I call you Chris?'), reasonable – yet another instance of how one's ogres tend to confound expectations on contact (I hope he feels the same about me). What a sea change there has been in the last 20 years. None of the old smug arrogance. No one now pretends the system is infallible. Ken Macdonald, the Director of

Public Prosecutions, actually began his contribution by saying that he kept a copy of *Error of Judgement* on his shelves as a reminder of what had gone before. I asked about the ever-threatened demand that suspects should be detained for up to 90 days and he replied, 'Twenty-eight days has been useful to us, but we're not asking for an increase. The police aren't asking for one either and yet it keeps coming back. I don't know where it is coming from.' We all know where it's coming from, of course – from posturing politicians seeking to appease the mob. I put that to him afterwards, and he didn't disagree.

Meanwhile, The Man flew to Sedgefield to announce the date of his re-entry into the earth's atmosphere. It is to be 27 June.

Friday, 11 May

A vast industry has grown up analysing The Man's place in history. So great is demand that a tented media village has been erected on St Stephen's Green. An average statesman, not a great one, is the *Telegraph's* grudging verdict. 'Progressives who can win elections are rare,' says the *Guardian*. 'He was a winner, that is not unimportant.' What do I think? That at his best he was courageous, far-sighted, brilliant, idealistic, personally attractive, but that his undoubted achievements are eclipsed by one massive folly: that he tied us umbilically to the worst American president of my lifetime with consequences that were not merely disastrous, but catastrophic. The Man was touched by greatness, but ultimately he blew it.

Monday, 14 May

Jack Straw buttonholed me at the parliamentary party meeting this evening and asked who I was intending to nominate. I repeated what I said to Nick Brown the other evening: Michael Meacher, but I bear Gordon no malice. He seemed most interested in whether I would transfer to John McDonnell if Michael went out. I told him I wouldn't, which seemed to satisfy him. Later, I heard that Michael had pulled out, having secured fewer nominations than John. Meanwhile Hilary Benn, my preferred candidate for the deputy leadership, is struggling to get on the ballot paper, having just over 30 nominations, well behind the other candidates.

Tuesday, 15 May

Ran into Michael White, who recommended Alan Johnson for deputy leader on the basis that he was capable of standing up to Gordon. He quoted someone who had worked for Alan: 'In any confrontation with Gordon he would say, "Let's go away and reconsider our positions." They'd come back, both having moved. The difference was that Alan would admit it and Gordon wouldn't.'

Now that Michael Meacher is no longer in the race I am much sought after by the McDonnell camp. I could end it all by simply nominating Gordon, but I'm rather enjoying the attention. A long call from my old friend Jon Lansman, followed by a slightly heavier email, invoking the spirit of '81 with just a hint of betrayal should I fail to comply. By evening I'd had enough and went off to nominate Gordon.

9 p.m., Room 219, Portcullis House

Hilary's HQ. From the window a stunning panorama extending from Big Ben, across Parliament Square to the Abbey. Dramatis personae include the following: Gareth Thomas, Jonathan Shaw (whose room this is), Hugh Bayley, Gordon Banks and Beatrice Stern (Hilary's special adviser) crammed around a small circular table. Ian McCartney's unmistakable, if at times incomprehensible, Scottish brogue emanates from a mobile phone on the table. I am seated somewhat to the rear, there being no room at the table. Hilary is in the room next door, chasing up stragglers, some of whom are hard to track down and who, even when cornered, are proving a mite slippery; occasionally his head appears round the door to report progress. Atmosphere: frenetic. We have less than two days to find another dozen votes from the diminishing pool of those who have yet to nominate. Beatrice has printed out a list and we are working our way scientifically through it. Two people have indicated that, while Hilary is not their first choice, they will if pressed provide the magic 45th nomination, but they are not willing to come aboard before then. Another two of our promises are abroad, but that still leaves us well short.

'Gwyneth Dunwoody?'

'Your generation, Chris.'

'You must be joking.' Fortunately they are.

'Who can talk to Bob Wareing?'

'Milosevic,' I venture.

In the end we delegate the task to Tony Benn.

And so it goes. We depart for the ten o'clock division, each with a little list of ears to be bent.

As I am sitting in the Noe Lobby, waiting to pounce, who should sweep by but Gordon, exuding bonhomie. 'How are you?' he calls, as usual not pausing long enough to catch my reply; then, just as he pulls out of earshot, 'You're a good man.' It is not often I get two sentences out of Gordon, so I spend a moment pondering the significance. Then the penny drops. He has just been informed that, along with just about everybody else, I have nominated him. Like others, I have done so not out of love, but out of recognition that his ascent is inevitable and we might as well make the best of it.

Wednesday, 16 May

Another meeting in Room 219. Hilary is still half a dozen nominations short. It's beginning to look as if he won't make it, though Beatrice is still sending out reassuring messages. Hilary looks tense, though personally I can't see what all the fuss is about. There is very little power at stake and being deputy to Gordon won't be much fun.

In Speaker's Court I ran into John Reid, alighting from his armoured Jag, surrounded by officials and protection officers. 'Sorry to see that you are exchanging all this for a bus pass,' I teased. The boys from the Branch were unamused, but John took it in good heart. 'Why?' I inquired, when we were alone. He said Gordon had been willing to leave him where he was, but he had been worried about becoming a focus of opposition every time he and Gordon had a row, which they did from time to time. Is that the explanation? Who knows? So few politicians surrender office voluntarily, especially one who is so at ease with power as John appears to be, that one is bound to be suspicious.

The Dispatch Box, Portcullis House, 3 p.m.

I am queuing for a cappuccino when a voice whispers in my ear, 'Tell Hilary I am still available to trade ...'

It is the ever-affable Alan Simpson. He is saying that, if we can put one or two nominations the way of John McDonnell (who is still languishing in the upper twenties), McDonnell's team will do likewise for Hilary.

'Impossible,' I say. 'Everyone on our side has already nominated Gordon.'

'What about you?'

'Me too.'

'Then you are guilty of premature articulation,' he says with a baleful smile.

'Besides,' I add, 'Hilary is opposed to such deals as a matter of principle.'

'In that case, he should tell his supporters to stop ringing me up,' says Alan, melting away into the crowd.

Thursday, 17 May

Awoke to the news that Hilary has acquired his 45th nomination, thereby ensuring his place on the ballot paper. As for the leadership, John McDonnell has conceded defeat, the Brown steamroller having acquired enough nominations to make it mathematically impossible for anyone else to get on the ballot paper. Which means that, in effect, we are going to have two prime ministers for the next six weeks, with all that entails in terms of media mischief. It remains to be seen whether it is in Gordon's interest, or the party's, to have a coronation rather than a contest. Although Gordon has been putting it about that he was relaxed about the possibility of a contest, the truth is that he and his henchmen have been doing everything in their power to avoid one. Blair, by contrast, positively went out of his way in '94 to ensure that there was a contest, even to the extent of encouraging his supporters to ensure his rivals got onto the ballot paper. That's the difference between The Man and Gordon. The one supremely self-confident, the other radiating insecurity.

Norine MacDonald, who lives in Afghanistan, came in for lunch. We ate in the atrium at Portcullis House. Norine is just about the only foreigner who travels in the southern provinces without a military escort. The people are starving, she says. No one goes near the camps into which the displaced have been driven. She is full of praise for our military, who she says are very pissed off with our Department for International Development for the lack of an effective aid programme and for refusing to let the military go where DFID fear to tread. Meanwhile the Americans, as ever, are bombing and burning enthusiastically, pushing more people into the hands of the Taliban. A few weeks ago, she says, the Brits dropped leaflets saying, 'We're not the ones who are burning your crops', which led to a dust-up with the Americans, resulting in our having to apologise.

Monday, 21 May

To Church House for the deputy leadership hustings, in the very room where Parliament once sat after the chamber was bombed. 'I am glad you succeeded in stopping 90 days, otherwise I would have had to resign,' whispered Peter Goldsmith, the Attorney General, who was sitting behind.

We started with the six deputy leadership candidates. Each gave a little spiel and then answered questions. The format was ludicrous – 25 questions before anyone was given a chance to respond. John Cruddas was called upon to reply first. He simply ignored the questions and said what he intended to say anyway. Then Hilary Benn impressed everyone by responding by name to all 25 questioners, at which point the remaining candidates began frantically scribbling. Hilary and Harriet performed best. Harriet is attracting a fair amount of support but her difficulty is that not everyone has forgiven her for the embarrassment she caused us by sending her son to a selective school, not to mention the row over cutting benefit to single parents; on top of which no one thinks she is remotely capable of standing up to Gordon.

Wednesday, 23 May

To breakfast with David Currie, the OFCOM regulator, who gave an analysis of the impact of the digital age on television, every bit as gloomy as we pessimists forecast during the passage of the Communication Bill. Telecoms and broadcasting had collided, he said. Audiences are fragmenting. News, regional programming and children's television were unlikely to survive on commercial channels in their present guise. The BBC, too, is at risk. Radio is going the same way as television. He talked of the 'difficulty of sustaining the regulatory compact' and concluded by asking, 'How can a public service broadcasting system survive in this new age?' The former BBC Director-General, John Birt , added fuel to the fire by talking of 'market failure' and 'the inevitable demise of public service broadcasting on commercial channels – as we approach the digital switchover'.

This afternoon to the School of Oriental and African Studies for the annual meeting of the Royal Africa Society. I walked back from Russell Square, through rush-hour mayhem, harassed every few yards by desperate migrants handing out freesheets. On a pavement in Kingsway, a begging Roma woman with what looked like a disabled child on her knee. Slowly, inexorably, inevitably the chaos beyond our borders is beginning to lap at our comfortable little world.

Thursday, 24 May

To breakfast at the Royal Commonwealth Club to hear Mo Ibrahim, businessman and philanthropist of Sudanese origin, whose foundation has recently launched a substantial annual prize for that rare bird: the African head of state who, having done something for his people, voluntarily relinquishes power. He pointed out that Ghana at independence was richer than Taiwan or Malaysia. 'What happened?

It is a crime. We Africans are responsible. Until we learn to put the public interest over family or tribe we are wasting our time. Everything goes back to governance. There is no point in going to the G8 and saying, "Give us the money." No point. It's about governance.' So refreshing to hear this coming from an African.

Wednesday, 30 May

Another little ray of light on The Man's style of governance. Robin Butler, who was Cabinet Secretary for the first eight months of our tenure, is reported in today's *Guardian* as saying, 'In the eight months I was cabinet secretary when Tony Blair was prime minister, the only decision the cabinet took was about the Millennium Dome. And the only way they got to take that decision was because Tony Blair had to leave the room to go to a memorial service and Prescott was left in charge. There were in fact more people against the Dome than for it and the one thing that Prescott could get cabinet agreement to was that they should leave it to Tony Blair. That was the decision.' Incredible? On second thoughts, no. All too believable.

Monday, 11 June

Twenty years today since I was first elected.

Jack Straw, addressing the parliamentary committee this evening, remarked *inter alia* that we are due a substantial pay rise and that he had said as much in a submission to the Senior Salaries Review Body, spouting some nonsense about comparators. And this when we are restricting the public sector to just over 2 per cent. Not on your Nelly, I thought. In fact I said so. So did a couple of others, prompting Jack to call us 'hair shirts'.

Tuesday, 12 June

This evening, with others, a meeting with John Reid in the Prime Minister's room at which he sought to persuade us of the need for yet more laws on terrorism, including a return of something strongly resembling the old, discredited 'Sus' laws and extension of detention without trial. Confidence was not inspired when, on entering, we were each handed a bit of paper recording the results of a Populus poll suggesting that the public favoured stronger measures by a margin of two to one. Is this the evidence base we are being asked to consider? I inquired where the pressure for an extension of detention was coming from, citing my exchange with the DPP in Birmingham last month. John replied that he took his advice from the police, not the DPP. According to Andrew Dismore, however, Met Commissioner Ian Blair says he is not looking for an extension either. Several people pointed out that it was Stop and Search that gave us the Brixton riots last time round. To be fair, John was fairly measured, promising to consult carefully and asserting that he had an open mind, adding that we faced an unprecedented threat from an enemy which had potentially unlimited capacity to inflict carnage and which acknowledged no limits.

The Man has made an interesting speech about 'the feral media' – something he's obviously been wanting to get off his chest for a long time.

Thursday, 14 June

To Number 10 with Tobias Ellwood, a bright, 30-something Tory MP who has a plan for phasing out opium production in Afghanistan. Keith Hill convened the meeting with officials from the Foreign Office, International Development and Defence. We sat in the Pillared Drawing Room, the very room in which four years ago The Man outlined to select committee members his intention to invade Afghanistan. Tobias, a former army officer who has been to Afghanistan four times, outlined his plan. He has also been in Washington, where he claims it is being taken seriously. He was heard politely, but there was considerable scepticism. The practical obstacles are immense, not to mention the Americans, who are a law unto themselves. On the way back Tobias described how a friend of his, a major, had been invited to dine with American officers at their mess in Bagram airbase. A large screen had a live feed from a helicopter gunship spraying bullets at alleged Taliban and there were cheers every time someone was hit. As Tobias said, they appear to regard the war as a video game.

Saturday, 16 June

Today's *Telegraph* carries an interview with Hilary Benn in which he is asked if he still believes it was right to invade Iraq, to which he replied with the same disingenuous formula that The Man uses, 'I can't look you in the eye and say that I regret Saddam Hussein is no longer there.' Fair enough, given that he's in government, but then two paragraphs further on he says piously, 'If we're not straightforward and direct, if we don't tell it like it is, then we're in danger of being overwhelmed by cynicism ...'

Monday, 18 June

Sunderland

Emma is 12 today. Before departing for London I presented her with a hand-drawn card depicting a small person immersed in a book entitled 'Harry Potter and The Tiny Nuisance'.

London

To the Cloisters to sign the remembrance books for The Man and JP. Some of the inscriptions are sickening in their sycophancy. Not wanting to appear hypocritical I kept my contribution short and to the point. To The Man I wrote: 'A pleasure serving with you ...' Later it occurred to me that I should have added, 'most of the time'. To JP merely 'All Good Wishes'. Anything more would cause a thunderbolt to come from heaven.

Tuesday, 19 June

The Coming of Gordon is anxiously awaited. Rumour and speculation abound, but absolutely no hard information. His camp is hermetically sealed. No one has the slightest idea what he has in store for us, although it is taken as read that the slaughter will be great. As for me, I look on with only mild curiosity.

Meanwhile The Man remains immersed in a whirlwind of activity. Speeches, summits, farewell visits, interspersed with weekly visits to Parliament for Questions, at which he continues to excel. He neither looks nor sounds like a man on the brink of oblivion, yet eight days from now it will all be over.

Wednesday, 20 June

Dropped a note to the Speaker in the hope of being called at PMQs. I wanted to ask The Man, apropos his 'feral' media speech, if with the benefit of hindsight he regretted not taking on the press barons instead of trying to appease them. Needless to say I wasn't called. So humiliating, all that bobbing up and down while the Speaker averts his gaze. What am I doing here?

To an upper committee room to listen to the Iraqi foreign minister, a plump, courteous man whose fluent English testifies to years of exile in London. He used words like 'difficult' and 'challenging' to describe the current situation, while asserting that in some provinces – and even in parts of Baghdad – something approaching normal life existed. Not a good idea, he said, for the US to talk to Iran and Syria, because those governments had a long agenda of which Iraq was only a small part. Instead they should let the Iraqis take the lead. 'I asked the key Iranian leaders, "Do you really want the Americans and the British to leave?" and they said, "No". They do not want disintegration.'

Then to the Groucho Club for a party to celebrate the launch of a Brook Lapping production entitled *The Rise and Fall of Tony Blair*. There I met a man who claimed to be a floating voter who predicted that Gordon would triumph over David Cameron because the public would eventually notice that Gordon was a heavyweight and Cameron was not. I record it because it is the first time I have heard a disinterested party predict that Gordon will triumph.

Thursday, 21 June

This morning, a bizarre report that Paddy Ashdown has been offered a place in Gordon's government which he has duly declined. Yesterday it was reported that Gordon had met with Ming Campbell and offered the Lib Dems several places, which Ming, wisely, also declined. There are also reports that John Stevens, the former Metropolitan Police Commissioner, has been offered something. It seems extraordinarily cackhanded. Just why would it be in the Lib Dems' interests to ally themselves to an unpopular Labour government? Why, for that matter, would it be in our interests, given that we have a majority of more than 60?

There are also reports that The Man may become George Bush's Middle East envoy. Surely not. That would be true poodledom.

As I was departing, I ran into Geoff Hoon, who recounted the scene at this morning's Cabinet, The Man's last. Tributes all round, to which The Man responded gracefully, but without sentiment. 'Some of my staff,' he said, 'think I have not yet adjusted to the fact that I am going. So if I wander in next week, please point me in the direction of the men in white coats.'

Friday, 22 June

To a local primary school to be photographed with a breakfast club. A bright, sunny place, full of happy little people. The head (a dynamic, attractive woman who says she has 'the best job in the world') gave me a tour. A growing proportion of the children were Bangladeshis with mothers who speak little or no English. I chatted to a young Bengali teaching assistant. 'Are girls of 14 or 15 still disappearing from the secondary school up the road and sent off to be married in Bangladesh?' I inquired.

'It was a problem, but less so now.'

How come?

'Because the government raised to 18 the age at which husbands or wives could be brought in.'

Yessssss.

Monday, 25 June

To London through a landscape sodden after days of torrential rain. It is said to be the wettest June on record.

This evening to a crowded meeting of the parliamentary party where we bade farewell to JP and The Man. Harriet Harman, our new deputy leader, was at the top table, positively glowing after her surprise victory on Sunday. Gordon, as ever, puffy and exhausted. The Man, by contrast, looking as though he were commencing rather than finishing a decade in office. JP's speech a white knuckle ride, leading down all sorts of dangerous alleyways, carried along by a tide of goodwill. The Man, brief, dignified, generous and received with rapture. Afterwards a presentation. A guitar for The Man, crystal decanters for JP. Another ovation. A historic moment – the most successful Labour leader in history taking his leave. No battery of cameras to bear witness. Just us, the foot soldiers whose loyalty has been tested to the limits. People snapped away with their mobile phones. No tears. Everyone, not least The Man himself, knows that it has to end. Just relief all round that the handover has gone so smoothly. It could so easily have been different.

Wednesday, 27 June

To the chamber for The Man's final appearance. I found a seat on the cross benches in front of the special gallery on the Opposition side, which afforded a grandstand view. Cherie and three of the four children were upstairs in the west gallery. My first sighting of Leo since he was a baby, a lovely little chap who hadn't a clue what was going on and kept having to be told to look at his dad. A brief flurry of excitement, waving of order papers on our side and boos from the other, when Tory defector Quentin Davies took his seat on the Labour benches. Otherwise a mainly subdued affair. All but a handful of ignoramuses avoided point scoring. Cameron asked about the floods, mercifully without seeking to pretend it was all the government's fault. Some nice moments. Nick Winterton, huffing and puffing about Europe, brought down to earth when The Man wished him farewell in three European languages. A foolish Lib Dem with wild hair asked a convoluted question about disestablishing the Church of England. The Man just looked at him, smiled, shrugged and said, 'I don't think I can be bothered with that', and promptly sat down to laughter. 'Bowlers outshone by batsman,' whispered the Lib Dem aristocrat sitting next to me.

Then the finale. Alan Williams, father of the House, read out a dignified little tribute to which The Man responded gracefully. And that was that. The end. The final curtain. He sat down and our side rose as one. Before we knew it the ovation had spread to the public galleries. On the Opposition side Sylvia Hermon was first up, then the Lib Dems began to rise, the Tories briefly floundered, Cameron was quick to catch on and was soon on his feet, gesturing to reluctant backbenchers to follow, which, with varying degrees of reluctance, they duly did, leaving only a handful of surly Scots Nats in their seats. Then he was gone, pausing only to shake hands with the Speaker, the applause continuing as he disappeared down the corridor and into history. Several people, Margaret Beckett for one, were wiping tears from their eyes as we filed out. I kept thinking of that leaked memo at which we all sniggered last September: 'He must leave with the crowds still wanting more.' At the time, given the low point we were at, it seemed impossible, ludicrous, fatuous … but it's happened. He's done it. For once the New Labour machine delivered.

Two hours later, having been anointed at the Palace, Gordon was in Downing Street, waving awkwardly in response to the demands of the media legions, prattling about the need for change. The clear implication being that he is repudiating everything that has gone before, even though he shares responsibility for much of it. He still doesn't look happy (what does it take to make Gordon happy?) and it still takes a second or two for a smile to travel from his brain to his lips.

Thursday, 28 June
All day word of Gordon's Cabinet has been filtering through. My interest being purely academic, I made no effort to discover the details, just picking up bits and pieces from people in corridors. Even

by nightfall, I had not seen a full list. Alistair Darling is Chancellor, a safe pair of hands if ever there was one. David Miliband is the new Foreign Secretary, which strikes me as unwise. To be sure he's bright and personable, but he's never been left anywhere long enough to achieve anything of substance. Jacqui Smith, the new Home Secretary, has always struck me as a lightweight, but then I know little or nothing of her; as Chief Whip she's been practically invisible. There is a great deal of change for the sake of change. People who were doing perfectly good jobs have been either dropped or reshuffled. The carnage is unprecedented – Des Browne is the only member of the outgoing Cabinet who remains in the same seat and even he has had responsibility for Scotland tacked on almost as an afterthought (no doubt the Nats will have something to say about that). Youth is (almost) everything. Jack Straw (Justice – surely he was hoping for something better?) is the only Cabinet minister on the wrong side of 60; several of the new boys and girls are in their thirties and have only been in Parliament for five minutes. The caravan has well and truly moved on.

Andrew Lloyd (Africa Director at the Foreign Office), who I ran into at Westminster tube station, reports that Dave Triesman is out, lasting just two months longer than I did. His replacement – our eighth Africa minister in ten years – is Mark Malloch-Brown, who is having to be inducted both into the Lords and the Labour Party in order to qualify. Still, at least he knows about abroad, which makes him better qualified than most.

Friday, 29 June

'Are you sure you want to carry on?' Ngoc asked at breakfast this morning. Until now we have always assumed that I have no choice but to serve another term if I want to see the children through university. It's true, I don't want to continue. To be sure there are days which are enjoyable, but they are rarely fulfilling. I mustn't kid myself that I am doing anything very useful beyond acting as a glorified social worker. As far as the big picture is concerned, I am entirely irrelevant. If I'm not careful I shall end my days as a Tea Room bore, regaling anyone prepared to listen with tales of triumphs past. For the first time, the balance has tipped in favour of retirement.

The full extent of Gordon's ever-expanding big tent is gradually becoming apparent. Malloch-Brown, John Stevens ... This evening there was a hilarious interview on the *PM* programme with Digby Jones, the former CBI Director General, who is going to be something at the newly christened Department for Enterprise. He has generously agreed to take the Labour whip in the Lords, but balked at party membership. His previous trenchant criticisms of government were read back to him one by one and he did not resile from any of them. He was repeatedly asked if he intended to vote Labour, but declined even to commit to that ... Should we laugh or cry?

Monday, 2 July

Jacqui Smith, our new Home Secretary, made a statement about the attempted bombings at the weekend. Everyone, including David Davis for the Tories, sang her praises, so much so that at times one might have imagined she had been called upon to dismantle the bombs herself whereas, so far as I can see, all she did was call for vigilance, praise the emergency services and chair a meeting of COBRA. Gordon, surrounded by his new Cabinet, addressed the parliamentary party. He thanked everybody copiously and, as ever, talked a lot about listening. The questions were mainly about affordable housing, where we have a big crisis brewing. Karen Buck said the housing shortage in London was driving racial tension.

Tuesday, 3 July

Gordon made a statement to the House outlining a huge programme of constitutional reform, including strengthening Parliament by giving select committees power to veto certain public appointments. He also talked of handing to Parliament responsibility for the Security and Intelligence Committee, something I've been pressing for years without getting anywhere. To judge by the unenthusiastic response from the chairman, Paul Murphy, the strongest resistance will come not from the agencies, but from the MPs already on the committee, the anointed.

To Admiralty House for JP's farewell do, compered by Gus O'Donnell, the Cabinet Secretary. Gordon, too, put in an appearance, accompanied by one of the Special Branch men who came with me to Somaliland. The place was crammed with officials and former ministers, many of whom had hair-raising tales to tell about the perils of working with JP. Oddly, however, they all seem to retain a sneaking regard for him.

Later, during a division, Bob Ainsworth regaled me with the tale of the fifth target that mysteriously appeared in the drugs White Paper. Bob, who used to be in charge of drugs policy at the Home Office, had devised four targets, only to discover that a fifth one – to halve poppy cultivation in Afghanistan – had appeared from nowhere over the weekend. 'Where the hell's this come from?' he asked his bemused officials. The answer, of course, was Number 10. Another spectacularly unenforceable New Labour wheeze dreamed up on the hoof. Opium production in Afghanistan is now at record levels.

Wednesday, 4 July

To the chamber for Gordon's first PMQs. Adequate, but lacklustre. Not the great clunking fist that we had been led to expect. The problem is that having spent ten years in a post over which he had total mastery, he can now be asked about absolutely anything and this will take some getting used to. At one point he was reduced to pleading that he had only been in the job five days (seven, actually). Not that it mattered very much, the occasion being overshadowed by events elsewhere. A lobby journalist remarked, 'The word upstairs is that to everyone's surprise Gordon could not have had a better start. A terrorist incident in which no one was killed ...'

Tuesday, 10 July

To the Labour HQ in Victoria Street for a spot of by-election telephone canvassing. There was only one other person, a keen youth, and we were heavily outnumbered by a bunch of master strategists sitting about chatting. We were presented with a fatuous script which I ignored in favour of simply asking how people intended to vote, but I could hear the keen youth going through every tedious detail. I doubt whether he had spoken to half a dozen people in the hour that I was there. Responses were surprisingly friendly (but then this was Sedgefield) until I noticed that I was being asked to contact people whose views had been ascertained as recently as yesterday. I drew this to the attention of the sharp-suited young master strategist who appeared to be in charge and who I doubt had ever knocked on a door in his life, and he confirmed that this was indeed the case. At which point I gave up and went off to hear William Hague lecturing on William Wilberforce. As Hague pointed out, Wilberforce had rejected offers of office, preferring instead to devote himself to his anti-slavery campaign, with the result that 200 years on he was still remembered with respect, while most of his contemporaries were forgotten. 'By not seeking power, he achieved much more than those who did.' Amen.

Wednesday, 11 July

Front-page headline in this morning's *Sun*: 'Cheshire housewife marries Bin Laden'.

Friday, 13 July

To the Stadium of Light for David Puttnam's final outing as chancellor of the university. A delightful man. One of that small band of life enhancers of my acquaintance (others include Liz Forgan and Charles Baker Cresswell). Merely to spend time in his company is to come away refreshed. At lunch David remarked that Sunderland and the north-east had regained its self-confidence during the last ten years or so. He told of an exchange with the late Bishop David Shepherd, regarding the revival of Liverpool, which might equally apply to us.

'How come?' he had asked.

To which the bishop replied, 'We stopped feeling sorry for ourselves.'

Sunday, 15 July

Mark Malloch-Brown, the new Africa–Asia–UN minister, has unwisely given an interview in the *Telegraph* in which he appears to be under the impression that he is a rather more significant figure than he actually is. By evening he had been firmly put back in his box by Miliband. Another little foretaste of the problems that lie ahead with these big tenters? In the Lords they are taking bets which one will be the first to throw his toys out of the pram and walk away denouncing us. The smart money is still on motormouth Digby Jones, but Malloch-Brown obviously can't be ruled out.

Monday, 16 July

Chief Whip, Geoff Hoon, announced at this evening's meeting of the parliamentary party that we were going to have to suspend the convention that parliamentary private secretaries should not serve on select committees because we didn't have enough people to fill the vacancies. For this parliament only, he said, but we shall see. So much for strengthening Parliament's ability to scrutinise the executive. The problem is that ever more backbenchers have been incorporated into the executive. The process began as a device for neutralising Parliament and has mushroomed under Gordon – a record number of ministers (including two and a half juniors at DFID doing the job I resigned from six years ago because there wasn't enough work for one), including ten unpaid; a record 57 parliamentary private secretaries, who while away their time planting questions (and sometimes even the supplementaries), half a dozen 'special envoys' for Cyprus, the rainforests and goodness-knows-where-else, and another half a dozen party vice-chairs. Barmy.

Thursday, 19 July

To the Treasury in an attempt to persuade Jane Kennedy not to allow the Inland Revenue to close their tax offices in the centre of Sunderland. The girl on reception had never heard of Jane and had to make a telephone call to discover who the ministers were ...

I pointed out that it made no sense for one part of the Treasury to be farming out civil service jobs to the blighted regions while another department in the same building was looking for ways of disposing of them and suggested that the two should talk to each other. Whether or not they will take any notice remains to be seen.

Then to the chamber, where I made a short and unintended contribution to the Zimbabwe debate. A dismal affair. A handful of the usual suspects, Nicholas Winterton et al, huffing and puffing, and the latest in a long line of hapless Foreign Office ministers, Meg Munn, who has never set foot in Africa, reading from a script about events with which she is utterly unfamiliar. Not her fault, poor woman. It's more than two years now since the Foreign Office had a minister in the Commons capable of answering questions about Africa.

In passing, a nice little story from George Young. He went to help out in the by-election at Ealing Southall, part of which he represented until 1997, and called at a restaurant he used to frequent. The proprietor, who hadn't seen him for more than ten years, didn't bat an eyelid and greeted him with the words, 'Usual table, Sir George?'

Home on the 20.00.

Friday, 20 July

Half a dozen or more members of the new Cabinet have 'fessed up' to smoking dope in their youth, including wide-eyed, innocent Yvette Cooper. This sudden bout of breast beating has apparently been prompted by plans to tighten the law on cannabis, combined with the emergence of a youthful picture of our new Home Secretary, Jacqui Smith, looking a little on the high side.

Monday, 23 July

The floods have reached Tory England, which means that any day now the media will be setting out in search of someone in government to blame, although David Cameron has provided a welcome distraction by disappearing to Rwanda even as the flood waters lap at his constituency.

A mesmerising performance from George Galloway in response to the Standards and Privileges report on his relationship with the former Iraqi regime. No one left the chamber during the one hour and 18 minutes that he was on his feet. In turns angry, humorous, outrageous. He would have gone on much longer, but for frequent interruptions from the Speaker urging him to address the report and stop slagging off members of the committee. Eventually the Speaker lost patience and named him, leaving George to slink ingloriously out from the chamber, whereupon George Young was called and proceeded to scientifically demolish the huge wall of bluster that Galloway had so painstakingly erected. He was duly excluded for a month without pay, for all his brilliance a busted flush.

Sunday, 5 August–Saturday, 11 August

Montréal du Gers

To France to stay with Ray and Luise Fitzwalter, clutching a copy of Alastair Campbell's diaries. I had intended to give it to Ray as a present, but he already had one that he and Luise were competing to read. We whiled away a pleasant week with outings and a couple of six- or seven-mile *randonnées* through fields of vines and sunflowers. Dinners by the pool, a concert in the church at Forces, medieval night in Montréal (beautiful, innocent, yob-free fun). Just as we were about to depart, Ngoc received a text from Saigon to say that her father was dead.

Sunday, 12 August
Sère, Gascony

Communication with Vietnam proved difficult but we eventually made contact on a bad line using the owner's landline. Grandpa will be buried tomorrow. Later, a text from Luise to say that Ray's daughter had given birth to a son. As one life ends, another begins ...

Monday, 13 August

This morning, at about the time Grandpa's funeral was taking place far away in Kontum, we went up the hill behind our cottage and held our own little service. We stood in a circle and Ngoc described his life with its dramatic changes of fortune, how he went from being a refugee to prosperity, before being reduced again to penury. I said a few words. Then we stood facing east, put our hands together and bowed. We were up there about an hour, a pale view of the Pyrenees on the distant horizon.

Wednesday, 15 August
Sère, Gascony

A short walk in the Pyrenees. We drove to the Col d'Aspen, picnicked in the woods and then the girls and I (Emma complaining all the while about the heat) walked a couple of miles to a viewpoint offering stunning 360-degree views, range after range receding into a blue haze.

Wednesday, 22 August
Sunderland

Ngoc has set up a little altar for Grandpa on the mantelpiece in the kitchen. A framed photo flanked by small candles, flowers and a bowl of fruit. Death in Vietnam is not so clinical and impersonal as it is here ... the body removed within hours, a trip to the crematorium, a buffet lunch for the mourners and then back home to get on with life

... In Vietnam it is much more complicated. The body remains in the house until the funeral, friends visit and must be entertained, monks are hired to pray and perform the rites. The dead are still believed to be present for the first three days and food must be prepared for them. The spirit doesn't leave the body until day 49, at which point it will be determined whether the departed ends up in heaven or hell. The ritual accompanying the 49th day is, therefore, especially important and Ngoc will be going home for that.

Wednesday, 29 August

Sunderland

A trickle of new Labour Party members, about a dozen this month. The first for a long time. Not to mention an eight-point lead in the polls. Gordon must be doing something right.

Thursday, 30 August

I rescued a woman and four young children facing eviction because their housing benefit claim had been rejected. So rare these days that I do anything useful apart from collecting the litter in the street.

Sunday, 16 September

A crisis brewing re Northern Rock, which is rumoured to be in trouble. On every television news bulletin, long queues of depositors trying to reclaim their money, despite the view of most commentators that there is not the slightest chance it will be allowed to go under. Anyway, deposits make up only about 20 per cent of the bank's income; the rest comprises mortgage repayments, which are proceeding normally.

Monday, 17 September

Alistair Darling has been on the bulletins all weekend, trying to reassure Northern Rock depositors that their money is safe. If ever there was a man for an hour like this, it is Alistair. Whoever heard of a crisis on his watch in any of the many departments in which he has served? Yet this morning, on Radio 4, I thought I detected just the merest tremor in his otherwise unruffled demeanour. Why, he was asked, did the government not increase the guaranteed level of compensation in the event of collapse if it wants to put an end to the crisis? No doubt this is being considered, but Alistair isn't yet in a position to say.

Tuesday, 18 September

The Great Panic is over, the government having announced that it will guarantee all Northern Rock deposits. Overnight the queues have disappeared.

Sunday, 23 September

Labour Party Conference, Bournemouth

Arrived to find the place in the grip of election fever. Until now I had assumed it was all got up by the media but it appears that the clever young master strategists around Gordon are furiously talking up the possibility on the strength of a couple of good polls and some crap about Gordon needing his own mandate. Pure insanity. We have a majority of more than 60 which is unlikely to be improved upon and more than two years of this parliament still to run. Apparently they are talking about early November. Good grief, it's hard enough persuading the citizens of Sunderland to vote on a sunny evening in May, let alone on a dark, rainy evening in November.

In fairness I should record that it isn't just the master strategists. At Waterloo I met a hotshot Labour lawyer from one of the big City law firms. 'Gordon should go now,' he said. 'The word in the City is that more banks will be in trouble by January – and Gordon will be blamed.'

Monday, 24 September

'Am I the only person who thinks all this election talk is bollocks?' inquired Alastair Campbell, who I came across holding court outside the Highcliff Hotel.

'No, Alastair, you are not.'

I asked about the diaries. Had he run them past The Man prior to publication?

'Yes, Tony saw it all. He wanted me to stick it on Gordon a bit more.'

'When might we expect the unexpurgated version?'

'Some of the stuff with Gordon is mind-blowing. Not sure I can even put it in the unexpurgated version. I saw a poll that said only 8 per cent of people now think we are divided whereas last year it was 60 per cent. The fact is that Gordon was the cause of the divisions. It was *all* Gordon. There wasn't a single member of the Cabinet who didn't at one time say that Gordon wasn't up to being prime minister.'

The Speech. A leaner, fitter Gordon, in contrast to the puffy, exhausted, driven figure we are used to. Relaxed, almost. No razzmatazz. Few jokes. Verging on the dour. Much talk of hard work, duty, honour. A great deal of shameless sloganising about Britain and Britishness. Some substance – increased maternity leave, an elected second chamber, a commitment to restore the link between pensions and earnings. Seemed to go down well with everybody, even the hacks. I guess just not being The Man is enough to get by for the time being.

Someone drew my attention to an extract from the latest volume of Tony Benn's diaries in today's *Daily Mail* in which he quotes me – accurately – as advising him not to visit Saddam and says, 'Chris is so right-wing now and so loyal and Blairite.' Incredible. The old rascal sells his soul to the *Daily Mail* and then accuses me of selling out.

Tuesday, 25 September

Breakfast with Tony Benn. I hadn't realised he was staying in the same hotel until he appeared at my table this morning. I couldn't resist pointing out what I have so far refrained, despite considerable provocation, from mentioning. Namely, that Blair had intended to appoint me, not Hilary, to the job at International Development and had only been talked out of doing so by the whips on the grounds that I had voted against the Iraq enterprise whereas Hilary had voted in favour and duly stepped into my shoes. I bear Hilary no malice – on the contrary I greatly admire him – but it is a bit galling to be accused of selling out on one page of Tony's diaries and on the next to find him celebrating Hilary's promotion. I am not sure how much of it sunk in, but he was kind enough to present me with a copy of the book, inscribed to 'A dear friend'.

Wandered down to the conference centre, but couldn't bring myself to go in. Instead I sat outside in the sunshine finishing off *The Inheritance of Loss*, this year's Booker winner. Gordon Brown walked by, deep in conversation with someone I didn't recognise, closely shadowed by a posse of acolytes and trailed discreetly by his grey official Jaguar and a black Special Branch Land Cruiser. No sign of election fever abating, but apparently polls from Scotland are indicating that the Nationalists would do well, which might prove sobering.

Took part in a panel discussion organised by Amnesty about extraordinary rendition. The others were the Amnesty General Secretary Kate Allen, Clive Stafford Smith, a lawyer who represents some of those in Guantanamo, and a bright young Muslim lawyer whose name I didn't catch. Inevitably there was a great deal of America-bashing, which began to get on my nerves after a while, so I pointed out that, terrible though it all was, none of this would have happened were it not for Islamist terrorists blowing up embassies, the twin towers, nightclubs in Bali etc. This was received in total silence. It's not what anyone wants to hear.

Then to Northern Night, where Gordon and Sarah made a cameo appearance. He made a nice little speech complete with a couple of self-deprecating stories; she looked awkward and rigid, obviously hating every moment of it.

A beautiful full moon in a cloudless sky, reflected in the sea.

Wednesday, 26 September

Breakfast at the Highcliff. Then out with Graham Bash, a delightfully amiable head-banger whose views haven't changed one iota since the early eighties, and a couple of his friends for a walk along the coast to Swanage, and back by bus.

This evening, passing the security checkpoint en route to the ITV reception, a policeman took me to one side and whispered, 'Can I just say, sir, that – as a London Irish person – I would never have had the confidence to join the police if it wasn't for your work with the Birmingham Six and the Guildford Four ...'

Thursday, 27 September

To London on the train with Derek Wyatt, who shares my view that an election now would be bonkers and whose view might be thought to have some relevance since he has a majority of 79. Like me, Derek thinks this madness is too late to stop.

Monday, 1 October

We seem to be talking ourselves into an election, come what may. Bill Crawford, Sunderland's local electoral registration officer, says November would be 'the worst possible time' from the point of view of the number of voters registered. The new register doesn't come into effect until December and across the City at least 6,000 people would be disenfranchised. The Association of Electoral Registration Officers has put out a statement saying that up to a million people could lose their right to vote if the election takes place on the old register. Might this provide Gordon with an excuse to back down without too much loss of face? I put in a call to Jack Straw, whose antennae are normally pretty good, to see what he thinks and register my concern. Jack was cautious: 'I have mixed feelings. It's Gordon's call. He is entitled to a mandate.' He added that, if we didn't go now, there was absolutely no case for an election in 2008, the moment for the mandate argument would have passed. He then went on to suggest that a November election was no big deal, citing the Americans and the fact that, at some time in the distant past, our borough elections used to take place in November. He also mentioned the impact of the Ashcroft money, to which I replied that the solution was not an early election but to use our majority to close the loophole that Ashcroft was exploiting. Jack said that he was just about to go into a meeting on that very subject, but we could only amend the law if we had the support of the Liberal Democrats and anyway it would take until March next year. He thinks the election will be on 8 November.

Tuesday, 2 October

Election fever mounts. It's had the unfortunate effect of forcing the Tories to put on a display of unity at their conference this week when they might otherwise have been tearing lumps out of each other. Overnight the new merciful, compassionate, green Conservative party has disappeared. All the talk now is of tax cuts. George Osborne has announced that under a Tory government no one leaving an estate worth less than a million will have to pay inheritance tax, which the Tory press are claiming exempts nine million people. Utter nonsense, of course, since in reality only about 6 per cent of estates pay death duties. In Sunderland I doubt whether it is 1 per cent – and most of them vote Tory already. All the same, a ruthless, clever move which will play well in the Home Counties.

Thursday, 4 October

It's becoming apparent that Gordon and the young master strategists have over-reached themselves. The Tories have had an unexpectedly good conference, their minds concentrated by the prospect of an election. Cameron turned in an impressive performance yesterday and by this evening there are reports that our lead in the polls is evaporating. The big question is can Gordon talk his way out of this folly without too much loss of face. He's going to look pretty foolish if he backs down, but if he ploughs on he risks oblivion. Either way this episode has showed him up for the desiccated calculating machine that he is.

I spent the day trying, with frazzled nerves, to breathe life into the new Sunderland Central constituency's somnambulant election machine, resenting every minute that I have to waste on this insane exercise.

Saturday, 6 October

There is to be no election, after all, Gordon announced this afternoon. With an entirely straight face he came up with some nonsense about how he wants to be judged on delivery rather than promise, as if an election was the last thing on his mind, when everyone knows he has thought of little else for months. He has done himself and the party real damage by encouraging this charade. So much for all this strong-man posturing. He looks weak and foolish. The Tories are resurgent; Cameron's ratings have soared. None of this would have happened had Gordon and his playmates concentrated on governing rather than manipulating. This episode has, however, had the solitary benefit of smoking out the Tories on tax. Their promise on inheritance tax was the mother of all election bribes – worth a cool £283,000 to any family worth a million or more. It had a devastating impact in Middle England, even among those who would never have been eligible. The depressing thing is that it worked. If the bribe is large enough, Middle England can be bought.

Monday, 8 October

A somewhat chastened Gordon addressed the parliamentary party this evening. 'If there is blame, I will take it,' he said. As well he may, since everybody knows that none of the acolytes (Douglas Alexander, Ed Balls et al) arrayed glumly behind him would lift a finger without his say-so. He just about managed to defuse the anger, but he's burned up a lot of credit in the process. At his joust with the media earlier in the day he asserted to general derision that the fall in our poll rating had not been a factor in his decision. Also, he's still prattling on about change. 'The country wants change,' he told us this evening, as though he has played no part in government for the last decade. He also argued, brazenly, that the Tories had shot themselves in the foot over tax since their promises were unaffordable. Oddly, he even suggested that we could match the Ashcroft millions, hinting that he had some big donors up his sleeve, but surely we don't want another arms race over funding. Look at the trouble we got into last time round. Instead of trying to outspend the Tories, we need to close the loophole in the law that enables Ashcroft to pump unlimited amounts of money into selected marginals between elections. Several people made this point afterwards, but Gordon didn't seem to get it. The only overtly critical contribution came from Mike Connarty. 'What have Gordon and the people around him learned about themselves?' he asked. He went on, 'No more spin. We've had ten years of it. Keep your spinners under control.'

Later, in the Tea Room, Alan Milburn remarked, 'Take this with a pinch of salt since it comes from me: Gordon has no policies and no strategy. He had – much to my surprise – done well on character, but now he's blown that too.'

A brief chat with Hilary Armstrong in the Members' Lobby. She made the same point as Alastair Campbell the other day. 'Gordon has the advantage of not having to contend with counter-briefing. There was hardly a day when Gordon's people weren't briefing against us. It's amazing that Tony lasted as long as he did.'

Tony Wright, who passed by while I was waiting at the bus stop this evening, said, 'It's awful. He's thrown away all that we gained over the summer. This could be a turning point.'

Monday, 15 October

Suddenly it's open season on Gordon. No longer Gordon the Mighty, Gordon the Invincible, Gordon *über alles*. Cameron and his Tories, who two weeks ago the pundits had all but written off, are sweeping all before them. It is Gordon who now looks vulnerable. There are even tentative signs that some of the Blairistas, who until now have kept their mouths shut, are beginning to brief against him. Hard to believe that such a dramatic reversal of fortune can have been caused by failing to call an election which no one wanted anyway. A temporary blip or a shifting of the tectonic plates? Who can tell?

Oh yes, and Ming Campbell has been removed as leader of the Lib Dems. His demise was announced by Simon Hughes in a terse statement outside Cowley Street. Ming himself was nowhere to be seen. That's two leaders they've disposed of in two years. What a ruthless bunch the Lib Dems are, for all that they like to cultivate a cuddly image. The good news is that a Lib Dem leadership election should take the pressure off us for a while.

Wednesday, 17 October

Lunch with the Cambodian Ambassador in preparation for Saturday's trip.

Ann Clwyd had an audience with Gordon this afternoon to report on her most recent visit to Iraq last July. She's supposed to be his Special Envoy – a carry-over from the Blair era – but, although Gordon hasn't formally dispensed with her services, she does not have the degree of access she once enjoyed. Ann reported that Gordon appeared uninterested, asked no questions and seemed ill at ease throughout her 20 minutes with him. 'I came away,' she said, 'with the impression that he isn't going to last.'

This evening I went, alone, to the Apollo cinema in Lower Regent Street to see *Atonement*. On the bus home a sharp-suited Tory MP who I didn't recognise leaned over and whispered, apropos of nothing, 'Here's the irony. He's got the job he has wanted for ten years and he can't do it.'

I don't agree. I think Gordon, inadequate though he is in many respects, can do the job and will go the distance.

Sunday, 21 October

Le Royal Hotel, Phnom Penh

Thirty-four years since I first set foot here. Then the city was surrounded. At night it shook to its foundations as B-52s pounded the countryside. From here you could drive to the front line after breakfast and be back by the swimming pool by lunch. Hard though it is to credit, the American position then – as late as August 1973 – was that they were facing a Vietnamese invasion and that the Khmer Rouge, if they existed at all, were insignificant. It was here at the front desk that Jon Swain opened a hero-gram ('Congratulations your eyewitness account of fighting on Highway Four ...') addressed to a British correspondent whose foreign desk seemed to be under the impression that he was in Phnom Penh when in fact, as we all knew, he was in Singapore or Bangkok rewriting agency copy.

We are here as guests of the Cambodian parliament. Seven of us: three Labour, three Tory and a pleasant Liberal Democrat woman from the Lords. Ann Clwyd is our leader. This is my fourth visit, which gives me a little edge over the others, but I must be careful not to appear a know-all. The protocol is totally OTT. We are being ferried about in a convoy of black Peugeots, one apiece, each driven by a white-liveried chauffeur and preceded by a motorcycle policeman with a low whining siren.

This afternoon we were treated to a whistlestop tour of the city. After which we persuaded our hosts to drop us at the old Foreign Correspondents' Club by the river. Later Peter Viggers, Andrew Robathan and I walked back to the hotel via the Phnom, the huge stupa from which the city takes its name. On the steps, half a dozen disabled beggars, mine victims by the look of them. I wanted to give them something, but none of us had any small change. When the others had gone I went back and put five dollars in the bowl of a man with no hands. When I got close I realised he was also blind in both eyes.

This evening a lavish welcome dinner. The woman sitting next to me, a member of the Politburo, said she had lost 30 out of 34 members of her family in The Great Terror. Although her place card identified her as 'Mrs' she was unmarried. 'There were not enough men left in my generation,' she said.

Monday, 22 October

A day spent racing around town in our ludicrous convoy, the ambassador's black Range Rover bringing up the rear. Calls on the presidents of the Senate and the National Assembly, meetings with senators and assembly members, a visit to the death camp at Toul Sleng, with its haunting photographs of the doomed. Finally, out to the compound beyond the airport where, at huge expense, the special criminal court is preparing to try the handful of surviving Khmer Rouge leaders. In the evening, after dark, we took a cruise on the river. I sat on the roof chatting to Lin, our delightful little Khmer guide, while the others remained below decks. Dinner at the Foreign Correspondents' Club, during the course of which there was a huge electric storm.

Tuesday, 23 October

Another day of calls. Forty minutes with the foreign minister, two hours with the prime minister, Hun Sen, who was long-winded but eloquent and charming. In the afternoon we began a round of the opposition parties. Gradually, a picture is emerging. This is a one-party state masquerading as a multi-party democracy to appease the donors on whom Cambodia remains heavily dependent. To be sure, the achievements are in many respects impressive, considering that they started from Year Zero. Phnom Penh is a city reborn, positively humming with life. But ... everywhere there is talk of corruption and land-grabbing. Vast tracts – 100,000 hectares in one case – are being handed over to so-called 'entrepreneurs' in return (it is widely suspected) for donations to the ruling party; peasants are being dispossessed, forests cleared – a process made easier by the absence of land records; fortunes are being made by a handful of oligarchs with the right connections. Even fishing rights on the Tonle Sap are allegedly being auctioned, to the dismay of those who have fished it for generations. One other observation: although the state lacks funds to provide much in the way of education, health care or mine clearance, which are to a large extent left to foreigners, it does appear to have the resources for some lavish – and it must be said surprisingly tasteful – public buildings. One can't help wondering if the donors are being taken for a ride.

This evening, a reception at the residence, a delightful old French mansion. Among the guests Ok Serai Sopheak, a former Funcinpec commander during the controversial coalition with the Khmer Rouge during the eighties. He described how it worked. The West supported the non-communist resistance and the Chinese bankrolled the Khmer Rouge. The Thais stole about 30 per cent of the foreign assistance that passed through their territory. Sopheak denied any knowledge of the rumoured SAS training in Thailand, saying that he sent his people to the Jungle Warfare School in Johore Bahru. The entire operation was supervised by an international contact group, membership of which included the Thais, Singapore, Malaysia, the UK, the Americans ... Relations with the Khmer Rouge and the Thais were close ('they had safe houses in Thailand ... everything'). Was he nervous about being allied to the Khmer Rouge? 'It was high politics. Even the Americans and Great Britain had voted for the Khmer Rouge at the UN.'

Wednesday, 24 October

A tour of the opposition parties. The royalists are in disarray and lack any kind of programme. The Sam Rainsy Party is said to be a one-man band – two if you count his formidable wife – and too uncompromising. Most impressive was the newly formed Human Rights Party, comprising refugees from the others. We are introduced among others to Pen Sovan, prime minister in the government installed by the Vietnamese when they cleared out the Khmer Rouge in 1979. After two years, he disappeared to Vietnam, where he was detained for ten years, much of that time in an underground prison. Why? 'Because I opposed Vietnamese control of Cambodia.' My goodness, what a tale he could tell. If only there were time to cross-examine him ... He has written his memoirs, but unfortunately they are in Khmer.

Highlight of today's itinerary, a tour of the royal palace, mercifully undamaged during The Great Terror. Stunning. On a par with the Forbidden City, though much smaller – and virtually unknown.

This evening, a lavish farewell banquet, including graceful traditional dancers and a voluptuous young woman singing 'Sex Bomb'.

Thursday, 25 October

Le Royal Hotel, Phnom Penh

7 a.m.: seen from the balcony of my room on the second floor, a plump monkey, trailing a long tail, striding purposefully across the gravel forecourt in the direction of the dining room. A security guard, radioing for back-up, gives chase. Monkey accelerates and disappears leaving security man peering in vain into the undergrowth.

The Residence, Hanoi

A full moon, lanterns hanging from a franjipani tree. A light supper by the pool in the courtyard. 'This is the country that has reduced poverty fastest in the world,' says the ambassador. At current rates of growth (8 per cent) it will be middle income by 2015. An astonishing transformation. 'After a terrible history,' the ambassador goes on, 'this is the happiest time anyone can remember.'

'What about democracy?' demands one of the Tories.

'Vietnamese have a very low expectation of government,' says the ambassador. 'They just want the government to get off their back, which it is beginning to do.'

Back at the hotel, tension. A meeting with trade unionists has been scheduled for tomorrow and the Tories are refusing to go, despite Ann's insistence that they must. The Tories are adamant. They aren't going and that's that.

Friday, 26 October

Hanoi

Ann has been taken ill so, on the basis of seniority, Peter Viggers has assumed the leadership of our little party. Potentially problematic since he is entirely out of his depth in this neck of the woods – indeed, one suspects, anywhere outside the Home Counties – but he was kind enough to allow me to make the speech at the lunch with members of the National Assembly. This morning's engagements included a session with an impressive senior Assembly official who cheerfully fielded questions about the one-party state. 'We may have only one party, but that does not mean we have only one opinion.' Yes, the party would have to relax its grip on the media: 'You cannot make decisions for 84 million people. They have to make their own.' Who is more important, I asked, the prime minister or the general secretary of the party? The prime minister, he replied. Since when? 'Since about the last seven or eight years.' As we were going down the stairs, he remarked that the traffic in Hanoi was a bigger problem than the one-party state.

The meeting with the trade unions was a serious embarrassment. Robathan and Liddell Grainger (much to my relief) continued with their boycott, but Peter Viggers – having been elevated to the leader-ship – decided, as he put it, 'to step up to the plate'. We were greeted by two intelligent women who were under the impression that we were seriously interested in the rights of workers in Vietnam, faced as they are by some of the world's most ruthless employers. Instead, Sir Peter appeared to regard them as enemy aliens. Before they could utter a word, he took control of the meeting, treating them to a pat-ronising, convoluted, nonsensical little homily about communism. 'To what extent do you think you are qualified to impress democracy on Burma?' he demanded. They looked bemused (and they were not alone). It hadn't occurred to them that imposing democracy on Burma was any part of their remit. Three times I had to remind him to wait for his remarks to be translated before moving on to his next point. The others did their best, but no one seemed capable of asking simple, relevant questions. I just wanted the ground to open up.

Later, a meeting with a junior foreign minister, who turned out to be the son of the former foreign minister, Nguyen Co Thach. An amusing episode at the end when we presented him with a glass bowl from the House of Commons souvenir shop. The box was opened revealing, in place of wrapping paper, a pair of Ian Liddell Grainger's socks.

Saturday, 27 October
To Haiphong, a city which still retains some of the innocence that Hanoi once possessed. Here the bicycle is alive and well.

We visited a secondary school, where a group of confident, shiny-faced youngsters treated us to a little sketch about the difference between love and friendship.

'What's that uniform?' barked Andrew Robathan at a shy young teacher. He was referring to children wearing red scarves.

Young pioneers, she replied.

'Like the Hitler Youth, I suppose.'

Fortunately her English was not good enough to enable her to understand what he was getting at. She told me afterwards that we were the first Englishmen she had ever met. Goodness knows what she made of us.

This evening, back in Hanoi, dinner with Mr Long, who used to be at the embassy in London. He took me home and introduced me to his wife and son. Such intimacy would have been unthinkable ten years ago.

Finally, a walk around the Hoan Khiem lake. The chaos is unbelievable. What was once a city of a million bicycles is now a city of a million Hondas. Thousands of young people circling endlessly, aimlessly, faces masked against pollution. The dice are heavily loaded against pedestrians. Outside the post office I naively waited five minutes for the green man to appear on the traffic signals before attempting to cross the six lanes of traffic, but when the moment came the traffic simply carried on regardless.

Alas, the Vietnamese are making a big mess of their new-found prosperity. It will take just one Honda in ten to turn into a car and nothing will move. At which point, I suppose, they will make their next big mistake and start chopping down the trees, demolishing the old French villas to make way for superhighways and even then, after the elapse another ten years, still nothing will move. What was once one of the world's most beautiful cities will become just another Bangkok, Manila or Beijing.

Tuesday, 30 October

London

Another grovelling apology over the revelation that there are apparently 300,000 more migrants from the new EC members than previously thought, although the truth is that no one knows. This means
that at least half of the several million new jobs we boast about having
created have gone to migrants. Result: Gordon, who has been going
around mendaciously proclaiming 'British jobs for British workers', is
well and truly hoist by his own petard.

Friday, 2 November

Sunderland

Sarah is 18 today. What a pleasure it has been watching her grow up.
What fun we have had together. I can't bear the thought that she will
be leaving us before long. She wants driving lessons, which we have
reluctantly conceded. I drew a birthday card showing her driving at
high speed through red lights with everyone leaping for cover. Also, I
enclosed a letter saying how much we loved her and offering 15 little
pieces of advice based on my (almost) 60 years' experience of life and
she shed a little tear. In the evening we went out for a meal at the
Prickly Pear.

A union rep from Northern Rock called in. He says that the mortgage business is down by 80 per cent and that many of the 1,500 staff
at the Doxford call centre are twiddling their thumbs. Redundancies
can only be a matter of time.

Tuesday, 6 November

On foot through autumn sunshine to Westminster, arriving just
before HM the Queen. As ever, I didn't go down for the State Opening,
but from my little office in the eaves I could hear martial music, interspersed with the sound of the police helicopter that is now an obliga-
tory feature of such occasions.

Wednesday, 7 November

To the Royal Commonwealth Club to hear Sir Nick Stern on climate change. A beautifully clear presentation. He left us in no doubt about the urgency, but instead of the usual doom and gloom his approach was rational, constructive and relatively upbeat. If disaster is to be averted, he says, we will need to reduce carbon emissions by at least 75 per cent (as opposed to our newly announced target of 60 per cent) by 2050. This is to be achieved by way of carbon trading, drastic reductions in deforestation and much greater energy efficiency. He stressed that he was calling for low carbon growth, not low growth. A global deal was essential and developed countries must take the lead. 'If we insist that a global deal depends on poor countries signing up to targets now, we will not get a global deal.'

Then to the House to hear Jack Straw and Jacqui Smith call for yet another extension of the time limit for detention of terrorist suspects without charge. The Tories and the Lib Dems are against and hopefully there will be enough of our people to block it. I pointed out that as recently as May the Director of Public Prosecutions had said that neither he nor the police were pressing for an extension, but it doesn't cut any ice. They are determined to go ahead.

Thursday, 8 November

To the chamber to see Eric Pickles, a rotund Yorkshire Tory of impeccable working-class origins, slaughtering Hazel Blears and Yvette Cooper. They spouted targets and task forces and he just poked fun. First, to general hilarity, he read from Hazel's blog a ludicrous item headed 'General Election – bring it on'. Then, in answer to the suggestion that Tories were against any new house building, he simply read out a list of Labour MPs who were objecting to housing developments in their constituencies. And so it went on. Yvette made an earnest intervention, but was brushed aside. It was painful to watch.

This afternoon, while I was awaiting a guest in the Central Lobby, a man came up and shook my hand, thanking me for sparing the time to see him. Clearly a case of mistaken identity.

'Who do you think I am?' I inquired.

'Norman Tebbit,' he replied in all seriousness.

Sunday, 11 November
Sunderland

A clear, bright day. To the Civic Centre for the march to the Cenotaph. A little put out to find that, for the first time in the 20 years I have been attending, the Members of Parliament were excluded from the civic procession. Instead Bill Etherington and I were unceremoniously bundled down the hill ten minutes before and put in seats to one side, instead of standing as usual alongside the Chief Executive and the Mayor. I shan't make a fuss, but if it happens again next year, I shall go and stand with the public rather than sit with the officials.

In the afternoon Ngoc and I took Emma and her friend Catherine for a walk in the autumn sunshine at Castle Eden Dene. We discussed the possibility of my standing down at the next election, which grows more attractive with every day that passes.

Wednesday, 14 November

Admiral Lord West, one of Gordon's big-tenters, was on the radio just after 8 a.m. saying that he had 'yet to be fully convinced' that there was a case for increasing the length of time for which terrorist suspects could be detained. I thought to myself, 'I bet he changes his tune within the hour.' Sure enough, by 09.10, after a visit to Number 10, he was telling the assembled media that he was now fully convinced. Much merriment all round.

A discreet chat with Charles Clarke behind the screen at the far end of the Tea Room. Apparently Gordon has been trying to tempt him back into the fold. He recounted a bizarre sequence of events. Talks began before The Man retired, with Gordon saying he wanted Charles back in government. Come the day, however, no job was offered but, on the very day that the new government was announced, Gordon invited him for another chat, repeatedly promising, in the face of Charles's scepticism, that he would be offered something big in the first reshuffle. Gordon then asked if Charles fancied being an ambassador anywhere, which he didn't. Or a special envoy to Burma, Darfur or China? Again Charles declined. Then in August, on the day that Gordon had his famous tea with Margaret Thatcher, he was invited back and asked to become a special envoy on migration – i.e. persuading countries like China, Iran and Nigeria to take back their illegal migrant citizens. It was put to Charles that this would 'create a trajectory for his return to government within a year'. There followed a visit to the Cabinet Office to discuss terms of reference and, since then, nothing.

Monday, 19 November

To the chamber for Alistair Darling's Northern Rock statement. As ever, he was cool, calm and collected. George Osborne, as ever, was obnoxious.

Tuesday, 20 November

To the Attlee Suite in Portcullis House to hear General Sir Richard Dannatt and a large contingent of the officer class deliver a presentation on the work of the army. Interestingly, both he and Colonel Richard Westley, commander of the regiment just back from Helmand, were at pains to stress that the government was investing 'significantly' in equipment, housing etc. If that was the case, I inquired, why do we keep reading apparently well-placed military sources saying the opposite in the *Telegraph*? Needless to say, he denied all, saying he had made clear to his staff that anyone who leaked would be out, but someone must be at it all the time – witness the lead in last week's *Sunday Telegraph*.

This afternoon another statement from a noticeably subdued Alistair Darling. The entire Cabinet, including Gordon, turned out. Glum faces all round. It appears some chump at Revenue and Customs has, against all the rules, put a disc or discs containing 25 million child benefit records – names, addresses, National Insurance numbers, bank account details, the lot – in the post and inevitably it has gone missing. The head of HMRC has resigned and search parties are out looking for the missing disc. So far there are no reports it has been misused, but the possibility remains. The Tories were torn between looking grave and hardly being able to believe their luck. As several people pointed out, with particular reference to ID cards, this kiboshes any notion that confidential information is safe in government hands. Alistair performed masterfully, but he must know that if the pit gets any deeper he may have to fall on his sword. God knows what the tabloids will make of it tomorrow. Our luck has well and truly turned.

Wednesday, 21 November

A hard rain falling. The media have gone bananas over the lost discs and, at Questions today, David Cameron worked himself up into a synthetic rage on the subject, though Gordon handled him well. Later, he made a rare appearance in the Tea Room, looking surprisingly relaxed, all things considered. 'You couldn't make it up,' he said with a wry smile. Apparently the National Audit Office, where it was supposedly sent, refused to allow a search of their offices for several days and the clerk who mailed the discs can't recall what address he put on it. So far as I can tell there is no great public panic underway as yet, though the media and the Tories are doing their best to organise one. The problem with all this is that it eats away at our reputation for competence and, once lost, it will not easily be regained.

To Committee Room 16 to hear Jacqui Smith, flanked by Tony McNulty and Alan West (he who has 'yet to be fully convinced'), set out the case for an increase in pre-charge detention, which she did quietly and competently. Most people acknowledged that the issue was being handled far better this time around than last. Nevertheless scepticism was widespread. Jacqui's case was not helped by the appearance of the former Attorney General, Lord Goldsmith, and the Director of Public Prosecutions, Ken Macdonald, before the Home Affairs Select Committee. They both said they could see no case for an extension.

To Clapham for dinner with John and Sheila Williams. Sheila, whose advice is usually sound, reckons I should serve another term.

Thursday, 22 November

To the City for a meeting of the Prison Reform Trust. Afterwards, I walked to the tube with Robert Fellowes, who is well connected in the City. He reckons the American economy is moving into recession and that it will take the rest of us with it.

Friday, 23 November

Awoke to hear the former chief of staff, Admiral Lord Boyce, on the radio denouncing the government, in the most intemperate and apocalyptic terms, for its alleged parsimony on defence spending and demanding huge increases. Apparently he was one of a posse of former defence chiefs who opened up on us in the Lords last night. A complete contrast to what we heard on Tuesday from General Dannatt and Colonel Westley. I immediately rang the *Today* programme and suggested they invite Dannatt or Westley to repeat what they told us on Tuesday, but I was told it was too late. I called the offices of Des Browne and Bob Ainsworth and left messages suggesting that they put up Dannatt and Westley, but nothing came of it. It makes my blood boil. Not least because at every election the officer class vote by a margin of three to one for a political party that promises lower taxes and cuts in public spending.

Monday, 26 November

A new disaster. It has emerged that a North-East property developer, David Abrahams, has been donating money to the Labour Party using the names of employees (one a Tory) to conceal his identity. This evening the General Secretary, Peter Watt, admitted he knew all about it and resigned. A huge new feeding frenzy is underway.

Tuesday, 27 November

Everyone is talking about our latest donor difficulties. It turns out that David Abrahams was a well-known, somewhat eccentric, figure in the region, although I haven't come across him. It's hard to believe that

Peter Watt was the only one in the know. A huge search is underway for a politician to pin it on and by this evening the hacks had discovered that Abrahams, under an assumed name, had given Harriet Harman £5,000 for her deputy leadership campaign, so now she's in the firing line, too. And of course all this is rubbing off on Gordon. The crises and cock-ups are beginning to accumulate. 'I am beginning to wonder whether we haven't got the Anthony Eden of our day,' remarked Andrew Mackinlay this evening. 'The trouble is we don't have a Macmillan to follow on.'

Wednesday, 28 November

Gordon took another big hit at Question time today. Cameron ranted away about his alleged incompetence, though in truth Gordon is blameless. Vincent Cable came up with a brilliant line: 'The House has noticed the Prime Minister's remarkable transformation over the last few weeks from Stalin to Mr Bean.' Part of our problem is that New Labour neutralised the party. General secretaries used to be substantial figures, capable of saying 'No' to the prime minister, but most party officials these days are young zealots who just say, 'Brilliant idea, Tony.' Dave Triesman was the last substantial figure to be General Secretary and he was eased out – partly for refusing to go along with the loans scam that got us into so much trouble.

Tonight there is talk of a new police investigation.

Thursday, 29 November

No sign of an end to the frenzy. A lobby journalist told me that the Tories are sending out unattributable leads on plain paper, some of which are turning out to be false. They've obviously got someone going forensically through our accounts and are spraying out allegations in all directions in the hope that enough mud sticks. The damage is enormous and we seem powerless to counter it. We just keep apologising all the time. 'Gordon's going to have to up his game,' remarked Dennis Skinner this evening. 'He needs to hit back. Not just take it on the chin. If he can't, he'll have to go.'

Friday, 30 November
Sunderland

To Hendon Valley Community School, a jewel in New Labour's crown. Alas, all is not well. The 'wrap around' nursery care, announced with much fanfare, is losing £8,000 a month and is faced with collapse when the subsidy runs out, as it will next April. Like many such projects, the theory was that after a few years it would become self-sustaining, but the area is so impoverished that there isn't a market for any more than a few hours a day. The neighbouring schools have similar problems. This must be happening all over the country. It's a design flaw. The only state nurseries that are paying for themselves are those in middle-class areas where everyone is working and they, being cheaper, have collapsed the private nurseries. Breakfast clubs have gone the same way. As soon as the subsidy was cut back, numbers fell dramatically. The Valley Road breakfast club was attracting 110 a day when free, but as soon as a modest charge – 30p a day – was introduced attendance fell to 40. Chris Young, the excellent head teacher, described herself as being 'raw with frustration' with the constant flow of unthought-out, underfunded government initiatives that rain down upon her. I was taken aback by how angry she was. It seems that just about all New Labour's proudest achievements are going belly up. She reported stiff resistance to the school meals initiative. So much so that they've had to start putting junk food back on the menu to stop kids voting with their feet. Mothers are telling their children *not* to eat healthy food. A couple even bent the ear of an Ofsted inspector on the subject. Came away deeply depressed.

Monday, 3 December

The media are still full of what they choose to call 'sleaze' stories about Labour funding. Wendy Alexander, Labour leader in Scotland, is being hounded for having accepted £950 from a donor based in the Channel Isles, although I doubt she realised he was outside the jurisdiction. Harriet Harman and Peter Hain have been dragged in for failing accurately to record the funding of their deputy leadership campaigns. In truth, most of this amounts to little more than sloppy accounting and scarcely merits the use of words like 'sleaze' and 'scandal', which are being sprayed about with abandon. Meanwhile the Tories, who have pioneered, with knobs on, just about every genuine funding scandal of the last 20 years, are getting off scot-free. Why, it's not so long since they tapped £8 million, *yes £8 million*, off a man suffering from dementia and refused to hand it back until ordered to do so by the High Court and no one has even been indelicate enough to mention the subject.

Gordon addressed this evening's meeting of the parliamentary party in a folorn attempt to rally the troops. He promised 'rigorously, surgically' to put an end to the abuses in our camp and legislation to limit individual donations, and close the so-called Ashcroft loophole which allows unlimited spending between elections. He also hinted that the trade unions will have to accept changes to the regulation of the political levy. Gerald Kaufman attempted to raise morale by saying that this wasn't much of a crisis compared with some he had lived through; good stuff, but no one quite believed him. I said we had to stop apologising and go on the offensive; it's not as though we are short of ammunition – I set out some of the more graphic examples and was, for the first time in ages, applauded.

Tuesday, 4 December

To Latymer Upper (day pupils only, fees £12,000 a year) to speak to sixth formers. My theme: 'In defence of politics', an uphill task in these difficult times. Lots of intelligent questions. One girl suggested we should legalise drugs and prostitution and buy up Afghani opium for use as morphine.

Back at the House: a truly awful debate on party funding, forced upon us by the Tories. A great deal of ya-booing and tit for tat. It did none of us any good. You only had to look at the grim faces in the public gallery to see how it will have gone down outside. I had put my name in to speak, but the quality of debate was so dreadful that, not wishing to become tainted by it, I asked the Deputy Speaker to cross my name off the list.

Wednesday, 5 December

Iain Duncan Smith remarked to me, as we shared a lift, that the Tories were wrong to have made such an issue of 'sleaze'. 'It will rebound,' he said. Several of the older, wiser Tories have been quietly saying the same. Iain drew attention to an interview with Tony Blair last Sunday in which he said that, with hindsight, he regretted making such an issue of 'sleaze' in the Major years.

'It's consuming all of us,' remarked one of my friends in the Press Gallery, 'including us journalists. We know we have only to put the word "sleaze" in the opening paragraph to get our story in the paper.'

Thursday, 6 December

After much hand-wringing the government have decided to have another go at increasing pre-trial detention: this time to 42 days, surrounded by all sorts of supposed (and hopelessly impractical) safeguards. Once again the Tories and the Lib Dems have come out against, though how many on our side will fall for it remains to be seen. I had to smile on reading the paper setting out the government's case, which remarks in passing that concerns have been expressed by community groups 'and others'. The others include the Director of Public Prosecutions, the former Attorney General, Lord Goldsmith, and not a few senior police officers.

Tuesday, 11 December

To the chamber to hear Ed Balls deliver a jargon-encrusted statement announcing a blizzard of new initiatives, action plans and official guidance to improve the lot of our schoolchildren. There are to be mentors, and parent-run school councils, and teachers are to be enjoined to keep in regular email contact with parents, every child is to have a 'red book' documenting his or her progress through the early years of their lives. Most teachers I meet are pleading for a respite from New Labour initiatives. Goodness knows what they are going to make of all this. It was tempting to get up and point out to him – apropos my recent visit to Valley Road – that much of the early-years care in the poorest parts of my constituency is on the point of collapse because funding is running out. Instead I confined myself to bending his ear on the subject in the Division Lobby.

Wednesday, 12 December

My 60th birthday. Grateful though I am for having reached the age of 60 with my health intact, the knowledge that my life is three-quarters over weighs heavily. I try not to think about it, but my name is recorded in the *Guardian* birthdays column and people have been congratulating me all day.

Meanwhile a great new iceberg is looming out of the mist. Jacqui Smith – no doubt on Treasury instructions – has upset the Police Federation by staggering their pay increase, with the result that they all lose out on a couple of hundred quid. Pretty small beer, really, but it's not how the Federation sees it. They have reacted by organising a huge uprising. We are being bombarded with letters full of words like outrage, disgust, betrayal (the Federation never does anything by halves). They are demanding Jacqui's head and there are calls for the right to strike, oblivious of the fact that the police are far better paid than those public servants who do have the right to strike. Privately most people agree that it's a mistake to upset one of the mightiest vested interests in the country for the sake of saving £30 million, but dare we back down in the face of a campaign of intimidation? And were we to do so, what would be the impact across the rest of the public sector? However, there is a bigger problem looming. The Senior Salaries Review Body is rumoured to be recommending above-inflation pay increases for ministers and MPs. The Treasury, needless to say, will recommend against, but (unlike other public servants) we get to vote on our own pay and conditions. If, as seems likely, we vote ourselves a generous increase while denying the same to others, all hell will break lose.

Thursday, 13 December

Gordon appeared before the Liaison Committee this morning and confirmed that there will be no backing down on police pay. Gerald Kaufman is fuming. He says he's written to Gordon, Jacqui Smith, Geoff Hoon, urging a climbdown but no one is listening. 'I've given this government my absolute, grovelling loyalty,' he fumed, 'but they've given me nothing in return.'

Lunch in the Churchill Room with Nick Kay, our new ambassador in the Congo. He claims to be optimistic, but it didn't sound as though much has changed on the ground. It seems the Chinese are moving in, offering infrastructure in return for natural resources, and Kabila seems to have bought the whole package without dwelling on the small print. Apparently, when he addressed parliament on the first anniversary of his election, Kabila made no mention of the donors or the 17,000 UN troops who have stabilised his country, but referred repeatedly and in glowing terms to China.

Home on the 20.00.

Monday, 17 December

My whip, Alan Campbell, reports that people previously thought of as Brownistas appear to be giving up on Gordon and casting about for a new wagon to hitch themselves to. Who? He mentioned a couple of names, people involved in the August '06 coup attempt. Alan also thinks that this parliament could run into the spring of 2010.

Today I collected my over-sixties Freedom Pass, which allows me free travel in London, courtesy of The People's Ken. Ludicrous, really. When I wait for a number 3 in the evening, at the stop by Victoria Tower Gardens, the only other passengers are usually other members of the Lords or Commons, plus a waiter from the dining room – and the waiter is the only one who pays.

CHAPTER FOUR

2008

Saturday, 5 January

Sunderland

To town, where clearing up is still going on after the usual seasonal mayhem. The plate glass in every one of the bus shelters in Fawcett Street, about ten in all, has been smashed; several telephone boxes are also without glass.

Monday, 7 January

General unhappiness at this evening's meeting of the parliamentary party. Barry Sheerman, an ultra-loyalist, led the charge. Why, he wanted to know, was the government going out of its way to upset some of the most articulate people in the country in an effort to save trivial amounts of money by cutting back on further education for those who already have degrees? Why had we taken on the police over a paltry £30 million which had already been budgeted for, someone else wanted to know. Someone else talked of 'political stupidity' on public sector pay in general, given that it was the bedrock of our support. The government seemed to be going around looking for people to upset, said another. 'If we want to save money,' said Mike Foster, 'why not make some big decisions, not death by a thousand cuts.' 'People like me, who are loyalists, are having their loyalty stretched to the limit,' said Adrian Bailey. Harriet Harman did her best to stem the tide with a little homily about not taking risks with the economy, but there was no banging on desks when she sat down. The natives are restless.

Also, a brief discussion on MPs' pay, on which, ludicrously, we shall be invited to vote later this month. I pointed out that it would be political suicide to award ourselves a larger increase than we were prepared to grant the rest of the public sector, which prompted some mild 'hear-hearing', but not enough to imply that the penny has dropped with most people.

Thursday, 10 January

Suddenly I am relevant again. For a moment or two at any rate. At Business questions I lobbed a little shot at Harriet Harman, asking how come we yet again find ourselves in the ludicrous position of voting on our own pay, having been repeatedly assured in years gone by that it would never happen again. To my pleasant surprise she responded generously, acknowledging that if my amendment six years ago – brushed aside by Robin Cook – had been accepted we wouldn't now be in this position. Afterwards, in the Tea Room, we agreed that I would table an amendment next week seeking to link our pay in future to the fortunes of our humblest constituents, probably pensioners. She also wants me to assist with lobbying colleagues against voting themselves an above-inflation pay rise, in defiance of government advice. Something I have been doing anyway.

Tuesday, 15 January

A meeting with the Home Secretary, Jacqui Smith, anxious to convince me to support her plans for extending pre-trial detention. We had a pleasant chat in her room for about 20 minutes. I was non-committal although my instinct is to oppose. I asked how she was coping with protection and she told a nice story about how, last summer, she'd taken her children to a camping site in Wales; another of our colleagues, Mike Foster, and his family were also there. Mike was in a tent, she was in her caravan and the Special Branch officers assigned to guard her were in a posh hotel up the road.

Tuesday, 22 January

To the Department of Justice in company with a delegation of Members whose seats are marginal, in an attempt to persuade Jack Straw to close the so-called Ashcroft loophole that allows the Tories to pour money into the marginals. Jack, however, is proving reluctant for fear of opening a new front on union donations. As he pointed out, the party is heavily in debt and we are now totally dependent on union funding, just about all other sources having dried up (what rich man wants to donate to Labour only to be monstered in the tabloids?). Someone argued that, if he didn't act soon, it would be too late and we would face defeat. 'What could be worse than an election defeat?'

'Annihilation,' replied Jack. Rightly or wrongly, he believes the Tories are out to destroy us.

Thursday, 24 January

A belated outbreak of sanity. We decided *nem con* to restrict our pay increase to 1.9 per cent, in line with the rest of the public sector, which means we can look the Police Federation in the eye and tell them to get lost. My amendment, linking future rises to the old age pension, wasn't called, but Harriet promised once again to try to find a way of sparing us the perennial embarrassment of having to decide our own remuneration.

Peter Hain has resigned, following the news that the police are examining unregistered donations to his deputy leadership campaign. His departure has triggered a mini-reshuffle. Typically, Gordon has opted for maximum complication. Four or five bright young things, most of whom had been in their jobs a mere seven months, have been moved. A crazy way to manage the business of government. We work in a lunatic asylum.

Monday, 28 January

Some *sotto voce* muttering about the youthful new appointees, sneeringly referred to in the media as being on work experience. 'What talents are required to be in the Cabinet?' inquired Eric Joyce as we filed into the Division Lobby this evening. Even Nick Brown, a Gordon loyalist, describes the new appointments as 'a big risk'.

Other news: the mixed-race woman selected by the Tories to succeed Ann Widdecombe at Maidstone turns out to have been seeking selection as a Labour councillor in Croydon as recently as 2005. I came across Gerald Howarth in the library, photocopying the relevant page of the *Mail on Sunday*. 'We've brought it on ourselves,' he said, 'with all this political correctness.' It's the second time the Tories have been caught out. Their candidate in the recent Ealing by-election had purported to be one of ours until a few months previously.

Tuesday, 29 January

A graphic account of life at the frenetic court of Gordon, from A Friend in High Places. Rumours of tantrums, harassment of minions, chaotic micro-management and telephone-throwing are true. Gordon, she says, is perpetually exhausted, incapable of relaxing, constantly micro-managing and takes disagreement personally ('Why are they doing this to me?'). He fires off up to 100 emails a day in all directions, demanding answers on every subject under the sun. He personally is said to have written Alistair Darling's pre-Budget speech. On New Year's Eve, with 30 guests waiting for him downstairs at Chequers, he spent the best part of four hours phoning all and sundry about the crisis in Kenya and then, instead of joining his guests, went to bed. By 7.30 a.m. on New Year's Day he was back on the phone again. According to my informant, far from being groupies, the officials who came with Gordon from the Treasury are cynical. They recount overhearing him on the phone to The Man, flatly denying responsibility for negative spin, even as his agents – sometimes operating from the same room – are colluding with the enemy. Relations between acolytes are not always good either. Douglas Alexander and Shriti Vadera are said to have been at loggerheads in DFID. On the credit side, unlike The Man, Gordon is willing to deliver tough messages – and (contrary to rumour) did so on his recent visits to India and China. He also has an extraordinary capacity to absorb information, never needing to be told anything twice.

Wednesday, 30 January

A huge furore over Derek Conway, a Tory Member, following a report by the Standards and Privileges Committee, which found that he had misused the office costs allowance to employ his 'all but invisible' student son.

Monday, 4 February

The stain from the Derek Conway business is spreading. The weekend press is full of tales about Members (mainly but not exclusively Tories) exploiting the allowances. Some outrageous scams have come to light. The rot runs deep. It is dragging us all down.

At this evening's meeting of the parliamentary party a row over four of our number – Frank Field, Kate Hoey, Gisela Stuart and Graham Stringer – who have got themselves mixed up with some sort of Tory front organisation that is planning to organise referendums on the Lisbon Treaty in ten, mainly Labour, marginals. An acrimonious discussion. Graham Stringer and Gisela Stuart reluctantly offered to withdraw, but Kate was defiant and Frank silent. David Winnick upped the ante, questioning whether they could remain on the whip. The Chief Whip, Geoff Hoon, was similarly uncompromising. Withdrawal was not enough, he said. Those concerned must disavow.

Tuesday, 5 February

Complaints about Members employing relatives are flooding in. At this morning's meeting of the Standards and Privileges Committee we agreed, as a matter of urgency, to require Members employing relatives to register their names. The Speaker has set up his own inquiry, but one only has to look at some of the names on it to see that nothing much will change, if it is left up to him. Increasingly, he is seen as an obstacle to reform. Meanwhile we are all tainted.

Wednesday, 6 February

Gordon is gradually getting the hang of PMQs. Unlike The Man, he'll never be a star, but he seems to have the measure of David Cameron, who today asked a laboured series of questions about the number of 'reviews' ordered by Gordon (in truth rather a lot) and was easily swatted aside. Pat McFadden, once a courtier, remarked, 'I think it's probably hit Gordon just how much stuff there is coming at you in Number 10. It's unrelenting. You can't just retreat into a shell, as he used to do in the Treasury. People demand answers. You have to respond.'

Thursday, 7 February

Norine MacDonald came in, hotfoot from Afghanistan. Situation bordering on the catastrophic, she says. Corruption and torture rampant. A culture of impunity. Karzai has lost the plot; surrounded by villains, he seems to believe the British are conspiring against him. She had heard from Afghani sources that he was only just talked out of expelling our ambassador. David Miliband and Condi Rice are there today, no doubt trying to talk some sense into him, but the possibility has to be faced that sooner or later NATO faces defeat in Afghanistan, with all that that implies.

Friday, 15 February

No one turned up to this evening's surgery at Pennywell. It was the same at Silksworth the other day and at Thorney Close. Five years ago there would have been a queue, but now we are lucky if we have two or three customers. Graham insists that this is because we encourage people who ring up to call at the office during the week. Maybe, but I wonder if something more fundamental is happening. Is it to do with my slide into obscurity or the rise of the internet? Who knows, but we are going to have to change our approach.

Sunday, 17 February

To Holy Island with the girls and Aunty Liz. Brilliant sunshine. This is said to be the sunniest February on record. On the way up we stopped in Alnwick, lunched in one of the little cafes overlooking the market square.

Arrived home to find that the top had come off one of the taps in the bathroom, causing water to shoot up in a great geyser. Ngoc called the fire brigade, who came swiftly to the rescue (she was full of their praises). Disaster narrowly averted.

Monday, 18 February

To the House to see Alistair Darling announce that he is proposing to nationalise Northern Rock. George Osborne made a fool of himself using words like 'catastrophic', 'disaster', 'back to the seventies' etc. The Tories and their media friends seem to think they scent Alistair's blood, but I don't see it myself. The *Financial Times*, which can usually be relied upon to talk sense at times like this, said, 'Anyone who suggests that the Labour government has gone back to 1970s socialism deserves ridicule. It has made a sensible, hard-headed, non-ideological choice.' The only criticism is that Alistair took too long about it.

Tuesday, 19 February

The Bill to nationalise Northern Rock went through all stages in a single sitting, finishing at midnight. The government had a comfortable majority thanks to the support of the Lib Dems. George Osborne, conscious perhaps that yesterday's rabble-rousing hadn't caught the mood of the hour, made a sober contribution. He seems to have wiped that facetious perma-smile off his face. Perhaps someone has told him.

Wednesday, 20 February

To an upper committee room to hear representatives of the Institute of Directors, the British Chambers of Commerce and the Federation of Small Businesses spell out their objections to Andrew Miller's bill, which seeks to provide some minimal protection for agency workers. The usual tosh about the need for flexibility and the likely loss of jobs were they to start treating people decently. Had fun inquiring if, by any chance, the organisations they represented had been opposed to the national minimum wage and for approximately the same reasons. After a bit of wriggling, they all agreed that this was so. The pinstripe from the Institute of Directors was particularly brazen, arguing that no one would ever know how many jobs had been lost as a result. I pointed out that unemployment in Sunderland was lower than it had been for 30 years. Came away with a spring in my step. In these days of big tent politics it is good to get the occasional glimpse of the class enemy.

Saturday, 23 February–Wednesday, 27 February

Five days laid low by a chest infection. For the first couple of nights I could only sleep sitting up. Ngoc has looked after me splendidly, holding my hand, feeding me soup and broth. By Wednesday, with the help of antibiotics, I felt well enough to creep round to the office and do a bit of paperwork, but I still don't feel right.

Monday, 3 March

Ninth day of the Lisbon Treaty. A tiny band of zealots – Bill Cash, David Heathcoat-Amory, John Redwood etc. – boring everybody stupid. Jim Murphy, at the Dispatch Box, calmly batting back every new piece of nonsense. I can't recall having received a letter from a single constituent on the subject.

Tuesday, 4 March

Lunch with Keith Hill, who remarked on the 'joylessness' of Gordon's style of government. His sources in Number 10, like mine, talk of perpetual grumpiness driven by lack of sleep, a tendency to micro-manage, a failure to make even the simplest of decisions until the last minute. Later, in the Tea Room, Hilary Armstrong said that The Man used to complain that 'Gordon depresses everyone'.

Kelvin Hopkins remarked cruelly, 'We have replaced a psychotic with a neurotic.'

Wednesday, 5 March

To Claridge's, in the company of half a dozen colleagues, to meet the Vietnamese prime minister. Our delegation was led by the lacklustre Ben Chapman, who might easily have been mistaken for a Politburo member in a one-party state. The prime minister by comparison, despite a lifetime inside the Stalin system, seemed bright, relaxed and energetic.

This evening the final votes on the Lisbon Treaty. The call for a referendum was comfortably disposed of, despite a small uprising on our side. To general satisfaction on both sides, the Lib Dems got themselves in a terrible mess. Several of their front bench spokesmen have lost their posts for defying their leader's instruction to abstain.

Monday, 10 March

Alistair Darling addressed this evening's meeting of the parliamentary party, in advance of Wednesday's budget. Cool and calm as usual, despite the storms raging around him. No one yet knows, he said, the full extent of the fall-out from America but, with one of the most resilient economies in the world, we were better placed than most. Jeff Ennis from Barnsley said we had to get a message to the white working class that we were on their side, because many of them were giving up on us. Barry Sheerman said the situation may be worse than we think, with banks not lending to each other and our manufacturing industry heading east.

Mark Kent, our ambassador in Hanoi, and his wife came in for dinner.

1. Late friends: Michael Foot – in the words of David Cameron, 'the last link with an heroic age of politics'. © Andrew Wiard

2. Tony Banks – who said of his re-incarnation in the House of Lords, 'Wonderful. I've gone from being a boring old fart to a young Turk in a single leap.'

3. Rupert Hanson, the man who brought music back to Sunderland, 'close to the top of my little pantheon of local heroes' – see entries for 17 June and 17 July, 2009.

4 & 5. *Out and about in the North: unveiling a plaque on the home of Joan Maynard, MP for Sheffield Brightside 1974–87; (above); with Sunderland lifeboat men (below).*

6. A visit from prime minister Gordon Brown with CM and former Sunderland mayor, 99-year-old Elizabeth Porter.

7. CM and Nicholas Soames in the Prince of Wales' garden at Highgrove, June 2006.

8. A visit from the Dalai Lama, 21 May 2008. 'The journey between engagements was like a triumphal procession. People lined the corridors and came running from all over.'

9. CM on his annual walk on the Cleveland Way.

10. 'My Dad' by Sarah Mullin.

15. *Goodbye to all that: a standing ovation as Tony Blair leaves the chamber for the last time, 7 June, 2007.*

16. *Gordon and Sarah Brown and family leave Downing Street: 'Sadly, the little lads are unlikely ever to remember the famous place that was once their home' 11 May, 2010.*

Tuesday, 11 March

Awoke to the news that the former Attorney General, Peter Goldsmith – normally such a sensible fellow – is proposing that our youth be required to swear an oath of loyalty to the Queen. Lord, spare us.

A leisurely lunch in the Adjournment with Bruce Grocott, now free of office for the first time in years. He shares the general doubts about the calibre of some of the new Cabinet. 'Name the stars,' he said.

'Miliband,' I offered.

'You'll be hard put to think of another.'

One of the problems, says Bruce, is that Gordon's acolytes are still chasing around after him, instead of running their departments.

Wednesday, 12 March

Alistair's first Budget. The mood was downbeat. Everyone complaining how dull it was, but maybe that's just what we need, instead of gimmicks and fatuous initiatives. The word 'stability' featured many times. To a large extent Alistair was boxed in by decisions already announced in Gordon's last Budget. Is it sensible to proceed with the tuppence cut in the basic rate, given that income tax is the fairest way to raise money and that the sums forgone are very large? This is ground that, once surrendered, can never be recovered, except perhaps by a Tory chancellor. And it means Alistair and his successors are forever condemned to search for stealthier, less acceptable ways of raising money.

Sunday, 16 March

Peter Camm and I cleared three weeks' worth of litter from the street. Two black bags full, plus a couple of smaller bags of recyclables. As we were delving into the undergrowth a posse of teenage mothers and their offspring came by, giggling. One inquired, 'Are you'se on community service?'

Monday, 17 March

Mounting fury in the ranks at the news we are about to be compelled to publish the last three years' worth of expenses claims, which will provide a huge new bout of sport for the tabloids. At the party meeting this evening Jane Kennedy described how, on a visit to a school in her constituency last week, she had been harangued by a woman complaining about the £10,000 we are all supposed to be allowed to spend on fitting out our kitchens. A fantasy born of this so-called John Lewis List maintained by the Finance Department, the existence of which none of us were aware of until the other day. 'We're going to have years of this,' said Jane. 'Can't anything be done?'

'We don't have a toenail to stand on,' replied Chief Whip Geoff Hoon. The Information Tribunal ruled against us comprehensively, even to the extent of allowing publication of our addresses. 'An atavistic atmosphere is developing,' remarked Harriet Harman. 'We've got to stand up and stop appeasing.' The trouble is no one knows how. In truth we have brought much of this on ourselves by voting for ever higher allowances. I pointed it out at the time, but no one wanted to know. There was bound to be a backlash sooner or later.

Tuesday, 18 March

A poll in today's *Guardian* gives the Tories their biggest lead in 25 years. It's the latest of several pointing in a similar direction. What's more, Boris Johnson seems to be on course to become Mayor of London. Have we reached the point of no return? It can't be far off.

A call from Ron Sandler, the banker in charge of Northern Rock, to say that he expects to lose about a third of the company's 6,000 jobs, but that the Sunderland office is likely to survive. Later, several of us were invited to a meeting with Alistair Darling, who said that Sandler had found Northern Rock to be in better shape than he expected, owing to a strong mortgage book.

This evening, to an upper committee room the hear Ed Balls talk about his 'Children's Plan'. We were handed a 'toolkit' containing several glossy brochures, a DVD and a jargon-crammed PowerPoint presentation. Much lofty talk of 'making Britain the best country in the world for children to grow up in' and endless references to consultations, parents' panels, expert groups, delivery agreements, outcomes frameworks etc. Quite what it all means is unclear and nothing said during the meeting made me any the wiser. I pointed out, not for the first time, that early-years care in Hendon – one of our previous initiatives – was on the point of collapse because the funding was drying up and Ed promised to pay us a visit, but I am not holding my breath. I do begin to wonder whether we haven't lost our way in this myriad of educational initiatives and whether the time has come to let someone else have a go.

Thursday, 27 March

A one-liner. The place deserted. No lights on the message board, messengers hanging around with nothing to do. A handful of Members in the chamber. In an otherwise empty library I came across John Reid, exuding pessimism about our prospects. 'Our position is irrecoverable,' he said, 'unless the Tories do something stupid.'

'Maybe,' I said, 'our historic mission is over and we are faced with a long period of Tory rule, until another party breaks through.'

'That's what we were becoming – a different party. One that recognised that much of the working class has become middle class. The danger is that, in Opposition, we will revert to being the party of the marginalised. You can't win power on that basis.' To my pleasant surprise he didn't blame it all on Gordon. 'Tony left behind a party that was unsustainable,' he said. 'Maybe you and I should devote the rest of our lives to trying to educate the party.'

'Either that or growing vegetables – and right now I'm on the vegetable side of the equation.'

Later, in the chamber, a brief debate about the Standards and Privileges Committee's recommendation, in the wake of the Derek Conway debacle, that we should register the employment of relatives. It went through *nem con*. I made a short speech saying that this was only a first step and that we have only ourselves to blame for the low esteem in which we find ourselves, a proposition which none of the handful of Members present disputed, but which no doubt some colleagues will find upsetting.

Monday, 31 March

A whiff of panic in the air. Gordon addressed the parliamentary party, unveiling a fatuous new slogan ('We must own the future') which he repeated about 20 times. He was assailed with complaints from all sides. Lindsay Hoyle said people might vote Green, but they weren't willing to pay for it, the implication being that we should dump all this Green nonsense and get back to good old pork barrel politics. Helen Jones said, 'We are politicians, not managers. Harold Wilson built the Humber Bridge to win a by-election. That's fine by me.' Several people complained about post office closures. Eric Martlew was applauded when he said it had been a mistake to do away with the 10 per cent tax band and Gordon was actually heckled when he tried to argue that no one was worse off.

Tuesday, 1 April

Second reading of the new counter-terrorism Bill, which, among other things, seeks to extend pre-trial detention from 28 to 42 days. Jacqui Smith spoke well, but she was under siege from all sides. She will be hard put to get it through, given that she faces the almost insurmountable problem that the Director of Public Prosecutions has said he doesn't want the powers she is determined to thrust upon him.

In the evening, dinner with a friend from my Foreign Office days. He says the spooks are frustrated at not being allowed to talk to Hamas, who did, after all, win the freest election in the Arab world for 20 years. He added that time is rapidly running out for a two-state solution in the Middle East.

Wednesday, 2 April

Eric Martlew recounts that Gordon invited him in to discuss his complaint about the abolition of the 10 per cent tax band. At the end he said, 'If you can think of a way out of it, let me know.'

To which Eric replied, 'If I do, you'd better make me Chancellor,' eliciting (he said) a half-smile.

Friday, 4 April

A call from my whip, Alan Campbell, to inquire whether I will be taking part in the smouldering rebellion over the abolition of the ten pence tax rate. I won't, as it happens, but this looks like doing us serious damage. As usual the trail leads back to Gordon. He announced it in last year's Budget in order to finance a two pence cut in the basic rate, which no one was seriously demanding. It was all about posing as a tax cutter in order to win a cheap round of applause. Another piece of short-term gimmickry that's come back to haunt us.

Saturday, 12 April–Sunday, 13 April
Bamburgh

With the girls to Northumberland for a couple of nights' B&B with Charles and Barbara. On day one we visited the Grace Darling Museum, strolled along the beach, despite an icy wind from the north, and walked the ramparts in Berwick. Most of Sunday was spent at Paxton.

Monday, 14 April

The girls went riding on the beach at Seahouses. We spent the hour before sunset on Ross beach, the best in Northumberland – the only people on five miles of golden sands with a castle at each end.

Tuesday, 15 April

Home to a great pile of drudgery. 'METHADONE CITY,' screams the front page of tonight's *Echo*. No wonder Sunderland has an image problem.

Wednesday, 16 April

Hardly a day passes without my contemplating retirement. The sad truth is there is no longer any serious role for me in Parliament. So far as the government is concerned I am entirely outside the loop and increasingly it looks as though it won't be long before the entire government is relegated to the Tea Room. If I am to make an announcement, it would need to be in the next couple of months. Before we start distributing leaflets in the new wards saying I'm the candidate.

Thursday, 17 April

Gordon is on a visit to Washington, which our media – the BBC is among the worst – have been trying from the outset to portray as a failure on the grounds that it has been overshadowed by the visit of the Pope. Actually, it seems to have been rather successful. He's addressed the United Nations, met all three presidential candidates, dined with the President and been generally well received. One naff moment. I caught a clip of an interview in which Gordon remarked how much he enjoyed watching American television. 'Thank you for your contribution to our culture,' he ended. Ugh. Why does he do it? To be loved, I guess.

Friday, 18 April

To the Stadium of Light for the annual dinner. Our best ever, 170 guests at £30 a time. David Miliband was star attraction. All day I was on tenterhooks, fearing that (as is the way with top people) he might cry off at the last moment. Already we had been told he would only be staying for the soup. Sure enough, as I was changing into my suit, the telephone rang. 'This is the Number 10 switchboard. I have the Foreign Secretary for you.'

'Where are you?,' I practically shouted at him.

He seemed taken aback. 'In sunny South Shields, where else?'

Anyway, it had the effect of making him turn up earlier. He had two Special Branch men in tow, one of them, Toby, who was part of the team that came with me to Somaliland three years ago. David worked the tables and made a fluent, thoughtful, if rather bland speech which was generally well received and departed in a convoy headed by a police motorcyclist. All told, a big success. There may be life in our old penny farthing machine after all.

Monday, 21 April

To a packed meeting of the parliamentary party to hear Gordon attempt to talk his way out of the growing furore over the abolition of the ten pence tax band. Until now he's been in denial, insisting there are few if any losers, but now there are signs that the penny has dropped, prompted by the prospect of a potentially ruinous uprising over Frank Field's amendment to the Finance Bill, which is down to be voted on next week. Much talk of 'listening' and 'understanding', vague promises of a review with a view to – eventually – compensating those who have lost out. Over and over he used the phrase, 'We get it.' But that's the point, does he?

From the floor a mix of pleas for ultra-loyalty and unrepentant scepticism. It's not as though this is the first time. We've been round this course several times before – the cut in benefit for single mothers, the 75 pence pension increase. Always the trail leads back to Gordon. Gerald Kaufman demanding loyalty, launching an intemperate attack on Frank Field ('I'm sick and tired of colleagues who have been in office rediscovering their social consciences as soon as their bottoms hit the backbenches'). That apart, however, the mood was comradely, if sombre. Frank called for 'a clear indication by Monday' of what the government was going to do to repair the damage. The difficulty is that there is no easy way out. Identifying and compensating the losers is technically complex and there is no money left in the kitty – it has been spent on tax cuts for the middle classes.

Earlier, Frank told me that when he first raised the issue privately, a year ago, Gordon had clenched his fists and screamed, 'There are *no* losers.' So we have travelled quite a long way.

Tuesday, 22 April

A visit from the new Eritrean ambassador. Like all Eritreans, he was charming but unbending on the question of the disputed border.

In the Library Corridor later, I came across John Healey, the local government minister, who was at the Treasury when the fateful decision on the ten pence tax rate was made. 'Why on earth did Gordon do it? Was he just after a cheap round of applause on Budget day?'

'No,' said John. 'Gordon wanted to portray himself as a tax cutter, with an eye to an autumn election. That's what it was about.'

Wednesday, 23 April

To the chamber to bear witness to the great U-turn. Chief Whip Geoff Hoon tipped me off about it last night. Sure enough, Gordon announced a plan to compensate those who were out of pocket due to the abolition of the 10 per cent tax band, starting with pensioners aged between 60 and 64 and young persons on the minimum wage. Sighs of relief all round on our side. Derision from just about everybody else. A triumph for Frank Field, who led the uprising – and for the collective power of us, the poor bloody infantry, when sufficiently provoked, and, by heaven, we have been sorely provoked these last few weeks.

Friday, 25 April

Much of the week has been spent responding to angry emails and letters from people who claim to have lost out as a result of the abolition of the 10 per cent tax band. Many conclude with a promise never to vote Labour again.

Sunday, 27 April

Awoke to the BBC review of the papers gleefully reporting the strike at the Grangemouth oil refinery and talking up the possibility of a new winter of discontent, cheerfully aided by spokesmen for the public service unions. Despite unprecedented prosperity, the pessimism is toxic.

Monday, 28 April

Came across Gordon striding down the Library Corridor on his way to address some Asian jamboree in one of the dining rooms. How isolated he looked. A protection officer with a wire coming out of his ear five paces behind. A female official scurrying to keep up. Someone else out in front. In the middle Gordon, alone.

The row over the abolition of the 10 per cent tax band resurfaced during the Committee Stage of the Finance Bill. The minister, Jane Kennedy, was suspiciously vague as to how we are going to compensate those who have lost out. It's beginning to dawn on all concerned that there is no easy way out of this mess. The losers are difficult to identify and it is impossible to devise a formula that will repay them all. This is going to rumble on for months and in due course there will be another round of letters and emails from people complaining that they've missed out. What a shambles.

Tuesday, 29 April

Nick Raynsford reckons that we face a Boris landslide on Thursday. He was out on the doorsteps on Sunday and says hostility to Ken Livingstone among the over-forties is intense. Only the young spoke up for him and most of them won't vote.

I was waylaid at the ten o'clock vote by Michael Meacher. 'We *must* talk.'

'About what?'

'The future.'

'I hope you're not planning another leadership bid?'

Naturally, he denied all, but it soon became clear that this was exactly the subject on Michael's agenda. He talked of assembling a group of 20 like-minded individuals and seemed surprised when I suggested it would be all over the *Guardian* the next day. Before long he was talking of going to see Gordon with a list of suggestions, as if that would make the blindest bit of difference. Good old Michael, I do so admire his energy and optimism, but I am not going to be part of any hare-brained conspiracy to overthrow our unloved leader. Not least because we are too far gone. It no longer matters who the captain is, we are fatally holed below the waterline.

Wednesday, 30 April

Rang Daphne Park to arrange lunch. We had a brief exchange re Africa. 'Why,' she asked, 'do we persist in feeling guilty all the time? We were a good colonial power, unlike the French or Portuguese.' She quoted a prominent Ghanaian she had once known who used to say that the British had given Africa two priceless gifts, the English language, enabling Africans to communicate across tribal boundaries, and the rule of law.

This afternoon to the chamber to hear Alan Simpson move an amendment to the Energy Bill giving the government a year to come up with a plan for feed-in tariffs. He spoke for more than half an hour without a note and with beautiful clarity, demonstrating real expertise and winning acclaim from all sides. One of the best speeches I have heard for a long time. A class act. Alas, he is not seeking re-election. We shall miss him when he goes. About 20 of us voted against the government, but it wasn't enough.

Friday, 2 May

Another local election drubbing. In Sunderland we lost five seats to the Tories, including Ryhope, a former pit village which hasn't returned a Tory in living memory. We now control nothing in the south of England outside of central London and for the first time there are tentative signs of a Tory revival in the north. Just before midnight, it was announced that Boris Johnson is to be the new

Mayor of London, which must send a shiver down some Tory spines. They are going to have to keep a tight rein on him, at least until the election.

Saturday, 3 May

A long talk with Ngoc, who thinks I should retire at the election, partly on the grounds that politics is now a despised profession and partly because I am not doing anything useful and am unlikely to in future. I am not bothered about the first, since I am content to be judged by those who know me, but the prospect of another six years hanging around the Tea Room waiting for the Division bell fills me with gloom. Two questions: can I afford to retire, and how am I to while away the years that remain? Ngoc reckons that, once the flat is rented, we won't be much worse off. As regards the beckoning void, there's always writing and perhaps a bit of lecturing, also that elusive walled garden. We more or less decided I should go. If so, I will have to move quickly. Probably as soon as Friday.

Sunday, 4 May

A big bout of self-flagellation underway. Much talk from Gordon and his senior henchpersons about listening and learning, feeling people's pain etc. One can overdo this humility lark, especially when it is so clearly phoney. The 10 per cent tax band folly apart, most of the things for which we are being blamed – fuel prices, food prices, the slump in the mortgage market – are due to factors way beyond the influence of mere national governments. The sad truth is that people have finally tired of us and no amount of pandering and breast-beating is likely to make any difference.

Tuesday, 6 May

To London, still agonising over whether to stay or go. What weighs most heavily is the inevitable accusation that I would be letting down the local party were I to depart, though, in truth, they will hold the seat whoever is the candidate. The local Tories, of course, are bound to allege that I am frit, whereas what I fear is not the prospect of defeat, but victory.

In the Tea Room, open talk of insurrection, mainly but not entirely from Usual Suspects. The difference is that they no longer trouble to lower their voices. If not Gordon, who? Graham Stringer favours Alan Johnson on the grounds that he is everything that Gordon isn't – personable, a southerner and possessed of a sense of humour. And if not Alan?

'Anyone.'

Wednesday, 7 May

To Hampstead for dinner with the Woollacotts. Among the guests, a young woman from the Cabinet Office who remarked that Gordon had run out of people capable of saying 'no' to him and that he had 'surrounded himself with control freaks and skivvies'.

Thursday, 8 May

I was joined at lunch in the cafeteria by a former member of the Blair court. 'Are people saying to you that Gordon should go?' he inquired. 'So many misjudgements,' he went on, and proceeded to list them – ranging in seriousness from the 10 per cent tax debacle to yesterday's reclassifying of cannabis, against official advice. Gordon's latest folly is his apparent intention to press ahead with the proposed extension of pre-trial detention from 28 to 42 days 'even though everyone is telling him he can't win'. My friend reckons that sooner or later there is bound to be an uprising, although I pointed out that history suggested otherwise. The dear, sentimental old Labour Party doesn't get rid of failing leaders. We go down with the ship, witness Foot in '83 or Kinnock in '92. We discussed alternatives. Ideally someone of southern origin or, as he put it, 'who can pronounce English place names correctly' – Miliband, Straw, Johnson, Denham, Hutton, but our preferred choice was Hilary Benn. Interesting to hear such insurrectionist talk from someone who is fundamentally a loyalist. 'I haven't had this conversation with anyone else,' he said.

Friday, 9 May
Sunderland

D-Day. Am I staying or going? If I am going, I have to tell the executive this evening. All week I have been counting down the hours, trying to put it out of mind. When I went out this morning I still hadn't decided. If anything, the odds were on staying. I toured Grangetown School, attended an anti-racism event at the Stadium of Light with scarcely a thought of what was to come. I stopped off briefly at home to return the car keys to Ngoc.

'Have you decided?' she asked.

'I don't think I can … I would be letting down too many people.'

'Have you ever, once, thought of your partner?'

'Of course, but …'

And with that the balance tipped. I went to the office, called my three staff together, swore them to secrecy for two hours and told them I would be going at the election. They took it remarkably well, considering they had no inkling of what was coming. Graham and I did the surgery and then I went over to the Civic Centre for the executive meeting. They were gob-smacked, stunned. They had thought they were coming to discuss our election campaign, only to find themselves faced with having to find another candidate and start again from scratch.

I went home feeling sick.

Saturday, 10 May

A hollow feeling. Like bereavement. Similar to how I felt after I made that fatal call to Hilary Armstrong in 2001, asking to be moved on or out – and discovering it was out. This time there really is no way back. Every bridge is blown. Unless I can find something useful to do, the days ahead will be empty, a long slow decline into senility and oblivion. Oddly, what nags at me most is that Sarah, who turned 18 six months ago, will now never have a chance to vote for her old dad.

When I told Emma she asked, 'What will you be then?'

'Nothing. I will be retired.'

'*Retired?*'

For as long as she can remember, indeed for her entire life, her dad has been the Member of Parliament for the place where we live, a big figure in her small world. Now he will be nothing and that's not cool.

A beautiful day. For the first time this year we had lunch in the garden.

Monday, 12 May

A late train to London. The mood at the meeting of the parliamentary party was ugly. A couple of thinly veiled calls for expulsions, one from an angry Scotsman who accused Kate Hoey of playing footsie with Boris Johnson, who wants to appoint her as some sort of sports adviser. Mike Gapes referred to Frank Field, who gave an unhelpful interview on this morning's *Today* programme, as 'a creeping Judas'. By and large they picked easy targets. No one mentioned Cherie and JP, whose unhelpful memoirs are all over the Sunday press. Harriet Harman spoke sensibly of 'the danger that in our disappointment people are looking for someone to blame and the media, as ever, are offering a sympathetic shoulder to cry on'.

Later, in the Division Lobby, I was assailed from all sides by people wanting to know why I was going. David Miliband playfully kicked me, remarking that it was only a couple of weeks since he attended my constituency dinner to help raise funds for my re-election. Steve Byers remarked that we couldn't afford to lose thoughtful people. Alan Milburn inquired how I was going to afford to get the children through university. To every inquiry I reply that I am past my sell-by date. Some people assume I am going to be a famous writer again, but I have no such expectations. The truth is there is no plan. Only the beckoning void.

In China there has been a huge earthquake. Thousands dead and missing, which puts our pathetic little problems into perspective.

Tuesday, 13 May

To the chamber to hear Alistair Darling explain how he is going to dig us out of the hole we are in over the abolition of the ten pence tax band. To everyone's pleasant surprise, he has opted for the simplest option, raising thresholds to the benefit of everyone except top-rate payers. The downside is that it will cost £2.7 billion, which will have to be borrowed. Also, it is too expensive to continue with indefinitely, so, come the pre-Budget statement in November, Alistair is going to have to come up with a new wheeze. The other notable feature of the statement was a handsome apology from Frank Field for his attack on Gordon on the *Today* programme.

Later, in the Library Corridor, I came across a loyalist colleague who was lamenting the 'awfulness' of Gordon. He added, 'The truth is that public spending has been out of control for the last three or four years because there are so many sacred cows ...'

This evening to the Prime Minister's room for an exchange with Number 10's deceptively youthful Head of Strategy, David Muir. His message: despite their lead in the polls the Tories were still vulnerable; if the focus groups are to be believed, Cameron is not in as strong a position as Blair in the mid-nineties; he is still thought of as a slick salesman rather than someone with whom most people empathise. Despite not liking us, most people still share our values. There is all to play for. Our problem is that 80 per cent of respondents think we are split and divided parties do not win elections; we had to stop talking about ourselves and start talking about the Tories. Easier said than done in the current Stygian gloom.

Wednesday, 14 May

With Chris Young, head teacher at Valley Road School, to see Ed Balls and children's minister, Bev Hughes. My purpose was so that they could hear at the first hand the impending collapse of early-years care in the poorest parts of Sunderland. To my pleasant surprise Ed listened attentively. His conclusion, however, was that the problem lies with the way the local authority is distributing the funds rather than any national shortfall. He promised to send a senior official to Sunderland to see what can be done.

Friday, 16 May

No great sorrow seems to have been triggered by the announcement of my retirement. No weeping and wailing or rending of garments. No one throwing themselves at my feet begging me to reconsider. A few emails, a letter or two (one from a dear old friend saying I have spared him the embarrassment of having to vote Labour again). A friendly leader in the *Echo*, a paragraph in the *Guardian* (describing me as 'the Editor of *Tribune*', a post I relinquished 24 years ago), but that's about all. Still a vague feeling of bereavement. Can't quite believe I've done it. As Bruce Grocott said, 'You are giving up more than a job, it's a way of life.'

A letter from party headquarters asking me to confirm reports of my retirement 'so that it can be reported to the National Executive Committee'. This I duly did. So that's it. My fate well and truly sealed.

Monday, 19 May

A minister – a middle-ranking female – joined me in the Tea Room full of gloom after a weekend campaigning in the Crewe by-election. Many people, she said, give Gordon as the reason for not supporting us. Did I think there was any chance that he might be persuaded to stand down? No, I said. We will go down with the ship. That is the Labour way. She said she had been on two outings with Gordon and been astounded to hear him ask the same three questions, same words, same order, of everyone he met.

Tuesday, 20 May

Chaired a meeting for Jacob Zuma, the likely next president of South Africa: his second visit to the UK in a month, affable, but cautious and long-winded. Ominously, he was whisked off to lunch by a Tory peer who bore a passing resemblance to Alan B'stard and who, according to the peers' register, has an unhealthily long list of business interests.

Wednesday, 21 May

A visit from the Dalai Lama. I chaired a meeting for him in Committee Room 14 and then escorted him to a press conference on the other side of the building. The journey between engagements was a triumphal procession. People lined the corridors and came running from all over, he stopped to shake hands with everyone, schoolchildren, tourists, policemen. He answered questions cheerfully, endearing himself to everyone with his simplicity and good humour. The hacks, needless to say, were principally interested in why Gordon (with characteristic ineptitude) has decided to receive him at Lambeth Palace, rather than Number 10, but HH refused to play and they soon lost interest.

Douglas Hogg, who is much nicer in private than in public, asked how I thought we were going to do in tomorrow's by-election at Crewe. 'Badly,' I replied. 'It's not fatal,' he said, 'but I don't think you'll win with Gordon.' His demeanour was kindly, not seeking to score points. I asked what he advised. 'Stick with him,' he said, 'because if you don't, the civil war will be bloody. It took us ten years to get over removing Margaret.'

Thursday, 22 May

Today's *Times* contains a beautiful colour picture of the Dalai Lama playfully resting his head on my shoulder during one of the lighter moments at yesterday's press conference. I am not sure what the joke was, but it may have been when one of the questioners introduced herself as being from Positive TV and when HH inquired what that was I pointed to the others and said, 'As opposed to negative TV.'

Friday, 23 May

Sure enough, we have been massacred at Crewe, the first time in nearly 30 years that the Tories have captured a seat from us at a by-election. It's bound to lead to another big bout of 'Gordon must go', but my hunch is that he will stay – to the bitter end.

Thursday, 29 May

A report on the front page of today's *Guardian* suggests that the Labour Party is £24 million in debt, that the Co-op Bank is demanding repayment of £2.6 million by the end of June and that National Executive members may be personally liable. The spectre of bankruptcy looms. Either that or utter dependence on the unions. All part of the Blair legacy. Ironic that New Labour has made us dependent on the unions to an extent unprecedented in living memory.

I took a day off. Ngoc and I drove to Barnard Castle, visited the gardens at Ecclestone Hall and finally to the High Force and back, via the wilderness, through Weardale.

Monday, 2 June

To a packed meeting of the parliamentary party to hear Jacqui Smith trying to talk us into backing an extension to 42 days of pre-trial detention. Much talk of 'tough decisions' and multiple 'safeguards', but the subtext is that, like all such issues, it is turning into a vote of confidence in Gordon and our loyalty is being appealed to. I hadn't intended to speak, but not wanting to be thought cowardly put my hand up at the last moment and said firmly that I would be voting against, referring to past mistakes. I spoke for about five minutes and was heard in respectful silence, but afterwards was buttonholed by Jack Straw and accused of being disingenuous, on the basis that the mistakes of the mid-seventies couldn't possibly happen today. I replied that we weren't only talking about the seventies – look at the Stockwell shooting.

Earlier Alan Campbell, one of the whips, tried to talk me round, saying I could be sure that the overwhelming majority of my constituents would want me to vote for 42 days. The last time I heard that argument deployed was when Hilary Armstrong tried to persuade me to vote for the Iraq enterprise – and look where that got us.

Tuesday, 3 June

A cup of tea with Ruth Winstone, who remarked that she thought that Labour's historic mission may be over and that it was downhill all the way from now on, à la Liberal Party in the twenties. The same thought had occurred to me of late, but it's the first time I have heard anyone else say it.

Wednesday, 4 June

This evening to the Crown Agents' annual bash at Marlborough House and then back to the House to be joined in an otherwise deserted Members' Dining Room by the Europe minister, Jim Murphy, who recounted how the Russians were relentlessly and ruthlessly buying up the world's energy supplies with a view to clawing their way back to superpowerdom.

Monday, 9 June

To London, where the government is making frantic efforts to dig itself out of the hole it has got into over its plans to extend pre-charge detention to 42 days. Nick Brown, who was on the train, says he believes they will lose.

Tuesday, 10 June

Desperate efforts re 42 days. Ministers have abandoned any attempt to argue the merits and are simply appealing to loyalty on the basis that we have to save Gordon, whose popularity – according to a poll in today's papers – has now sunk below that of Iain Duncan Smith at his nadir. Gordon himself has been ringing all and sundry. Even Diane Abbott received a call, which shows how desperate he must be. He spent this afternoon in his room seeing people at 15-minute intervals, some for the second or third time. Extraordinary tales of inducements. Offers of places on committees, ministerial visits, increased compensation for ex-miners with industrial diseases. There was even a pledge to take a lead on getting the US to lift sanctions against Cuba …

rumours of offers to the Ulster Unionists in return for their votes. Several people emerged saying how demeaning and embarrassing it was. And he takes it all so personally. 'You did it for Blair, why can't you fucking do it for me?' he shouted at one colleague. 'He was plead-ing,' someone said. 'Weird, worrying, is he ill?'

'Maybe,' someone suggested, 'he suffers from a mild form of Asperger's. That would explain the difficulty he has relating.'

I am just about the only dissident not to have received a call, having made my position crystal clear at the parliamentary party the other day, although Jack Straw bent my ear in the Tea Room, making no effort to dispute my assertion that we should never have embarked on this foolish, fatuous exercise. 'Some day I'll tell you about it,' he said.

Even John Reid, who no one could accuse of being a softy, is pri-vately seething. 'This will make it more difficult to fight terrorism,' he said. 'It discredits the government and the party.' He described as 'mad' the latest concession, compensation for those held beyond 28 days and then released.

Wednesday, 11 June

To the Cabinet Office to hand over a memory stick containing the ministerial parts of my diaries, which must be vetted before they can be published. As I was going in, I ran into another 42-day wobbler who was treated to an interview with Gordon yesterday.

'What brings you here?'

'Oh, I've just been to a security briefing with the spooks ... well, not actually the spooks ... they've given me something to think about.'

'Perhaps I can give you something to think about,' I ventured. 'How do you think the Great British Public are going to react when some tinpot jihadi, who turns out not to be a terrorist, is released on the 43rd day with an IOU in his pocket for £36,000 of taxpayers' money?'

'Mmmm,' he replied, 'that is a point.' But I suspect, from his demeanour, that he had already sold his soul.

I had thought that people would no longer confide in me now the news is out that I am keeping a diary, but on the contrary several have made clear they were talking *because* I keep a diary. All day long tales emerged of bizarre encounters in the Prime Minister's room. Some were called back two or three times. Andrew Mackinlay was called in twice even though he made clear from the outset that his mind was made up. Gordon, noting Andrew's interest in the accountability of the Security and Intelligence Committee, asked if he would like to go on it, even though, so far as anyone is aware, there are no vacancies. He then inquired about Andrew's interest in the War Graves Commission, the implication being that there might be a place on that if Andrew was interested. Andrew thought it was hilarious. 'A bring and buy sale,' he said.

Meanwhile rumours are swirling about what has been offered to the Democratic Unionists in return for their nine votes. Concessions worth up to £200 million are being spoken of.

In the event it was the Unionists who saved the day – the government won by just nine votes. Thirty-six of our side – myself included – voted against, more than expected, plus an unknown number of abstainers. Attention will now focus on exactly what price was paid for the support of the Unionists. The Tories were on the case within minutes.

Thursday, 12 June

A stroll around Kennington with Sally Banks, who is looking for a house. Then to the House to be greeted by the astonishing news that David Davis has resigned both as Shadow Home Secretary and from Parliament. Apparently he had a blazing row with Cameron over whether they should persist in their opposition to 42 days – the details are not yet clear. Suddenly the heat is off us and back on the Tories. Could this be the turning point?

Wednesday, 18 June

Emma is 13 today.

A victory: after months of badgering, Liam Byrne has granted indefinite leave to remain to a desperate Congolese who has been living on charity in Sunderland for the last couple of years. Official incompetence prevailed until the end. Liam says they were refusing to provide him with the file, claiming they didn't have the staff to track it down. In the end, he set a deadline, saying that, if they didn't produce it, he would grant the man's claim regardless and in the end that's what happened.

Thursday, 19 June

The media are full of economic gloom. An inflation rate of 3.3 per cent is being presented as a catastrophe. Tanker drivers, after a four-day strike, have reached a deal giving them an outrageous 14 per cent. As a result everyone is at it. Dave Prentis, the Unison general secretary, was on the bulletins last night threatening to tear up a three-year deal only just signed on behalf of health workers. A summer of discontent looms.

Friday, 20 June

Sunderland

To the Minster for the funeral of a young soldier killed in Afghanistan. The best part of a thousand people turned out, some watching on screens outside. A handsome young chap, only a year older than our Sarah. His poor mother was distraught, sobbing inconsolably over the coffin.

The Congolese who I helped rescue came in. I thought he'd be overjoyed, but he wasn't. It turns out that a grant of indefinite leave to remain, unlike asylum, will not allow him to bring in his wife and two small children, who have been marooned, in penury, in Kenya for four years. So I have to go back to Liam Byrne and start again.

Monday, 23 June

Alan Milburn was on the station at Newcastle. He has seen polling not yet in the public domain and says it's awful. Alan reckons there is a 40 per cent chance that Gordon won't make it to the election. What might persuade him to stand down? 'The cabinet would have to tell him.' Who? Most people capable of delivering bad news are outside the Cabinet. We discussed possible successors. Alan reckons the candidates would include Harman, Miliband, Straw. Not Alan Johnson ('a nice guy who recognises his own limitations. People assume he has hidden depths, but he doesn't'). Jack he ruled out on the grounds that he's *ancien régime*. Miliband, the strongest possibility, lacks the common touch. Who else? Alan himself perhaps? 'Probably not' (note the 'probably'). 'I'm too divisive.' All of which suggest that we will stick with Gordon. Incredibly, Alan still thinks we have a slim chance of holding on: 'It depends whether you think the public are comfortable with the Tories.'

Tuesday, 24 June

Lunch with Daphne Park, who regaled me with more tales of her extraordinary life, including the time she had smuggled a South African who was facing execution out of the Congo under the back seat of her Volkswagen. Once again I broached the possibility of taping her memoirs and, again, she brushed aside the idea. I should have dropped the subject, but as I was helping her back into her electric wheelchair I made a little joke about hiding a bug under the table next time we met. 'You've let the cat out of the bag,' she said curtly, and sped off without saying goodbye. I hope I haven't offended her.

Friday, 27 June

A friendly note from Daphne, thanking me for lunch and the books I sent her – *The Year of the Fire Monkey* and a recent edition of *A Very British Coup*, which I recklessly addressed to 'my favourite spook'. Anyway, she doesn't seem to have taken offence.

Monday, 30 June

To Newcastle in good time to catch the 09.31, as usual, to London. A slight delay and a last-minute change of platform was announced. I duly crossed to the other side. A train came in. I boarded – only to discover that it was bound for Edinburgh, first stop Berwick-upon-Tweed. It was 16.30 by the time I reached London.

In mitigation I must add that at least one other person made the same mistake.

Tuesday, 1 July

An email from Alastair Campbell: 'I still have a gut feeling that the country won't elect Cameron. But then I had a gut feeling that Labour could not possibly elect Harriet Harman as deputy ...'

Wednesday, 2 July

Lunch with My Friend in High Places, who speaks of tantrums, paranoia, hyperactivity and a constant demand for eye-catching gimmicks. Also, an extraordinary account of a recent visit to the Chinese embassy to sign the condolence book for victims of the earthquake. While Gordon and his party were inside word reached them that David Cameron had turned up and was waiting outside for his turn. Whereupon Gordon, fearing that his limelight was about to be stolen, went into a great sulk, strode out of the embassy, barely acknowledging Cameron, and climbed into his car. Once inside he began pummelling the headrest in front of him, causing his protection officer's head to ricochet, bleating about 'treachery' and 'conspiracy' and demanding to be told, 'Who did this to me?'

A hapless official tried to placate him, but Gordon would not be placated. Eventually the official inquired who was in this conspiracy. To which Gordon, without batting an eyelid, replied, 'The Tories, the Chinese and the Foreign Office.'

Thursday, 3 July

An unusually crowded House for a Thursday, but then of course we are discussing pay and rations. On pay, despite weeks of media lies, we were a model of restraint – rejecting the 'catch up' recommended by the Senior Salaries Review Body, and opting instead for a modest 2.25 per cent plus a promise, which no one quite believes, that we will never again have to vote on our own wages. On expenses, however, modest reforms proposed by the Members Estimates Committee were rejected in favour of a motion from Don Touhig more or less supporting the status quo. As always, I voted with the hairshirts, but in truth Don Touhig's motion wasn't all that wicked; the main reforms (transparency and receipts) are already underway and it is debatable whether we need to bring in outside auditors at enormous public expense.

'Gordon won't lead us into the election,' remarked Eric Martlew as we filed into the hairshirt lobby. 'Most people know we can't win with him. There's no malice. People are sad about it.'

'What makes you think the dear old Labour Party will ever muster the resolve to get rid of him, just because we face certain defeat?' I inquired.

'The difference is,' said Eric, 'that in those days we didn't have many seats to lose. This time we do.'

Who does Eric favour by way of replacement?

'Miliband or Johnson.'

Monday, 7 July

The Americans are reported to have bombed a wedding party in Afghanistan, killing a large number of women and children. They are still in denial, but no doubt it will be confirmed in due course. This will be the third wedding they have bombed – one in Iraq and two in Afghanistan.

Tuesday, 8 July

I initiated a little debate in Westminster Hall on the impact of the Rating (Empty Properties) Act, which came into force on 1 April and threatens to put a number of local companies out of business. Pallion Engineering, for example, faces an increase from £55,000 to a potentially ruinous £277,000. Another huge own goal, the fuse for which was lit during Gordon's time at the Treasury. I've been raising it with ministers privately for months and getting nowhere, so I decided to go public. The hapless junior minister put up to answer whispered in the margins that he agreed with my analysis, but the problem was the Treasury – who needless to say were nowhere to be seen. Apparently the Treasury have budgeted on receiving £950 million, which they can ill afford to lose, from taxing unused or underused offices and industrial sites and are in denial about the likely damage.

Wednesday, 9 July

At the suggestion of the local government minister, John Healey, I wrote to Alistair Darling, asking him to assess the impact of charging rates on empty business property and to announce the outcome in his pre-Budget report. Peter Candler (of Rivergreen Developments), who came in for dinner this evening, says it's mad and will kill off regeneration in the North-East. The regional development agency and the chambers of commerce say much the same. Apparently, the idea came from two very clever people – Sir Michael Lyons and Kate Barker – who were commissioned by the Treasury to work out a way of forcing surplus commercial property onto the market. With characteristic Treasury brilliance, it was dreamed up at a time when the economy was buoyant and launched in a downturn.

Thursday, 10 July

Mum would have been 88 today. I thought of her all day.

A chat with Dennis Skinner about Tuesday's meeting of the organisation subcommittee, which, after a long debate, decided to impose another all-women shortlist on Sunderland. He says it's all down to Harriet, who is determined to increase the quota of female MPs, at whatever cost. Dennis said he would have retired last time and only stayed because Harriet was determined to impose an all-women shortlist on Bolsover, which would have excluded the local front runner.

Friday, 11 July
Sunderland

The head teacher of a local, and much improved, secondary school called in to complain that his school has appeared on a list of schools allegedly threatened with closure if they don't reach 30 per cent A–C grades, including English and maths. This just seven months after receiving a letter from the schools minister, Jim Knight, congratulating the school on being 'amongst the top-performing' based on added value. The letter goes on: 'Please pass my thanks and congratulations to your pupils, staff and governors for all their hard work and success.' Should we laugh or cry?

Saturday, 12 July

Attended two fairs and a meeting of the 'Friends' of our various parks. I enjoy getting out and about. It's what I do best, but in truth it's all rather pointless since, in a year or so, I will be gone – just another prematurely retired pensioner.

Monday, 14 July

Another day, another initiative. The latest is Jacqui Smith's suggestion that youths found with knives may be made to visit stab victims in hospital. Yesterday she was all over the media with it. Today, however, she is retreating in the face of near universal ridicule. Shades of our late great leader, marching anti-social youths to cashpoints ...

Wednesday, 16 July

Came across a former Cabinet minister in the Library Corridor to whom I told the story of Gordon's visit to the Chinese embassy. 'He's got to go,' he said. He repeated this a couple of times and then went on quietly to relate that preparations for a coup are underway. 'The plan is for four or five ministers to go and see him and threaten to resign if he doesn't go. I'm talking to some of them. Jack Straw, Alistair Darling and Geoff Hoon were among the names mentioned. I'm against involving Alistair because I think he'll be loyal to the end, even though he's been badly treated.' Who, if not Alistair? James Purnell was another possibility, though it was unclear whether he has already been sounded out. 'I'm going to say that if they don't remove him the backbenchers will. I'm gathering names of people prepared to sign. About 80 so far.' He said he would come back to me. When? 'End of August, beginning of September.' For now, Gordon's fate hinges on the outcome of next week's by-election in Glasgow East, though even a narrow victory there may not be enough.

Monday, 21 July

With cousin Jo to a garden party for backbench members and spouses at Number 10. A relaxed-looking Gordon worked the crowd for nearly two hours, which was impressive considering that his day had started with an address to the Israeli parliament. He joked that the prime minister, Ehud Olmert, has a current poll rating of just 8 per cent, which makes his look positively rosy.

Wednesday, 23 July

Lunch with a friend from Foreign Office days. He ran into Jack Straw ten days ago who gave him the clear impression that an uprising is afoot. Jack's assessment of the current state of play was unequivocal: 'We're fucked.'

Friday, 25 July

Awoke to the news that we have lost the by-election in Glasgow East to the Scottish Nationalists on a swing of over 20 per cent. At 7.20 a call from the *Today* programme, who haven't been interested in anything I've said or done for two years. I have only to pronounce the words 'Gordon must go' to be all over the bulletins. Instead I let the answerphone take the call. Fifteen minutes later up popped Martin Salter, sounding very statesmanlike. 'We must keep our nerve' was his message. We loaded up the car and set off for Norfolk.

Saturday, 26 July

Burnham Market

The papers are full of speculation about the possibility of a September coup in the wake of yesterday's by-election result. Patrick Wintour in the *Guardian* is particularly well informed, reflecting the conversation I had last week, citing unnamed 'friends of Jack Straw'. A couple of flies in the ointment: (a) even in the unlikely event that Gordon were to be dispatched with minimal bloodshed, there is no evidence that we stand the remotest chance of winning under anyone else; the best that can be said is that we might save a few seats; (b) far from being postponed, defeat would be hastened by the fact that a new leader would find it impossible to resist demands for an early election.

Glorious sunshine. We spend the day on Scolt Head Island, a long spit of dunes, marsh and sand cut off from the mainland at high tide.

Monday, 28 July

After a weekend of feverish speculation Jack Straw has issued the following statement: 'I am absolutely convinced that Gordon Brown is the right man to be leading the Labour Party.' All day I kept my ears peeled for the sound of a cock crowing.

Wednesday, 30 July

Great excitement in the media about an article in today's *Guardian* by David Miliband which is alleged to be evidence that he is positioning himself in the event that an accident were to overtake Gordon. But then, of course, it is the silly season.

Thursday, 31 July

Burnham Market

Emma's friend Catherine lost her purse containing about £35. Close questioning revealed that it was last seen two days ago when we visited the shrine town at Walsingham. So, without much expectation of success, off we went back and retraced our steps down the main street, calling at half a dozen shops, to no avail. We were on the point of giving up when I casually asked a young man who was locking up his shop whether a purse had been handed in and sure enough one had. He unlocked, went back in, reached behind the till and there it was. Another 30 seconds and our paths would never have crossed. A minor miracle. Appropriate perhaps, considering the location.

Tonight's TV news shows David Miliband signing autographs and looking very prime ministerial. My first thought when his article appeared in yesterday's *Guardian* was that the fuss was all got up by the media, but on reflection there does seem to be something in it. His protestations of innocence were not quite as heartfelt as they might have been. Bob Marshall-Andrews and Geraldine Smith were also on the bulletins tonight, demanding that Miliband be sacked for disloyalty.

Wednesday, 6 August

Sunderland

My assistant, Michael Mordey, placed on my desk a file of about 30 letters and emails from party members asking that I think again about my decision to retire. Actually, it's not so many considering that he's been running a little campaign behind my back. Anyway there's no going back, though no day passes without my wondering if I should have stayed put.

Later, to Thompson Park in Southwick to bear witness to the opening of a new playground, where I was assailed by three local councillors asking that I reconsider.

Monday, 11 August

The Russians have invaded Georgia. The television news is full of pictures of Russian armour rolling through the Georgian countryside and demands for Western intervention from Georgia's smooth, English-speaking president. Just like old times. Or is it? It appears that the Georgians started this with an attack on South Ossetia, a disputed enclave, 90 per cent of whose citizens hold Russian passports, timed to coincide with the opening of the Olympics. Also, the Americans have been messing around, training and arming the Georgians right under Russian noses.

Thursday, 14 August

Montréal du Gers

Sarah's A level results, obtained from the internet: three As. She will be going to Oxford. I am so proud of her. If only her Granny and Grandpa had lived to see this day.

This evening, a four-mile guided *randonnée*. We started outside the *mairie*. About 40 people, all but a handful French. Fine views of the floodlit church up on the ramparts as we returned in darkness. We ended with a cup of lemonade and biscuits in the square. What a lovely spirit there is about these little French towns with their fairs and fêtes. I could happily live here.

Monday, 18 August

Sunderland

Home to an unexpected bonus. A Tory think tank, Policy Exchange, has published a report suggesting that governments should give up trying to regenerate cities like Sunderland and encourage people to move south. Needless to say, the author, an academic from the London School of Economics, has never set foot in Sunderland. This has provoked a huge outbreak of local patriotism and embarrassed wriggling from the Tories, local and national. A wake-up call for those foolish people who believe they will behave differently next time round. We must exploit this for all it is worth.

Tuesday, 19 August

Rain all day. Indeed it has been raining all month. An overwhelming sense of grey. For the second year running summer has been all but wiped out. A poll in today's *Guardian* says that replacing Gordon with Miliband would make no difference. People actively prefer Cameron.

Saturday, 23 August

With Emma and half a dozen party members, I spent a couple of hours pushing through local letter boxes a leaflet mendaciously entitled 'What the Tories think of Sunderland'. It consists almost entirely of press reports with headlines like 'Write off the North in favour of the South' and 'Cities in North doomed, says favourite Tory think-tank'. Low politics, I am afraid, but hey, why not? They've shafted us often enough.

Sunday, 24 August

Tonight's television news showed an American warship carrying 'relief supplies' docking at a port in Georgia. Two more are said to be on their way. A dangerous, stupid game. Before we know it the Russians will be back in Cuba.

Wednesday, 27 August

The Georgia crisis is hotting up. Awoke to the news that Dick Cheney is on his way to Georgia and David Miliband is in Ukraine, 'building a coalition against Russian aggression'. Here we go again. Why do we have to dance so enthusiastically to the tune from Washington? Today's *Guardian* reprints an article from the *Washington Post*, purportedly by Ukrainian President Yushchenko but probably drafted by the same PR agency that the Georgians have been using. It says, 'We need to be embraced by NATO.' Like hell they do.

In Afghanistan meanwhile the Americans have had another of their 'accidents', the biggest so far, killing about 90 civilians, including 60 children.

Sunday, 31 August–Friday, 5 September

With John Williams for our annual walk in the hills. Along the Cleveland Way from Sutton Bank to Robin Hood's Bay, 75 miles and a good deal of up and down. Mist on day one, but after that fine views across the Vale of York and north to Teesside and far beyond. On day two, at Bilsdale, a perfect rainbow, with a beginning, a middle and an end. Four days across purple moors and two down the North Yorkshire coast, through idyllic little settlements – Runswick Bay, Staithes, Whitby and finally to Robin Hood's Bay, a small masterpiece: a mix of fishermen's cottages and fine Georgian houses linked by a maze of passageways, clinging to the cliff side.

Unscathed save for a blister on my right big toe, the first since I acquired my Brasher boots eight years ago. Weather generally good until the final day, 14 miles along precipitous cliffs lashed by unremitting rain.

Saturday, 6 September

Upsidedown Cottage, Robin Hood's Bay

Torrential rain for much of the night. The television news depicting scenes of flood and pestilence with predictions of more to come and yet, miraculously, we awoke to find sunshine breaking through the grey gloom After breakfast John and I strolled up the cliff path, water streaking off the cliff tops, Ravenscar wreathed in cloud. Then we went our separate ways.

St Bede's Terrace, Sunderland

Home to find that last night's storm has ripped another huge branch from the ash tree by our garden gate, mercifully no one injured and no damage to the neighbours' cars. Also, a message from Fraser Kemp saying that he, too, is standing down, aged just 50. So that's all three of the Sunderland MPs going. Astounding. Later, we spoke by phone. Fraser seems to have no clear plan, but like me sees no point in hanging around the Tea Room for the next five years. Re the general situation, he sees no way out. On the contrary the pit is getting deeper with every day that passes: Charles Clarke has been sounding off again and there are endless, irresponsible demands from trade union leaders which, if conceded, would only serve to narrow our base still further. We appear to have developed a death wish.

Friday, 12 September

Fraser Kemp to lunch. Like me, he thinks the damage is irreversible and that we are faced with a lengthy period, if not an eternity, in opposition. This evening, news that Siobhan McDonagh, hitherto an ultra-loyalist, has been sacked from the whips' office for calling for a leadership election. Amazing. So far as I am aware, until now there is no recorded instance of her ever having stuck her head above the parapet on anything.

Saturday, 13 September

Joan Ryan, another ultra-loyalist, has joined the call for a leadership election. It's beginning to look like orchestrated subversion. So far only a handful are implicated, but could this be the beginning of the long-awaited uprising?

Tuesday, 16 September

The world financial system is on the brink of meltdown and we have little or nothing to say. Instead we are preoccupied with our own local difficulty. Tonight we lost our first minister, David Cairns, from the

Scottish Office. So obscure that it wasn't until he appeared on the television news that his face rang a bell. All the same, this continual drip, drip is very debilitating. Meanwhile, our television screens are showing erstwhile Masters of the Universe emerging ashen-faced from Lehman Brothers' gleaming tower in Canary Wharf, carrying their possessions in cardboard boxes. Tonight there is talk that the American insurance giant AIG is on the point of collapse. Other names are being mentioned, notably Halifax Bank of Scotland. Ironically, all this market turmoil is likely to shore up, rather than undermine, Gordon's position. After all, can we afford to entertain the nation with a protracted bout of navel gazing when the economy is collapsing around our ears?

Wednesday, 17 September

The American administration has effectively nationalised AIG. It occurs to me that if we want to demonstrate our relevance and put some clear blue water between us and the Tories, we should abandon our hitherto slavish pandering to the City and come up with a plan to bring the Masters of the Universe within the rule of law. There will never be a better opportunity. I devoted an hour to drafting a letter addressed to Gordon enumerating half a dozen areas where we needed to strike – bonus culture, unsecured mortgages and so on – but in the end balked at sending it since for me this is *terra incognita*.

Thursday, 18 September

Awoke to the astonishing news that Lloyds are being allowed to take over Halifax Bank of Scotland to prevent impending catastrophe. Only yesterday, the top man at HBOS was proclaiming that all was well, although now I come to think about it he did look a little ashen. The new bank will control a third of the market and competition laws are being waived to allow the deal to go through, which may well store up problems for the future, but what else can we do in the face of this tsunami? Meanwhile our beloved prime minister has at last found his voice and is now talking for the first time of 'cleaning up the financial system', although whether his enthusiasm will outlive the current crisis remains to be seen.

An email from Claes Bratt in California saying that ABC is reporting that 68 per cent of Americans believe in angels, 46 per cent think they have a personal angel and 20 per cent say they have met either an angel or a devil. He adds, 'Meanwhile we hear little these days about "the wisdom of the market". Or the brilliant idea of privatising social security.'

Saturday, 20 September

J. K. Rowling has donated a million pounds to the Labour Party in recognition of our child-care policies and in protest at Tory plans to skew the tax system against unmarried mothers. Hooray for J. K. Rowling. At a time when so many of New Labour's fair-weather friends have melted away, when the polls are showing us 20 per cent behind the Tories, she rides to our aid. A rare shaft of light in these days of unremitting gloom.

This afternoon Emma and I went to the Stadium of Light as guests of Niall Quinn, to see Sunderland beat Middlesbrough 2–0. 'You've brought us luck. You can come again,' he said to Emma.

This evening, supper in the garden, during the course of which I berated Emma for neglecting her reading, to which she replied, 'I am the intellectualest [*sic*] person in my class.'

Monday, 22 September

A fascinating piece by David Marquand in the current issue of the *New Statesman*, arguing that our current woes are not primarily due to the failings of our leader: 'They stem from a profound intellectual and moral malaise that has gripped the Labour party for at least half a decade.' He goes on: 'Labour lost its soul under Blair, not Brown. I hoped Brown would help the party to find it, and I am sad that he has not. I now realise that the task is beyond the capacity of any leader.'

The core issue is, according to Marquand, 'a fatal mismatch between public expectations and political rhetoric on the one hand,

and the realities of tightening resource constraints, destructive climate change and the mechanics of global capitalism on the other. We live in a society where everyone believes they have a divine right to ever-rising living standards; that we have finally reached the sunlit uplands of ever-increasing consumption, and that if the good times come to an end, our leaders must be to blame.'

He continues: 'The age of abundance will pass whatever we do ... The choice lies between a gradual controlled, but still painful transition to a new age of austerity, and an infinitely more painful and destructive transition at a somewhat later date. The first option is patently the right one yet it involves a transformation of the moral economy – a revolution of mentalities as radical as the reformation or the implosion of communism – of which there is as yet, no sign. The real charge against Brown is that he has failed to grasp this ugly truth.'

The party conference is underway in Manchester. I am now so utterly irrelevant that, for only the second or third time in 38 years, I cannot bring myself to go.

Tuesday, 23 September

At the conference in Manchester a big effort is underway to show (a) that, contrary to the evidence, Gordon is really a normal human being and (b) that he is capable of leading us, if not to the promised land, then at least out of the current mire. Today his big speech. As one of the commentators remarked, he's having to reapply for his job. Sarah was prevailed upon to come on stage and introduce him, à la Michele Obama. A lot of talk about fairness and stability. 'A new settlement for new times' was the latest vacuous slogan. By most accounts it went well. Talk of an uprising has receded ... for now.

I drove up to Cragside for lunch with Joyce Quin and then we walked seven miles in the Simonside Hills.

Thursday, 25 September
London

To the Cabinet Office to discuss the diaries. I was taken to Ed Miliband's grand apartment on the third floor, where a very pleasant woman, whose job it is to vet memoirs, left me in no doubt that she disapproved of the entire enterprise. She also thought it churlish and ungrateful that I should have been so unenthusiastic about my first visit to government. Surprisingly, however, she asked for very few deletions.

Meanwhile, the hacks are attempting to organise a new crisis around the suggestion that Ruth Kelly is leaving the government in protest against Gordon's leadership. Pure fantasy, as they very well know, but they're all at it. 'Kelly's exit reignites Labour's civil war' (*Guardian*), 'Reshuffle in chaos as Kelly resigns' (*Daily Telegraph*) ... and so on. Her very plausible explanation that she wants more time with her four children aged eleven and under has simply been ignored.

Monday, 29 September
Sunderland

My assistant, Michael, just back from the party conference in Manchester, reports that Gordon (who doesn't know him from Adam) shook his hand half a dozen times, on each occasion chanting the same mantra, 'Thank you for all you do.' He seems to say that to everyone he meets. Bizarre.

To London on an evening train.

Tuesday, 30 September

To breakfast at Simpson's-in-the-Strand to hear a very fluent Chinese (with close ties to the regime) justify what he claimed was China's benign Africa policy. China, he said, believed in non-interference and unlike the West did not lecture Africans on how they should run their countries. But as the businessman who proposed the vote of thanks remarked, 'with power comes responsibility'.

A lunch for Ray Fitzwalter at the Café des Amis to celebrate his book on the rise and fall of Granada. A dozen guests, mainly refugees from the golden age of television. Everyone in despair about the lamentable state of commercial television. The fear is that, without serious competition, the BBC will deteriorate, too. Much discussion of whether the government should use part of the licence fee to bale out Channel Four. Apparently there is some large pot of gold left over as a result of the impending switch to digital TV which could be dipped into. Andy Burnham has to make a decision in the next few months. As it happens, I ran into Andy this evening at Liz Forgan's farewell do (as chair of Heritage Lottery) in the National Gallery and he did not seem keen. Quite right, too. With only the merest exceptions – the 7 p.m. news and the occasional drama or documentary – Channel Four, too, has succumbed to the tidal wave of junk sweeping the airwaves. Why should the taxpayer save it?

Wednesday, 1 October
To the School of Oriental and African Studies for a talk by Richard Dowden, who has published a book on Africa. Two points of note. First, that most Africans remain cheerful despite the ruinous state of their continent. 'There is more hopelessness in Highbury – where I live – than there is in the whole of Africa,' he remarked. Second, Richard quoted former American Assistant Secretary of State Hank Cohen as saying of US policy in Africa, 'We want to see human rights, democracy and free markets. But if you get the last one right, we give you a discount on the other two.'

Friday, 3 October
Gordon's long-awaited reshuffle. Des Browne at Defence is out, replaced by John Hutton. Margaret Beckett is back – as housing minister (a bit of a comedown for a former Foreign Secretary). Nick Brown returns as Chief Whip and Geoff Hoon replaces Ruth Kelly at Transport. The big story, though, is that Peter Mandelson is back – for the third time. It caught everyone (not least Peter himself) by surprise.

I chaired a drugs conference in the Moses Room at the Lords, gave a talk to a large party of A level students and then went for a pizza with Claes, en route from California to Sweden for his annual visit to his aged parents. After a couple of glasses we got around, as always, to lamenting the state of the planet, a subject given a new urgency by the current crisis of capitalism. Claes believes – as I do – that soon nature will exact a terrible range on the human race for the havoc we are wreaking. Question: will it happen on our watch? Or our children's?

Saturday, 4 October

To the Dean's Hall at Berkhamsted School to speak at the Graham Greene festival. About 100 people in attendance, mostly of a certain age, including several of the great man's relatives. I stayed for dinner and sat at the same table as his daughter, Caroline, who assured me that, despite allegations to the contrary, Greene's politics were broadly left of centre and he remained, throughout his life, on the side of the underdog.

Sunday, 5 October

The media are beside themselves at The Return of Mandelson. He has dominated the headlines for three days so far. Apparently he recently ran into George Osborne while they were both on holiday in Corfu (Peter, inevitably, as a guest of the Rothschilds) and was 'dripping pure poison' about Gordon. Now he is going around saying that he and Gordon are 'joined at the hip'. His appointment is either a masterstroke or an act of desperation. Perhaps both. No one doubts Peter's exceptional talents, but the question is will they be deployed on Gordon's behalf or used to undermine him? The problem with Peter is twofold: (1) he has a tendency to go gaga in the presence of rich men and (2) he can't resist briefing against colleagues. Has he learned from catastrophes past? We shall see.

Monday, 6 October

At long last Parliament resumes. After ten weeks' absence we are all but irrelevant. The markets are in free fall. Alistair Darling, unruffled as ever, made a statement on the banking crisis. The Tories looked subdued. I guess it's gradually dawning on them that this could end badly for them – after all (as Frank Dobson remarked), they are the political wing of the City. Later Gordon addressed a crowded meeting of the parliamentary party, sounding calm and confident. The crisis has given him a new lease of life. He has a story to tell. There is a job to be done. People are listening again. His poll ratings, though still dire, have stabilised. Most people seem to think he is better qualified to cope with the crisis than the sleek David Cameron or the perpetually smirking George Osborne. He was well received. George Howarth, one of the summer plotters, declared that 'hostilities are over'. Ian Davidson congratulated him on forming 'a government of national unity' – a reference to the return of Mandelson and other senior Blairites.

Tuesday, 7 October

Keith Hill, who joined me at lunch in the cafeteria, pointed out that most of those signatories who attempted to bring down The Man now have jobs in the government. Doesn't that say it all?

As I was leaving this evening Chief Whip Nick Brown whispered that Alistair would be making another statement tomorrow on the long-awaited rescue package. 'Not just big, huge.'

I walked with Alan Milburn as far as Vauxhall. We discussed the remarkable upturn in Gordon's fortunes. Alan said, 'For the first time in his premiership, Gordon has been lucky.'

Wednesday, 8 October

PMQs. Serried ranks of grim-faced Tories. David Cameron doing his best to sound statesmanlike, but it cuts no ice. Cries of 'pathetic' from our side evoke no return fire. Nothing. Not a peep. The party of free markets and non-intervention is suddenly lost for words. They can do nothing but limp sadly along in our wake, signing up to measures that a week or two ago they would never in their wildest dreams have contemplated.

'No one wants our banks to fail ...' says Cameron.

From our side shouts of 'Where's your plan?'

Gordon, by contrast, is in his element. This is stuff he knows all about. Effortlessly he swats the fleabites from the other side, dominating the chamber, just like old times.

A lone Tory backbencher bravely attempts a sling shot, picking up on one of Gordon's phrases. 'Will the Prime Minister tell us when this age of financial irresponsibility began?'

'In 1979,' shouts one of our backbenchers to huge cheers. Even a few Tories can't resist wan smiles.

'This may be a turning point,' whispers my neighbour, Tony Wright.

Then it's Alistair's turn. Calmly he announces his plan for stabilising the banking system. The sums are mind-boggling: £200 billion for the Bank of England's Special Liquidity Scheme; a £25 billion taxpayer contribution to a Bank Recapitalisation Fund, but only in return for a preferential stakeholding; a £250 billion guarantee to encourage new lending.

And that's not all. 'In return for our support, we will be looking at executive pay, dividend payments and lending practices ...'

The Tories look sick. George Osborne's face has been wiped clean of that perpetual smirk that has been with him since his public school. When his turn came he entertained us all by demanding 'absolute assurances that no bonuses will be paid' to the bankers who have got us into this mess. From our side hoots of laughter. As everyone knows, the Tory party is *par excellence* the party of the bankers, hedge-funders and derivative traders. City slickers have paid for champagne receptions, chartered aircraft and even helped fund the office of the Shadow Chancellor himself. Why, one of them is even party treasurer. Yet here they are waxing indignant about the very hands that feed them.

'Who knows where we shall be in a year's time?' says Tony Wright. 'But for the moment let us enjoy.'

Later, in the Tea Room, a brief exchange with Alistair, in good shape despite only three hours' sleep last night. 'Congratulations on delivering the 1983 manifesto,' I said.

'Yes,' he said cheerfully, 'and with Tory support.'

Sotto voce he added, 'It is by no means clear that the banks will start lending again. We're not out of the woods yet.'

Thursday, 9 October

To Westminster in bright sunshine, a circling police helicopter the only blemish on a clear blue sky, sun illuminating the turrets and towers, glinting on gold leaf. Much of the media are choosing to imply that yesterday's rescue package – worth £400 billion or £500 billion, depending on which newspaper – is a gift from the taxpayer to the bankers, whereas it consists mostly of guarantees or repayable loans and investment in equity which may eventually earn the taxpayer a profit. Even the BBC was at it last night, with foolish vox pops from ill-informed punters demanding to know why such sums couldn't be found for the NHS. Overall, however, the coverage is friendly and does seem to have stabilised the markets – at least for now.

Dennis Skinner joined me on the terrace at lunchtime. He thinks that, come the election, we are still in with a chance.

Friday, 10 October

Sunderland

To a community centre in Grindon, where the councillors are supposed to have arranged a coffee morning for people wishing to meet their MP. Unfortunately, they have failed to publicise the event (save for a leaflet in the window), so it's just me and them around a big table discussing the wickedness of the world. A lot of talk from one about 'making punishment fit the crime'. In vain, I pointed out that most types of crime – notably burglary and car theft – have gone down dramatically in the last ten years, without the aid of the birch. Eventually a couple of passing ladies with problems that need solving are persuaded to call in and tell me about them.

Then to the Lazarus Centre, run by former local hard man George Craig, which treats people addicted to drugs and alcohol. A GP attached to the centre says the local waiting list for drug treatment is almost non-existent nowadays, whereas a few years back an addict seeking treatment could wait months. He ascribes the improvement entirely to the undoubted efficiency and dedication of the practitioners and only at my prompting recalls the huge increase in government funding which must have something to do with it. Another little benefit from a Labour government which no one will notice until the Tories are re-elected and start slashing budgets.

Saturday, 11 October

Markets around the world continue to slide, losing up to 10 per cent in a single day. The FTSE has fallen by a fifth in the last week – the biggest fall in its history. Iceland, whose banks are sheltering at least a £1 billion of British local authority money, is bankrupt. The media are full of pictures of hysterical traders, charts and graphs pointing remorselessly downwards. Meanwhile the G7 finance ministers are meeting in Washington in a desperate attempt to stave off the collapse of the entire financial system. Who knows where it will end?

The only good news is that Barack Obama is pulling ahead in the opinion polls, but the mood in middle America is ugly. Tonight's television news showed John McCain being hissed by his own supporters for resisting the suggestion that Obama is 'an Arab' and a terrorist. Which gives rise to the thought: if Obama wins, how long before 'a lone nut' tries to kill him?

Monday, 13 October

What extraordinary times we live in. Today, cheered on by the Tory party and the City, we nationalised *three* high street banks. The headline in tonight's *Standard* reads: 'SHARES RISE IN BANKS BUYOUT' over a story which begins: 'A wave of relief surged through the City this afternoon after three high street banks were effectively nationalised.' Wonderful. Dear old Harry Perkins would be green with envy.*

This afternoon, another statement from Alistair, looking for all

---

*Fictional Prime Minister in my first novel, *A Very British Coup*.

the world as if he had spent the weekend relaxing in his garden whereas in fact he is just back from a meeting of finance ministers in Washington and spent much of last night finalising his takeover of the banks. Gordon, by contrast, looks crumpled and exhausted, yet he too is a new man. 'Looking very much in charge,' as one commentator remarked when he visited Canary Wharf this morning to tell the bankers what's what. There was even applause from onlookers.

All the same, mustn't get too excited. There is a long dark winter coming. For the first time in a decade, a boarded, unsaleable house has appeared in St Bede's Terrace.

After Alistair's statement I nipped down to the High Court for a party to mark the retirement of Graham Zellick as head of the Criminal Cases Review Commission. Igor Judge, now Lord Chief Justice, presided, exuding charm and goodwill. (It was not always so. 'Do you know this man, Mullin? Is he a communist?' he once inquired of Charlie Falconer.) Professor Zellick remarked that during his five years in office he had served three Home Secretaries and six ministers, 'some of whom had gone before we even met them'. Back at the House, a new mood re the Tories. Time to go on the offensive. Tony Lloyd convened a meeting with a couple of Number 10 spinners. Their message: Cameron is vulnerable. The word from the focus groups is that, while people like his energy and dynamism, there is a sense that he's not quite from the same planet as most of us. 'Those pictures of him biking to work followed by a limo have stuck.' Likewise, the suggestion – in Gordon's conference speech – that 'this is no time for a novice'. Also, 'it is a myth that he has decontaminated his party'. Whatever they think of Cameron most people don't trust the Tories. Our task is to 're-couple' Cameron with his party. 'Is Gordon still bombarding everyone with emails and pre-dawn phone calls?' I inquired. 'It's got better,' said one. 'The emails mostly arrive by 9 a.m., then you know what you have to do all day. Also, you learn to distinguish between those that matter and those that don't.'

This evening, a shameless, brazen performance from Jacqui Smith (following an almost three to one defeat in the Lords) announcing that the government was abandoning attempts to persuade us to allow 42 days' pre-trial detention. A belated outbreak of common sense, delivered with maximum ill-grace, implying that those of us who had resisted were somehow soft on terrorism. She also, risibly, asserted that she had the support of the entire anti-terrorist establishment. I was so angry that, uncharacteristically, I kept my mouth shut for fear of saying something I might later regret.

Tuesday, 14 October

To the Treasury, to see Angela Eagle about the impact of the decision to impose full Business Rates on empty property. From all over come stories of developers adopting a policy of scorched earth to avoid having to pay on buildings that, in the current economic climate, are unlettable. Pallion Engineering, based in the old shipyard and kept alive these last 12 years by heroic efforts, is faced with a fivefold rate increase; the head of the local regeneration agency is predicting a bill for £840,000 on buildings acquired in preparation for the third phase of our city centre re-development, and all speculative building – an essential feature of regeneration – has come to a halt. Pure insanity. Angela seems to have got the message, but her officials, whose view is relentlessly London-centric, still appear to be in denial. The question is, can she persuade Alistair, who is understandably distracted by other matters, to be merciful?

Wednesday, 15 October

Caroline Dawnay, from United Agents, rang to say that Pat Kavanagh, who has loyally stuck with me through many fallow years, has an inoperable brain tumour. Pat of all people. So sharp, bright and always in such good shape. Only this year she and Julian walked across Sicily.

This evening, in an upper committee room, Jack Straw outlined his long-awaited Bill, intended to tighten the regulation of postal voting rules, shake up the much complained about Electoral Commission and, hopefully, put an end to the so-called Ashcroft loophole. Jack's Bill also has implications for trade union donations to the Labour Party – which could be fatal. This provoked a full-frontal assault from Don Touhig, an amiable but traditionalist Welshman, who demanded that the Bill be abandoned, that the Electoral Commission be done away with and that we 'stop dancing to the tune of the *Daily Mail*'. Jack responded robustly, pointing out that the Electoral Commission, for all its faults, was our baby. 'We are the party of regulation. When the Tories were in power we made a big issue about transparency and disclosure of donations, none of which could be implemented without a Commission. We simply can't abolish it.' He added archly, 'My only interest is in making sure the Labour Party is protected.' On postal voting he said, 'The blunt truth is that there has been industrial-scale fraud among the Asian community and it needs sorting.'

Thursday, 16 October

Ed Miliband, on his first outing as Secretary of State for Climate Change, delivered a statement conceding just about all the demands of the environmental lobby – higher emissions targets, feed-in tariffs and the inclusion of emissions from aviation and shipping – for strengthening his Climate Change Bill. Congratulations flowed in from all around, though naturally the Tories and the Lib Dems claimed to have thought of it all first. Can it be that, after all, we are serious about tackling climate change? Afterwards, I tackled Mike O'Brien, who is just commencing his second stint as energy minister, and says there are some huge renewable energy programmes in the pipeline – windmills on Dogger Bank, the Severn Barrage and so on. At the moment they are stalled because some of the big investors are pulling out as a result of the current banking crisis, but the good news is that the more enlightened Gulf states are starting to take an interest.

Friday, 17 October
Sunderland

A visit from two constituents recently made redundant from a local call centre servicing a national chain of furniture stores. About 130 jobs have gone altogether. Actually, the whole thing is a scam. The company have called in receivers and are setting up an arm's-length operation in Cardiff under some of the same management, employing people on a casual basis to avoid having to pay pension contributions, holiday or sickness pay or any of the other benefits that we used quaintly to associate with civilisation. My constituents complained that they had been gulled into staying on until the end in return for a promise of a decent pay-off – one had even turned down another job – only to find that all the lines had suddenly gone dead and none of their former management were responding to calls. Needless to say, virtually no one was a trade union member. We're in for a lot more of this as we march resolutely backwards to the nineteenth century.

Monday, 20 October

In the Tea Room this evening Des Browne told me the following tale about a constituent, a signalman on the railways, who early each morning took a short cut to his signal box across the estate of the local laird. One day he was intercepted by the said laird on horseback.

'What are you doing on my land?'

'I'm on my way to work,' replied the signalman, adding insolently, 'a concept that may be unknown to you.'

'You're on my land.'

'How did you come by it?'

'My ancestors fought for it.'

'Well,' replied the Bolshie signalman, 'if you come down off that horse, I'll fight you for it.'

At this the laird, recognising that he had met his match, rode away.

Pat Kavanagh died this morning.

Tuesday, 21 October

George Osborne is in trouble for allegedly soliciting a donation for the Tories from a Russian oligarch who he met in August while staying at the Rothschild villa on Corfu. The source of his embarrassment is an extraordinary letter in yesterday's *Times* from Nat Rothschild, but the feeling is that Osborne's real offence is to have caddishly leaked to the *Sunday Times* an account of the conversation he had with Peter Mandelson while they were staying with the Rothschilds in Corfu. *L'affaire* Osborne dominates today's media. Such is the effect Peter has on British politics.

During tonight's Division, a former Treasury minister whispered to me that, about a year after we were elected, he took part in a two and a half hour meeting at which officials briefed Gordon that our apparent prosperity was built on unsustainable levels of debt and that, sooner or later, the bubble would burst unless reined in. Gordon rejected the advice and the rest is history. In fairness, let it be said that Gordon no doubt took the view that this was an attempt by officials to nobble Labour's spending plans before we had our feet under the table.

Wednesday, 22 October

Much merriment at George Osborne's discomfort, not least because it has provided the media with an excuse to reprint pictures of those arrogant, spoiled, upper-class louts in the Bullingdon Club, featuring both the youthful David Cameron as well as George Osborne and Nat Rothschild. At today's PMQs Osborne was sitting sheepishly beside Cameron as our side taunted him with cries of 'Roubles'.

Keith Hill encountered him in a lift yesterday. 'Hi, George. How's your day been?'

To which, quick as a flash, Osborne replied, 'Wait until he starts on you.'

Thursday, 23 October

The broadsheets are full of tributes to Pat Kavanagh. Everyone talks of her modesty, integrity, elegance and the awe she inspired in authors and publishers alike (so it wasn't just me). Someone wrote: 'Pat died as she had lived: with no fuss and most efficiently.'

Friday, 24 October

To police HQ at Gillbridge Avenue for one of my occasional meetings with the divisional commander, Dave Pryer. Apropos our growing compensation culture, he related the following tale: he was on a bus in County Durham which came to a sudden halt, throwing the passengers forward. Nothing serious. Everyone initially declared themselves unhurt. Until up got a smart alec who asserted that anyone with an injury could claim up to £5,000. Whereupon some of his fellow passengers started murmuring that perhaps they had been injured after all. At which point up got Dave and drew everyone's attention to the security camera. 'I don't know whether or not it records sound as well as pictures, but you could be in serious trouble if you tell lies.' Suddenly, all talk of compensation died away.

Saturday, 25 October

Sarah, who, as is the fashion among today's youth, is generally contemptuous of her old dad, was telephoned by a boy she met on a recent visit to Edinburgh. 'I've just seen a great film,' he said. The title? *'A Very British Coup.'* 'Oh,' said Sarah, 'my dad wrote that.' Whereupon, never previously having shown more than a passing interest in my life's work, she took the DVD down from the shelf, went upstairs and watched it. One up for Dad.

Sunday, 26 October

To St Aidan's Church to hear a talk by a Christian woman from Bethlehem in which she described how the city had been virtually cut off from the outside world by the accursed Israeli wall. She illustrated her talk with slides. It is only when you see the pictures that the enormity of what the Israelis have done strikes home. She showed the settlements, all built on stolen land, advancing remorselessly, connected by roads on which only Israelis are permitted to travel. I came away boiling with impotent rage. Even if, by some miracle, Obama is elected next week nothing is likely to change, such is the strength of the Israel lobby in Washington.

Monday, 27 October

Sterling is plummeting as the colossal extent of our economic cataclysm unfolds. So much for the idea that we are better placed than other comparable economies to weather the tsunami. Ngoc reports that the cost of an airline ticket to Vietnam is up 20 per cent and rising, thereby jeopardising our planned expedition next summer.

Thursday, 30 October

Michael Chertoff, the US Secretary for Homeland Security, addressed a meeting of the Henry Jackson Society in Committee Room 14. The Friends of Israel were out in force, to judge by the applause that greeted his response to my question about the Israeli wall. He compared the fight against Islamist terror to fascism in the thirties and the Cold War. 'We face a similar ideological struggle, not with Islam – a great religion – but with people who infuse Islam with fascist ideas.' The struggle would be long and arduous. 'It is important not to become complacent or resigned as we did in the struggle against communism in the seventies.' There was talk of good and evil, freedom and democracy, and a passing reference to 'the difficulty of Vietnam', but his message was that we had to stand up to Islamist terror as Reagan and Thatcher had stood up to communism. Despite occasional simplicities, it wasn't an unintelligent presentation. But in parts he reminded me of Alden Pyle in *The Quiet American*.

Sunday, 2 November

Sarah is 19 today. I drew a card depicting her in her current incarnation as a Sainsbury's checkout person with a conveyor belt of shopping stretching along the front of the card and round the back. With Emma we went to lunch at the cathedral café in Durham and afterwards walked along the river toward Houghall Woods.

Monday, 3 November

John Hutton, our new Defence Secretary, looking more than usually gaunt, addressed the parliamentary party. The situation in Iraq, he said, had changed fundamentally (he used the word about ten times). The Sunnis were now onside. The troop surge had worked and the Iraqi army was gradually becoming a credible force. So much so that he had recently been able to walk around the centre of Basra, escorted only by Iraqis. Afghanistan, on the other hand, was another story. No end in sight, but withdrawal too awful to contemplate. Re defence spending he spoke of imminent 'difficult decisions'.

Wednesday, 5 November

Awoke to the news that Barack Obama has been comfortably elected President of the United States. Everywhere rejoicing crowds, people cheering, weeping, embracing. In Chicago, his home town, a quarter of a million gathered to hear him claim victory. A seminal moment. Hope has triumphed over fear. America has rejoined the world.

Thursday, 6 November

Lunch with Tom Watson in the Cabinet Office. A rotund, delightfully self-effacing fellow, he enjoyed a brief moment of fame when he was credited with triggering the attempted coup in September 2006. The truth, he insists, was a little more prosaic. Despite being a junior defence minister, he agreed to sign a letter drafted by Chris Bryant, calling on The Man to go, and then, with touching naivety, set off for an official visit to the Earl Haig poppy factory in Scotland. Having time on their hands, Tom and his wife decided to make a weekend of it and booked themselves into a smart hotel. While they were about it, they decided to call in on Gordon and Sarah to hand over a present for their newborn son. Meanwhile, back in London, word leaked out about the Bryant letter, bearing the signatures of Tom and 14 colleagues (half of them office holders of one sort or another). All hell duly breaks loose. At which point Tom receives a call from a *Daily Mail* journalist asking if, by any chance, during his sojourn in Scotland,

Tom had called on Gordon. 'As it happens,' says Tom, 'I did.' Bingo. A conspiracy is born and Tom is deemed to be up to his ears in it. That's his story, at any rate, and I am inclined to believe him.

Not that it's done him any harm. Along with most other participants in the '06 uprising he has been wafted into Gordon's government. A fact which, of course, only compounds the conspiracy theory.

I asked what caused him to lose faith in The Man. He mentioned several things. The bill for Cherie's hairdresser,* an article in *The Times* in which The Man talked of going on indefinitely (which seems to have been the trigger for the Bryant letter), but the straw that broke the camel's back was unbelievably trivial. 'I was sitting in a meeting in the MOD, idly chipping away at the gold star on my security pass. "Don't do that, Minister," remarked one of the army top brass. "That star is what will get you admitted to the bunker in the event of a nuclear war."'

'Where is the bunker?'

'Seven floors down from where we are now sitting. We can arrange a tour, if you'd like.'

'Have the Blairs been round?'

'Yes, they took a look at the prime minister's quarters.'

'And were they satisfied?'

'No, as it happens. Mrs Blair didn't like the décor. We had to redo it.'

And that, according to Tom, is what tipped him over the edge.

Tom, incidentally, believes there will be no election until the autumn of next year at the earliest – and probably not until 2010.

Friday, 7 November
Sunderland

Awoke to the news that, contrary to expectations, we won the by-election at Glenrothes. The majority was a comfortable 6,000, which brings the Nationalist bandwagon to a sudden halt.

To St Aidan's School to address the sixth form and then

---

*During the 2005 election campaign Cherie Blair was attended upon by a hairdresser for whose services she billed the Labour Party £7,500.

to Pennywell Youth Project, the success of which is celebrated by ministerial visits and on government websites. And yet, despite heroic efforts by all concerned, the centre is in danger of folding. Why? Because no one is willing to provide core funding. There is no shortage of money available for new capital projects – indeed, the National Youth Agency has £1.9 billion to spend – but little or nothing for paying the bills once they are up and running. I hear this complaint everywhere I go. Unless a solution can be found, Sunderland in years to come will be dotted with derelict youth and community facilities, every one a monument to folly.

Saturday, 8 November

Sunderland

Everywhere I go people are lamenting my impending retirement. I haven't met one who thinks it's a good idea. 'You're leaving us!' remarked a prominent local woman. She repeated it several times, as though I were a deserter.

Monday, 10 November

To London in bright, cold sunshine, which by Doncaster had given way to grey mist and swollen rivers.

The headline in today's *Times* reads, 'Council homes for life to be scrapped,' over a story that suggests that Margaret Beckett is considering plans to give new tenants fixed-term contracts, subject to review every few years. Much muttering in the Tea Room. Hard to think of anything more barmy. As though we are searching for ways to alienate that part of our core vote that we failed, despite best efforts, to alienate when Gordon abolished the ten pence tax band. It seems to have been dreamed up by one of the ubiquitous think tanks and I'd be amazed if someone as sensible as Margaret falls for it, but it needs knocking on the head pronto.

Huge relief at the Glenrothes result. Gordon Banks and Frank Roy, who masterminded our campaign, were lavishly praised at this evening's party meeting. Also, a mini-uprising over a suggestion by

Chief Whip Nick Brown that in future anyone who has voted against the government in the last year will not be considered for a place on a select committee.

Nick is already in retreat. 'You know I won't do it,' he said to me as we passed through the Aye Lobby this evening, but that's the point. He already has.

Tuesday, 11 November

The 11th day of the 11th month. I ventured out into Whitehall for the two-minute silence, hoping to catch sight of the three old boys, Bob Stone, Harry Patch and Henry Allingham – aged 108, 110 and 112 – the last survivors of the Great War. Alas, the crowd was vast and I was too far away.

To Wingfield House, the American Ambassador's magnificent residence in Regent's Park; unfortunately the wrong time of year for a tour of the garden but from the windows a distant glimpse of the Post Office Tower across acres of lawn. Ambassador Tuttle will shortly be receiving his marching orders, given the outcome of the presidential election and the fact that his is a political appointment, but he and his wife were gracious. The house, a vast solid, thirties mansion, was built by the Woolworth's heiress Barbara Hutton, who sold it to the US government for the princely sum of US$1. A long chat with a friendly Tory who gave me a lift back to the House. He described Cameron and Osborne as 'oppositionists' with no long-term strategy and reckons they will fall out in due course.

Wednesday, 12 November

Lunch with My Friend in High Places, who reports that the banking crisis has done wonders for Gordon's morale. No more tantrums. A marked fall in the number of pre-dawn emails and telephone calls. She attributes the change partly to the calming influence of Sarah, who, she says, is now far more visible, and to the fact that Gordon now operates out of an open plan office in Number 12, which causes people to be nicer to one another. The dreaded Shriti Vadera, on the other hand, continues to upset just about everyone, even – unwisely – the ladies on the Number 10 switchboard. Apparently, however, she is very good at dealing with bankers.

Thursday, 13 November

A belated outbreak of common sense, re the Post Office. James Purnell announced that he was scrapping plans to put the card account out to tender. Had the contract been awarded to the private sector, as it almost certainly would have been, several thousand more post offices would have closed with goodness-knows-what political consequences. At last our young masters are starting to behave like politicians rather than managers in thrall to every new corporate wheeze. I guess it is the collapse of the banks that's caused a little light to come on. The Tories looked very glum. Another of their foxes has been shot.

John Prescott was on the tube. We travelled together to King's Cross. He seems to have adjusted well to the loss of office. I asked if he missed it, but he says he doesn't. I guess in a way he's relieved that it's all over.

Monday, 17 November

What a roller coaster British politics has become. One moment Gordon is lord of all he surveys, next he is plumbing depths never before visited by a British prime minister. Now, suddenly, he is back on top again. Once again it is Gordon *über alles* and Shadow Chancellor George Osborne's turn to plumb the depths. The media are full of whispers that he is not up to it, too lightweight, that the City and Tory backbenchers have lost confidence in him etc. This about a man until recently portrayed as a master strategist, leading the Tories back to the sunlit uplands. No doubt the tide will turn again 'ere long, but we should enjoy this new mood while it lasts.

Margaret Beckett in her latest incarnation as housing minister addressed this evening's meeting of the parliamentary party. One after another southern members rose to describe the housing catastrophe, rising repossessions, record waiting lists, a generation priced out of the market, a dwindling supply of social housing decimated by the right-to-buy. Tales of desperate local authorities forced to lease back – at many times the original rent – former council properties from tenants who had exercised their right to buy, sold up and disappeared to sunnier climes. Margaret left us in no doubt that, for the first time in a decade, it is again respectable to talk about building council houses. Another New Labour nostrum bites the dust.

Tuesday, 18 November

A scary talk with an economist-cum-tax specialist who works for the Trades Union Congress. He said that on 5 October, the day that Lehman Brothers went under, he went out and stocked up with enough tinned food to last six weeks. He had thought there was a strong possibility that all the banks would go down and that there would be no means of exchange, civil disorder, troops on the street. There was still a danger that some major corporations – several names were mentioned – would go under and have to be bailed out by the taxpayer as the banks have been. Also, that several countries – Hungary, Belarus, Ukraine, Moldova, even Italy – were either bankrupt or on the point of bankruptcy and there was a danger that desperate people would start to move west or, as someone present put it, 'We could end up with a sort of Congo on the edge of Europe.' He also thought that sooner or later pressure on our currency would force us into the euro.

Dennis Skinner, just back from a meeting of the party's National Executive Committee, remarked that the party is in better heart than it has been for a long time. 'Something is happening. It's just possible we could win. I can feel it.'

Wednesday, 19 November

The battle lines are becoming clearer. At PMQs Cameron, following on from his announcement yesterday that the Tories are abandoning the pretence that they would match Labour's spending on public service investment, hammered Gordon for his alleged profligacy. To judge by the glum expressions behind him, he didn't make much impact, but it is early days yet. The Tories are now free to go into the next election posing as the party of fiscal restraint – or 'cuts' as our side were shouting at him – while painting us as the party of tax increases. So far they haven't had much luck in pinning the blame for the crisis on us, if only because (as Gordon pointed out on Monday) 'even the Americans agree it started in America'. That could all change once the bills start to come in.

Monday, 24 November

To London for Alistair Darling's pre-Budget statement. Actually, there was nothing 'pre' about it. It was a Budget. Bigger than any in living memory. Mega. Billions splashed about everywhere in a desperate attempt to kick-start our ailing economy. A 2.5 per cent cut in VAT which alone will cost more than £12 billion. Several billion on bringing forward capital projects, child benefit up, pensions up, tax cuts for basic rate payers. All the old rules torn up. No mention of prudence. Of course it will all have to be paid for, but not until well after the next election. In due course there will be increases in National Insurance for those earning over £40,000 and a 45 per cent tax rate for those on £150,000, but not nearly enough to pay for it all. The Tories went wild at the suggestion that the public finances wouldn't be back to current levels until 2015, and only then if Alistair's optimistic predictions about a return to growth come good. A huge gamble and, despite much cheering on our side, no one seems confident that it will work. For now we take comfort in the thought that all this is the work of finer minds than ours, but is it?

Tuesday, 25 November

Predictable headlines. 'Middle Class Tax Bombshell' (*Telegraph*), 'The Day New Labour Died' (*Mail*), 'Middle Britain Bashed' (*Express*). More ominously a restrained leader in the *FT* warning of much pain in years to come, questioning the impact of the cut in VAT, suggesting that Alistair's sums don't add up. For the Tories, George Osborne was on his feet demanding an emergency debate, which the Speaker, rightly, conceded. Extraordinary that our masters should think they could get away with spending on this scale without giving Parliament a say. Also, and scandalously, much of what has just been announced was leaked in advance.

Wednesday, 26 November

Suddenly politics has come alive. Talk about clear blue water. It couldn't be bluer or deeper. A return to old politics. The Tories going on about a tax bombshell, to which we respond by labelling them the 'do nothing' party. How it will all end is anybody's guess. Gordon saw the enemy off easily at PMQs today, shooting Sir Peter Tapsell, one of the grandest and most pompous, straight between the eyes.

Thursday, 27 November

To Sunderland on an early train, nose running like a tap. My annual cold and as usual it is going straight to my chest. I dragged myself over to the Stadium of Light to hand out awards to Sandhill View School leavers. To bed, shaking with fever. So much so that I could barely hold a cup of water.

Friday, 28 November

The bulletins are full of an attack by jihadi terrorists on the Taj hotel and several other prominent targets in Bombay. At least 100 dead, fires raging. It's been going on for two days and no one seems to know where the jihadis have come from or what their cause is, only that they appear to be well armed and highly motivated. Pakistan, of course, is the number one suspect.

Monday, 1 December

Still congested, but just about functioning. This afternoon to Monk-wearmouth School, where I talked to a class of 14-year-olds. A mix of delightful, bright-faced, enthusiastic youngsters and indifferent, inso-lent youths. In keeping with this age of celebrity, much interest as to whether I had appeared on TV and how much I earn (Answer: 'Less than your head teacher, but more than your form teacher'). One bright little blonde asked, 'What was the most important decision you've ever taken?', which left me floundering for a moment until it dawned on me that nothing I had ever been called upon to decide as a minister was as significant as, for example, voting against our involvement in Iraq or as useful as banning smoking in public buildings.

Tuesday, 2 December

To London on an evening train. The news is dominated by a huge row over a police raid on the office of Damian Green, the Tory immigra-tion spokesman, who was the beneficiary of a string of leaks from a civil servant in the Home Secretary's office. The Tories have spent the first few days trying mendaciously to present the incident as evidence of an authoritarian government seeking to suppress legitimate oppo-sition, despite the insistence of the police that they acted off their own bat, without the knowledge of anyone in government. Now the finger is beginning to point at the Speaker.

Wednesday, 3 December

A third day of sub-zero temperatures. I walked in with a scarf wrapped round my face.

The Queen's Speech was overshadowed by the growing row over the arrest of Damian Green. The Speaker made a statement that only dug the pit deeper. It turns out that the police had no warrant and that Speaker Martin appears to have given the go-ahead without even taking legal advice. Ominously, and ungallantly, he appeared to be dumping on the Serjeant at Arms, Jill Pay, who was looking very mis-erable. Tory indignation knows no bounds. Led by Michael Howard, they were jumping up and down with points of order and endlessly intervening on the Prime Minister as he attempted to introduce the government's programme. Several people on our side pointed out that there were one or two other principles at stake, besides the rights of Members: the impartiality of the civil service, for example; not to mention the operational independence of the police, something the Tories used to be very keen on, not least when the police were conducting their honours inquiry. But the bottom line is that Mr Speaker Martin has let us all down. If we'd had someone like George Young, this would never have happened.

Harriet Harman quietly (actually, not all that quietly) suggested I try to persuade Jacqui Smith to forget about her latest foolish wheeze – elected police authorities. 'There's no support for it,' she said. 'No one is asking us for it. It can only get us into trouble.' In that case why are we going ahead? 'There's some support in Cabinet.' Like who? 'Hazel Blears.' Say no more.

Thursday, 4 December

M from Washington called in. Very upbeat. He says Obama is unlikely to pursue 'Star Wars' or to be pushing to get Ukraine and Georgia into NATO. He will also want to cool the confrontation with Iran, even at the risk of letting the Iranians get on with their nuclear programme. He won't take on the Israelis, but he won't allow them to mess with Iran. 'All Obama wants,' says M, 'is calm so that he can get on with sorting out the economy.' Pakistan, he says, is the big problem that no one knows what to do about. Also, Bill Clinton is a potential embarrassment, swanning about the globe, mixing with all sorts of undesirables. 'Out of control,' according to M.

Sunday, 7 December

Spent the afternoon reading Nigel Lawson's sceptical look at global warming, *An Appeal to Reason*. Beautifully written, scrupulously footnoted. His thesis is that (a) the evidence is ambivalent; (b) if global warming is happening, there are beneficial as well as adverse impacts; (c) the proposed cure – drastic cuts in carbon emissions – is worse than the alleged disease and anyway impossible to implement since the biggest emitters will never co-operate; and (d) that adaptation rather than mitigation is the way forward. Much food for thought. Without doubt a case to be answered.

Monday, 8 December

This evening to Congress House for the Prison Reform Trust's annual lecture, delivered by an extraordinarily eloquent black American law professor. Some shocking statistics: since 1972 the American prison population has risen from 200,000 to 2.3 million, including (incredibly) 73 children aged 13 and 14 serving life without parole. The Welfare Reform Act 1992, signed into law by Bill Clinton, no less, denies welfare to anyone with a drug-related conviction, resulting in widespread destitution. And no end in sight. Even if he lasts the full eight years, Barack Obama is unlikely to have a chance to appoint enough new Supreme Court judges to make a difference. His message: don't go down the American road.

Tuesday, 9 December

To Buckingham Palace, where I watched in awe as the Right Honourable Keith Vaz managed, in a crowded field, to inveigle himself into The Presence. HM, radiant in lime green, worked the crowd, in a gallery lined with Rembrandts and Van Dycks, for an hour and a half, managing to look bright and interested throughout.

A brief exchange with Sarah Hogg, who once worked for John Major. She confirmed that he had toyed with banning foreign ownership of our media, but said I wouldn't find any paperwork. They knew it was dynamite and committed nothing to paper.

A poll in today's *Times* put us comfortably ahead on economic competence, though still four points behind on voting intentions.

Wednesday, 10 December

To the Almeida theatre in Islington for Pat Kavanagh's memorial meeting. Strictly by invitation in order to exclude the *Evening Standard* and the dreadful Jeanette Winterson. Giles Radice and I were the only politicians. The rest were literary glitterati – Carmen Callil, Robert Harris, Ian McEwan and, of course, Pat's husband, Julian Barnes. A minimalist ceremony, no introductions, no applause, no fuss; beautifully choreographed, just right for a woman of such poise, elegance and so few words. At the end someone read out a list of epigrams found in her notebooks. One said: 'If you want to succeed in society, you need to let yourself be taught a lot of things you already know.'

This evening to Number 10 for Christmas drinks. Just about every light in the Ministry of Defence still blazing when we emerged at 9.30 p.m. So much for all those military big-wigs ringing up the *Daily Telegraph* every five minutes, saying how starved of funds they are.

Saturday, 13 December

Every day the news grows worse. The pound is plunging against the euro. Woolworth's has gone under. Nissan and Toyota on short time; nine-month sabbaticals at Vauxhall; meanwhile the US car giants are in meltdown. Today there are reports that Bernie Madoff, a Wall Street fund manager, is going bust to the tune of US$50 billion. Apparently it was all a scam.

Sunday, 14 December

Gordon has spent the weekend on a whistlestop visit to Kabul, Islamabad and Delhi. Unless I am mistaken, at all three stops he was still sporting the same purple tie that he was wearing when I chatted to him briefly at Number 10 last Wednesday.

Monday, 15 December

Keith Hill joined me at lunch. The Man, who he saw on Friday, is on good form, apparently. The Man's analysis of the present situation is that we are in uncharted waters. Government and Opposition have adopted starkly different approaches to the economic crisis and no one knows who is right. And even if Gordon's approach is right, it is far from clear that it will lead to a recovery in time for the inevitable election. 'Scary,' says Keith.

Miliband the Younger addressed the parliamentary party this evening, saying that action on climate change represented a chance to win back some of the middle-class votes that we had lost over Iraq. Also a chance to reassert moral authority. I asked if he had read Nigel Lawson's book. He hadn't, but promised to.

Tuesday, 16 December

'How are we doing?' I asked Dennis Skinner in the Tea Room this afternoon.

'We're on a knife edge,' he replied. 'At any moment we could slip and slice our balls off.'

This evening I tapped out an email to the Labour Party General Secretary, Ray Collins, re all-women shortlists in the light of recent experience in Sunderland, asking whether we might have stretched the elastic as far as it will go. I know what the answer will be, but I ought to get something on the record.

Saturday, 27 December

The Israelis have attacked Gaza, in response to incessant rocket fire from Hamas. 'This is only the beginning ...' said a spokesman ominously.

CHAPTER FIVE

2009

Tuesday, 6 January

The Israelis are laying waste to Gaza. A picture on the front of this morning's *Guardian* shows a distraught father standing over the bodies of his three small children, looking for all the world as if they were asleep, killed by tank fire. They are killing on a ratio of 100 to one, dropping huge bombs into crowded housing, systematically demolishing what remains of Gaza's ramshackle infrastructure, destroying mosques, all in the name of fighting Hamas. It is nothing new. They did the same in Lebanon 18 months ago. These are crimes and the people responsible are war criminals. Yet still no one of any consequence speaks out. From European governments, our own included, just a lot of mealie-mouthed calls for a ceasefire. From the US, which as everyone knows could put a stop to this overnight, blatant connivance. Even as the bodies pile up and death and destruction rain down, Bush speaks only of Hamas violence. Silence too from President-Elect Obama. Tonight it was reported that three schools have been hit, including one run by the UN, killing perhaps 40 people, many of them children. The UN school was clearly marked, the flag was flying, the co-ordinates had been sent to the Israelis, but still they bombed it. Within the hour an Israeli spokesman is justifying the carnage on the grounds that someone in the school fired at them – clearly a lie. It is striking how articulate Israeli spokesmen are. How apparently reasonable. How calm. How utterly, utterly shameless. Nothing fazes them. Over and over they repeat that Israel does not target civilians. Of course they don't. They are just completely careless. No point in getting angry with them; they just calmly repeat their mantras.

The difficulty is, of course, that there are no heroes in the Middle East. Extremists abound on all sides and, for all the talk of roadmaps, there is no solution in sight. Even in the unlikely event of a settlement there is no shortage of lunatics waiting to destroy it. As my old friend Wilf Burchett* used to say, 'Every morning I get up and thank God that he never made me an expert on the Middle East.'

Wednesday, 7 January

An email from Claes Bratt expressing pleasant surprise at Obama's choice of Leon Panetta to head the CIA. 'I've met Panetta many times … a thoroughly pleasant man with an ironic sense of humour, widely respected for his integrity and decency … very intriguing choice. I don't imagine they are celebrating at Langley.'

On the radio yesterday someone remarked of George Bush that he was only coherent when talking of war, revenge, punishment or baseball.

Saturday, 10 January

To Worcester College, Oxford, to address the annual dinner of the Study of Parliament Group. The gathering consisted of clerks and librarians past and present and a smattering of academics, including David Butler, about 60 or 70 in all. I gave an irreverent account of my life and times, laced with jokes and a shameless plug for the diaries; it went down wonderfully. 'Why are you retiring?' people kept asking. To which I could offer no adequate reply.

Earlier, I caught a bus to Headington to visit Daphne Park in the convalescent wing of St Luke's Hospital. She was in sparkling form, holding court in her dressing gown, regaling me with tales of her wartime service with the SOE, training agents who were parachuted into France and later, in Berlin and Vienna, searching out German

---

*One of the great war correspondents. See his memoirs, *At the Barricades*, Quartet, 1980.

and Austrian scientists before the Russians could kidnap them. She joined the SIS in 1948. I asked if she had known Violette Szabo, the young shop assistant from Brixton who was executed in February 1945, a bust of whom has recently appeared on the embankment, near Lambeth Palace. 'No,' she said, 'but I knew Odette.'

Sunday, 11 January

A pleasant morning mooching round Oxford. Most of the colleges were closed so I had to make do with tantalising glimpses of secret gardens, courtyards and pillared quads. Everywhere bright-faced, prosperous-looking youngsters, many on bicycles. This time next year my Sarah will be one of them. Then back to London for dinner with Liz Forgan and Rex Cowan. Rex, who is Jewish, is boiling with anger about what Israel is up to in Gaza; he and Liz had been on one of the recent demonstrations outside the Israeli embassy. 'These are not war-lords,' he said. 'This is a disciplined army ... a government in control. They must be held to account. We should stop pretending we have any leverage and start organising sanctions. The trouble is everyone is afraid of The Lobby.'

They kept on at me to make plans for an afterlife. '*Now*,' said Liz. 'If you leave it until after you've retired, it will be too late.'

Monday, 12 January

David Miliband made a statement on Gaza, full of well-meaning but ineffectual guff about the need for an end to violence by both sides and concern about civilian casualties. Feelings were running high. On all sides talk of war crimes and from some quarters calls for sanctions and for the withdrawal of our ambassador. Gerald Kaufman, himself a Jew, was the most outspoken. I – taking a lead from Rex yesterday – said that we were kidding ourselves if we imagined that we – or anyone else in the EU – have the slightest influence on the Israelis. Sanctions are the only hope of getting their attention.

Later, Gordon Brown addressed a crowded meeting of the parlia-mentary party. He was on good form (better than I've seen him in a long while), talking confidently of plans to get banks lending again, boosting public investment, bashing the Tories with gusto. Points from the floor included pleas not to part-privatise the Royal Mail and calls to reconsider plans for a third runway at Heathrow.

Tuesday, 13 January

To Great Smith Street, to the offices of the Committee on Standards in Public Life, to bend the ear of Sir Christopher Kelly about the iniquitous 'communications allowance'. A final throw of the dice, having failed to persuade the Electoral Commission to do anything about it. He was affable, but non-committal. Afterwards we discussed Members' allowances, which he is interested in reforming. He said they had been waiting to see if the House would reform itself, bringing in outside auditors etc., but we had funked it. I pointed out that transparency was already changing old habits, but he seemed to think a shake-up was called for. He talked ominously of 'being brave' about salaries in return for trimming the allowances. Being brave, of course, means another big, above-inflation increase which would trigger another great wave of public indignation and ridicule. I replied that all we need to do is tie future increases to those of typical constituents – teachers, nurses, pensioners – and leave it that way for ever.

Wednesday, 14 January

To Committee Room 10 to hear Peter Mandelson explaining why he is proposing to give the private sector a stake in Royal Mail. He was calm and fluent, if a trifle disingenuous, refusing to admit that what is proposed amounts even to partial 'privatisation' (which of course we have forsworn). His argument – shades of Air Traffic Control – was that it wasn't just about investment, but it was good management that is woefully lacking in the Royal Mail. 'It just doesn't have the gene pool' was how he put it. He was heard respectfully, but there was much scepticism. 'If private sector management is needed, why don't we just buy it in?' someone asked. Someone else pointed to the mess the private sector had made of the buses. Despite all the huffing and puffing, the reality is that it's more or less a done deal because the Treasury have insisted that they won't rescue the Post Office pension fund unless the private sector are given a stake.

Thursday, 15 January

To Labour Party HQ in Victoria Street to discuss all-women shortlists with the General Secretary, Ray Collins. Undaunted by the fact that the embargo on male applicants in Sunderland Central resulted in just five applications, Harriet and the sisters have decided to repeat the experience in the neighbouring seat, Houghton and Sunderland South. All three Sunderland seats have now had all-women shortlists imposed. In every case local wishes have been ignored and two of our three are among the safest seats in the country. Somewhere alarm bells ought to be ringing. I said, 'When are we going to admit we have a problem? Will it be when there are only four applications for a safe seat? Three? Two? One?' He concedes there is a problem, but remains committed to the policy. Wider advertising of vacancies is his solution.

On party finance, Ray says that last June we came within a whisker of bankruptcy. He's managed to stabilise the situation, but it's still precarious.

This afternoon, a debate on Gaza. So many people wanted to take part that we were limited to six minutes each and still not everyone was called. Only two or three people spoke up for the Israelis – Louise Ellman, reading from a script which might have been supplied by the embassy. The two front benches used weasel words like 'unacceptable' to describe what is going on. Almost everyone else talked war crimes and sanctions.

Friday, 16 January

Sunderland

A visit to the community centre at Plains Farm. The usual story, no core funding, the person in charge – a dynamic woman called Julie – desperately writing begging letters to charitable trusts, to no avail:

everyone wants to fund new projects, but no one is interested in sustaining existing ones. Having no money at my disposal, all I can do is offer one or two mildly helpful suggestions and a friendly letter of reference.

Later, a delegation from the long streets in Hendon complaining about mayhem which is gradually rendering life unbearable in what were once streets of owner-occupied cottages inhabited by working-class citizens who actually worked, but are increasingly being taken over by some of the city's worst landlords. Then at the surgery this evening, agents for two of the town's biggest (and in one case worst) landlords, 400 properties apiece, complained that the payment of housing benefit direct to tenants was making rent impossible to collect and that as a result they were threatened with bankruptcy. I managed to keep a straight face and forbore to mention that it was I who persuaded the Prime Minister (I still have his handwritten note thanking me for the suggestion) to stop the flow of housing benefit direct from the public purse to landlords' bank accounts, which was causing the destruction of our inner cities. To be sure, there is a problem – and I will investigate. But I also wondered whether in these particular cases bankruptcy might be in the public interest.

Saturday, 17 January

Gradually it is dawning on Emma that life beyond the cosy confines of St Bede's Terrace may be a mite tougher than she has hitherto supposed. Last week, in citizenship class at school, she took part in an online test to determine the sort of career she was aiming for. She duly filled in the questionnaire and up popped a list of the careers for which she was suited. In first place: car park attendant.

Monday, 19 January

To the chamber to hear Alistair Darling announce a huge new bail-out for the banks, this one said to be worth £100 billion, the earlier £37 billion having been absorbed without trace. Mostly, he was heard in dead silence. The Tories, too, were subdued. It's all too obvious they don't have any better ideas. If this doesn't work, a full-scale takeover of the entire banking system is the only card we have left.

Ken Clarke is back on the front bench. Throughout the Chancellor's statement he sat prominently wedged between George Osborne and Oliver Letwin, his unhealthily red face contrasting with Osborne's pallid features.

Meanwhile the Royal Bank of Scotland, which owns NatWest among others, has announced the biggest corporate loss in British history – a cool £28 billion.

Tuesday, 20 January

Barack Obama, a man whose father might once have been refused service in a Washington restaurant on the grounds that his skin was the wrong colour, was today sworn in as the 44th president of the United States. The event was witnessed by vast, cheering crowds stretching from the steps of the Capitol, away down the Mall as far as the eye could see. Even here, as the hour drew near, the excitement was palpable. All over the building Members, Tory and Labour alike, security guards and Tea Room staff clustered around TV sets to bear witness. Some nice moments. The shining little Obama girls bursting with pride for their dad, the smaller of the two giving him the thumbs up. And the sweetest moment of all when George and Laura Bush were seen off the premises, escorted by the Obamas to the helicopter that whisked them away on the first leg of their journey home to Texas. You have to hand it to old George W, though. He has behaved with great dignity throughout the handover, which can't have been easy given how keen everyone was to see the back of him. Where the Obama presidency will lead remains to be seen. Expectations are so high they cannot possibly be fulfilled. But it was a moment to savour.

Wednesday, 21 January

To Dining Room A for an all-party media group breakfast with Ed Richards, chief executive of OFCOM, who I first came across when he worked in Number 10. The news is every bit as bleak as I had supposed. We are moving helter-skelter down the American road – hundreds of television channels with nothing worth watching on any of them. Google and satellite television are between them gradually dragging down the terrestrial channels, except for the good old ring-fenced BBC, and to judge by the comments of the Tories present, they have plans for putting paid to that, too. 'I worry about what will unfold in the next two years,' said Ed. He went on, 'There is a risk of a rapid cycle of decline, cuts in ITV and Channel Four and soon we will be in a position where only the BBC will have resources for original programming, which won't be good for the BBC either.' Someone suggested a levy on Google, which is sucking several billions a year out of our economy, but, as Ed pointed out, there is nothing to stop Google upping sticks and moving to Luxembourg if they don't like our tax regime. He said there were three options for public service broadcasting: continued subsidy, managed decline or privatisation. The Tories present (John Redwood, Philip Davies and a clutch of reactionary peers) were in no doubt which option they preferred. The only sign of Tory dissent was Elspeth Howe, who flashed a thin smile in my direction every time one of the headbangers took the floor. Alas, she is the past. They may be the future.

The Aye Lobby

An extraordinary exchange with one of that small band of *über* New Labourites whose systematic abuse of the franked envelopes for purposes that were blatantly party political led to our stationery being strictly rationed.

'I bet you don't use your allocation,' she said.

'No, I don't.'

'Would you mind ordering a thousand franked envelopes in your name and letting me have them?'

I demurred, pointing out that I was a member of Standards and Privileges, the committee that adjudicates on precisely such abuses.

She was unfazed. 'Strictly between you and I. No one would know.'

'I can't.'

'Other people do it for me.'
She just didn't get it.

Thursday, 22 January

The London *Standard* has been bought by a Russian oligarch. Someone from *Guardian Online* rang to ask if I thought this was a threat to free speech. 'Can't be worse than the Rothermeres,' I replied. Later, in the Tea Room, Bruce Grocott held up the early edition of tonight's *Standard*. The headline was was 'Good news: gas prices cut by 10 per cent'.

'When was the last time you saw good news on the front of the *Standard*?' asked Bruce. When indeed.

Saturday, 24 January

Today's *Telegraph* contains an interview with Denis Healey in which he recommends doing away with Trident. Now he tells us ...

Sunday, 25 January

The *Sunday Times* is leading with allegations that four Labour peers agreed to accept cash in exchange for amending, or persuading the government to amend, legislation. Cash for questions all over again, only this time it's our turn.

In the morning I dug out the compost heap. After lunch Ngoc and I drove to South Shields and walked along the cliff top in bright sunshine, stopping on the way back for a drink at Marsden Rock. It was warm enough to sit outside on the terrace watching the waves.

Monday, 26 January

Jack Jones and Michael Foot, both aged 95, came to this evening's meeting of the parliamentary party. It was moving to see the two old boys, both big figures in their day. Jack positively glowing, but not entirely with it. Michael a poor old ruin, wild, skeletal, no longer in control of his movements. It seemed almost cruel to expose him.

Superlatives flowed. There were several standing ovations. People clicked away with their mobile phone cameras, knowing this is probably the last glimpse we shall see of either of them. To the New Labour generation, of course, they are ancient history, ghostly reminders of a past long ago repudiated, but everyone entered into the spirit of the occasion. Neil Kinnock, as ever too loud and too long, did the introductions. Gordon Brown made a simple, effective little speech. Then, with Gordon clutching his right arm, Michael spoke. Strong and clear. Only a few sentences, but enough to show that his mind is still alive inside that ruined body. Dear old Jack just smiled benignly.

Tonight's bulletins feature a tape of Lord Taylor of Blackburn, one of the accused peers, hawking his services for upwards of 100 grand. Everyone is livid with the silly old fool. This is going to do us enormous damage. As someone remarked, we are unravelling, exactly as John Major's government did. Our luck has well and truly run out.

Tuesday, 27 January
Members' Lobby

As I was leaving this evening Ed Miliband, Secretary of State for Climate Change, bent my ear about tomorrow's vote on a third runway for Heathrow. 'The author of *A Very British Coup* wouldn't vote with the Tories, would he?' I explained to young Ed, who despite his present eminence hasn't been with us all that long, that there is not a Tory lobby and a Labour one, but an Aye and a Noe Lobby – and yes I would be voting for the Tory motion since it reflected my views. He then attempted, in a tone that suggested exasperation, to persuade me that expansion was conditional on the toughest emission constraints in the world and they would be legally binding. To which I protested that the airlines would find a way round whatever constraints he saw fit to impose, as they had with all previous restrictions. Whereupon he walked off, shaking his head in disbelief at my naivety.

Wednesday, 28 January

An excellent debate on Heathrow. The Tories cunningly tabled a motion worded precisely as the early-day motion which a large number of us had signed some weeks ago, thereby causing much squirming and wriggling among the fainter hearts. Geoff Hoon turned in a bullying, over-the-top performance which didn't do the government's case any good and, with the exception of Ruth Kelly, just about everyone who spoke from the floor opposed a third runway. The west London members, whose constituencies are already blighted, were particularly outspoken. The whips were scuttling about, trying to talk people into abstaining rather than vote against the government. Even the Prime Minister was deployed. According to Mark Fisher, he was pleading, 'Do this for me. If we lose, it will go round the world that we are unfit to govern.' Nick Brown invited me in for a gentle chat, disclosing a piece of paper which suggested the government was within a single vote of losing. When I got back to my room I found an urgent email, several hours old, bidding me ring Number 10. Happily, however, it was too late. In the event the government won by 19.

Friday, 30 January

Gordon's fatuous slogan, 'British jobs for British workers', has come back to haunt us. Workers at a refinery in Lincolnshire have downed tools in protest against the employment, by an Italian subcontractor, of Portuguese and Italian workers at a time when local unemployment is rising rapidly. The television bulletins are full of angry white males holding up placards and alleging that Gordon has betrayed them. Workers at power stations and refineries all over the country are coming out in sympathy. So far it is all fairly good-natured, but that could change. A gift for the BNP and our poisonous tabloids. This is where cheap populism gets you.

Monday, 2 February

To London, through a bleak freezing landscape, though, for once, the north got off lighter than the south, which is under six inches of snow. Much of the capital paralysed. No buses, only half the Underground, even the Members' Tea Room closed because the staff could not get in. The *Evening Standard*, which has reverted to type after its brief flirtation with good news, was ranting on about 'chaos', but actually it all seemed quite peaceful apart from one or two minor inconveniences.

A statement from Pat McFadden about the 'British jobs for British workers' row. He conceded little, urging everyone back to work and saying we must never succumb to protectionism. Much talk from the Tories of chickens coming home to roost re Gordon's foolish pledge. Our position is that he was referring to making the British workforce job-ready. Like hell he was.

Tuesday, 3 February

Walked in from Kennington through the snow. Victoria Tower Gardens was dotted with snowmen and at the Lycee someone has constructed a massive pillar of snow, about ten feet high.

This evening a meeting re Gaza with Foreign Office and DFID ministers, Bill Rammell and Mike Foster. The Israelis are still blockading and increasingly contemptuous of the outside world. To begin with the meeting went predictably with a certain amount of huffing and puffing from most colleagues, with Bill sticking skilfully to the official line. Then Ken Purchase took the gloves off and said – as I did in the debate last month – that we should stop deluding ourselves that we had any influence with the Israelis and start distinguishing clearly between right and wrong. This triggered a much more robust discussion in which several people pointed out that there was no sign that the Israelis are interested in a two-state solution, otherwise why would they be encouraging settlements across the West Bank? Increasingly, one hears it suggested that the days of a solution based on two states are over and that the only way forward is a single secular state in which all sides learn, however painfully, to live together.

Wednesday, 4 February

Another stinking cold which, as ever, has gone straight to my chest. I've been coughing and spluttering all week.

This evening, to dinner with the spread-betting magnate and mega-donor to the Tory party Stuart Wheeler and his wife, Tessa, in their Mayfair penthouse. Despite his great wealth, Stuart is a shy, modest man who appears to be entirely motivated by principle rather than self-interest. The purpose was to thank those involved with the All Party Rendition Group, of which he has been a generous supporter. A delightful evening, even though I was placed – to much merriment – opposite a large portrait of Mrs Thatcher. I find it one of the most attractive features of our democracy that decent people whose views on many issues are diametrically opposed can combine in support of a just cause.

Thursday, 5 February

The African Union has chosen Gaddafi as this year's president in succession to the villain from Congo-Brazzaville. Really, it's too much. Why should we take them seriously, if this is the best they can do?

A brief chat with William Hague on the train. Re Afghanistan, which we debated this afternoon, he says that General Petraeus – the American who is credited with recent progress in Iraq – was our only hope. The Americans are fed up with Karzai and want him replaced. They are likely to press for a big troop surge. We've seen this film before. A liberal American president inherits a small war and then gets sucked into a big one. I can't see a way out of Afghanistan in my lifetime. The trouble is, if we pull up stumps now – as some advise – there would be millions of refugees.

William also remarked re the alleged crisis in defence spending that the MOD are having to dip into future years' budgets. Sooner or later something will have to give. 'How about scrapping Trident?' I ventured. 'We could never do it, but your lot could.' He didn't think it likely, although he happily agreed that the Tories stood a better chance than us of getting away with it.

Monday, 9 February

A new feeding frenzy following the revelation – in one of the Sundays – that Jacqui Smith is claiming the Additional Costs Allowance against her family home, while lodging with her sister in London. Peter Oborne has a piece in today's *Mail* describing the arrangement as 'corrupt'. A foretaste of what we can expect later this year when our expenses are published three years in arrears.

Also, a big storm brewing over the news that the bankers – even those whose banks are largely state-owned – are going ahead as usual with their obscene annual splurge of bonus payments, unfazed by the ruin they have wrought. Mounting public fury, demands for government intervention. So far all that has been promised is 'a review'. This evening, a meeting with a harassed-looking Yvette Cooper, who explained that the government was doing its best, but that unravelling existing arrangements was complicated. No doubt it is, but if we are not careful the government is going to find itself in the unhappy position of defending a profession that – for the time being at least – is even more reviled than ourselves.

Peter Mandelson addressed the parliamentary party, but without referring to the issue on most people's minds – the proposed part-privatisation of the Post Office. It came up soon enough in Questions and though Peter's response prompted mild heckling, he was generally well received and so reticent about the Post Office that I begin to wonder if a U-turn is being organised.

Tuesday, 10 February

Today's papers report a fall in profits (to a mere £61 billion) for Barclays, the directors of which have, thus far, avoided throwing themselves on the mercy of the taxpayer. However, buried in *The Times* report on the subject is the following chilling sentence: 'Total Barclays assets and liabilities each mushroomed to more than £2 trillion, both now larger than the UK domestic product …' With stunning understatement the report goes on: 'The size of its balance sheet would pose problems for British taxpayers … in the unlikely event that the bank were to fail.' Ye gods.

Wednesday, 11 February

Just four – repeat four – women have applied to succeed Fraser Kemp in Houghton and Sunderland South, one of our safest seats.

Wednesday, 25 February

To the Home Office with Molly Meacher and Lord Cobbold to discuss the forthcoming UN drugs summit in Vienna with Alan Campbell. On the wall in the waiting area I counted pictures of no fewer than 26 post-war Home Secretaries, one every two years on average. While we were there the news came through that David Cameron's severely disabled son had died. PMQs was called off. Instead Gordon made a brief, moving tribute and the House was suspended.

Monday, 2 March

A storm raging over the discovery that Sir Fred Goodwin, the former chairman of the Royal Bank of Scotland, which has just recorded the biggest loss in British corporate history, escaped with a pension of £693,000 a year, payable from the age of 50. He is brazenly resisting calls to return at least some of his ill-gotten gains. Harriet was in the media over the weekend, suggesting that the government would force him to, but it appears that she has rowed out too far. Treasury lawyers are advising that Sir Fred's position is watertight. 'A nightmare,' remarked Yvette Cooper at the Treasury committee.

Also a big row brewing over plans to sell off 30 per cent of the Royal Mail. The general reaction is incomprehension. How could we be so daft? Just at the moment when the private sector is on its knees along comes Peter Mandelson (or is it Gordon?) with plans to part-privatise one of our most loved institutions. So far no sign of movement. On the contrary, the pit gets deeper every day and it's hard to see how we are going to dig ourselves out.

Tuesday, 3 March

Another bank, HSBC, has published its results alongside the news that five of its bankers shared bonuses of £32 million despite a slump in profits and the bank having to write off £17 billion in bad debt. The chairman was quoted as saying, 'People had given up focusing on whether something was the right thing to do, focusing only on whether or not it was legal.'

A chat with my good friend Keith Hill re all that anti-Blair spin emanating from the Treasury in the bad old days. The Man, says Keith, didn't believe it was coming from Gordon, although the courtiers kept telling him that it was. After Gordon became leader, it all stopped. 'That's the proof,' says Keith. He added that in the early days The Man had probably hinted, if not explicitly stated, to Gordon that he would only serve a term and a half – and that, of course, is the root of it all.

Hilary Benn remarked to me, apropos Alastair Campbell's diaries, how struck he was by how dependent The Man was on Alastair, how frequently he rang for advice, how insecure he appears and what a contrast with the brilliant, confident performer that we saw so much of in public. Hilary was also struck, as was I, by the extraordinary degree of access Piers Morgan – and other tabloid lowlife – enjoyed and what a waste of time it all was.

Thursday, 5 March

The Bank of England has cut interest rates to just half a per cent, prompting howls of anguish from savers. More ominously, the Bank has embarked on a mind-boggling £75 billion programme of 'Quantitative Easing', which apparently means printing money and using it to buy gilts from the banks in the hope that they will start lending again. Whether they will or not remains to be seen. We are entering unknown territory.

Wednesday, 11 March

A brief exchange of fire with Lance Corporal McAvoy re my reference in the *Diaries* to his girth. He (twanging his red braces): 'If you talk about my fat belly, I'll talk about your speccie baldness.'

'Be my guest, Tommy.'

As we were going through the Aye Lobby this evening, Michael Meacher recounted an exchange he had with The Man, shortly before the '97 election, when Michael was front bench spokesman on environment. A crisis had blown up, he couldn't remember what, and he had rung up Blair to clarify what he should say. According to Michael, The Man replied, 'You'll just have to lie.' Michael was gobsmacked. 'I've never forgotten it,' he said, adding, 'And I don't mind if you put that in your diary.' A small addition to the growing body of evidence – remember the 'Bobby' incident* – that, in extremis, The Man did not always tell the truth.

Friday, 13 March

I am trying to rescue a young woman from Benin who the UK Border Agency is trying to remove to Lagos, despite the fact that she has never set foot in Nigeria. She has a 17-month-old son. If she goes she will be destitute. The toddler, presumably, has none of the immunities needed for life in a Nigerian slum. No one seems to have given a thought to what will become of him. It's literally a matter of life or death. She was due to be bundled onto a flight at 10.30 tomorrow, but I managed to track down the immigration minister, Phil Woolas, in his constituency and persuade him to give the poor woman another week. I have until Tuesday to make representations.

Saturday, 14 March

Sunderland

In today's *Telegraph* a half-page review of my *Diaries* by Roy Hattersley alleging that 'page after page exudes the conviction that he is morally superior to those around him'. Roy, I suspect, has not yet fully recovered from our differences in the eighties. Also, as so often with 'great'

---

*The codename given to Peter Mandelson during the 1994 leadership election to enable his involvement in the Blair campaign to be denied.

men, one never knows whether they have actually read the book or just dipped into it in search of material that supports their prejudices.

Monday, 16 March

A postcard from Simon Burns, a Tory MP: 'You might think I'm sad, but I've just spent a weekend gripped by the diaries ...' Similar messages coming from all over. People knocking on my door asking me to sign copies. One Tory, a publisher by profession, described it as 'a phenomena'.

Tuesday, 17 March

Binyam Mohamed, late of the dark prison in Bagram and Guantanamo, came in for a quiet chat with Andrew Tyrie and myself. To avoid recognition he has shaved his beard and is in the process of changing his name. In remarkable shape, considering his extraordinary ordeal. Ethiopian by origin, but came here from America. How come he ended up in Afghanistan? His story is that he had been living in London and had fallen in with a crowd who were doing drugs. Eager to escape, he had joined the local mosque, where someone suggested he head out to Afghanistan if he wanted to see Islam at its purest. After a few months in training camps for foreign jihadis in Jalalabad and later Kandahar he was then sent to man the second line of defence near Kabul – against the Northern Alliance – before being taken ill with malaria. He says he was in hospital when the American attack began and the Taliban took him to the border. He was picked up in Karachi, as he was about to board a plane back to the UK. He never saw any fighting and claims to have had no interest in an anti-America jihad, on the contrary his ambition had been to help the Chechens against the Russians. The rest is history. Now he just wants to regain his life and resume his engineering studies. He's apparently good at football, having once been trialled by Chelsea. It could all have been so different ...

Wednesday, 18 March

Alan Johnson relayed a message re the *Diaries* from his special adviser, a 32-year-old woman: 'You've really lightened up my bedtime.' And I didn't think there was any sex in it.

Thursday, 19 March

Awoke to the news that unemployment has crossed the two million mark, about where it was when we came in – and rising faster than ever before. Odds are it will hit three million by this time next year. If this carries on, everything will unravel. Another lost generation of hopeless, unemployable, misbehaving youth. The Tories, with characteristic shamelessness, are dusting down their 'Labour isn't working' poster from the late seventies. All we can say in reply is that we won't be as beastly to the unemployed as they were. That plus our latest fatuous slogan: 'Real Help Now'. Not enough to save us, I fear.

Friday, 20 March

Sunderland

An hour with Paul Prest, 'chief executive' of the new academy at Pennywell. A messianic, driven man, vaguely resembling the BBC's Robert Peston, who commutes from York and back each day. Already he is making waves. His first act was to insist that the kids remain on the school premises throughout the day, instead of roaming the streets at lunchtime. The inevitable rebellion was ruthlessly suppressed with mass suspensions, which seems to have done the trick. So far only one permanent exclusion, which is a good sign. The culture shock is proving too much for some. About 40 per cent of the staff have fled, but he didn't seem sorry to have lost most of them and claims to have no trouble finding replacements. A fair amount of business-speak. As is the way these days, his deputies are 'strategic directors' and his speech is laced with references to American research which may or may not prove relevant to the stark realities of life on the streets of Pennywell. Early days yet. The new school, which will take children aged eight and upwards, will not be ready until

September and so for now they are still operating out of the same tired, asbestos-ridden '60s buildings. I came away mildly optimistic. My worry is that he will burn himself out. An early test of his commitment will be whether he gives up commuting from York and moves nearer his place of work.

Sunday, 22 March

Jade Goody, foul-mouthed star of *Big Brother* and various other vulgar extravaganzas, has succumbed to cancer. In keeping with the spirit of the times, the Prime Minister put out a statement mourning her loss.

Ken Clarke, meanwhile, has caused a storm by appearing to wobble on the Tories' commitment to raise the upper limit on inheritance tax to £1 million – a litmus test issue in the meaner parts of Middle England. By evening he had been prevailed upon to put out a statement 'clarifying' his position. Useful confirmation, were any needed, that Tory priorities remain unchanged, despite our present travail.

Monday, 23 March

Everywhere the stench of decay. Yesterday's *News of the World* devoted three salacious pages, complete with colour photos, to the antics of Nigel Griffiths with an unnamed woman in his Commons office. Meanwhile yet another row over expenses. This time the culprit is the employment minister, Tony McNulty, who, incredibly, has been claiming the second home allowance on a house in which his parents are living, even though he lives in Hammersmith and represents a constituency no more than ten miles from Westminster. This evening he put out the usual bald statement, *de rigueur* on these occasions, that everything was within the rules, but it won't wash. As even he seems to admit, it is indefensible. There is, I fear, much more of this to come.

This evening, at the meeting of the parliamentary party, a chastened John Denham explained how the Learning and Skills Council has been merrily giving the nod to new higher education building projects without any proper accounting and as a result has commitments many times over budget. The chief executive has resigned, mercifully *sans* bonus, and all new building has been put on hold while the mess is sorted.

Meanwhile the diaries have crept into the *Sunday Times* best-seller list – at number 10. My publisher, Andrew Franklin, emailed to say he had ordered another reprint, the second in a fortnight. Gisela Stuart, just back from Bahrain, says that each of the three Tories on her delegation had their noses buried in a copy.

Tuesday, 24 March

To an upper committee room for a presentation by Greg Cook, the party's pollster. Our overall position is dire, but there are small reasons for cheer: despite the best efforts of the Tories and their friends in the media, an impressive 82 per cent of the population believe that the origins of the recession are global rather than local; and the punters, by a margin of nearly three to one, stubbornly persist in the belief that the bankers rather than Gordon are primarily to blame.

Wednesday, 25 March

Gordon is en route to the Americas to sell his call for a 'global fiscal stimulus' at the G20 summit next month. Unfortunately his clarion call has been somewhat undermined by Bank of England governor Mervyn King's statement yesterday that we cannot afford any more such grand gestures. Music to the ears of the Tories, who made much of it at Questions today. In Gordon's absence, it was left to Harriet to hold the line, which she did with some success, battering Hague with his party's pledge to raise the inheritance tax threshold to a million, thereby benefiting 3,000 of the country's most prosperous citizens to the tune of £2 billion.

Rob Marris and I were joined at lunch in the cafeteria by Douglas Alexander, a close confidant of Gordon's. He asked what was exercising us and we both mentioned the proposed part-privatisation of the Royal Mail. Had it yet been discussed at Cabinet, I inquired. 'Not as such,' replied Douglas. Astonishing.

In the Aye Lobby this evening, Brian Donohoe recounted how Richard Branson had once poured a glass of water over his head at a private dinner for complaining when the Great Entrepreneur had announced, for the umpteenth time, that he was about to purchase new rolling stock for the West Coast line. Some time later, finding himself sitting on in a meeting between the Transport Secretary and Branson, Brian placed a glass of water conspicuously on a table between them and just as Branson was in full flow, raised the glass slowly, nodded towards Richard … and put it to his lips.

Thursday, 26 March

To the *Guardian*'s glassy new palace at King's Cross to record my first ever podcast. On the way out I ran into Duncan Campbell. 'Do you still see Julie?' I inquired, recollecting that Julie Christie had once taken a shine to my Vietnam novel. 'I'm married to her,' he replied.

Saturday, 28 March

'THIS COUNTRY OF FEAR AND ANGER' is the main headline in today's *Daily Mail*. All part of a sales strategy aimed at keeping their readers permanently apoplectic.

More seriously, the billionaire investor George Soros, interviewed in today's *Times*, describes next week's G20 summit as 'a make or break occasion … a last chance to avert disaster'. If it fails, he says, the global trading and financial system could fall apart. Britain, he suggests, is particularly vulnerable. Another trip to the IMF cannot be ruled out. He goes on: 'This is a crisis unlike any other … a total collapse of the financial system with tremendous implications for everyday life … the size of the problem is actually bigger than the 1930s.' Mercifully, he resists the temptation to blame it all on Gordon, saying only that 'he underestimated the severity of the problem, but then so did most people.'

Tonight it was announced that Scotland's biggest building society has gone bust.

Sunday, 29 March

Another great feeding frenzy re Jacqui Smith's expenses, which, apparently, include a claim for two pornographic videos. Her husband, the culprit, has duly owned up, but she must have signed the form and, if she hadn't been claiming on the family home, she wouldn't be in this mess. 'It's good that you are leaving,' Ngoc remarked this evening. 'People hate MPs.'

Tuesday, 31 March

The tabloids are working themselves into a frenzy over our expenses. 'What planet are they on?' (*Mail*); 'Credit Crunch? Not for MPs on £208,000 a year' (*Express*). 'THEY ARE ALL AT IT' (*Mirror* – actually, the only place I've ever worked where they were all at it was Mirror Group Newspapers in the seventies). Much of it is pure lies. The twisting, scheming, malevolent hacks have simply added staff salaries, office rent and all other office costs to our overnight expenses and pretended it is all salary.

Back to London to find an email from the New Labour high command offering, get this, a photo opportunity with Jacqui Smith. What planet are they on?

Wednesday, 1 April

Sunshine, pink blossom, a cloudless sky. The only jarring note, as I walked in from Kennington, a helicopter hovering above Downing Street, where Barack Obama was breakfasting with Gordon. Then to the Treasury in an attempt to persuade Stephen Timms not to let the Inland Revenue evacuate its city centre offices in Sunderland, thereby inflicting gratuitous damage on our fragile economy. He was amiable, but unrelenting. On the way I ran into Douglas Hurd, who said that after my visit to Nigeria in January 2005 the High Commissioner, Richard Gozney, had written to Number 10 saying how well the visit had gone and urging that I be kept on. I wonder if his note was drawn to the attention of The Man? If so, he probably thought that I put Richard up to it, but actually it is the first I have heard of it.

The rulers of the world are assembling in London for the G20 summit. It's being billed as struggle between the fiscal stimulators (Brown, Obama) and the regulators (Sarkozy, Merkel). Everyone agrees that the stakes are high. At times like this Gordon excels. He was on excellent form at Questions today, bashing the Opposition all round the chamber. One can just begin to glimpse the possibility that all may not, after all, be lost.

Thursday, 2 April

The fiscal stimulators appear to have won out at the G20, although not to the extent that Gordon seemed to be hoping for. Also, much talk of cracking down on tax havens and boosting the IMF. Rather less about greening the planet. Some minor rioting in the City. Overall, however, a triumph for Gordon. Even the congenital cynics seem to have been temporarily silenced.

With Sarah to Heathrow, where I put her on a plane for Ho Chi Minh City, via Singapore. A moment I have been dreading. Just about managed to get through without blubbing. She will be gone five months.

Friday, 3 April

An email from Andrew Franklin at Profile to say that he has ordered another reprint of the *Diaries* – the third in 20 days. Where are they all going?

Saturday, 4 April

An ignoramus called Ian Cowie has a full page on the front of the financial section of today's *Telegraph* headed 'Them and us', asserting that the Inland Revenue treats politicians differently from their constituents. Among his many false or misleading assertions is the following: 'Now that the average MP claims £135,000 a year for expenses – yes, that's right, more than five times national average earnings – this means they avoid paying £54,000 a year tax which HMRC would demand from anyone lucky enough to receive such payments.' What he does not say, of course, is that most of this is office costs – staff salaries, rent of office, utility bills etc. – none of which ever touches our bank accounts. In what other profession are staff salaries and office rents regarded as income? How can we counter this blizzard of lies which is gnawing at the very foundations of parliamentary democracy? The trouble is, of course, we have brought so much of it on ourselves that it is now open season.

Tuesday, 7 April

To Manchester, where I delivered an after dinner speech to 200 members of the Political Studies Association. Is this to be my future? A light entertainer.

Easter Sunday, 12 April

A new feeding frenzy brewing, entirely self-inflicted. Damian McBride, one of Gordon's shadowy henchpersons, has been caught attempting to devise some sort of smear campaign against leading Tories. He was gone by nightfall, but I doubt whether his head will be sufficient to appease the mob.

Easter Monday, 13 April

Sure enough the airwaves are thick with demands for a personal apology from Gordon, although there is no evidence that he had anything to do with the misbehaviour of his henchperson. At least not directly. The problem is that, for all his high-minded posturing, everyone knows this is Gordon's *modus operandi*. As someone remarked, there is a dark side to Gordon.

Saturday, 18 April

Alice Mahon, who represented Halifax until the last election, has announced she is leaving the Labour Party after more than 50 years.

She said she had hoped the party would return to its core values under Brown, but it had not turned out that way. The McBride business seems to have been the final straw.

Monday, 20 April

Lunch in the cafeteria, where I was regaled by John Reid with an account of how, as his star rose in the run-up to The Man's retirement, unpleasant stories about him began to appear in the *Mail* and the *Sun*. Then came a call from Rebekah Wade (the then *Sun* editor) ostensibly about other matters, who started quizzing him about the coming leadership election, at one point blurting out, 'Why don't you withdraw then?' At this stage John hadn't declared any intention to run against Gordon and, in the event, he didn't. The implication was clear. The smears would stop, if he let Gordon have a free run.

A subdued mood at this evening's meeting of the parliamentary party. Denis MacShane appealed for colleagues to stop trying to appear holier than thou re expenses. Joan Humble said she had been knocking on doors over the recess and that the public appeared to hate MPs; moreover, party members weren't that keen on us either. The chairman, Tony Lloyd, opened with a ritual denunciation of Damian McBride and called on colleagues to exercise restraint. Alistair Darling gave a little pre-Budget speech, the gist of which was: 'These are difficult times, but we will get through them; at least we have a plan, unlike the Tories.' He was received politely, but without enthusiasm. Nick Raynsford made a plea for future announcements to be confined only to matters on which we could deliver. I asked where the pre-Budget leaking was coming from (all weekend the media have been full of authoritative pronouncements) and was fobbed off with a jokey reference to the diaries. The answer, I suppose, is that these leaks emanate from the same source as most others: Number 10.

Tuesday, 21 April

Gordon has come up with some great new wheeze for sorting out – at a stroke – the great expenses crisis. He's proposing that our second home allowance be abolished and replaced with a *per diem* based on attendance. As people have been quick to point out this is likely to give rise to a whole new genre of scams, à la European Parliament and House of Lords, where members just turn up to sign on and then make a run for it. Bizarrely, Gordon made the announcement on YouTube. He is proposing a vote next week so that a new system can be in place by summer, but I would be surprised if he gets away with it. I fear we are in for a lot more misery before this is resolved.

This evening, a drink on the terrace with Sama Akaki, a Ugandan acquaintance. He brought a copy of the diaries for me to sign. 'If you had written a book like this in Africa,' he said, 'you would either have disappeared or been charged with treason.'

Wednesday, 22 April

Budget day. A budget anticipated like no other in recent history. A last throw of the dice as we confront oblivion. Alistair's delivery was, as ever, low key, but the news was unremittingly grim. All previous estimates are out of the window. He is now predicting that the economy will shrink by 3.5 per cent (as recently as November, he was suggesting only 1 per cent), borrowing is predicted to rise to a shocking 11.9 per cent of GDP and the books are unlikely to balance again for another decade or more. So much for having ended boom and bust. The Tories were surprisingly subdued. As well they might be. This could be their inheritance. Their usual pre-election promises of tax cuts will cut no ice with anyone. The cupboard is bare. Some crumbs here and there. A 50 per cent tax rate for those earning £150,000 and over. A small boost for child care, clean energy and the pensioners' winter fuel allowance, but overall not much sign of the trumpeted fiscal stimulus, for the very good reason that the coffers are empty. Cameron's response ('the government has run out of money and moral authority') was devastating, provided of course that one forgets that this all started with his irresponsible friends in the City. This evening, on the television news, interviews with unemployed youngsters in South Wales, a fifth of whom are without work. Another lost generation beckons. This is where we came in.

Jack Jones has died, aged 96.

Thursday, 23 April

Alistair's Budget attracts a uniformly hostile press. 'Labour's leaving present,' says the headline above a piece by Larry Elliot in the *Guardian*. He goes on: 'This package delivers a poison pill to the next government whoever forms it.' Jonathan Freedland, also in the *Guardian*, writes: 'To see Alistair Darling delivering his budget was like watching a man pushed from a skyscraper, falling calmly, even gracefully ...' The rest of the papers are less elegant. 'They Ruined Britain' (*Express*), 'Alistair in Wonderland' (*Mail*), 'Return of Class War' (*Telegraph*). 'Red all over' (*The Times*). Only the *Sun* ('At least it's sunny') finds anything to smile about.

Friday, 24 April

Sunderland

The regional director of the UK Border Agency rang to say that, after further consideration, he is going ahead with plans to deport the young woman from Benin and her 17-month-old baby. The agency have ceased pretending that she is the person whose name was on the passport she used to enter the country, but they are still insisting she is Nigerian, although she claims never to have set foot there. What will become of her when she steps off that plane in Lagos tomorrow evening? 'We've been in touch with the Nigerian social services,' he said cheerfully. I pointed out that there are virtually no functioning public services in Nigeria, but it cut no ice.

Saturday, 25 April

Official figures suggest a 1.9 per cent fall in GDP in the first quarter of this year, compared to the 1.5 per cent predicted by Alistair as recently as Wednesday, which, as commentators have been quick to point out, doesn't entirely inspire confidence in his other forecasts.

Monday, 27 April

An outbreak of swine flu in Mexico has temporarily distracted the media from their otherwise unrelenting assault on the government. Instead the tabloids vie with each other to scare their readers witless. The *Express*, as ever, is the clear winner, predicting up to 120 million fatalities. Death toll so far: 103.

A visit from M. He remains confident that Obama will abandon 'Star Wars', but stealthily. Cyber wars are apparently the next front line. Already the Pentagon has set up a special unit. The threat comes not from China and Russia (collapsing the economies of the Western world is not in their interests) but from al-Qaeda and assorted franchisees.

Much pissed-off-ness at this evening's meeting of the parliamentary party over Gordon's latest plan for an attendance allowance in lieu of expenses. The whips have managed to persuade him that it is unworkable and a retreat is being hurriedly organised, but only at the cost of several days' bad publicity and, to save face, we are to be forced to vote on a series of other half-baked initiatives. Nick Brown did his best to calm the waters, but there is no mistaking the anger.

Tuesday, 28 April

An exchange with Treasury minister Angela Eagle in the Tea Room about what I regard as the greatest of Gordon's many follies, the decision (in his final Budget) to cut the basic rate of tax, thereby throwing away a cool £9 billion a year in return for no more than a cheap round of applause. 'A last genuflection to bollocks,' said Angela. She added, 'We have come to a fork in the road. There are only two things we can do. Raise taxes or cut services.'

Wednesday, 29 April

Walked in with John Morris,* who remarked, apropos the current morass over allowances, 'Our founding fathers would be turning in their graves.'

---

*Former Secretary of State for Wales and Attorney General, now in the Lords.

In an upper corridor I encountered Doug Hoyle. 'Gordon must go,' he said. 'He's not even talking to his friends and even getting small things wrong.' In response to my protest that the dear old Labour Party never gets rid of failing leaders, Doug responded, 'You can't carry on if you are below 30 per cent in the polls for any length of time. I never thought I'd say it, but I'd go for Alan Johnson.'

For the first time in more than two years I was called at Prime Minister's Questions and took the opportunity to inquire whether this might be the moment to reconsider whether we could afford to spend £20 billion on a new generation of nuclear weapons. This was received with stony silence on the Tory side and only muted hear-hearing on ours. Gordon gave a considered response, not quite ruling it out, but giving no encouragement.

This evening a new crisis: the government was defeated by a Lib Dem motion demanding that Gurkhas and their dependants be given a right of residence in the UK. In vain the immigration minister, Phil Woolas, pointed out that it would cost another £1.4 billion which we could ill afford, that we had more than doubled Gurkha pensions and that in any case we had eased the immigration rules to allow several thousand more into the country. None of which cut any ice. Most sickening was the sight of the Tories, who have ruthlessly and unscrupulously used immigration and asylum against us at every election in recent memory, demanding that Gurkhas and their families be treated as honorary Englishmen and saying how disgracefully the government was treating these brave, loyal soldiers. As Phil Woolas pointed out just five, repeat *five*, Gurkhas were granted British citizenship prior to 1997. The whole thing has been got up by the tabloids and the *Telegraph* – which, ironically, are rabidly opposed to entry for just about every other category of foreigner – and the dreadful Joanna Lumley, who all week has been emoting over our television screens. In the end the government lost by a handful of votes, mainly due to abstentions on our side.

Thursday, 30 April

We spent the day debating our allowances (never an edifying spectacle at the best of times). Gordon's plan for an attendance allowance has been quietly junked, but we are to press ahead with votes on other less controversial reforms, without waiting for Sir Christopher Kelly to report. The Speaker was persuaded not to call an amendment, proposing that decisions be left to the Kelly inquiry, and, as a result, the government motions were duly carried by large majorities, allowing the whips to claim massive triumph. Though, in truth, it was all about saving Gordon from himself. Meanwhile the fall-out continues from yesterday's defeat on the Gurkhas, which is being presented by the Tories and their friends in the media as yet more evidence of Gordon's crumbling authority, whereas actually it was a cock-up by the whips, who failed to realise how many of our colleagues had allowed themselves to be intimidated by tabloid skinheads.

Friday, 1 May

Blow me down. Today's papers report that Cameron is tentatively thinking of abandoning Trident or least cutting back on it.

Sunday, 3 May

We are imploding. Everyone running round like headless chickens. Charles Clarke is being quoted as saying that he is 'ashamed' to be a Labour MP, David Blunkett is making speeches alleging that we lack any social policy and this morning Hazel Blears is all over the papers with her prescription for recovery, which is, of course, being interpreted as an attack on Gordon – to which she has had to issue a hasty denial. To crown all, Paddy Ashdown is alleging that senior New Labourites are threatening to defect to the Lib Dems, were Labour (in Opposition) to lurch too far leftwards. If we carry on like this, catastrophe beckons.

Tuesday, 5 May

A brief chat with the Chief Whip, Nick Brown, who complained that he is being briefed against for his alleged failure to be robust over the part-privatisation of the Royal Mail (he has apparently informed Gordon that the policy is unsaleable – at least to Labour members). 'Where is the pressure coming from?' I inquired.

'Us. The management and the unions are fine. It's coming from the government. I am told we need the money, but it's only half a billion and frankly we could print that.' As Steve Byers pointed out later in the Tea Room, we won't get much for it given the current state of the markets. Steve also revealed that The Man is lobbying hard to be Euro president and has a good chance of getting it. Amazing, just as New Labour sinks beneath the waves The Man is reborn as King of Europe.

Later, I talked to John Denham, who confirmed that there has been no recent discussion in Cabinet of our plans for the Royal Mail. Gordon's foolish plan for an attendance allowance had apparently been run past the Cabinet – in Glasgow the other week; several people had asked questions, but no one said it wasn't a good idea. That's a large part of the problem: no real debate at Cabinet. A trend that began under Blair, or was it Thatcher?

Finally, an exchange with Jim Cousins. 'We are in meltdown. It's going to be worse than '83. We're going down not with a bang, but with a whimper. There *is* a big political case to be made against Gordon, but nobody's making it. It's all so personal and trivial.'

Wednesday, 6 May

Poor Gordon took another battering at PMQs today – and all so personal. You could see it was getting to him. The question that really got under the wire was the suggestion that he's been blowing his top at Number 10 switchboard operators and officials. At the end he just picked up his papers and stormed out without so much as a nod to anyone. Afterwards I went over to Millbank to record a piece for the BBC's *Week in Westminster*. Of course, it was all about Gordon and whether or not he will survive. I was very loyal and insisted that he would, but to my surprise George Mudie, who I had always taken to be in Gordon's camp, thought that there was a chance he would go of his own accord were he to encounter 'a perfect storm' – a combination of catastrophic Euro election results and defeat over the Royal Mail might, he suggested, be the catalyst.

Afterwards, George described how a few weeks back he and a handful of Friends of Gordon had been invited to Number 10, thinking they were being asked for advice, but when they got there they soon realised that he wasn't looking for advice, only help in ramming through whatever ill-thought-out initiative he was currently grappling with. 'It's like trying to help an alcoholic,' said George. 'You can only help someone who wants to be helped.'

Thursday, 7 May

A friendly letter re the diaries from Richard Mottram, the former Permanent Secretary at the Transport Department, re the Martin Sixsmith affair and the fall of Steve Byers about which he was memorably quoted. He disputes my suggestion* that Steve's downfall may have had to do with misinformation from officials. 'There was no misinformation by officials. Rather it was possibly a case of a certain New Labour style to leak Sixsmith's resignation and then choose to confirm it in TV studios, even though it had yet to be finalised. From that moment on we were wrong-footed. Perhaps that might be why, as Stephen headed for the TV studios, I uttered to a "colleague" five expletives in quick succession.'

Friday, 8 May
Sunderland

A massive new feeding frenzy. The *Telegraph* has got its hands on a computer disc of our unexpurgated expenses and this morning it has begun publishing highlights. Page after unedifying page. Naturally, the *Telegraph* is claiming public interest, even though the whole lot

---

A View from the Foothills, pp. 261 and 286.

was due to be published anyway in a couple of months. Needless to say, they have begun with Labour members, and prominent ones at that, and much more is promised over the next few days. The damage is incalculable. Not just to us, but to the entire parliamentary system. We are sinking in a great swamp of derision and loathing. No matter that the guardians of public morality at the *Telegraph* appear to have paid a large – and so far undisclosed – sum of money for discs that appear to have been stolen, open season has been declared on us wretched, despised servants of the people.

Saturday, 9 May

The *Telegraph* is continuing its unrelenting assault and most, but not quite, all the media are joining in. So far, with one minor exception, only Labour Members have been targeted and there is an air of banality and overspin about some of the allegations. One or two of the more perceptive commentators are beginning to question whether or not the pudding is being over-egged, but there is no doubting the overall impact.

Sunday, 10 May

On the evening news, the first indication that the *Telegraph* is at last preparing to turn its attention to the Tories. First up, Oliver Letwin, who apparently claimed £2,000 to install a drainage pipe under his tennis court. As Nick Robinson remarked, 'The political class have lost control of this story. No one knows where it's going.'

Monday, 11 May

To Westminster. Entire place traumatised. No one talking about anything but expenses. The Speaker gave a right bollocking to Kate Hoey and Norman Baker for allegedly colluding with our oppressors in the media. A good five minutes' worth. I've never seen him so worked up. Actually it was way over the top. Gave the impression he is rattled, which I imagine he is.

To a jam-packed meeting of the parliamentary party. Chairman Tony Lloyd opened with a little pep talk, remarking that there was 'a duty on us collectively not to give in to despair'. (Yes, that's how bad it is.) Then Gordon, eyes half closed with fatigue, spoke. This was Gordon like I've never seen him before. He spoke with real passion. As good as Blair at his best, coming out fighting. While acknowledging that we had to clean up our act, he spoke of 'a deliberate campaign of distortion' and he went on, 'A year from now what people will remember is whether a Labour government was able to take us through the economic crisis. What's being tested is not just me, but the strength of our beliefs. We have to prove that we are worthy.' He sat down to a thunderous, heartfelt standing ovation, entirely spontaneous. Anyone who thinks Gordon will go quietly, however rough the going gets, is badly mistaken.

Tuesday, 12 May

For the second day running the spotlight is on the Tories. Not for them sordid little claims for bath plugs or plasma TVs. No, they've been at it on an altogether different scale, with outrageous claims for repairs to tennis courts, swimming pools, housekeepers and even a suggestion that Douglas Hogg claimed for cleaning out his moat. The papers are suddenly full of pictures of Home Counties mansions set in acres of manicured lawns, straight out of *Country Life*, allegedly maintained at taxpayers' expense. Proof, in case anyone has forgotten, that the class divide is alive and well. A reporter from the BBC has even had fun surveying the Tory estates by helicopter. We laugh, but it is dragging us all down.

Lunch with My Friend in High Places. She says Gordon has been behaving better of late, but he is still the same exhausted, tantrum-prone, hyperactive Gordon. 'The debate among those around him is whether he is basically a good man who feels obliged to do bad things in the interests of the greater good or whether ...'

Damian McBride's departure, she says, has left a gap. McBride was good at dreaming up stories to feed to the hacks, 'otherwise they start inventing stuff. They were a big embarrassment on the recent

Washington trip, pumping out "Obama snubs Gordon" stories. The White House couldn't believe it.'

'Why not leave them at home?' I suggested.

'Because they would start saying the Prime Minister's never here, always travelling etc.'

A long, sad, whispered conversation with Defence Secretary John Hutton, who has decided not to contest the next election, which means he will have to stand down come the reshuffle in a few weeks. 'I'm in a job I love,' he says, 'but I can't go on.' Like most of us he sees electoral catastrophe looming and believes Labour will be led into the wilderness for a generation – or perhaps for ever – under someone like John Cruddas or Harriet Harman ('I'm not even sure I'd vote Labour if Harriet became leader'). The New Labourites, he reckons, will not hang around. Realignment – a pact with the Lib Dems is even a possibility. Gordon, he says, is obsessed with conspiracies. 'Forcing Tony Blair out was the stupidest thing we ever did.'

Whole place sunk in gloom. Pleasure at the latest revelations about Tory excesses is tempered by the knowledge that we are all vulnerable. Once the national media lose interest the local papers will start. Already the *Journal* is ringing round North-East Members, asking us to volunteer our expense claims in advance of publication so they can trawl through them at leisure, picking us off one by one.

Wednesday, 13 May

Payback time. A bidding war has broken out between the main parties to see who can display the most repentance. Cameron (who has himself repaid the cost of having his wisteria trimmed – Tory excesses are so much more elegant than ours) is leading the field with an ultimatum to eight of his Shadow Cabinet that they repay the cost of maintaining their tennis courts, swimming pools, moats etc. – or else … On our side Hazel Blears (who surely will not survive the coming reshuffle) has agreed that she will, after all, be paying capital gains on one of her several former residences and tonight an ever so 'umble Phil Hope announced he would be repaying a staggering £40,000 – the record so far.

Thursday, 14 May

To Clarence House, to be entertained to drinks and a stand-up lunch by the Prince of Wales. Fellow guests included a number of Tory grandees (Nick Soames, James Arbuthnot, George Young, Bernard Jenkin – the latter two and their spouses arriving by bicycle). The fate of Speaker Martin was much discussed. A definite mood on the Tory side that he must go. My instinct thus far has been that, woefully inadequate though he is, we must not allow the media to bring him down, but I begin to wonder if the line can be held. Undoubtedly the plates are shifting. A couple of brief exchanges with HRH. He remarked that he had recently encountered a woman who shouted, 'Abolish the monarchy', and had only just restrained himself from replying, 'Fine – then I can run for president.' One can't help feeling that he would prefer that to being king. In the current climate he'd walk it and then at least he would have a mandate.

I strolled back through the park with Kate Hoey. 'A pity you are standing down,' she said. 'You'd make an excellent Speaker.'

To my astonishment today's roll call of The Fallen includes Elliot Morley, who appears to have been charging for a mortgage that was long ago repaid.

Friday, 15 May

Sunderland

A couple of hours touring Alex Smiles's recycling plant, which processes 40 per cent of our domestic waste, but the rest still goes to landfill. Plastic, he says, remains the big challenge. The more I learn, the more it dawns that coping with waste is one of the great challenges – perhaps the greatest – of the twenty-first century and we are not yet winning.

This evening's *Echo* highlights the expenses of local MPs. The only figures mentioned are the London allowance totals for last year, which show me in a good light, my claim being just over half that of my neighbours. There is also an editorial remarking on my general saintliness. I derive no satisfaction. We are all vulnerable in this climate.

I scribbled a note to Elliot Morley, who, whatever his sins, is a decent man and was an excellent minister. 'Remember,' I wrote, 'you are not short of friends.'

Monday, 18 May

Growing crisis re Speaker Martin. This afternoon he stumbled through a statement saying he was 'profoundly sorry' for the mess we are in and acknowledging his part in it. Then Douglas Carswell, the Tory backwoodsman who has tabled a motion of no confidence, rose and demanded that time be made available for a debate. 'It's not a substantive motion,' the Speaker replied. 'Oh yes it is,' came voices from all sides. Extraordinary. I've never seen the Speaker heckled before. One after another, Members rose to demand a debate. The Speaker consulted the clerks and said that only the government could table a substantive motion. Sir Stuart Bell rose. Always a bad moment since his interventions invariably dig the pit deeper. 'A majority of Members will support your statement, Mr Speaker,' but this attracted only mild hear-hearing (all from the Labour side). Sir Patrick Cormack, without whom no great occasion is complete, compared the mood in the country to that at the time of the Norway debate in 1940. The Speaker, unlike last week and despite considerable provocation, responded calmly, but there is no doubt that the mood is ugly. It was like watching Ceauşescu's final appearance, when the crowd turned against him.

Later, to a packed meeting of the parliamentary party. Everyone traumatised, awaiting a call from the *Daily Telegraph*. This weekend's revelations include the news that Gerald Kaufman had claimed an outrageous £8,500 for a Bang and Olufsen television 'home cinema' and Ian McCartney, whose working-class origins are impeccable, has claimed for champagne flutes.

Frank Dobson was first up. 'Be warned,' he said. 'The Lib Dems and the Tories have not abandoned party politics.' There was, he alleged, a three-part strategy. When they had disposed of the Speaker, they would demand Gordon's resignation. If they got that, they would demand an immediate general election on the grounds that we couldn't have yet another Labour leader without an electoral mandate.

'And anyone who thinks that an immediate general election would be of benefit to the people who voted us in is not on this planet.' He sat down to applause.

Gordon was received warmly. For the first time since the crisis began, he appears to have a plan. First, he said, we had to support each other – the party would make available legal and financial advice for colleagues in trouble; there would also be help in handling the media. Second, we had to show ourselves worthy of public trust. No more excuses. We have to clean up the system. There would be an independent examination of the last four years' claims and those that were found to be unjustified would have to be repaid. In the meantime, there would have to be limits on what could be claimed. Finally, we had to abandon self-regulation, which was no longer credible. 'There is no other way,' he said. 'We are being tested as never before.' At last, some leadership. We went away mildly cheered.

Tuesday, 19 May

To a crowded chamber to hear the Speaker announce his resignation. A short, dignified statement lasting all of 30 seconds and then back to business as usual. Except, of course, that there is nothing usual about today's business. The place is buzzing. Some of our number regard what has happened as a coup by the Tories and the media.

Re the succession, names in the frame include Alan Beith, Vince Cable, Ming Campbell, Frank Field, Alan Haselhurst, Ann Widdecombe, George Young and, most remarkable of all, John Bercow, who many on our side favour as a way of getting back at the Tories. 'It's got to be someone younger and untainted,' remarked Steve Byers, who favours Bercow. A brief exchange with Alan Milburn, who reckons its all over ('We're fucked, utterly fucked') and that all that remains is to nail down what can be nailed down and plant the odd booby trap.

I should also report that one other wildly improbable name has been mentioned: *moi*. 'Mr Speaker Mullin,' called BBC political correspondent Nick Robinson as I was on the phone in the Members' Lobby and when I laughed he said, 'Several people have mentioned your name.' And tonight, on *Newsnight*, Jeremy Paxman asked if I was running. I can't, of course, because in a little while I will be gone …

Wednesday, 20 May

The Paxman interview has set a hare running. North-East media very excited. Apparently the story has been on the local radio all day. Ngoc reports that teachers in Emma's school were talking about it, also the nurse at the clinic when she took Emma for her injections. Several encouraging emails. Actually, although a long shot, it is not an impossible dream. Or at least it wouldn't be were I staying. The field is not so strong. The Tories aren't at all keen on Bercow and our lot won't have Frank Field. Vince Cable, who would walk it, has ruled himself out. Alan Haselhurst, who performed brilliantly when he stood in when Michael was ill, has had trouble with expenses. George Young, who I favour, is regarded by many as too establishment. Most people seem to think we need a break with the past. Undoubtedly, there is a gap in the market.

Lunch in the cafeteria with Douglas Alexander, who I like more every time I see him. He says Jack (Straw) was the best minister he ever worked for 'because he knew how to delegate and he treated fellow ministers as politicians and not as underlings'. Even after 12 years at the top, says Douglas, Jack is not jaded or cynical; his appetite for government remains undimmed

The *Telegraph* reports that I claimed for a black-and-white TV licence, which has been the subject of much amusement among colleagues, many of whom dwell in the world of plasma screens.

Today's tabloids are particularly vicious. Not for them magnanimity in victory. 'Arise Lord Gorbals', sneers the front page of the *Mail* over a story focusing on the size of the Speaker's pension.

Thursday, 21 May

Sure enough, having disposed of the Speaker, the Tory media have launched a campaign for a snap election – exactly as Frank Dobson predicted. The *Sun* is leading the charge with a coupon demanding an immediate election which readers are invited to cut out and send to Gordon. It couldn't be more blatant.

This evening, as I was departing, I ran into Chief Whip Nick Brown. 'Between you and me,' I said, 'given that we are going to lose the election, we ought to be planting a few booby traps.' I had in mind a few modest measures such as the election of select committee chairmen.

'I think we've done that with the PSBR,' replied Nick, smiling wickedly.

Friday, 22 May

Awoke to hear Tory MP Nadine Dorries on the radio predicting a suicide or two if the hysteria continues.

The *Telegraph*'s revelation (as part of its expenses probe) that I still possess a 30-year-old black-and-white TV has provided a little light relief from the usual shock horror. A full page in today's *Mail* and a friendly leader in the *Guardian*: 'At a time when the political class is so discredited, it is worth recalling those like Mr Mullin who do some good. What a shame he steps down at the next election.' Indeed.

Wednesday, 27 May

The bidding war continues, each leader striving to prove he is more in command than his rivals. Today the unctuous Nick Clegg is proposing that errant MPs be subject to instant recall – a recipe for tabloid rabble rousing if ever there was.

Thursday, 28 May

Two more heads have rolled: Julie Kirkbride and Margaret Moran have announced they will be stepping down come the election.

Friday, 29 May

Like the Big Brother house we wake up each day and turn on our television set to see who is in danger of eviction. Today's candidate is Bill Cash, who has been renting a flat from his daughter, but assuming he has been paying no more than the market rent, it is hard to see how the taxpayer is out of pocket. He didn't sound all that repentant.

Monday, 1 June

Day 24 of the *Telegraph* assault on the political classes. Today they are leading with a new attack on Alistair Darling. Apparently he claimed for a service charge, paid in advance, on his flat in Kennington shortly before moving to Number 11 Downing Street. The suggestion being that he should have remembered to repay the money. As if he didn't have one or two other things on his mind, given that he'd just been made Chancellor of the Exchequer. Nevertheless, the *Telegraph* are making a meal of it. This looks like an attempt to bring him down. It is rumoured that Gordon is lining up Ed Balls to replace him.

As I walked in through Speaker's Court, who should I see but The Man, looking tanned and fit, surrounded by bag carriers and bodyguards. Just like old times. He must be glad to be out of it. Even his considerable skills couldn't dig us out of the big, dark pit into which we have fallen.

Awful scenes at tonight's party meeting. Barry Sheerman started with a long rant, demanding to know why no one had consulted us about this latest batch of initiatives (Gordon is talking codes of conduct, electoral reform etc.). A fair point, but he did go on. Before long everyone was at it. Someone demanded the head of the man in charge of the Fees Office. Several people complained of feeling isolated and abandoned. Jim Dowd started heckling Harriet Harman, who occupies a neighbouring constituency, for allegedly showing him up. A woman from Wales, voice trembling, treated us to a rambling account of the trouble she'd got into over furniture. On and on they went. So much so that the meeting had to be extended by half an hour. I've never seen such demoralisation. We are a besieged subculture. Everyone looking for someone to blame, except of course ourselves. ('Nobody loves us and it's all their fault,' one wag behind me whispered.) Harriet (who has performed well throughout this crisis) did her best to calm things down: 'If we start arguing among ourselves, we will not get through this.' Here and there shafts of light. 'Stop all this whingeing,' said Gisela Stuart. 'It's not just a Labour crisis, it's a Tory one, too. Our constituents just want MPs who don't fiddle their expenses.'

Ian Davison, in a rare moment of levity, inquired, 'Where did all this constitutional reform shite come from?'

Malcolm Wicks said, 'The survival of the party is the big issue, not whether or not we win the election.'

Dennis Skinner claimed to detect a faint hope of victory, if only we could get on to the economy and off our expenses. 'I plead with the people at the top table,' he said. 'We cannot, should not, be talking about this issue.'

The difficulty is, of course, that no one inside or outside the Westminster village wants to talk about anything else.

Tuesday, 2 June

The wheels are coming off. This morning it was confirmed that Jacqui Smith will be standing down as Home Secretary come the reshuffle, which is feverishly anticipated as soon as the Euro elections are out of the way. No great surprise, but how come it leaked out now? A little while later Beverley Hughes announced that she, too, would be standing down. A surprise, given that she is so far unscathed by the expenses meltdown and might reasonably have expected preferment. Then Tom Watson in the Cabinet Office announced that he, too, would be leaving the government and Patricia Hewitt let it be known that she would not be contesting the election. As if all that wasn't enough, the 'Star Chamber' set up by the Labour Party National Executive announced that four of the big expenses offenders would not be permitted to contest the next election – three going quietly, but Ian Gibson, who still has the backing of his party, protested loudly and is threatening an immediate by-election.

A chat with Larry Elliot (economics editor of the *Guardian*). Interestingly, he sees definite signs of green shoots. The stock market is rising, the banks and the housing market have stabilised. 'The measures taken last autumn have stopped an immediate crisis.' The downside is that he reckons it may not be sustainable. 'None of the domestic policy instruments in place will prevent a repetition in three years' time.' He added that the government's core economic message is that 'Tory cuts will be bigger than ours.' Not a very encouraging basis for election victory. He reckons the Tories will put up tax – probably VAT – as soon as they are in, just as Geoffrey Howe did in 1980.

Rumours that unnamed backbenchers are organising a round robin letter calling on Gordon to go. Treat with caution. The last time this happened – when Blair was looking wobbly – it turned out to have been concocted by the media.

Wednesday, 3 June

An editorial in today's *Guardian* calling on Gordon to go. Meanwhile the Cabinet seems to be reshuffling itself, without waiting for Gordon. Today Hazel Blears announced her resignation. Exquisite timing (one day before Euro elections) from this so-called ultra-loyalist, but then she has had the black spot on her ever since she had to cough up £13,000 in unpaid Capital Gains Tax to the Inland Revenue. Inevitably, her departure – along with yesterday's others – have triggered a huge media frenzy about Gordon's future. My guess is he will survive, but it is touch and go. Removing him by force would be very messy and leave us with embittered henchpersons wandering about causing trouble. Talking of which, people are asking why the *Telegraph* has been having a second bash at Alistair Darling. Is he being briefed against with a view to installing Ed Balls at the Treasury? Surely they can't still be at it.

'What's your majority?' I asked a colleague.

'It's 6,100'.

'Iffy,' I gently suggested.

'I'm past caring,' she replied.

Came across Ann Coffey, Alistair Darling's PPS, in the Library Corridor. 'Tell Alistair to stay put,' I said. 'He's been an excellent Chancellor and Gordon isn't strong enough to move him.' She undertook to pass the message.

Still no sign of the rumoured 'Gordon must go' letter that's supposed to be doing the rounds, though the hacks are asking people if they've signed.

Thursday, 4 June

Sunderland

Euro election day. Huge slaughter anticipated, although the results will not be known until the weekend.

A call from the *Mail on Sunday*. 'Would you like to write a piece on the poisonous atmosphere at Westminster?' I laughingly pointed out that they are not short of staffers who have devoted their lives to doing precisely that and they don't need any help from me.

Also a spoof email, purporting to be from Alistair Darling, inviting me to sign up to a 'Gordon must go' campaign. Someone has even gone to the trouble of setting up an Alistair Darling mailbox to receive replies. My guess is that this is a Sunday newspaper sting. I doubt any of our number will fall for it, but you never know.

This evening, no sooner had polls closed than up pops Barry Sheerman demanding that Gordon stand down. Minutes later comes word that Work and Pensions Secretary James Purnell has resigned, leaving behind a message calling on Gordon to go. At least he had the decency to wait until the election was over. How much more of this can we take?

Friday, 5 June

Awoke to hear Paul Farrelly, the backbencher fingered by Number 10 as being behind the 'Gordon must go' round robin, indignantly denying that he had anything to do with it. So far nobody has taken up James Purnell's challenge, but the day is young ...

Much anger re expenses at this evening's meeting of the local party. Several people demanded that errant MPs be prosecuted until I pointed out that several cases had already been referred to the police. At which point they switched to demanding that they be sacked, until I pointed out that this would leave us with a number of tricky by-elections. Someone suggested we pass a motion in support of Gordon, but no one could think of anywhere to send it, so the idea was dropped. One member remarked afterwards that every other person she met during a recent bout of door knocking was complaining about Gordon.

Home to discover that Caroline Flint has flounced out of the government, complaining that she'd been used as window dressing. Only last night she was featured on the evening news bulletins swearing undying loyalty.

Saturday, 6 June

After days of angst the deckchairs on the *Titanic* have finally been rearranged. Alistair Darling is staying put at the Treasury, having successfully faced down Gordon's shameless attempt to replace him with Ed Balls. Peter Mandelson will henceforth be known as the 'First Secretary', which means he is effectively deputy prime minister. Incredibly, he has found a way of making himself indispensable – again, although one must reluctantly acknowledge his talents are considerable and urgently needed. Alan Johnson becomes Home Secretary. Bob Ainsworth replaces John Hutton at Defence and Peter Hain returns as Welsh Secretary. Among the departures ('for personal reasons') are Margaret Beckett, our safest pair of hands, Geoff Hoon (tipped to be our next EU Commissioner) and Tony McNulty, who has much explaining to do re his expenses.

I should also mention Alan Sugar has been appointed 'Enterprise Tsar' in place of the unlamented Digby Jones. Another classic piece of Gordon gimmickry which will inevitably backfire. Whatever next? Susan Boyle for culture minister?

Sunday, 7 June

Nick Raynsford was on television this morning calling for Gordon to go. A sure sign that the plates are moving if someone like Nick, a man of sound judgement and natural caution, thinks the game is up.

Tonight's Euro election results produced the predicted meltdown. Labour polled a derisory 15 per cent, beaten into third place by UKIP. In Wales we came in behind the Tories for the first time since 1918. On this showing, or anything resembling it, we face annihilation come the general election unless we can persuade the nation to talk about something other than our expenses and the character of our leader. It's not that the Tories are popular. It's just that we're so hopeless. Damage limitation, not victory, is all we can reasonably hope for. We need to do something bold that will strike a blow behind enemy lines, such as switching from first-past-the-post to alternative voting. The Tories, of course, would cry 'foul', but the Lib Dems could probably be persuaded to back it, all the while protesting that they prefer some purer form of PR. It might easily find favour with the public, many of whom are nervous about governments with unfairly large majorities. We would need a referendum, of course. That could be held in the autumn and, if it goes our way, a Bill could be through by spring. Who better to promote it than the new Home Secretary, Alan Johnson? The fact that he has always favoured electoral reform should protect us from charges of opportunism. It won't save us from defeat, but it might save us from ruin.

Monday, 8 June

Alan Milburn was on the train, firmly of the view that Gordon must go. 'We're in a pit and still digging,' he said. By the time we reached London, another minister – Jane Kennedy – had gone.

In the library I came across Tom Watson, Gordon's amiable henchperson, who has just vacated his job in the heart of government. 'Why?' I inquired.

'My wife,' he said. 'The final straw was when the *Sun* went through my waste bins. All they found was a lot of dirty nappies, but for her that was it.'

Then to a jam-packed party meeting, billed by some as the final chance for a showdown. The corridor outside was crammed with lobby journalists and even a couple of Tories observing from a discreet distance. The entire Cabinet was jammed into the space behind the platform, Peter Mandelson in pole position just behind Gordon, scribbling away as usual. Harriet Harman (who has had a good crisis) looking fresh as a daisy in contrast to Ed Balls, the man who would be Chancellor, looking bleary-eyed and miserable. Beyond him, upbeat and cheerful as ever, Neil Kinnock, a man who knows a thing or two about leadership crises.

Gordon, it must be said, was looking remarkably relaxed considering the storms that rage around him. He was greeted with warm applause (Mandelson glancing round carefully to see who was not participating). He spoke calmly and confidently, right hand in trouser pocket, scarcely glancing at his notes. If only the public could see him like this. There was a note of humility. 'I have my strengths and I have my weaknesses. I know I need to improve. There are some things I do well and others not so well. I know I have got to keep learning. I've learned we need the talents of everyone.' Hastily adding, for avoidance of doubt, 'I've learned something else. When you've got a problem, you don't solve it by walking away, you solve it by facing it.' He called for unity. 'I am not making a plea, but an argument. When we are divided we lose. Unlike times past, there are no great ideological differences between us. Not one resignation letter that I have seen mentioned a policy difference. I'm not coming here begging for unity for my sake, but because we have a common purpose.' He sat down to much applause and banging on table tops.

Some courageous contributions from the ranks. A mixture of pleas for unity and calls for Gordon to go. By and large all sides were heard respectfully, though Charles Clarke, who has shot his bolt once too often, attracted some mild heckling. 'The country has not made up its mind about Cameron,' said former minister Tom Harris, 'but it has made up it's mind about you.'

Fiona Mactaggart said bluntly, 'Unity is not the problem, Gordon. The problems are integrity and authenticity. I don't believe you when you say you've learned the lessons ...'

David Blunkett, pleaded for an end to blood-letting, but added, 'Please engage with people with whom you don't necessarily agree.' It sounded like a job application, but someone said he had been made an offer and turned it down.

Frank Dobson repeated his warning of three weeks ago that we should be under no illusion: the real goal of the Tories and their friends in the media was an immediate general election 'and anyone who thinks we would benefit from that needs care in the community'.

Many of the pleas for loyalty were conditional. Several people called for plans to part-privatise the Royal Mail to be abandoned (surely Gordon's got that message by now?), others remarked that unity was a two-way street. Margaret Beckett, who, it appears, resigned after being refused a place in the Cabinet (another massive misjudgement on Gordon's part), prefaced her support for him by remarking, 'I am uniquely qualified to agree with Gordon that he doesn't get everything right.'

There was a moment of light relief when Geraldine Smith, who urged support for Gordon, added, 'Something extraordinary has happened. I am learning to love Peter Mandelson.' This drew laughter from all save the maestro himself, who, looking up from his notes, permitted a wan smile briefly to cross his otherwise pallid visage.

Last up, in what was clearly a piece of choreography, was Neil Kinnock, who spoke of 'a permanent, immovable truth – in politics disunity attracts the death penalty. People will say, "If they can't govern themselves, how can they run the country?" What you see tonight is a man who has endured a firestorm, the likes of which none of us have ever experienced ...' He was just launching into rhetorical full flow when the chairman asked him to wind up.

By now it was clear that Gordon was safe, but it was a close-run thing. If Johnson or Miliband had jumped ship, the game would have been well and truly up. The hope is that we can make it to the summer recess without any more self-inflicted calamities. After that, who knows?

Tuesday, 9 June

To Simpson's-in-the-Strand, where, along with Paddy Ashdown and Charles Glass, I addressed 250 well-heeled Home Counties pensioners at an *Oldie* literary lunch. 'Gordon must go,' whispered Paddy as we hovered in reception. 'He's damaging the government, the party and himself.' Back at the House I ran into Charlie Falconer, who is saying the same, adding, 'There is a blackness about Gordon.'

This evening Iain Duncan Smith put his head round my door, wanting me to sign a motion urging that the Speaker be given power to control the parliamentary timetable. So far the only declared candidates are Alan Beith and John Bercow, though George Young is beavering away discreetly in the background. Iain says that Bercow has no support whatever on the Tory side and that, if he is elected, they will simply remove him if and when they form a government. He agreed that the difficulty with George, though he would make an excellent Speaker, is that he will be seen as an establishment shoo-in – and an Old Etonian to boot – just when the public are crying out for change.

Wednesday, 10 June

Hilary Armstrong drew my attention to a wickedly funny cartoon in today's *Times* entitled 'New Cabinet Meets', depicting an outsize Peter Mandelson clad in what appears to be an olive green Mao suit, stroking a large white cat with Gordon's features seated on his lap, and poking out higgledy-piggledy from around him the tiny figures of Harman, Balls, Cooper, Darling, Straw, Johnson and Miliband. Hilary, who is usually cautious, remarked that James Purnell had gone with dignity and that Hazel Blears had gone because she was being briefed against. She added, 'Half the new Cabinet don't believe what they are saying and the public know that.'

Gordon, it must be said, was on good form at Question time, having been dealt a winning hand by the Tory health spokesman, Chris Grayling, who let slip on the radio this morning that the Tories are planning 10 per cent cuts across the board with the only exceptions health and international development. Thus armed, Gordon bashed Cameron around the chamber and, for once, came out on top. He followed this with a statement outlining a blizzard of initiatives designed to clean up expenses and reform Parliament and even the electoral system itself. It was classic Gordon, four or five closely typed pages, read at breakneck speed, a mixture of the practical and the wildly impractical. Is he serious or was it intended merely as a distraction from our – or, more precisely, his – present woes? I pointed out that, if we want to regain public confidence, there was one simple measure we could adopt at once – September sittings – putting an end to the Gladstonian summer recesses we continue to award ourselves. This prompted a note from Jack Straw (who it must be said is the sole member of the government sympathetic to September sittings) pointing out that in Gladstone's day the recess stretched from early August to February.

This evening, to dinner in Wimbledon with James and Margaret Curran. Among the other guests, David Cowling, a pollster working for the BBC, who said that, contrary to what most of the commentariat are suggesting, there is still every chance of a hung parliament. The Tory share of the vote in the recent Euro elections had gone down, and they only did well because the Labour vote had collapsed.

Thursday, 11 June

The race for the Speaker has suddenly come to life with the announcement by Margaret Beckett that she will stand. Ann Widdecombe has also joined in. The Tories are desperate to stop John Bercow, who some think already has enough support on our side to carry off the prize on the first ballot. My instinct, thus far, is to back George Young.

Saturday, 13 June

Sunderland

David Miliband is all over the media this morning saying that he considered leaving the government last week. Do we really need to know this? Surely he could have saved it for his memoirs? We need to shut up and start governing.

Called at Boots for a bottle of Listerine. 'Will you be putting in a bill for that?' inquired the young woman on the till. 'Only joking,' she added hastily, but of course she wasn't.

Sunday, 14 June

Sunshine. We lunched in the garden. I cut the hedge, picked up the rubbish in the street and visited our neighbour, Millie Brodie, who is visibly fading. She doesn't get many visitors, having outlived most her contemporaries and having no children or close relatives. She sits all day alone in her big room in the nursing home in Mowbray Close, her eyesight, hearing and perennial optimism gradually failing, but a little flame still flickers.

Monday, 15 June

To the Attlee Suite in Portcullis House to listen to the candidates for the Speakership. They all spoke well enough, but no one argued convincingly for prising this place free of the tentacles of the executive. I asked what they would do about our 80-day summer recess, which I regard as a litmus test of how seriously we take ourselves. Ann Widdecombe said she would explain to our constituents that we were really working, but we've tried that and no one believes us. A couple of others talked half-heartedly of 'rebalancing' the parliamentary timetable, but no one gave a commitment to September sittings. Naive of me to inquire, I suppose, given that any such promise would probably be fatal to a candidate's chances, with our deeply ingrained habit of voting for our own convenience over the public interest.

Later, at the party meeting, Jim Sheridan complained about the self-indulgent interviews given by Mandelson and Miliband in the weekend press. 'If members of the Cabinet have nothing constructive to say, then would they please shut up,' he said to mild hear-hearing.

Tuesday, 16 June

This morning, a magnificent outburst from Nicholas Soames. 'Can we stop calling this place a gentlemen's club? I run a gentlemen's club which has been in existence since 1712 and, if it was run the way this place is run, it would have died 200 years ago.'

John Bercow, Margaret Beckett and George Young are emerging as the front runners in the race to be Speaker. Bercow is engaging and energetic, but suffers from the near-fatal weakness that he has virtually no support on his own side, which is precisely why many of our lot are proposing to vote for him. As for Margaret, no one doubts that she could do the job, but she is no reformer and has only recently emerged from 30 years (in government and opposition) in the warm bosom of the executive. Which leaves George Young, a Tory gent of the old school – honourable, fair-minded, firmly on the side of Parliament and acceptable to all sides. If we'd had the sense to elect him last time we might not be in our current mess. Of course he is vulnerable to the charge that he is an Eton-educated toff, but it speaks volumes that his children were educated at comprehensive schools. As my old friend Joan Maynard used to say, 'It's not where you are coming from that counts – it's where you are going to.' I have nominated him.

Wednesday, 17 June

A talk on the telephone with Rupert Hanson, who has been diagnosed with terminal cancer and has only weeks to live. Rupert is close to the top of my little pantheon of local heroes. A man of enormous energy and infectious optimism, he has made a huge impact on the cultural life of Sunderland. Despite his dire prognosis he still managed to sound positive and upbeat as ever, making plans to keep his various orchestras going after he has gone. I count it an honour to have known him.

For the third week running Gordon came out on top at Questions today. Cameron made the mistake of conceding that there is a recession across Europe (and not just in the UK, as the Tories have been pretending for months), triggering huge cheers and cries of 'More' on our side. It was also Speaker Martin's last appearance and he read out a long, somewhat bitter valedictory statement, followed by tributes, some of which had a hollow ring given recent events, but he has just about managed to get out with his dignity intact.

This evening to Harrow to talk to the local Labour Party. On the way back I heard that the *Telegraph* has claimed another victim – Kitty Ussher, a Treasury minister.

Thursday, 18 June

The House authorities have at long last published their version of our expenses, so heavily blacked out as to be all but useless. What's the point? The *Telegraph* has them all anyway. The only result has been to trigger a huge new wave of anger and derision.

'Who are you supporting for Speaker?' I asked Dennis Skinner in the Tea Room this evening.

'I am voting Labour,' he said. 'It's a no-brainer. I'm grateful to Margaret. She's got me off the hook.' He was referring of course to the possibility of having to sully his hands by choosing between two Tories. As usual, Dennis was speaking in a manner which brooked no contradiction, so I forbore to mention that I had nominated George Young, although he will find out soon enough.

Friday, 19 June

Whose idea was it to black out so much detail from our expenses? I never asked anyone to remove anything from mine. On the contrary, I had to insist they reinstate a letter that explained one of my larger claims. The only effect has been to lend credibility to what the *Telegraph* have done, since we can no longer argue that it was all due to be published anyway. The House authorities made fools of us all.

Monday, 22 June

To London, dreaming of the speech I would give, were I a candidate in this afternoon's election for Speaker. My opening line: *I think I can say without fear of contradiction that I am not the candidate of the whips* ... I would go on: *We need a Speaker who will prise loose from this place the tentacles of the executive ... Someone who by the very fact of his or her election would indicate to the world outside that something has changed. I believe I am that candidate.* In passing I might deny any intention to install a black-and-white TV set in Speaker's House.

The air is thick with allegations of plots by the whips to install Margaret, but evidence is thin (although I did come across one Member who had been sounded out). Just this once the whips may have been traduced. In the event it was an uplifting occasion. Ten candidates, ten speeches, most with something original to say, even the no-hopers. The general expectation had been that it would come down to a choice between Bercow and Beckett in the final round, with the odds on Margaret, but she unexpectedly trailed in the first ballot and so by the third it boiled down to a choice between John Bercow and George Young.

'What do you advise?' I asked Dennis Skinner, who after the second ballot, now, unexpectedly, finds himself in the (for him) uncomfortable position of having to choose between two Tories.

'I think it's "stop the old Etonian" who has been educated beyond his intelligence,' declared Dennis, who knows full that well that I am backing George.

In the event Bercow won comfortably. Much cheering from our side and from the Lib Dems, while most of the Tories sat stony-faced, arms ostentatiously folded. At David Cameron's urging, some struggled grudgingly to their feet, applauding without enthusiasm, but most refused to budge. Tribalists on our side were openly baiting them. The Tories have been well and truly shafted and they know it.

Tuesday, 23 June

The junk journalists have wasted no time getting stuck into our new Speaker. 'SO MUCH FOR A FRESH START,' rages the *Mail*. Inside, across two pages, a piece by Quentin Letts headed, 'Impossible. They voted for someone worse than Gorbals Mick.' The *Telegraph*'s report is headed, 'New Speaker "flipped" his home twice to avoid tax'. And on Sky News I heard Peter Oborne denouncing John Bercow as 'a major expenses cheat … a disgraceful appointment'. My guess, however, is that it will all calm down in a few days and that, unless Bercow does something very silly (which can't entirely be ruled out), he will survive.

A small flame still flickers. On a whim, I put my name down for election to the select committee being set up under Tony Wright to consider strengthening the powers of Parliament and, to my pleasant surprise, out of 22 candidates for the eight Labour places I came second. 'A chance to leave a little legacy,' says Tony, who is also standing down at the election.

Wednesday, 24 June

Yet more evidence of the growing insanity. Ann Clwyd says she was telephoned by a local journalist who asked if it were true that three years ago she had claimed 29 pence for two oranges. Mindful of the possible headlines she got up at 3 a.m. and started going through her receipts, eventually to her dismay coming across one which listed the offending oranges. On checking with the Fees Office, however, she was told that she hadn't claimed for them and that the receipt should not have been published. A close-run thing. By such slender threads do political reputations hang in these feverish times.

Gordon received a bashing at PMQs. The problem is he appears to be in denial about the public finances, pretending that only the Tories will make cuts while we will go on spending. His minder, Peter Mandelson, was up in the gallery, grim-faced, feverishly taking notes. Peter is always making notes. What does he do with them?

Cousin Tony came in for lunch. Although he is 15 years older than me I realise that we have much in common. A dry sense of humour, a keen sense of the absurd, a love of fresh air and country walks – in his case on the Sussex Downs. He writes a four-line topical poem each day, a little like those Matt cartoons on the front of the *Telegraph*. Herewith today's:

> Cover-ups and blackings-out,
> However daft, I've heard them.
> But concealing addresses of second homes?
> That's redactio ad absurdum!

My Tory neighbour on Upper Corridor South is loudly complaining of being traduced by the *Telegraph*. For days I have had to listen through our paper-thin walls to his relentless wailing. 'I'm being vilified … my honour is at stake … my constituents need to know that I am straight and honest. I can only tell them that I am.' And so on. It's getting very wearing.

This afternoon, a rowdy debate on the Iraq inquiry. The government has retreated from its earlier insistence that it be held in private, but inevitably it wasn't enough to satisfy the Opposition or a number of refuseniks on our side. Much hot air expended, but in the end the government won comfortably. The sad truth is that, whether it's held in public or private, any outcome that fails to confirm that Blair is a liar and a war criminal is liable to be denounced as a whitewash.

Thursday, 25 June

I came across Angus, the Speaker's Secretary. 'How are you coping with the new management?' I inquired.

He smiled and whispered, 'It could have been you.'

Friday, 26 June

Sunderland

To the funeral of Peggy Weatherstone, an old party stalwart. Afterwards I gave an elderly lady a lift back to Beaumont Lodge, the sheltered housing where Peggy used to live. 'Everyone's complaining about Mr Brown,' she said, 'but I'll say one thing: since you lot came to power the pensioners are better off than they've ever been.' By pensioners, of course, she meant the poorer ones like herself and Peggy, not the Disgusteds of Tunbridge Wells, whose bottomless outrage fills the *Daily Telegraph* letters column day after day.

Monday, 29 June

Today would have been Dad's 89th birthday.

Awoke to leaden skies. It has been like this in the North-East all weekend while the rest of the country is bathed in a heat wave. Gordon made a statement entitled 'Building for the Future', making all sorts of improbable promises about house building and giving parents the right to demand one-to-one tuition for their children, all designed to put clear water between us and the Tories. The problem is that everyone knows that, whichever side wins, there are going to be big cuts in spending, and by refusing to own up we come across as being in denial.

Later, Jack Straw introduced a Bill to set up a new quango called the Independent Parliamentary Standards Authority in the hope of quenching public outrage re the abuse of our allowances. It is being rushed through in three days in order to get it on the statute book by the recess. No one seems happy about it. Not even Jack, who privately refers to it as 'a Something Must Be Done Bill'. Only Frank Field had the courage to vote against it, while the rest of us – from all parties – trooped lamely through the Aye Lobby, complaining as we went.

Wednesday, 1 July

Plans to sell off a third of Royal Mail have been shelved, 'until the economy picks up'. Peter Mandelson announced the news in a state- ment to the Lords in an elegantly executed U-turn. The real reason, as everyone knows, is that our masters have finally grasped that we, the poor bloody infantry, are just not having it. Yesterday Alan Johnson announced that ID cards would not, after all, be made compulsory. Let no one say we humble backbenchers are without influence.

Lunch with a noble lord, who recounted a tale about an occasion when Gordon was at the Treasury. Apparently he had insisted on tabling a self-congratulatory amendment in the teeth of resistance from the Clerk's Department, whereupon the Speaker had (unusually) refused to call it, resulting in a terrible tantrum. Later, a Treasury offi- cial remarked, 'What you don't realise is that it cost us £2,000 in fur- niture repairs.'

Friday, 3 July

Sunderland

Rupert Hanson is dead, barely a fortnight after his cancer was diag- nosed. Derek Foster, who has known him for 60 years, says that Rupert came from one of the poorest families in Sunderland. I was in the process of trying to get him an honour, but of course it's too late now. He deserves the biggest send-off we can organise.

Monday, 6 July

To the meeting of the parliamentary party, where Gordon Prentice demanded to know if the government was proposing to reverse a Lords amendment to the Political Parties and Elections Bill prohibiting political donations by tax exiles. Jack Straw promptly confirmed that this was his intention, saying that anyway it wouldn't deal with the Ashcroft problem, and that we had to proceed by consensus, otherwise the Tories would go after the trade union levy, without which we are dead. This provoked mild heckling. Several times Jack prayed in aid the General Secretary, Ray Collins, who nodded vigorously, leaving a feeling that we may have some dirty secret of our own to hide. Dale Campbell-Savours, the peer who threw the spanner in the works, described Jack's contribution as 'a bloody outrage'.

Later, we were addressed by Alistair Darling, who remains confident that the economy will begin to grow again by the end of the year, but – he added – 'there is much uncertainty'. Our debt, he said, would rise to 80 per cent of national wealth 'because we took a deliberate decision to increase spending up to 2011. We will need to halve the deficit over a five-year period. The next spending review will be tight.'

Tuesday, 7 July

This afternoon a spectacular storm. Thunder, lightning, hailstones. People gathered at windows to watch. An inch of rain in half an hour. Water cascaded through the light fitting on the committee corridor, outside Room 9, and wastepaper bins were commandeered to catch it. Later, a trickle of bedraggled, sodden refugees arrived back from the Queen's garden party, which caught the full force of the storm.

Wednesday, 8 July

This evening, along with a dozen others, a meeting with Ray Collins, who stuck firmly to the line that we must not ban donations by tax exiles. He confirmed that a ban wouldn't just hit the Tories – a number of our donors would be affected and, given the parlous state of Labour finances, it could inflict serious damage.

Thursday, 9 July

The *News of the World* has been caught out paying huge sums of money to people whose phones it has been tapping, in return for their silence. An old story, but the suspicion is that it is the tip of a very large iceberg. What really gives it legs is that the editor who presided when the scandal was first exposed was none other than Andy Coulson, David Cameron's chief spin doctor. Much happiness on our side. A rare chance to inflict a blow on both Murdoch and the Tories. The latter looked very sheepish when the subject came up at Question time. Their spokesman, an unhappy-looking Chris Grayling, quietly conceded that there were 'questions to be answered', provoking howls of ridicule from our side. An unexpected bonus, fun while it lasts, but I doubt it will make much difference in the long run.

This evening, with half a dozen others, to Jack Straw's room on the Upper Ministerial Corridor in a last-ditch attempt to try and talk him out of reversing the Campbell-Savours amendment. Gordon Prentice and Martin Linton led the way, saying how bad it would look for a Labour government to be amending the law in favour of tax exiles. At first Jack resisted, saying that it was gesture politics, but in the end, to our pleasant surprise, he backed down and we went away with an assurance that he would see what could be done. He asked me to stay behind afterwards for a brief chat. I said we had to end the growing dependence of all the main parties on the favours of rich men. Jack said there was a proposal to allow tax relief on small donations, to which he was sympathetic, but it had fallen because the Treasury weren't keen. An issue to which we must return, if British politics isn't to become fatally corrupted.

Saturday, 11 July

To Durham for the miners' gala, a reminder of that golden age of working-class solidarity, in the days before the triumph of selfishness, consumerism and global markets. I stood in sunshine in front of the County Hotel as the bands and banners flowed down Old Elvet. Then to the cricket ground to listen to the speeches, most of which were devoted to a blow by blow re-fighting of the '84–5 strike. Only Dennis

Skinner rose to the occasion with a magnificent rant that somehow managed to end on a positive note.

Sunday, 12 July

A growing list of casualties from the war in Afghanistan. Every week the coffin plane arrives at RAF Lyneham. The newspapers carry photos of fresh-faced young men killed in action, victims mainly of roadside bombs, at which the Taliban are becoming increasingly adept. Among recent casualties, several officers, including a highly regarded colonel who leaves two small daughters. A growing chorus of voices calling for us to get out and leave the Afghans to their fate. The Liberal Democrat leader, Nick Clegg, always quick to spot a bandwagon, is calling for withdrawal.

The case for getting out is that we aren't achieving anything. The case for staying is that a Taliban-controlled Afghanistan will provide the jihadis with a base from which to organise a takeover of nuclear-armed Pakistan, a prospect too awful to contemplate.

Monday, 13 July

The Tories and their friends in the media are becoming increasingly shameless re 'our boys' in Afghanistan. Liam Fox, their defence spokesman, has been at it all weekend, brazenly accusing Gordon of sending our soldiers into battle without adequate protection. This morning's *Telegraph* splashes photos of the latest casualties across the front page under the heading 'BROWN'S DERELICTION'. It's entirely cynical. As most of those on the front line seem to acknowledge, we are pouring resources into Afghanistan – an officer in Helmand, interviewed on the radio this morning, asserted they were 'better equipped than ever'. Bob Ainsworth, the Defence Secretary, remarked at Questions today that we can give our soldiers all the armour and helicopters in the world, but to achieve anything they have sooner or later to get out of their armoured cars and engage with the locals.

Increasingly the same paralysing, risk-averse culture that has infected so much of the public sector is being applied to warfare.

There are no acts of God any more. Lawyers, cheered on by sections of the media and some of our more disreputable politicians, are everywhere trying to persuade grieving parents that the death of their beloved sons was the fault of someone in authority who must, of course, be avenged by way of legal action. If we are not careful, our armed forces will be neutered.

There is the usual hypocrisy on spending. The loudest demands for increases coming from members of a political party that is simultaneously demanding savage cuts. Also a bit of snobbery about Bob Ainsworth. A feeling that he is NCO rather than officer material – which I don't accept for a moment.

This evening to Number 10 for Gordon's annual garden party. I go mainly to see the garden, steering a wide circle round Gordon and his entourage. This year, between the roses and the Cabinet Office, a healthy bed of vegetables has appeared. Whose idea was that? Not Gordon's, surely?

Tuesday, 14 July

The latest coffin plane arrived from Afghanistan, bearing the bodies of eight young men who died on the same day. The television news showed them being unloaded, draped in the Union flag, followed by the ritual procession of hearses through streets lined with silent crowds and sobbing relatives.

Wednesday, 15 July

Lunch with Grey Gowrie at White's in St James's, a little corner of the Establishment that I have never previously penetrated. Very old world. Fawning factotums calling everybody 'My Lord this' and 'My Lord that' and strictly no women, although the Queen was allowed in once and a picture of her with the committee hangs in the loo. Only a couple of faces I recognised. According to Grey, the clientele these days tend to be gentry rather than Tory politicians. David Cameron's father once chaired the management committee, but father and son resigned in protest at the vote to maintain the ban on women. Grey, a civilised one-nation Tory, was a minister in Mrs Thatcher's government. I owe my invitation to the fact that he enjoyed the diaries.

A huge increase in unemployment – up 281,00, the largest monthly increase on record. At this rate it will cross the three million mark by the time we leave office.

Thursday, 16 July

All day long I have had to listen to my Tory neighbour dictating Pooterish letters re his spats with the *Telegraph* and now *Private Eye*. To be sure, he has been traduced. I wish him well in his attempt to exact retribution, but I do wish the walls were thicker. Why can't he just sit in front of a computer and tap out his own missives?

William Hague was on the train going home. 'You may be the one who has to extricate us from Afghanistan,' I said.

He did not demur. He thinks Obama will give the war another two years and then review the situation.

Friday, 17 July

Sunderland

To the Minster, packed to the rafters for Rupert Hanson's funeral. A little too much God for my liking, but fine music, moving tributes from his children, at the end of which Rupert, as befits a maestro making his final curtain call, was carried away to applause and shouts of 'Bravo'.

The generals have opened fire on us re Afghanistan. Richard Dannatt, the head of the army, has been at it all week. Today it was the turn of the Chief of Staff, Sir Jock Stirrup. More helicopters is their immediate demand, but they are also rumoured to have asked for a couple of thousand more troops and been given only 900. The problem is, of course, that the military are not prepared to give up anything in return. They want more of everything – aircraft carriers, the latest jet fighters and (most of them) a new generation of nuclear missiles. The Tories, needless to say, are making the most of our difficulty, while remaining notably silent on how they would fund an expansion of our already enormous arms budget.

Sunday, 19 July

St Bede's Terrace, Sunderland

Our annual get-together for the movers and shakers in the local Labour Party. The last after 22 years. As usual Ngoc laid on a huge spread. The sun shone, after days of heavy rain. Among our guests a local GP who says she is inundated with patients claiming to be stricken with swine flu and demanding sick notes. Few, if any, have it, she says, and some are talking enthusiastically about the possibility of up to two weeks off work that the 'flu' affords

Monday, 20 July

A ray of sunshine amid the gloom. Nissan today announced they are to build a factory, adjacent to their car plant at Washington, to make 60,000 lithium-ion batteries a year, a first step towards the manufacture of electric cars. It means 350 new jobs immediately and the prospect that the new electric models will be built in Sunderland. The Prime Minister, accompanied by Peter Mandelson, paid a flying visit to celebrate the good news.

Wednesday, 22 July

A glimpse into the depressing world of benefit culture. Every week the *Echo* carries a column offering advice to readers who write in with queries about benefits. The adviser, John Gordon, is a true professional. He gives concise, precise answers, never commenting or moralising. Many of the requests come from pensioners struggling to survive on modest incomes who simply set out what they are already claiming and end with the sentence: 'Is there anything else I can claim?'

This week several particularly shameless examples, including this from the father of an 18-year-old school leaver who is preoccupied not with encouraging his son to better himself through work or higher education, but with introducing him to what could be a lifetime of dependency: 'Last week you told me that my ... son could not claim benefit until September. This would be when child benefit stopped and I would be responsible for him until then. Could he claim sooner, however, if he were to go and live with my sister and we were to give up claiming child benefit ...?'

Thursday, 23 July

To the Empire to see Emma and friends in the *Wizard of Oz*. She plays a Winkie, a role which seems to require her and others to march back and forth across the stage dressed in a Ku Klux Klan-type outfit, chanting, 'YO-WE-O'. Unfortunately the great actress seemed to have lost her voice by the end of the third performance – that plus the ominous news that one of the cast has gone down with suspected swine flu. That's all we need. We are off to Vietnam on Saturday.

Friday, 24 July

To London, through torrential rain. En route the inevitable news that the Tories have won the Norwich North by-election on a 16 per cent swing. A wholly self-inflicted disaster. The by-election was triggered by the resignation of Ian Gibson after the black spot was put on him by the party's so-called 'Star Chamber' following controversy over his expenses. He was widely respected and there is a general feeling that he was badly done by.

Saturday, 25 July

The Lycee, Kennington

'MPs attack Brown over expenses defeat,' reads the headline in today's *Telegraph*. Amusing to see how sympathetic the *Telegraph* is towards Ian Gibson ('popular figure, independent-minded') when it suits their purpose. Just goes to show that expenses are a weapon that can be switched on and off at will, deployed for or against, depending on the needs of the hour.

Emma awoke early complaining of a temperature and a sore throat. Catastrophe looms. We are due to depart for Vietnam tonight. Rang the swine flu hotline and got through with surprising ease – considering that the media are full of stories about supposed meltdown. A calm, sensible young woman noted Emma's details and then read out a long list of symptoms, most of which Emma didn't have, but she ticked three boxes and Tamiflu was therefore recommended. I was given a code number and an address in Vincent Square. I drove straight there. No queue. Rolls-Royce service. The man on reception even stood outside, protecting my car from a predatory traffic warden. I was back at the Lycee within the hour.

The patient was up by nine, consumed a light breakfast, shivery, speaking in a whisper, 50 per cent normal cheerfulness. Should we postpone? Singapore Airlines threatening a huge surcharge and at least a week's delay if we do. We decide to press on.

Sunday, 26 July
Transit Lounge, Changi Airport, Singapore

Space age. So sedate one feels one should speak in whispers. Headline in the local press about a Buddhist monk explaining to a court how he came by cash, cars, credit cards and a condo. Small patient, dosed with paracetamol, back to 75 per cent cheerfulness. Touch and go whether we will be allowed into Vietnam. Alarming stories of swine flu suspects being whisked off into quarantine.

Tan Son Nhut Airport, Ho Chi Minh City

Big panic underway. Officials wearing face masks. All passengers must pass a heat-seeking machine, which allegedly identifies those with abnormal temperatures, but Emma passes without incident. Within an hour we are comfortably installed in Aunty Hong's house. The small person on course for a remarkable recovery. Thank goodness we kept our nerve.

Monday, 27 July

Ho Chi Minh City. Saigon as was. The change since I was last here is astonishing. Entire neighbourhoods transformed. Everywhere banging and hammering, drilling and digging. In the city centre sky-scrapers tower above the little French shop-houses that have so far, but for how much longer, survived the onslaught of market forces. And the traffic ... motorcycles flow in a great, unceasing river. When they come to an obstacle they simply meander around it, along the pavements, down alleyways, across forecourts ... an irresistible force. And the roar, punctuated by the incessant hooting of horns, is constant, day and night.

A few surviving air pockets of tranquillity. Notably the magnificent French colonial-style post office. A vast, airy hall, with shuttered windows, ceiling fans, walnut writing desks and 20 separate windows for the multiplicity of transactions which were once possible here. My favourite is labelled 'Domestic Flower Delivery'.

Tuesday, 28 July

When I first came here 36 years ago I made my own way and got by. Now I have become utterly dependent on Ngoc, who, like all Vietnamese wives, keeps a tight hold on the purse strings. I have not a penny in my pocket or, more to the point, a single dong. This afternoon outside the Continental Palace Hotel I was waylaid by a one-legged beggar who simply would not believe I had no money. In the end I had to turn my pockets inside out to convince him and he looked at me with contempt. From now on I will insist that I am allocated a small supply of dong so that I can at least pay off the beggars (of whom, it must be said, there are a great many fewer than in times gone by).

Wednesday, 29 July

Awoke at 5.30 a.m. and went up to the roof, where the air is cool, to read. By 7.30 it was too hot and I retreated. I am reading Cherie Blair's autobiography, *Speaking for Myself*, which, despite some snide reviews, seems an honest, generally self-deprecating account of her remarkable life and the tensions at the heart of the New Labour court. On the penultimate page a revelation: 'Tony has a very quick temper.' Now that is something I never noticed in nearly ten years of dealings with him.

This evening to Tan Son Nhut Airport to welcome Number One Daughter back from Laos. A browner, leaner, more self-confident Sarah Mullin than the one to whom I bade farewell at Heathrow four months ago.

Friday, 31 July

Emma, Sarah and I took the hydrofoil down the Saigon river to Vung Tao. Past warehouses, cranes, oil storage tanks, container ships, tugboats, barges loaded with aggregate to within an inch of the waterline. Giant pylons march through the mangrove swamps towards the city, whose demand for electricity is growing exponentially. Under the huge new suspension bridge, which at the moment seems to lead nowhere, but undoubtedly presages the conquest of yet more territory by this most voracious of cities.

By early evening we are back in the chaos of Saigon. Actually, to call it chaos is not quite fair. It does work, kind of …

Wednesday, 5 August

Kontum, Ngoc's childhood home. First we must pay our respects to Grandpa, who died two years ago. He lies in a marble tomb in a cemetery a few miles along the road to the north. Death in Vietnam, like marriage, is now big business and from a distance the cemetery resembles a crowded town, with lavish tombs crammed together creeping up the hillside. We carry offerings of fruit, which we leave in a neat pile on the tomb, and take turns to light joss sticks. Sensing the possibility of a handsome gratuity, a woman appears from nowhere and starts vigorously clearing weeds from the area around the tomb. She is duly rewarded and her weeding becomes less vigorous from the moment the money touches her hands. Also, a group of children, eyeing the fruit we have just left. Ngoc delivers a stern lecture about allowing a decent interval to elapse before they steal it, but we know that it will disappear as soon as our backs are turned.

Then to Mangden, high in the hills, where a statue of the Virgin has been unearthed, causing a miracle to be declared and attracting pilgrims from all over. She stands on a plinth, surrounded by flowers, candles and seats with memorial plaques containing the names of sponsors, gazing out over virgin forest which will not be virgin for much longer. A mile or two back along the road, the forest is being cleared to make way for a new resort; vulgar houses of Californian dimensions are in the process of construction.

Thursday, 6 August
Kontum

This evening we visited Mr and Mrs Lai, a handsome couple who run a photography business in the main street. They have brought up ten children, all happy, healthy and successful. A large photograph of the family, taken on their golden wedding, has pride of place on the wall. Given the tragic history of their country, to have reared so large a family and emerged unscathed is no small feat. But you can go down as well as up. Ngoc is shocked to learn that our laundry is washed by a former classmate of her sister's ('a handsome boy, very privileged') whose family were once among the most successful in the town. Yet when the father died they could not even afford a coffin.

Friday, 7 August
Kontum

Occasionally I fantasise about retiring to Vietnam. Not to the heat and chaos of Saigon, but maybe to Kontum. I would buy a couple of hectares overlooking the Dakla river and build a wooden house with a veranda and wooden shutters, open on all sides to let the air flow through, solar panels on the roof – my only concession to the twenty-first century. The gutters would lead into an underground reservoir to ensure a plentiful supply of water. Around it I would plant a tropical garden growing avocados, grapefruit, rambutan, papaya and, of course, coffee, not to mention jasmine and bougainvillea. There I would fade into obscurity, surrounded by my wife's large and loving family.

The case for not doing so is (a) there is not the slightest chance that I could get my slowing brain around more than a few words of this most complicated of languages; (b) it would mean almost permanent separation from my children and grandchildren; and (c) I am not sure I could cope with the world beyond my compound, the dirt, pollution, the relentless march of consumerism and its attendant destruction of the natural environment. Oh, I know it is wrong to begrudge the Vietnamese their new-found prosperity and I don't. In time, no doubt, they will adjust, but not, I am afraid, in my lifetime.

We called at Grandpa's plantation, a sad place now. No sign of the coffee bushes that made his fortune. Only a poor man and his family scratching a living growing vegetables. There is a rumour that it is to be sold for a car showroom.

Number One Daughter, Sarah, who speaks Vietnamese, has been playing tricks on her younger sister. *'Con dien khung'*, she has taught her to say, telling her that it means 'I don't speak Vietnamese.' Only after Emma has happily repeated this on several occasions does she discover that it actually means 'I am crazy.' She is not amused.

Saturday, 8 August

A tearful goodbye to Aunty Yen and then we set off down Highway 14 through the Truong Son Mountains to the junction where the borders of Vietnam meet those of Laos and Cambodia. It was through these mountains that the Ho Chi Minh trail once ran, along which thousands of North Vietnamese soldiers travelled on their way south. Unlike us, of course, they walked and many perished en route under the relentless bombing.

As we leave the mountains the cloud that has been with us all day lifts and we emerge into a land of luminous green rice paddies, tended by peasants in conical hats. Soon we are skirting Da Nang, a monstrous, ever-expanding city playing host to vast, vulgar entertainment complexes with names like Vegas and Queen's Palace. The coastal fringe, where the huge American base once stood, is being developed by Japanese and Korean joint ventures into condominiums where the

Asian rich besport themselves, immune from the stark realities beyond their compounds.

Sunday, 9 August
Hoi An

Narrow streets, ancient courtyard houses and pagodas, merchants' mansions. A glimpse of what once was and will never be again. A sliver of old Vietnam that has somehow survived the depredations of the twentieth century and which the powers-that-be have in their wisdom (and with the help of UNESCO) decreed shall be protected from the merciless onslaught of the free market which rages all around. If only old Hanoi had been preserved like this.

Monday, 10 August

Up early for the long drive south along Highway 1, surely one of the world's most dangerous roads. Much of the driving is psychopathic. I lost count of the number of times we had to veer off the road in order to avoid head-on collisions, sometimes on blind bends.

The landscape, if we can but notice, is classically Vietnamese. In the blue haze to our right, the Truong Son Mountains, from which we emerged two days ago, green rice fields, wallowing water buffalo, duck farms, sampans negotiating narrow rivers. We are in the narrowest part of Vietnam. At times the mountains close in upon the road, squeezing the land available for cultivation.

By evening , thanks to the lightning reflexes and steely nerves of our driver, San, we have been delivered safely to Doc-let, a beach resort just north of Nha Trang.

Tuesday, 11 August
Doc-let

Sunrise. Blue sea, gentle waves, a cool breeze, a lone wooden fishing boat cruising offshore. The bay is half enclosed by a thin spit of land at the end of which is an island. Already the beach is full of chattering

Vietnamese, who, unlike the still sleeping foreigners, are well aware that this is the best time of day. Three hours from now and the heat will be unbearable. An old man is dredging for cockles. If he is lucky, he tells Ngoc, he will earn 10,000 dong, about 40 pence, enough to buy a kilo or two of rice.

Our beach, needless to say, is pristine. Further along it is a different story. I walked a mile along the shore to a nearby fishing village, only to find that the beach is a huge garbage dump, thick with plastic and other twentieth-century detritus. The industrious, ingenious Vietnamese, who over centuries have seen off wave upon wave of invaders, have themselves been defeated by the accursed plastic bag. They simply can't cope with it. Until not so long ago all garbage was degradable. If you bought a snack from a pedlar, it came wrapped in a banana leaf. Today it is likely to be encased in plastic. Plastic garbage litters the outskirts of every hamlet, every village, every town. In places it has been scattered by the wind, caught in trees and scrub, despoiling the landscape. Sooner or later a state of emergency is going to have to be declared.

Thursday, 13 August
Ho Chi Minh City

To Le Van Sy to report to Granny on our travels. A minuscule old lady in silk pyjamas, her spine is so crippled that she cannot sit for more than ten minutes at a time; mainly she lies on a bamboo sofa. Her mind, however, remains crystal clear.

Tuesday, 18 August

To the Caravelle Hotel to address the monthly lunch of the Britain–Vietnam Business Group. The Ambassador has come down from Hanoi for the occasion. My talk is entitled 'My 35-year love affair with Vietnam', though in truth the romance has worn thin over the years. The heat, the chaos, the relentless consumerism have taken their toll. To be sure, however, I will always love the Vietnamese for their energy, generosity and optimism.

This evening to Cholon to meet the parents of Thao, cousin Duy's wife. They were both Viet Cong, disappearing into the countryside in 1961 and reappearing only after Saigon fell in April '75. They lived for years in Tay Ninh Province, close to the border with Cambodia, sometimes retreating into Cambodia to escape the relentless bombing. They describe seeing friends blown to pieces, the terror of never knowing when death would come from the sky, people caught by the shockwaves vomiting blood, and treating napalm victims (he was a medic) with unspeakable injuries. They estimate that only 50 per cent of those who went with them into the bush survived and of those who did many were seriously damaged. Miraculously they emerged alive and sane. 'We were born under a lucky star,' they said.

Wednesday, 19 August

This evening we entertained the family – aunts, uncles, cousins, nephews – to a farewell dinner in a Hue-cuisine restaurant in District 3. Granny even put in an appearance, taking her place at the head of the table, so tiny that she was only just visible. We delivered her back to Le Van Sy and she stood at the door waving goodbye. It is unlikely that the girls and I will ever see her again.

Thursday, 20 August

Singapore

Suddenly we are in a world where great order prevails under heaven. Where traffic signals are obeyed. Where there is little or no litter and efficient public transport. Where everything works as it is supposed to. Like Vietnam, Singapore is a one-party state (although, unlike Vietnam, it masquerades as a democracy). The presence of the state is considerable, although generally benign – unless you are a drug trafficker, in which case you can expect to be hanged.

We are staying with our friends Kieu and Joergen. She worked with Ngoc at Saigontourist in the old days. He was the Danish Ambassador to Singapore before retiring and settling into academic life. From their ninth-floor balcony, huge views across the island to the downtown skyscrapers, a veritable Manhattan.

Saturday, 22 August

To the war graves cemetery at Kranji. Row upon row of identical tombstones, each bearing the name of a British soldier who perished in the Japanese invasion. According to Joergen, we were unlucky. The commander, poor fellow, surrendered without knowing that the Japanese had only 24 hours' worth of ammunition left.

Sunday, 23 August

Joergen remarked that British diplomacy had been degraded in the last ten years. 'British ambassadors used to be the best. Now they are glorified commercial counsellors, lacking weight.' As if to prove his point, an article appeared in today's *Straits Times* headed 'Rise of Britain's pink diplomacy'. It carried a picture of Chris Bryant, who, as the article points out, rejoices in the nickname 'Captain Underpants' after posting that unfortunate picture on a gay website. 'New minister in Foreign Office tells ambassadors to push for gay rights,' says the headline. The article concludes: 'The old Western belief that certain values are beyond dispute and must be exported as quickly as possible remains very much alive, if not in Washington, then at least in London.'

We spent a pleasant day at the bird sanctuary and after a leisurely supper Kieu took us to the airport and waved us off for London.

Tuesday, 25 August

A poll in today's *Guardian* shows Labour trailing the Tories 42–25. The Tories are ahead on all fronts – economy, education, law and order – save health, where we retain a narrow lead. They are said to be in the lead among all social classes in all regions. Most Lib Dems, it appears, would rather see a Tory government than a Labour one. All of which suggests that, barring miracles, we face meltdown.

Friday, 28 August

To Edinburgh for the festival. In contrast to the Labour conference, where I am a total irrelevance, I am much in demand on the festival circuit. This weekend, three engagements: a session on the diaries this afternoon, one with Polly Toynbee tomorrow on the class divide and on Sunday (at the television festival) a debate about politicians and spin. The diaries event attracted 600 people (at £7 a head) and was followed by a pleasant hour of book signing.

Saturday, 29 August

Edinburgh

Everyone is talking about last night's speech by James Murdoch, son of Rupert, in which he launched a great broadside on the BBC and what he called 'state-sponsored journalism'. His main complaint was that the BBC is using the licence fee to fund a free website which makes it impossible for other broadcasters (notably his own BSkyB) to charge for theirs. He also laid into the regulator, OFCOM, demanding outrageously that BSkyB be freed from the obligation to produce impartial news. One has only to look at Fox News to see where that will lead. There is some sympathy for his point about BBC Online, but it does stick in the gullet to see a mini-oligarch like Murdoch junior posing as a champion of competition and free speech.

Sunday, 30 August

To the Dean Gallery of modern art (much of it junk) in search of paintings by Dawyck Haig (I found one), then back, via the Waters of Leith, to the conference centre for a session on spin. Sky's Adam Boulton in the chair. The other panellists were Lance Price, who used to be Alastair Campbell's deputy at Number 10, Peter Oborne (who believes that the entire political class is corrupt and useless) and Heather Brooke, the woman who forced the disclosure of MPs' expenses. A good-natured discussion, but predicated on the proposition that the only spinners were politicians whereas, as I did my best to point out, political journalists are the biggest spinners of all. Afterwards a drink with Adam and Anji Hunter, who is now a corporate bigshot. Adam reckons that Gordon will stand down at the last minute rather than face annihilation. Angie, Lance and I strongly disagreed. Letting go is not in Gordon's DNA.

Monday, 31 August

Sunderland

Among the chores that awaited on return from Vietnam, a month's supply of the *Echo* to leaf through. Chock full of underclass mayhem – lootings, burnings, stabbings, rapes plus a killing or two. The good news is that our Nissan plant seems to be in line to produce the company's new electric vehicles. Thank goodness for Nissan.

Friday, 4 September

This evening, at the monthly party meeting, we were addressed by representatives of the probation officers' union, who talked of impending 'meltdown and devastation' as a result of the government's proposed spending plans. One had to pinch oneself to realise that all that has been proposed so far is a reduction of 2.4 per cent and this on top of a 70 per cent real terms increase in spending on probation since we were elected. When I put this to them, they immediately conceded that it was so but claimed that most of the increase had been wasted on a computer system that didn't work and an increase in bureaucracy, which may or may not be the case. The moral of the story seems to be that, however much the government invests in the public services, it can never expect the slightest credit from those in the front line.

Sunday, 6 September

Today's *Sunday Times* is leading with a story lambasting Gordon Brown for (apparently) refusing to demand that the Libyans compensate the victims of IRA bombings. The latest instalment of a foolish game that's been going on since the release of Abdelbaset al-Megrahi, the man convicted of the Lockerbie bombing, on the grounds that he is dying of cancer. The more interesting issue, upon which almost no one has touched, is whether or not Megrahi had anything to do with Lockerbie. The case against him was wafer-thin and he had an appeal pending which might well have resulted in his conviction being quashed.

Thursday, 17 September

To Millbank for a meeting of Reform of Parliament Committee, where, under the masterly chairmanship of Tony Wright, we spent the day discussing how to prise Parliament loose from the tentacles of the executive. Time is short and Tony is anxious that we should focus on a few measures rather than big-bang proposals which will get nowhere. We homed in on two issues: (1) how to recapture control of the parliamentary timetable and (2) how to increase the independence of select committees. Needless to say, it is all more complicated than it appears at first glance and there are those (not I) who remain to be convinced that there is a problem that needs solving. My suggestion for September sittings, thereby putting an end to the scandalous 82-day summer recess, provoked friendly nods from some of the lay experts, but not much enthusiasm among the elected.

This evening to the Methodist Central Hall for a lecture by General David Petraeus, the American in overall charge of military operations in Iraq, Afghanistan and much else besides. A civilised, thoughtful, decent man, far removed from the Rumsfeld/Cheney way of doing business. Already he is being spoken of as a future president.

Friday, 18 September

To Sunderland on the 11.27 Grand Central train from King's Cross, only to grind to a sickening halt outside Retford, having collided with a pedestrian. A suicide. Apparently he stood with his back to the train, arms outstretched, awaiting the awful impact. A car with a note inside was found nearby. Pity the poor train driver, who must have seen him from a long way off but been powerless to stop in time. The body must have been dragged some way because we could hear stones hitting the undercarriage. It went on for a long time.

A poll in today's *Times* says that most people now believe that the NHS would be better under the Tories. Should we laugh or cry?

Sunday, 20 September

An unseemly bidding war has broken out to see which party can inflict the most damage on the public sector. For weeks the media have been demanding that Gordon admit that public spending must be slashed and last week, at the TUC, he obliged. Now the ludicrous Nick Clegg is at it. Yesterday he was demanding 'bold and savage cuts'. This morning he was on *The Andrew Marr Show*, prattling about the need to 'treat people like grown-ups'. This isn't leadership. It's follow-that-opinion-poll. A cynical ploy to shore up support among the southern middle classes. I can't believe it is going to win him any votes. If you want bold and savage cuts, the logical thing to do is vote Tory.

Monday, 21 September

On the radio this morning, Shirley Williams talking sense about our current travails: 'This is not a British crisis. It is a global crisis. A crisis of capitalism. One of the things I feel most resentful about is the way in which the Tories have managed to present it as a British crisis, a crisis caused by Gordon Brown, when in fact it is a crisis of capitalism caused by a world banking system that is deeply sick and we have got to save it.' Come back, Shirley, all is forgiven. If only our current crop of ministers were so fluent and credible.

A visit to Dave Thornton, the head teacher at Farringdon School. He's taken on a bright new maths teacher and as a result driven Farringdon's '5 A-C' rating up from 32 to 47 per cent in a single year. Languages, he says, have been the big casualty of the drive to focus on practical outcomes – only 20 of 180 eligible students opted for a language – but the good news is that those who have are doing better than ever because they are no longer distracted by the surly and disaffected.

Tuesday, 22 September
House of Commons

To a Royal Africa Society breakfast at the Institute of Directors to hear Andrew Mitchell, one of the best and the brightest on the Tory front bench, outline his party's plans for international development. Sincere, fluent, well informed, he went out of his way to emphasise that there is not a Tory or Labour policy on overseas aid, but a British one. Amazingly, the Tories have committed to ring-fence aid spending and endorse the UN target – 0.7 per cent of GNP. A measure of how far they have travelled since the bad old days of the Pergau Dam and aid-related arms deals etc. Also, a tribute to Clare Short's success in utterly transforming British aid policy. She must surely go down as one of New Labour's most successful ministers. Oh, the irony.

Afterwards I walked back with Andrew across the park. He says that David Cameron is entirely signed up to protecting the aid budget. Should we believe him? Maybe, at least as long as Andrew remains in post, but what happens after that remains to be seen. He also remarked, apropos my diaries, that he had recently run into John Vereker (a.k.a. Sir Two Buzzes*), who had generously remarked that 'Chris Mullin was a much better minister than he pretends'. A fitting epitaph for my four undistinguished years in government.

Wednesday, 23 September

According to Channel Four's Gary Gibbon, David Cameron at a recent press conference cited my diaries as a reason for his proposed cutback of the government car service. So, I do still retain a smidgeon of influence. Alas, however, with the wrong party.

Later, a coffee with John Hutton, who claims to have heard whispers of yet another plot to bring down Gordon. This one involving a

---

*See *A View from the Foothills*, p. 181.

challenge to the chairman of the parliamentary party, Tony Lloyd, by someone standing solely on a 'Gordon must go' ticket. The thinking being that, since the election is by secret ballot, people would be free to give vent to their true feelings, unintimidated by The Apparatus. Much depends on who the candidate is, of course. Personally, I don't think it will happen and, if it does, the odds are Gordon would survive, even more damaged than he is already. And were Gordon to be ousted, we would face a legacy of bitterness that would linger for years. Ken Baker, who I ran into last night, said it took the Tories ten years to recover from the ousting of Thatcher. Even John agreed that replacing Gordon at this late stage was unlikely to make much difference, though he did add that it might be the difference between meltdown and survival.

Thursday, 24 September

'Obama snub for Brown'. Yes, the junk journalists at it again. Believe it or not, this latest piece of nonsense is the lead in the *Guardian* and *The Times*. The BBC's Nick Robinson is also at it. Gordon is at the UN in New York. The White House apparently couldn't find a slot for an audience with the President, no doubt on the very sensible grounds that if he received Gordon there would be similar demands from Sarkozy, Merkel and Berlusconi et al. Not to mention the fact that they are all off to Pittsburgh for the G20 summit the next day, where there will no doubt be plenty of opportunities for 'face time'. Needless to say, our hacks have chosen to interpret this as a snub. It's all a silly game, designed to demonstrate that everything poor Gordon does turns to dust. Last time he visited the US, the lobby hacks filled the airwaves with spurious demands that he apologise for 'causing' the recession. Oddly, in the US itself – and in Europe – an entirely different perception of Gordon prevails. While others dithered, he is seen as the one leader who knew what to do when the banking crisis struck. On this evening's bulletins, brief clips of Gordon receiving an award for statesmanship, but scarcely a word of this has reached the British electorate. A triumph of spin over substance, if ever there was.

Friday, 25 September

To Middlesbrough's magnificent Victorian town hall, for a meeting of the Grand Committee. Parliament comes to the North-East. The whole shebang, clerks, *Hansard* reporters, ushers in morning suits and a quorum of the region's MPs. I was sceptical, at first, but it turned out to be an uplifting occasion. Nick Brown, our 'Minister for the North', answered questions and then opened a debate on the region's economy to which most of us, in turn, contributed. And the speeches were good. Well informed, positive, focused on the real world – exactly what the public demands of its elected representatives. Alas, however, we may have been talking to ourselves since the region's media, preoccupied as they are with tales of mugging, murder and mayhem, were largely absent. According to Dari Taylor, before the proceedings had even started, one of the few journalists present was threatening an 'only ten MPs bothered to show up' story. Actually, it was 14 but it remains to be seen whether this made any difference.

Someone, a senior civil servant, drew my attention to a programme on BBC2 last night (*For Love of Money*) in which various important foreigners, including the former American Treasury Secretary Hank Paulson, were interviewed and said that last autumn the world economy came within a whisker of meltdown. The Americans had a plan, but it was deadlocked in Congress, and it was the decisive action taken by the British government that prevented catastrophe. If true, it means that Gordon and Alistair got right the biggest decision of the twenty-first century, bar none. Why is that a secret in this country? How come only foreigners know?

Sunday, 27 September

Our demoralised, depleted army is gathering in Brighton for the annual conference. Alistair Darling has given an interview to the *Observer* in which he likens us to 'a football team that has lost the will to live'. Gordon's latest wheeze is 'a Fiscal Responsibility Act' that commits us to halving the public spending deficit within four years. Meanwhile, The Noble Lord Mandelson has let it be known that, if by any chance Labour were to be defeated, he would be prepared to continue serving the country in some unspecified capacity. I bet.

Monday, 28 September

Brighton

My last Labour Party conference after 39 years. Journalists and lobbyists outnumber delegates by two or three to one. Doom and gloom everywhere. Everyone knows this is the end. Many of the speeches from the floor have a surreal quality – fluent but those reading them seem unfamiliar with the text. As though written by an unseen hand, which I suspect may well be the case. An excellent speech from Alistair Darling. Calm, credible, reassuring and what's more he took the fight to the Tories. As well he might. On the economy and the financial crisis we have a much better story to tell than most people will admit and the Tories have made the wrong call each turn. We ought to be rubbing their noses in it.

Peter Mandelson was the improbable star of the day. Emerging briefly from the shadows where he has always preferred to operate, he treated us to a minor masterpiece that was in turns witty, theatrical, self-indulgent, laced with faux modesty ('I make enemies sometimes needlessly ... I was sometimes too careless of the feelings and views of others ...' – where did he get that from?*). From time to time pausing to inject a sinister smile. Gordon sitting behind him, eyes half closed, affected amusement, nodding vigorously. If I were Gordon, I'd be thinking, 'What's this bastard up to now?' At the end Peter was rewarded with a heartfelt standing ovation. A historic day. The party has learned to love him. It's taken a while (about 20 years) and may not last, but it has come to pass and I have lived to see the day. Praise the Lord and pass the ammunition.

On the way to the station I passed an *Evening Standard* billboard. It read: 'BROWN: DEAD MAN WALKING'. Hooray for British journalism.

---

*See *A View from the Foothills*, p. 314.

Tuesday, 29 September

Brighton

Gordon's big day. Rarely can a leader have been under such pressure. One can't but sympathise. For the second year running Sarah, who everybody loves, did the warm-up. A mixture of charm and American-style vulgarity ('I know he loves our country and he will always, always put you first'). Then Gordon. Everyone was willing him to do well. And he did. He began by rattling off a list of what we had achieved (working the hall up into a frenzy) and rounded off with a list of things to come, a mixture of substance (restoring the link between pensions and earnings) and cheap populism (a right to recall errant MPs). Of spending cuts, there was scarcely a mention, which leaves us just a teeny bit vulnerable, since much of what was promised seems to involve more, not less, public spending. At the end there was the usual lengthy ovation followed by a somewhat contrived encore. Elation mixed with relief that he had pulled it off, but of course the big question is how will it play outside our little bubble? Is anybody listening? As I was leaving the hall, Jeremy Paxman thrust a microphone under my nose and demanded an instant reaction. Suspecting that he was taking the piss I offered an anodyne but friendly comment which I knew would not be used. I then asked what he thought, whereupon he came over all professional, as though he were some sort of lofty neutral observer, rather than the congenital cynic that he is. Sure enough, the *Newsnight* report of Gordon's speech was one long sneer.

By late evening word reached us that the *Sun* had come out for the Tories.

Wednesday, 30 September

How should we respond to news of the *Sun's* 'conversion'? My first reaction was mild amusement. Until last night I hadn't realised the *Sun* has been on our side these past 12 years and any student of the writings of Mr Trevor Kavanagh could be forgiven for thinking otherwise. The obvious response is to laugh, but there is a case for going on the offensive. How dare a billionaire American/Australian oligarch subvert our democracy? Who elected him? Etc. The difficulty with this line of attack is that New Labour have spent too long sucking up to Rupert. My pre-'97 strategy would have been to nod in all the right places, laugh at his jokes – and strike with deadly force in the first week: one daily, one Sunday per proprietor, ownership confined to EU citizens only, no one who owns a national newspaper allowed more than 10 per cent of a TV company ... and so on. The weakness, of course, is that (a) there is no shortage of unlovable megalomaniacs queuing to gobble up whatever comes on to the market and (b) forcing Murdoch to choose could well result in the closure of *The Times* and *Sunday Times*, not that the latter would be a great loss, but *The Times* would be.

Thursday, 1 October

A snippet from yesterday's *Guardian*: 'The US secret service is investigating who was behind a Facebook poll on whether President Obama should be killed. The page offered four options: Yes, No, Maybe, and "If he cuts my healthcare". More than 700 people responded...'

This evening, to a book festival in Appledore. I was once – 39 years ago – the Labour candidate in North Devon. About 140 people attended, but I recognised no one from the old days.

Monday, 5 October

Sunderland

A visit from a soldier just back from Afghanistan. 'We had a delegation of Tories out,' he said, 'just interested in looking for sticks with which to beat the government.' He added that there had been a big improvement in the quality of the equipment – fewer casualties from roadside bombs since the new armoured vehicles (Mastiffs) had been introduced. Still a shortage of helicopters, though.

Tuesday, 6 October

The bulletins are full of George Osborne's address to the Tory confer-ence, talking up the crisis in public spending, promising only blood, sweat and tears and blaming it all on the government, as if the global banking crisis never happened. All day a procession of Tories flowed through the studios, giving interviews casually studded with refer-ences to 'Labour's debt' and 'the mess that Labour has got us into' without anyone being indelicate enough to suggest that most of the deficit had been incurred baling out the Tories' friends in the City. Nor did anyone question whether our debt is really as bad as they keep alleging. Or whether a rise in the basic rate of tax (which has steadily fallen in recent years) might not also be part of the equation. Even government spokesmen, in so far as they are visible at all, seem only to be arguing that our cuts will be better than theirs – a recipe for defeat, if ever there was.

Wednesday, 7 October

George Osborne was on the radio posing as 'Mr Honesty', talking incessantly of the need to 'level with the public'. But that's just the point. He hasn't. The analysis he has offered so far is entirely dis-honest. This isn't a uniquely British crisis, it's global.

Thursday, 8 October

Today, at the Tory conference, it was the turn of David Cameron to put the frighteners on Middle England. He spoke of massive debt, social breakdown, attacked what he called 'big' government and even had the nerve to pose as a champion of the poor. How dare he? Broken Britain, my foot. In Sunderland we are still clearing up the mess from the Thatcher decade.

Friday, 9 October

To London on the 06.41. As we went down the east coast, a stunning sunrise – a gradually enlarging streak of deep, rich pink across a black/

blue horizon; far out to sea a cluster of lights from a passing ship or an oil rig, and after Hartlepool the long black silhouette of the Cleveland Hills.

Saturday, 10 October

I am staying (post an appearance at the Cheltenham Literary Festival) with Jean Corston in her lovely fifteenth-century house on the edge of the Cotswolds. From the window fine views across the Severn Valley towards the Forest of Dean. She related how, towards the end of The Man's tenure, Gordon presented a list of cronies who he wanted promoted to the Cabinet. 'Do you want them because they are allies or because they are the best available?' inquired The Man. To which there was no clear answer. In the end, The Man refused, saying that if Gordon wanted them in the Cabinet he should wait until he was prime minister and promote them himself.

Monday, 12 October

House of Commons

Everyone waiting with trepidation for a letter from Sir Thomas Legg, telling us whether or not we have to pay back over-claimed expenses. Initially we were told they would appear on the letter board in the Members' Lobby by noon, but as the day wore on there was no sign of them. People kept passing by, surreptitiously glancing. Smirking journalists hovered. In the event they didn't turn up until early evening. More than 300 of us – including Yours Truly – are being asked to make repayments. Growing anger at the news that Legg appears to have changed the rules retrospectively and that the entire political class is being criminalized. Meanwhile, Stuart Bell has made another of his disastrous interventions – he is all over the media saying how unfair it all is. Unfair it may be, but the fact is we have only ourselves to blame and the public are in no mood for self-pity.

Gordon addressed the parliamentary party. His message was that everyone should co-operate with Legg and get the expenses issue out the way once and for all. 'Have confidence,' he kept saying. 'Once we get through, the public will see that it has been dealt with and it will not be an issue at the election.' But many of our number weren't having it. He was heckled, sporadically at first and then more generally. Twice he paused to let the hubbub die down. 'Have faith,' he said. But the longer he went on the worse it got. It became apparent that he had lost the attention of the meeting or a large part of it. He sat down, ashen-faced, to desultory applause. I have never seen that happen to a prime minister before. His authority is draining away before our eyes. Demoralisation is palpable. We are in a deep, deep pit and there just isn't the will to climb out of it.

Earlier I passed John Denham in the Library Corridor and remarked that it seemed to be a secret, known only to foreigners and viewers of BBC2, that Gordon and Alistair saved the world financial system last autumn. To which John replied, 'If we haven't got the confidence to say so, why should anyone else?'

Tuesday, 13 October

Another great feeding frenzy re expenses. Media outrage at Jacqui Smith being required only to apologise. The front page of today's *Telegraph* splashes a carefully cropped – and I would have thought actionable – picture of her under the word 'theft'. The truth is that, although she should not have claimed on her Redditch home, there is no evidence that the taxpayer lost out as a result of her doing so. On the contrary, as Home Secretary she was entitled to the use of a grace-and-favour house in Belgravia which would no doubt have cost the taxpayer a great deal more. But of course no one is interested in any of that. Meanwhile a great pall of gloom hangs over the place. There is anger with Gordon for having set up the Legg inquiry. Anger with Legg for allegedly rewriting the rules retrospectively and for letting off some of the worst offenders scot-free. Loathing of the media for effectively criminalizing us. In a matter of months we have been transformed from upright, self-confident tribunes of the people into a besieged subculture.

Wednesday, 14 October

Much foreboding that PMQs would deteriorate into a discreditable slanging match which would provide yet more amusement for our many tormentors. In the event there was no mention of expenses, not even from the self-righteous Nick Clegg. Instead Gordon began by reading out a roll-call of The Fallen in Afghanistan since July – 37 names in all, received in absolute silence. And that set the tone for the entire half-hour, enabling Gordon to sound positively prime ministerial. Not that it will make any difference with the punters, but these days merely to get through without disaster is some kind of triumph.

An amusing little vignette re the government car service. Apparently, it has been suggested that, as a result of the EU's Working Time Directive, each minister may be required to have two drivers. Much confusion. Ministers fretting about how they are going to get home. And what to do about the boxes, which can't be taken on public transport? All madness, of course. The drivers spend most of the day sitting around anyway. This is surely the moment for a long-overdue shake-up. Only ministers who require protection should have a dedicated car; the rest should have use of the car pool as and when they need it. I feel a mini-campaign coming on.

One other piece of lunacy: Glenys Kinnock, after a mere five months as Europe minister, has been moved sideways to cover Africa and replaced by Chris Bryant. That's twelve Europe and nine Africa ministers in 12 years. How on earth can we expect to be taken seriously by our foreign counterparts?

Thursday, 15 October

To the Reform Committee, where we spent 75 minutes wrangling about how to get the appointment of select committees out of the hands of the whips. We were presented with six options – two of which we immediately ruled out. Needless to say, the two Lib Dem Members homed in on the purest, most complicated, least deliverable option and clung to it as though it were a matter of life and death, although in truth it is almost impossible to devise a system which is entirely beyond manipulation by the whips or their agents. No satisfactory conclusion was reached and it was agreed that the Clerk would circulate the four surviving options and invite each of us to list them in order of preference.

Afterwards, at a table in the atrium of Portcullis House, I came across Mr Speaker Bercow and his wife, Sally, and I took the opportunity to bend his ear on the need for September sittings and several other matters dear to my heart, such as removing parliamentary private secretaries from select committees. He in turn sounded me out on his plan to expose Lords ministers to questioning by Commons Members and, more controversially, permitting civil partnership ceremonies in Speaker's House. On the last point I advised caution. His tenure is by no means assured and that is very definitely a second-term issue.

Tuesday, 20 October

To Number 10, with other northern Members for a pow-wow with Gordon. He looked surprisingly well, all things considered. Hilary Armstrong in the chair, under the portrait of Walpole, the rest of us arrayed along the opposite side of the Cabinet table, I at the near end sandwiched between Fraser Kemp and one of the pillars. Gordon, in listening mode, furiously noting every point in black felt pen (cf. The Man, who always left note-taking to the underlings), occasionally banging his hand on the table for emphasis. There was no common theme, every issue was raised, from airport tax to the devastating job losses in the steel industry on Teesside. Re the postal workers' uprising, he was unbending: they must agree to modernise and that's that. The only note of optimism was injected by Fraser, who talked hopefully of electric car production at Nissan. We were there a little over an hour. Gordon responded to every point, refusing to be hurried, despite a stream of notes from officials urging him to wind up.

That was, surely, my last visit to the Cabinet Room.

This afternoon Pat McFadden – gaunt, dour, uncompromising – made a statement on the threatened postal strike. Meanwhile, it has emerged that the Royal Mail management are in the process of recruiting 30,000 casual workers. Both sides seem to be digging in for a long struggle.

Nick Soames says he has so far bought about 30 copies of the diaries for distribution among friends.

Wednesday, 21 October

Lunch with Keith Hill, who reckons that, if (as we all expect) the Tories do form a government, they are unlikely to last more than one term. He believes they are shallow and will be unable to cope. I do not share his optimism.

At this afternoon's meeting of the Reform Committee, an informal session with Mr Speaker Bercow. A refreshing contrast to the tired, do-nothing regime of his predecessor. He urged us to be bold and was very sound on September sittings – even wanting to sit for the full month, rather than the modest eight days for which I have been pushing. Afterwards, a session with the former Chief Whip, Hilary Armstrong, who brought us back down to earth with a passionate defence of the status quo.

This evening, during a division, John McFall, chairman of the Treasury Committee, remarked that he had been at a seminar in the City this morning and that the chairman – a banker – had gone out of his way to express gratitude to the government for its intervention last autumn, without which (he said) the entire banking system would have gone down. If only they'd say that out loud …

Thursday, 22 October

At Business questions I asked Harriet about September sittings. Speaker Bercow, a twinkle in his eye, knew what I was up to and called me first. I asked for a debate 'so that we can get the excuses out of the way as early as possible'. Harriet, needless to say, conceded nothing. Astonishing how pig-headed the Establishment are on this. Electing select committee chairmen, appointing a business committee – desirable though they are – will ring no bells at all with the public, but September sittings do. How else to convince people that we are not all sunning ourselves in the South of France when Parliament is not sitting? If we care about how we are regarded, and surely we do, this is an easy win.

Friday, 23 October

A great hullabaloo underway re the appearance of BNP leader Nick Griffin on *Question Time* last night. The Beeb have mishandled it from the beginning. Having invited him to take part, on the grounds that his party had won two seats in the European Parliament, they proceeded to hype the event for all it was worth, resulting in a trebling of the usual audience. They then made matters worse by completely setting him up, arranging a panel and an audience that was entirely hostile. It was so blatant that they managed to make the odious Griffin appear a victim, which has triggered a wave of sympathy among white working-class voters, precisely the audience to whom he seeks to appeal. Result: the BNP are claiming a surge in membership inquiries and a poll in which 20 per cent of respondents say they would consider voting BNP.

Wednesday, 28 October

Lunch with Charlie Glass, the former *Newsweek* man who was kidnapped in Beirut 22 years ago. Charlie, who has spent much of his career reporting the Middle East, reckons Lockerbie was the work of the Iranians, not the Libyans – in revenge for their passenger plane shot down by the Americans. 'We'll only find out when the regime falls,' he says. Re Iraq, Afghanistan etc. he remarked that there is not a single example of American-inspired regime change, anywhere in the world, that resulted in better government.

Thursday, 29 October

Ditchley Park, Oxfordshire

Shades of *Gosford Park*. A carriageway winding through a mile or more of parkland to an exquisite eighteenth-century mansion. A log fire burning in the Great Hall. Servants making off with our baggage, which reappears miraculously in our rooms. Below, in the basement, black-and-white photos of Clemmie and Winston Churchill sitting with the then owner, Ronnie Tree, on the south terrace. Apparently he came here a lot during the war.

Nowadays, Ditchley plays host to a foundation designed to promote Anglo-American understanding. A place to which the Great and the Good repair to put the world to rights. I am here, courtesy of something called the Better Government Initiative, to take part in a discussion about improving the quality of government and its accountability to Parliament. We are assembled in the library, about 40 of us seated alphabetically around a long circular table, watched over by a portrait of the founder and a pair of Raeburns, depicting an eighteenth-century couple, a woman in a lace cap and a bewigged gentleman, no doubt members of the family who once inhabited this place. The cast list is impressive. A mix of retired mandarins, clerks of the House, distinguished academics and a smattering of politicians. Most of us being of a certain age, practitioners are heavily outnumbered by pontificators. I am seated between Sir David Omand (late of the Home Office, GCHQ and the Joint Intelligence Committee – a deceptively youthful man who knows where many bodies are buried) and Sir Richard Mottram (a fellow survivor from the Department of Environment during the reign of John Prescott; subsequently chairman of the Joint Intelligence Committee). Others on the cast list include the ex-Cabinet Secretary Robin Butler, the current chairman of the Joint Intelligence Committee, Alex Allan, and the Comptroller and Auditor General, Amyas Morse. Politicians include Andrew Adonis, Charlie Falconer, Chris Huhne, Francis Maude, Nick Raynsford, George Young and Shirley Williams.

We talked from late afternoon until ten, with a break for dinner. None of it rocket science. All predicated on the belief that there is an urgent need to redress the balance between Parliament and the executive and the recognition that, given the current disgrace of the political classes, a small window of opportunity has opened. At dinner I sat next to Shirley Williams, the first proper conversation I have ever had with her (we were on opposing sides during the civil war of the late seventies and early eighties). We talked of Cambodia, Laos, Vietnam and Russia – where she lectures twice a year – and, of course, the banking crisis and Gordon's handling thereof. As I have long suspected, a delightful woman, full of humanity and common sense (or am I just getting soft in old age?). The one member of the Gang of Four we could ill afford to lose.

Later, until after midnight, Charlie Falconer hilariously entertained Richard Mottram, Andrew Adonis and me with impersonations of Gordon, Alistair and The Man, and Richard gave his version of the fall of Stephen Byers.

'What possessed Blair to embroil us in Iraq?' I inquired of a friendly mandarin who had a ringside seat throughout. 'Was it because he believed, at all costs, in keeping in with the Americans?'

'No,' he replied. 'The Neo-Cons in Washington came up with this idea that they could carve out some sort of democracy that would eventually bring peace to the Middle East and Blair bought into the delusion.' He added that a Pentagon official, Doug Feith, had even gone so far as to set up his own intelligence operation, behind the backs of the CIA, tasked with finding 'evidence' of a link between Saddam and al-Qaeda. Some wag had christened the exercise 'Feith-based analysis'. He said that there were still those in the SIS who believe that Saddam had all along possessed chemical and biological weapons and that they might yet turn up – perhaps having been smuggled out into Syria for safe-keeping.

Friday, 30 October
Ditchley Park

Daylight reveals a vast lawn sloping down to a lake, with a backdrop of golden beech and red maple and, on the rising ground beyond, a pillared folly. I ventured out just after dawn, in search of the walled gardens. Alas, they were long abandoned to bramble and dereliction; the walls, however, are pretty much intact. A pleasant way for some retired gentleman with time on his hands and a grant from the Heritage Lottery to while away his twilight years ...

Today's session focused on reforming Parliament (yesterday was government). The issues were those preoccupying Tony Wright's committee – beefing up select committees, seizing control of the parliamentary timetable, pre-legislative scrutiny. As usual, I put in a word for reducing our disgracefully long summer recess and, as usual, it failed to register. George Young, the only person of real influence present (given that he is likely to feature in a Cameron Cabinet), kept his powder dry. After lunch David Omand and I went for a walk around the lake, he recounting how (according to Alanbrooke's diaries) the chiefs of staff used to have to drive down to Ditchley to brief Churchill and would find themselves kept waiting until late into the night while he watched a film. They then had to drive back to London through country lanes (no M40 then) in the blackout and be back at their desks in Whitehall the following morning to resume the conduct of the war. Who, I inquired, was the best minister he had worked for during his long career at the heart of government? Without hesitation he named Peter Carrington. Honourable mention also went to Jack Straw.

Sunday, 1 November

A big row brewing over drugs policy. All stemming from Gordon's ludicrous decision, last year, to reclassify cannabis against the advice of the experts. Now Alan Johnson has sacked the head of the Advisory Council on the Misuse of Drugs for publicly disagreeing. Other council members are said to be on the point of resigning in sympathy. This is what happens when you rely for scientific advice on the *Daily Mail*.

Monday, 2 November

Sarah is 20 today.

This evening to a basement dining room in the Carlton Club to record a programme for the BBC – *Dinner with Michael Portillo*. The other guests were Gyles Brandreth, Roy Hattersley, Anthony Howard, Oona King, Jean Seaton and a *Sunday Express* journalist, Julia Hartley-Brewer. Subject of discussion, political diaries. Hattersley was resolutely against on the grounds that they were a betrayal of trust, an ego trip and anyway unreliable. I had thought he might murder me, but actually we got on well, better than I can ever recall. Pleasing how old animosities melt away with the passing of time. I suspect he has always had a lower opinion of me than I have of him. I always thought he would have made a good Home Secretary, save for his one blind spot about the Birmingham Six.

Tuesday, 3 November

'Cameron reneges on EU Treaty vote pledge,' says the main headline in today's *Telegraph* over a report than the Tories are about to abandon – surprise, surprise – their 'cast iron' promise to hold a referendum on the Lisbon Treaty. All very pleasing. Europe remains the fault line running through the Tory party. They just can't shake it off. One has only to toss the word 'Lisbon' across the chamber and the grey pinstripes rise like a lot of Pavlov's dogs. The only other thing that gets them all going is mention of Margaret Thatcher.

Rang Tony Benn, who sounded back to his old form, though he's not yet allowed out on his own. 'I don't find David Cameron attractive,' he said. 'You can't be a rich, white Obama.'

Wednesday, 4 November

The Kelly Report has been published to much wailing and gnashing of teeth. We each received a personally addressed copy in a brown envelope. As expected, he proposes a ban on the employment of relatives and an end to claims for mortgage interest (both to be phased in over five years). The latter is likely to prove expensive from the taxpayers' point of view, given that most people's mortgage interest is far below the likely rental values (mine is currently £231 on a flat that would cost £1,100 a month to rent). One piece of good news, which has passed almost unremarked: he proposes to end the dastardly 'Communications Allowance'. I think I can claim some credit for that, though I shan't do so too loudly, since not all my colleagues will be grateful.

At PMQs much fun over Cameron abandoning his 'cast iron' pledge to hold a referendum on the Lisbon Treaty. The Tories looked uncomfortable. Through the thin walls of my office on Upper Corridor South I can hear my backwoods Tory neighbour dictating a response ('I am sure that David Cameron is an honourable man ...') to protests from the angry Little Englanders in his constituency.

After Questions Speaker Bercow announced the appointment of Professor Sir Ian Kennedy to head the independent body that will in future regulate our terms and conditions. There was uproar at the news that he is to be paid £100,000 for a three-day week.

Thursday, 5 November

Jack Straw emailed me a draft of a written statement he is proposing to make tomorrow, announcing that he is abandoning the requirement that applicants for the judiciary should have to disclose whether or not they are Freemasons. Apparently he has been advised that he has no choice, given a ruling by the European Court regarding a case in Italy. Instead he is planning to introduce a register of interests for judges, but that won't be ready for some time. I sent him back a note suggesting that he delay amending the questionnaire until the register is in place. And also that he'd better get a move on with it or the idea will be forgotten as soon as he is out the door. Interesting that, in this age of transparency, the Masons (and the judges) are heading resolutely backwards.

To the Reform Committee, where for more than two hours we debated the final text of our report, which has to be ready by next week. It is becoming apparent that some of our members are not interested in change of any sort.

Saturday, 7 November

Today's *Telegraph* unleashes an assault on Professor Sir Ian Kennedy. The main charge seems to be that he is a friend of Alastair Campbell's, but what has upset them is the suggestion that he is proposing to take his time over the Kelly proposals and may not implement them in full. Let us pray he doesn't drag this out too long. We urgently need closure. There also seems to be a growing chorus of demands that we deserve a huge pay rise. Mostly they are anonymous and appear to be coming from colleagues (mainly Tories) who have a grossly inflated view of their own worth. Ominously, however, the former head of the Senior Salaries Review Body, Sir John Baker, has added his voice, saying we should be paid £100,000 a year. Like hell we should. It is hard to think of anything that would bring our profession into greater discredit than the suggestion that we should receive a whacking pay rise in return for not cheating on our expenses.

Sunday, 8 November

Sunderland

To Mowbray Park for the Remembrance Day service. My 23rd and last. I have outlasted half a dozen council leaders and three chief executives, but now it is my turn to fade away. Never again shall I process down Burdon Road behind the Mayor in his finery, in the company of assorted bigwigs, or sit in the front row listening to the last doddery veterans paying homage to The Fallen in calm, clear voices that belie their infirmity. Today's parade, bigger and better than ever, was given added poignancy by the place of honour accorded to the relatives of the half-dozen Sunderland lads who have been cut down in Iraq and Afghanistan.

Afterwards I chatted to Lee Martin, who, come the election, will contest Sunderland Central for the Tories. He reckons there is a thousand votes in it either way.

Monday, 9 November

A huge, largely synthetic row has been whipped up by the mother of a soldier who has complained that Gordon's letter of condolence was full of spelling mistakes and generally illegible. Needless to say, she has poured out her heart to the *Sun*, which is stirring the pot for all it's worth. 'The reason these things happen,' remarked a senior minister, 'is because Gordon's staff are scared of him. They don't dare say anything because he shouts at them.'

'Has he shouted at you?'

'Yes, there have been occasions when we've had to shut the door. Once or twice I have had to put stuff in writing because I can't have a conversation with him. Then he rings up and shouts at me.'

This evening I found myself in the same lobby as David Cameron (voting against secret inquests). He says he has nominated the diaries his *Observer* Book of the Year and seemed particularly tickled by the account of my struggle with the government car service, which he says he plans to reform.

Tuesday, 10 November

Lunch with a banker who I came across in Vietnam last summer. He reckons that the economy is doing better than the official statistics suggest, saying that our economic indicators are notoriously inaccurate compared to those in America and the EU. Re the Tories, he said they appear to have no serious plan for managing the economy and that Osborne is regarded as a lightweight in the City.

Wednesday, 11 November

The *Sun* has declared open season on poor Gordon, publishing a transcript of his 13-minute telephone conversation with the woman who rejected his letter of condolence. The whole thing reeks of a set-up (although we are assured it wasn't) and there are signs that, for once, public sympathy may be with Gordon – even the *Sun*'s own website has a narrow majority in his favour. On the radio this morning Peter Mandelson astutely remarked that – so far as the *Sun* was concerned – the real enemy was not the Taliban, but the British government.

Thursday, 12 November

A perfect autumn day, the sky cloudless. Victoria Tower Gardens carpeted with golden leaves from the plane trees. A whiff of roasting coffee beans wafting across the river from the little floating café opposite the entrance to Lambeth Palace. These are the things I shall miss when the curtain falls.

To the Grimond Room for the final session of Tony Wright's Reform Committee. We wrangled for three hours, several of our more assiduous colleagues wanting to nail down every dot and comma, as though we were compiling a legal document. Then Natascha Engel and Peter Atkinson moved a wrecking amendment, suggesting that we simply give up and leave all decisions to some future parliament (imagine the ridicule!); happily they attracted no support. Finally, we were left with a document recommending that select committee chairmen be elected by the whole House and that a backbench business committee be established to give MPs more say over the timetable. Even these modest proposals were too controversial for some. Several people (ominously all, save Natascha, former whips) voted against the business committee and another ex-whip abstained. On September sittings we were split down the middle and opted for a fudge. Overall, a disappointing outcome. We may one day be allowed to elect select committee chairs, but not much more.

Later, I was sitting in the Tea Room when Henry Bellingham came in, fuming at the news that John Bercow's wife is to stand as a Labour candidate for election to Westminster Council. Breathtakingly reckless for an inhabitant of Speaker's House. Is anything more likely to antagonise the Tories, on whom her husband's survival may soon depend? Until now, I thought he would survive, but I begin to wonder. As Henry said, if sufficiently provoked, the Tories won't hesitate to dethrone Mr Speaker Bercow and install one of their own.

Friday, 13 November
Sunderland

An hour with the City Hospitals chief executive, Ken Bremner. Thus far, he says, there have been just 53 confirmed cases of swine flu (so much for all those tabloid scare stories). The number of patients presenting at A&E continues to rise, despite the money lavished on primary care centres. Orthopaedic waiting lists (up to two years when we came in) are now down to 18 weeks or less. He still has problems with some consultants whose NHS work-rate is significantly less than their private sector turnover, though the fact that there are more of them gives him slightly more leverage than he used to have.

Sunday, 15 November

This evening I had the following exchange with Emma (aged 14½) re her failure, despite repeated reminders, to refill the bird-feeders:

'I am trying to teach you responsibility.'

'I have lots of responsibilities.'

'Such as?'

'Homework, my health, my social life ...'

Tuesday, 17 November

A poll in today's *Guardian* suggests that, for the first time, many people are attracted to David Cameron for positive reasons, rather than simply because they don't like us. By a narrow margin, a majority even appear to believe that the Tories are more likely to lift people out of poverty. Which only goes to show that God has a sense of humour.

To the Inner Temple to hear a lecture by Lord Hoffman. On the tube I fell in with a couple of Law Lords and Douglas Hogg. Despite initial misgivings, the Law Lords seem happy with their new abode in what was once Middlesex Town Hall; they get many more visitors and still have the use of the club facilities in the Lords. Douglas told me a shocking story. One evening, not long after he had relinquished the Lord Chancellorship, his father opened his front door to a man who was aggressively ranting and raving. As luck would have it, just at that moment a police car drove past and the man ran off. The next night, however, he knocked on the door of a county court judge and murdered him.

Back at the House I came across Bruce Grocott, who remarked apropos New Labour's Faustian pact with Murdoch, to which (as the Campbell diaries confirm) Bruce was wholly opposed, that it reflected The Man's total lack of confidence that we could win an election under our own steam and that, even if we won a first election, we couldn't hope to win a second.

Wednesday, 18 November

To Westminster for the State Opening. Ominously grey skies, a strong wind whipping up whirlpools of fallen leaves. I arrived just as a coachload of portly Beefeaters was disgorging by the Victoria Tower, along with convoys of ambassadors and high commissioners in gleaming, flag-flying limos. In an inner courtyard a tiny old lady on walking sticks was being helped out of large black car. 'The Lord Chancellor's mother,' a policeman called to a colleague. Jack's dear old mum, come to see him strut his stuff for the last time.

Never having attended a Queen's Speech and this being the last opportunity, I decided that this is another little box that needs ticking.

So I hung around in the Members' Lobby waiting for Black Rod to summon us to the upper house, and as soon as the top brass had passed fell in behind, through the Central Lobby crowded with onlookers, and just managed to squeeze into The Other Place, climbing up three steps, from where I had an excellent view. The scene resembled one of those giant costume dramas that the BBC does so well. Her Majesty, motionless, resplendent in white, seated upon the throne; beside her the sprightly Duke in full dress uniform. To the left a gaggle of pageboys, fresh-faced young aristos in red, and to the right two po-faced ladies-in-waiting, also in white, and the Lord Great Chamberlain, also motionless, holding upright the bejewelled Sword of State. Arrayed before them, peers of the realm, great and small, all in red gowns, which (so David Clark told me later) have to be rented at £150 a time by those who cannot afford to buy them.

The Speech was a long wishlist, much of which – as everybody knows – will never see the light of day, more appropriate to an election address than a programme of legislation. Most ludicrous of all a Bill requiring a future government to halve the public debt within four years. Some involve nonsensical, undeliverable target-setting, a habit that New Labour just can't kick. There is no shortage of people pointing this out.

Afterwards, in the Library Corridor I ran into Alan Milburn and his wife, Ruth. Alan said that shortly after Gordon became leader he advised him to go for an early election. 'I suggested September, before the party conferences, to deny the Tories the oxygen of publicity. If he'd done that, he would have had a majority bigger than Blair's, Cameron would have been toast and the Tories would have been in turmoil.' Alas, his advice was not taken, and the rest is history …

I had intended to speak in the debate, but after sitting for three hours in an almost empty chamber my morale nose-dived. I went to the Chair and asked Alan Haselhurst to cross my name off his list. 'But you're next on your side. I am sure the House will want to hear from you.'

'I am afraid not,' I replied, gesturing at the empty benches. If nothing else, a timely reminder of why I need to give up.

Thursday, 19 November

To St Martin-in-the-Fields for Peter Townsend's memorial. Beautiful music, generous tributes from friends and colleagues, one of whom remarked, 'Peter remained dedicated to the Labour Party all his life, despite its almost bottomless capacity to disappoint.' Then to the atrium at 4 Millbank to talk to some American students. Back at the House, I put my head inside the chamber to see how the debate on the Queen's Speech was going and was shocked to find not a single Labour backbencher, just a couple of junior ministers, a whip and a PPS; on the other side half a dozen Tories and two Lib Dems; otherwise a sea of green benches. The public gallery was empty, too. And this on a day when we were discussing health and education, two of Labour's big issues. Truly, this is a dying parliament.

Monday, 23 November

In today's *Telegraph*, leaked Ministry of Defence documents which shed fascinating light on relations between British officers in Iraq and their American counterparts. This from Major General Andrew Stewart: 'Our ability to influence US policy in Iraq seemed to be minimal.'

And this from Colonel J. K. Tanner, who commanded the British contingent in Basra in 2004: 'I now realise that I am a European not an American. We managed to get on better with our European partners and at times with the Arabs than with the Americans. Europeans chat to each other whereas dialogue is alien to the US military. Dealing with them corporately is akin to dealing with a group of Martians. If it isn't on the PowerPoint slide, then it doesn't happen.'

Tuesday, 24 November

To the Standards and Privileges Committee, where it was agreed, at the suggestion of Nick Soames, that I should be appointed acting chairman in place of David Curry, who has had to stand down owing to expenses trouble. News of the appointment went out on the lunchtime bulletins, resulting in a flurry of congratulatory emails. Alas, it

won't last. This afternoon Soames reported that he had failed to persuade the Tory whips to leave me in situ for the duration. A senior
Tory will be nominated shortly.

Wednesday, 25 November

To the Royal Lancaster Hotel for the annual dinner of the Institute of
Directors. Not my natural territory, but curiosity got the better of me.
A lavish event, 700 black-tie businessmen, four courses, good wines.
Entertainment by Ronnie Corbett and Ken Clarke. Not much evidence of recession, despite several references from the platform to
'hard times', accompanied by the usual demands for lower taxes and
less 'government interference' etc (except, presumably, when it comes
to rescuing the banks). Ken Clarke, entertaining as ever, complained
for 20 minutes about the government's allegedly catastrophic levels
of debt without once conceding that much of it was down to the cost
of rescuing the economy from the consequences of the greed and
avarice of his party's friends in the City. At one point, only slightly
tongue in cheek, he compared the government's fiscal policy to that
of Robert Mugabe. Even in this most Tory of institutions, not everyone was signed up to the mantra coming from the platform. At the
mention of Shadow Chancellor Osborne, someone at my table whispered, 'If that guy had been in charge last autumn, there would have
been meltdown.'

Later, a naval officer expressed concern about the weekly parade
of coffins from Afghanistan through Wootton Bassett. 'It's turning the
army into victims,' he said.

Thursday, 26 November

Final day of the Queen's Speech debate. George Osborne led for the
Tories, mocking us mercilessly for the proposed Bill to cut government debt by half (another of Gordon's pointless little wheezes) and
the continuing stream of unfeasible spending commitments. The
Tory case, however, suffers from a central core of dishonesty – a flat
refusal to acknowledge that the state of the public finances has

anything to do with the fortune we have spent rescuing the banks. I made this point when my turn came, forcing Ken Clarke into a grudging admission that the debt crisis might, after all, have something to do with the profligacy of the bankers. Vince Cable ('St Vince' as he is known on our side), on the other hand, was very fair in his assessment: 'Although I have major disagreements with the government's management of the economy up to the crisis, I agree with its management of the economy during the crisis.' He is so much more credible than Osborne.

Friday, 27 November

Customers at this evening's surgery included an agency worker who had been paid off for the winter and faced not being able to meet his mortgage payments. The sum involved was tiny – £260 a month – but way beyond his means. He was a decent, dignified man who had worked all his life, latterly for a plastics factory making components for Nissan, from which he had been laid off when the market collapsed last autumn. He had signed up with an agency and been taken on by the council to pick litter in Mowbray Park, but the work was seasonal and now he faced a winter on the dole – on benefit of just £64 a week. An ominous trend this. The growth of 'outsourcing' is producing a class of employee who can be picked up and dropped at will without qualifying for holidays, sickness or redundancy pay or any of the other hard-won benefits we used quaintly to associate with civilisation. Slowly, but surely, we are heading backwards towards the nineteenth century.

Monday, 30 November

To London, past swollen rivers and flooded fields after 30 hours of wind and rain.

M, hotfoot from Washington, called in. He's been at the Iraq inquiry and pronounced it a rare example of greater openness in the UK than in the US. There has been nothing similar in the US so far, in keeping with Obama's policy of not raking over the past. Obama, he says, is doing well considering his awful inheritance and the general paralysis in Congress. Re Iran he is keeping a low profile, in order not to inflame the situation. Re Afghanistan, he's proving very thoughtful. Re Pakistan, M says the US is much more heavily involved than is generally admitted. The drones which have been used against targets in the tribal areas are based in Pakistani military bases and US special forces, probably about 750 in number, are operating inside Pakistan. M added that he had recently spent an hour and a half with the Pakistani president, Zadari, and found him deeply unimpressive.

Tuesday, 1 December

The main headline in today's *Daily Mail*: 'WHY DOES LABOUR HATE MARRIAGE?'

To much hilarity the Lib Dems have performed a U-turn on their so-called 'mansion tax'. They were proposing to impose a levy on all houses worth £1 million and over; today they announced it will be restricted to houses valued at £2.5 million and over – i.e. those in Tory-controlled Notting Hill, Kensington and Chelsea as opposed to Richmond, Twickenham and Kingston upon Thames, which are, of course, Lib Dem strongholds. It couldn't be more blatant. They look complete ninnies.

Wednesday, 2 December

After months of cogitating, Obama announced an extra 30,000 troops for Afghanistan, bringing the US contingent up to 100,000. We are sending another 500. There is also talk of a phased withdrawal beginning in 2011, increased pressure on Karzai to clean up his government and lots more Afghan troops who will eventually take over, but no one is very optimistic. The trouble is that we've seen this film before. A liberal president inherits a war in a faraway country, the generals demanding extra troops for one more heave. On the radio yesterday, an archive clip of Lyndon Johnson announcing a big build-up in Vietnam. This is not Vietnam, of course, but there are uncomfortable echoes. The trouble is, no one can think of a credible alternative.

Gordon on excellent form at Questions today. Razor-sharp sound bites – 'Tory tax policy dreamed up on the playing fields of Eton', 'the more the Right Hon. gentleman talks the less he says' and one lovely line, 'The voice is that of a modern PR man, but the mind-set is that of the 1930s'. We went away greatly cheered, though how this plays outside is anybody's guess, but, as Keith Hill remarked at lunch, the dividing lines are becoming clear: cuts versus steady as we go on the economy; toffs versus commoners; plus of course the EU.

Monday, 7 December

A curious paragraph in today's *Times* reporting that the notorious photograph of the Bullingdon Club, featuring Boris Johnson, David Cameron and assorted other Tory toffs has mysteriously been suppressed. 'For commercial reasons,' according to the owners of the copyright. Which I interpret as meaning that someone has paid a large sum for it to be taken out of circulation until after the election. I guess the spinmeisters have noticed that it is incompatible with the image of the new, merciful, compassionate Conservative Party that is alleged to have arisen from the ashes of the lean, mean and greedy one.

At this evening's meeting of the parliamentary party, a long, whingy discussion about the Kelly and Legg inquiries. Much resentment at the fact that Legg has simply ignored many of the representations made to him and is proposing to publish a list of offenders which will lead to another round of media hysteria. The demoralisation is palpable. Try as he might, chairman Tony Lloyd just couldn't close down the discussion. Eventually some light relief in the form of the Transport Secretary, Andrew Adonis. One of that almost extinct species – a happy minister. Fizzing with energy and ideas, in contrast to the tired, demoralised complainers who can talk of naught but allowances.

Later, an exchange with a Tory barrister re The Man, who I hotly defended against the charge that he lied over WMD. This prompted the following response: 'He always had a flexible concept of truth and principle. He was well known for it at the Bar.'

Tuesday, 8 December

An exchange with Nick Soames, just back from a lightning visit to Bombay. 'The Indians have got us by the throat.'

'How so?'

'One day they'll overtake us. They work like hell, believe in education and they're not chippy. Absolutely no resentment.' His evidence for this last proposition was as follows: 'As I was being conveyed through the streets in a Rolls-Royce bigger than the Queen's, with gold-tinted windows, no one gave me the V sign. But they were all trying to see inside.' I bet.

Wednesday, 9 December

Alistair Darling delivered his pre-Budget report. A bit of banker bashing, an increase in National Insurance, VAT back up to 17.5 per cent, much talk of 'protecting front-line services'. Surprisingly tame, considering the direness of our plight. Re the deficit (a whopping £178 billion), containment rather than reduction is the strategy. It will not go down next year, but he did talk vaguely of halving it in the four years thereafter. The economy, he predicts, will return to growth (after shrinking by 4.7 per cent in the last 12 months). The great unanswered question and one we would prefer not to discuss until the election is out of the way is, of course, how we are going to extricate ourselves from the vast swamp of debt into which we have been sucked by the avarice and stupidity of the bankers. Our excuse for not taking immediate action is that we don't want to jeopardise the fragile recovery.

George Osborne was talking Armageddon. Demanding 'tough decisions', invoking the name of Roy Jenkins (who in 1970 balanced the books and lost us the election). For all his bombast, one suspects that George, too, is none too keen to go into detail this side of an election as to precisely how the Tories would tackle the deficit. The electorate would run a mile, if only they knew.

Only Vince Cable affected to remain above the fray, pouring scorn in equal measure on both our houses while at the same time leaving us none the wiser as to what he would do either.

This evening, to Number 10 with Julie Elliot, hopefully my successor, and a local businesswoman. A brief, good-humoured exchange with Peter Mandelson and then we all lined up to have our photograph taken with Gordon, who chatted amiably with Julie and her guest without addressing a single word or even a glance in my direction.

Thursday, 10 December

This morning's headlines: 'Middle classes hit hard' (*Telegraph*), 'The axeman dithereth' (*The Times*), 'Labour's war on workers' (*Express*), 'The Buck Passers' Budget – Darling vows to hammer the middle classes' (*Daily Mail*) and the *Sun*, with characteristic vulgarity, 'Darling just screwed more people than Tiger Woods'. Alistair is simultaneously assailed, sometimes on different pages of the same newspaper, for being (a) too tough and (b) too timid. No hope of a rational discussion in this climate.

Lunch with Grey Gowrie, who told the following tale. In the late seventies, when Margaret Thatcher was within sight of office, Denis without consulting her went out and bought a Rolls-Royce. Margaret, sensing an imminent PR disaster, ordered him to get rid of it, sharpish. Now I come to think of it, in Trafalgar Square one evening in about 1978, I recall seeing Denis drive by at the wheel of a Rolls-Royce with Margaret sitting in the passenger seat and thinking, 'Odd that no one knows their family car is a Roller.'

Monday, 14 December

Alistair Darling addressed the parliamentary party. His speech was gently laced with references to unspecified 'difficulties', but nothing too upsetting. One has to listen carefully to detect any hint of the immensity of the task ahead, but there were clues: 'If you are worried that we are reducing the debt too quickly, I wouldn't be.' Some useful progress to report on tax evasion: Liechtenstein has so far yielded about £1 billion and Alistair has other tax havens in his sights.

Wednesday, 16 December

This evening, a drink in the Pugin Room with a former Special Branch man of my acquaintance who was once part of the team protecting Gordon. He said that, despite the tantrums, workaholism and the difficulty he had relating, Gordon is a decent man.

Thursday, 17 December

To the BBC to record a 'review of the year' with Michael Howard and Matthew Taylor. Afterwards Michael remarked that John Major's great achievement had been to hold the Tory party together at a time when it was in danger of splitting. 'You can't have a Europhile leading the Tory party. If Heseltine had become leader, we would have split.'

In Copenhagen the talks on climate change are deadlocked. It's being billed as the last chance to save the planet. Dire warnings of floods, famine and pestilence unless we change our ways, but will we? Can we?

Friday, 18 December

Sunderland

A stinking cold which, as usual, has gone to my chest, Arctic winds, streets coated in a thin film of snow and ice. I spent an hour and half tramping the streets, inspecting the efforts of a local regeneration agency to upgrade the poorer parts of Hendon by means of selective demolition, buying out some of the worst landlords and face-lifting entire streets of crumbling Victorian houses with garden walls, railings and new facades. Came away much cheered. Who says Labour governments don't make a difference?

The climate change summit is still deadlocked. Today's *Guardian* claims to have discovered a secret UN report saying that whatever is agreed won't be enough and that half the earth's species will be extinct and hundreds of millions displaced by flood and famine by 2050 – well within the lifetime of my children.

Saturday, 19 December

Sunderland

The Copenhagen Summit has broken up in disarray, with an agreement only to 'note' a series of desirable objectives rather than to actually do anything. Could this be the decisive moment? The moment when the world decided to let nature take its course, rather than face up to the difficult choices that have to be made if calamity is to be avoided. Agreement or no agreement, maybe it is already too late and forces are already at work which no amount of summitry can ever reverse.

Sunday, 20 December

To the Wildfowl Park at Washington for Christmas lunch as guests of Pam and Roger Wortley. Outside the snow lay deep and crisp and even. The lane leading back to the main road was iced over and it took about ten goes, plus a push from Pam, Roger and a couple of helpful staff members to get the car up the slope.

The Great Freeze is playing havoc with public transport. The Eurostar trains are up the creek (no less than five having got stuck in the Channel Tunnel) and the bulletins are full of desperate travellers marooned at Paddington, Gare du Nord and the airports.

Monday, 21 December

Sunderland

To Pennywell for a meeting with Gordon Langley, manager of the youth project, which is in financial difficulties. I had been expecting to see just him but he had assembled most of the management committee to underline the seriousness of the situation. A familiar problem. No shortage of money for new initiatives, but little or nothing is for core funding. The New Labour obsession with innovation afflicts much of the voluntary sector. Tried and tested, well-established projects are dying on their feet while endless sums are lavished on bright new wheezes that flash across the firmament and disappear quicker than you can say 'tick that box'. I pointed out to Bev Hughes (the children's minister) some time ago that it will end badly and now it seems the day of reckoning is close. Gordon is deeply demoralised. He has used up much of his reserves and is beginning to lay off staff. And this at a time when the number of unemployed, semi-literate youths is again on the rise. If we are not careful, we shall be back where we started 20 years ago.

Tuesday, 22 December

Half a dozen calls re Pennywell. A friendly council official, in charge of 'Youth Provision', assured me that all was for the best. I fired off a note, copied to all and sundry, in the hope of breaching the wall of complacency and was promised a reply in the New Year.

The Great Freeze continues. Everyone coughing and spluttering. My chest is completely clogged. Ngoc spends much of the day with a blanket round her shoulders. Sarah has had a hacking cough since she came home and now it has spread to Emma. The back lane is so slippery that I have had to leave the car in the street at the front of the house for the last three nights.

Friday, 25 December

To the snowy wilderness above Haltwhistle for Christmas with the Todds. The roads were clear, but the track to Malcolm and Helen's house was impassable so we had to park on the verge and transfer our baggage to Malcolm's car, which had snow shoes on the front wheels. Ruth and Naomi have grown into self-confident and mature young women. Only yesterday, or so it seems, they were little girls playing happily together on our front lawn. And so it was again today as, for two short hours, they went sledging on the steep slope behind the house.

Saturday, 26 December

Birch Trees, Coanwood

Malcolm and I walked five miles through a frozen, snow-covered landscape to the Lamley Viaduct and back. We watched as, far below in the valley, two deer raced in leaps and bounds across a field, their brown hides contrasting with the pristine whiteness.

Tuesday, 29 December

In today's *Daily Mail*, between reports of 'high street chaos' (re the impending re-instatement of VAT at full rate) and lies about the number of people 'threatened' with death duties, the following gem: 'Britain's top prosecutor faced charges that he is a "socialist" yesterday after he flatly rejected Tory plans to give home-owners the right to kill burglars.'

The mind boggles.

Wednesday, 30 December

The Lycee, Kennington

I called on Uncle Peter, who is dying of liver cancer, in his little flat opposite Goodmayes Park. Drowsy, visibly fading, he was sitting in an armchair in the living room, a huge oxygen bottle on one side. A gentle, kind, other-worldly man, Peter is the last member of Mum's immediate family. Somewhere, there is picture of them all taken around 1930, Grandpa and Grandma Foley, and their seven children: Eileen, Terence, Maureen, Brian, Cyril, Mum and Peter, a little cheeky chappie in short trousers. When Peter is gone, as he soon will be, there will be no one left from the large happy family that lived for over 100 years at 44 Ripley Road, Ilford.

Thursday, 31 December

This evening, with John and Sheila Williams, Emma and two young friends, to the terrace of the House of Commons (which Speaker Bercow had graciously decreed should for the first time be opened to Members and their guests on New Year's Eve), from where we had a grandstand view of the fireworks. Afterwards, we made our way home over Lambeth Bridge, ankle-deep in discarded champagne bottles and other New Year detritus.

CHAPTER SIX

2010

Friday, 1 January

So begins the countdown to oblivion. My own and New Labour's.

A call from Claes Bratt, visiting his family in Gothenburg, as ever dreaming of retirement to a sunny, unpolluted clime. His freelance camera work for the American networks is gradually drying up, destroyed by the internet. 'No one cares about quality any more. No one wants to pay for anything. There is a lack of ambition. Even the *New York Times* is laying off journalists.' The only hope, says Claes, of saving serious journalism is that sooner or later someone will find a way to charge for access to internet news. 'That's the one thing about which I agree with Murdoch.'

Emma and I packed up the car and sped north to Sunderland, the last 30 miles through a blizzard.

Saturday, 2 January

Awoke to hear John Major and Shirley Williams on the radio discussing how to restore trust in politics. Their remedies included increasing MPs' pay (????!!!!), more power for select committees, backbenchers etc. No mention, though, of what to do about the tabloid virus (by no means confined to the tabloids) – the daily cocktail of misrepresentation, trivialisation and relentless cynicism – which is gnawing at the foundations of our democracy. In such a climate even a parliament composed entirely of Mother Teresas and Nelson Mandelas would have difficulty in inspiring trust.

Sunday, 3 January

Gordon appeared on this morning's *Andrew Marr Show*, desperately trying to sound upbeat, refusing to contemplate the possibility of spending cuts or tax increases. A position which is wholly incredible. He looked tense and exhausted, which makes you wonder what he's been doing over Christmas.

Monday, 4 January

A phoney war has broken out. Gordon and Ed Balls talk only of future spending plans (although there are rumours of a rift with Alistair and the Treasury over this approach). Even the Tories are at it, simultaneously lamenting the state of the public finances (which they shamelessly attribute entirely to Labour profligacy, without reference either to the global meltdown or to the part played by their friends in the City). At the same time they promise a freeze on council tax, tax breaks for married couples and all sorts of other expensive goodies. To cap it all, the Tories have launched a nationwide poster campaign featuring a large, airbrushed photo of David Cameron alongside the fatuous slogan: 'I'll cut the deficit, not the NHS.' Both camps appear to have concluded, and they may be right, that no rational discussion of spending cuts or tax increases is possible this side of an election. Whether they can keep this up for five months remains to be seen.

Tuesday, 5 January

To the Chamber to see Alistair Darling introduce the Fiscal Responsibility Act, which obliges the government to halve the deficit within four years. Surely the most pointless piece of legislation ever devised. Not least since it imposes no sanction if the target is not met. To be fair to Alistair, this is not his doing. It shows every sign of having been dreamed up in the fun factory at Number 10. He managed to keep a straight face throughout as George Osborne shredded it mercilessly. Osborne was followed by Frank Field, who made an apocalyptic speech comparing the current state of British politics with the phoney war of 1938–9 and predicting the imminent collapse of the currency.

By way of evidence he cited (as did Osborne) an announcement by Pimco, a big player in the bond market, that it would not for the time being be purchasing any more gilts.

'He's losing it,' whispered former Treasury minister Geoffrey Robinson as Frank sat down.

'Is he? I rely on you for advice about the bond market.'

'The government will get the money it needs, but it might be a quarter of a per cent more expensive, that's all. Pimco's statement is just a negotiating ploy.'

Let's hope so.

Wednesday, 6 January

Another coup attempt. Just before Prime Minister's Questions, I was sitting in the atrium at Portcullis House when up came Barry Sheerman (who has been calling for Gordon's head for months), saying that Geoff Hoon and Patricia Hewitt were about to put out a statement demanding a vote of confidence in our beloved leader. Sure enough, we emerged from PMQs (at which Gordon did well) to find an email from Geoff and Patricia demanding a ballot. By evening it had become clear that this latest putsch had failed. Most senior members of the Cabinet put out statements saying they were content with present management, though several took their time and were suspiciously lukewarm. Among the ranks there is fury, particularly with Geoff, a former chief whip, that he and Patricia should choose to upset the applecart, just as the heat was going out of The Gordon Question. Now it's back in the headlines again.

Thursday, 7 January

Much vitriolic email traffic re Hoon/Hewitt as colleagues vie to demonstrate their loyalty to the regime. One can't help noticing, however, that many waited until it was clear that the coup had failed before registering their upsetness. This morning's crop of loyalist emails was brought to an end by Eric Joyce, who wrote: 'Thanks, all. That's enough expressions of outrage. Especially those with insane punctuation.'

A scathing editorial in *The Times* headed 'A Last Opportunity': 'Labour MPs must finally have the courage to act – or else the electorate may do it for them.' The problem, as we all know, is that it is too late.

Drove Sarah to Oxford, where the snow in the side roads was a foot deep, and then made my way north through a bleak winter landscape, arriving at 2 a.m.

Friday, 8 January

A note from Bruce Grocott re the diaries, which, he says, 'reminded me why we have so enjoyed each other's company over the years'. A relief. I feared Bruce might disapprove.

Saturday, 9 January

Sunderland

The great freeze in its fourth week. A temperature of minus 18 was recorded in Oxfordshire the other day. The back lane a sheet of ice. Three weeks since I was able to put the car away. Ngoc has set to work plugging the many gaps in our leaky Victorian house, taking the old Brixton Road curtains out of storage. Mr Honeysett has been summoned to put up rails and the said curtains now hang across the front and back doors. We dwell in twilight. In the living room the shutters remain closed all day, curtains drawn. For the fourth time I cleared the steps and dug out paths to the front and back gates. The nearby main road eerily silent, even at midday.

Sunday, 10 January

Yet another assault on poor Gordon. This time from Peter Watt, the fresh-faced New Labour zealot who became General Secretary in the final years of The Man and who was unceremoniously dumped following the latest funding hoo-ha. With exquisite timing, Watt has chosen this moment to get his own back – across several pages of the *Mail on Sunday*. Among the damaging revelations, an inside account of the election-that-never-was. He quotes Douglas Alexander as saying of Gordon, 'The truth is, we have spent ten years working with this guy and we don't actually like him.' Douglas is naturally denying all and Watts admits he is paraphrasing, but it all adds fuel to the fire.

Monday, 11 January

The latest uprising has fizzled out, but there is no rejoicing. We all know that we are badly – fatally – damaged. This evening's jam-packed meeting of the parliamentary party was seething with anger towards the plotters.

'No personal attacks,' cautioned chairman Tony Lloyd, only to be greeted with cries of 'Why not?'

Gordon, flanked by the grim-faced Cabinet – Harriet Harman, Douglas Alexander and the Noble Lord Mandelson to the fore – attempted to raise morale and was warmly received by we who are about to die. 'We can win. We will win. We must win,' he concluded, but despite the applause and the table-thumping, no one believes him. The trouble is that nor do we believe that anyone else could lead us back to the promised land. It is too late for that. Actually, Gordon was on good form. As fluent and relaxed as I have seen him. If words any longer mattered, he would easily have passed the test, but we are beyond words now. He was followed by our election 'co-ordinators', Douglas, Peter and Harriet, each anxious to demonstrate (despite credible reports to the contrary) that they are working as a team and, just as important, that Gordon is no longer in sole charge. Indeed he may not be in charge at all. There was a clue, buried deep in his speech: 'I am not a team of one. I am one of a team.' Somewhere in the middle there was a nice little joke, hinting that Geoff Hoon and Patricia Hewitt might be destined for a salt mine in Staffordshire, which, everyone said afterwards, someone must have scripted for him. That's the problem – when Gordon cracks a joke no one believes that he could have thought of it by himself.

Tuesday, 12 January

Lunch with Kim Howells, late of the Foreign Office, now chairman of the Security and Intelligence Committee. We chuckled over the irony. His father was (until 1956) a Communist. Kim himself was in the CP for 18 months (until being politely asked to leave after exhibiting evidence of a capacity for independent thought). As a student at Hornsey College of Art he led a sit-in, not to mention that he was heavily involved in the miners' strike. Somewhere in the bowels of the security service there is bound to be a nice fat file on him and yet here he is presiding over the very committee to which the secret services are obliged to account. How times change.

Douglas Alexander, fresh from a meeting of the political Cabinet and armed with the latest focus group findings, attended the Northern Group. He spoke of an anti-politics mood in the country. A deep cynicism. 'A desire for change so strong that anything we say that implies we are insiders can only do us damage.' As if that wasn't bad enough the recession has changed everything – 'all the assumptions about growth have been torn up'. Even so, he added, people want a better future and somehow we have got to offer them one. But how, given that the public coffers are bare and the party just this side of bankruptcy?

Wednesday, 13 January

To a massive knees-up in Canary Wharf in aid of Jim Fitzpatrick's re-election fund. I had the following exchange with a pleasant but vacuous young woman, active in Jim's constituency party, who was seated on my left.

She: 'What do you do?'
'I am a Member of Parliament.'
'How long have you been an MP?'
'Twenty-three years.'
'That's interesting. You should write a diary.'

A huge earthquake in Haiti, casualties run to tens, maybe hundreds of thousands.

Thursday, 14 January

I have a split in my shoe, at the point where the leather joins the sole. My only other pair have a similar split in precisely the same place. I have tried getting them repaired, but no one wants to know. Actually, the split appeared several weeks ago, but the recent snow has made it impossible to ignore any longer. This morning, upon reaching the office, I had to take off my sock and dry it on the radiator. It's not that I'm too mean to replace them. I just can't bear the waste. In Vietnam or India no one would dream of throwing away two pairs of otherwise good shoes. I would take them to a man at a little stall by the side of the road and he would repair them without fuss.

This evening to Belfast for a book event at the arts festival tomorrow.

Friday, 15 January

Belfast

A damp, dull, grey day, the city much changed since I was last this way. The barricades have gone, investment is flooding in and the city centre no longer closes down at 9 p.m. Some things, however, never change. The police HQ is still barricaded with steel and concrete, the politics deadlocked – and relentlessly introverted. The first half-dozen pages of this morning's *Belfast Telegraph* are taken up with the crisis in the Democratic Unionist Party arising from the misdemeanours of Iris Robinson – the earthquake in Haiti is on pages 18 and 19.

Sunday, 17 January

Awful scenes from Haiti. An entire nation reduced to rubble. And this only the latest in a long series of catastrophes. Aid pouring in from all over the world, but the port has been destroyed and the airport capacity is limited, with the result that very little has yet reached the destitute.

Monday, 18 January

A depressing little discussion about electoral reform at this evening's meeting of the parliamentary party. All we were being invited to discuss was whether to include a provision for a referendum on alternative voting in the Constitutional Reform Bill that is currently going through or leave it to the manifesto. This provoked a host of objections to any change whatever. The Parliamentary Labour Party is really a most conservative institution. In truth, however, it is all an irrelevance since, whatever we do, no Tory government is going to take the slightest notice. If tinkering with the electoral system is such a good idea, we should have done it years ago. Now it's too late and stinks of desperation and self-interest.

Wednesday, 20 January

Awoke to the news that the Democrats have lost the by-election for Ted Kennedy's seat in Massachusetts, the equivalent of the Rhondda returning a Tory. A huge blow for Obama, since it means he loses control of the Senate. American voters are said to be 'angry', but if so their anger seems bizarrely irrational. It took the Republicans eight years to destroy the economy, organise two foreign wars and alienate just about the entire world. Surely they can't have been expecting him to put everything right inside 12 months? Later, a quiet chat in the Tea Room with a Foreign Office minister who says HMG is privately disappointed with Obama for (a) not standing up to the Israelis re settlements ('he blinked first'), (b) turning up empty-handed at the climate change conference in Copenhagen and (c) taking so long to make up his mind about deploying extra troops to Afghanistan.

At PMQs I found myself sitting next to Tony Wright, who whispered that he had been on an overseas trip with one of the new, modern young Tories who had boasted of emailing a third of his constituents before breakfast. 'That's why the new intake are so keen on conducting phoney surveys. They aren't interested in the opinions of their constituents. They just want to harvest email addresses.' He added with a weary smile, 'I am so glad I am going.'

Thursday, 21 January

Jack Straw gave evidence to the Iraq inquiry. Attention focused on a recently published 'Secret and Personal' memorandum that Jack addressed to The Man in March 2002 – a full year before the invasion – setting out with remarkable prescience the pitfalls and questioning the legality of the enterprise. Loyal courtier that he was, Jack wasn't quite opposed, but he clearly wasn't enthusiastic either. Jack is the one member of the War Cabinet who may emerge from this debacle with his reputation enhanced. The man who kept his head while all about him were losing theirs.

Tuesday, 26 January

To Simpson's-in-the-Strand for a slap-up lunch at which I – and four others – were presented with an 'Oldie of the Year' award. A dubious accolade since I had never previously thought of myself as old, but I guess I must get used to it. A huge cast of gracefully ageing glitterati, including Kate Adie, Anna Ford, Peter O'Toole, Moira Stuart and Terry Wogan. Most of the acclaim was for the dreadful Joanna Lumley for her Gurkha campaign, which is predictably proving to be a disaster, destitute Gurkhas arriving daily at Heathrow with a wholly unrealistic idea of the life that awaits them. Most of those at today's event were blissfully unaware of the misery she has caused and she was duly fêted, whooping and hamming it up for all she was worth, a token Gurkha in tow. I steered well clear of La Lumley for fear that, if I got too close, I might not have been able to restrain myself from strangling her.

The Iraq inquiry is hotting up. Today Sir John Chilcot took evidence from the Foreign Office lawyers Sir Michael Wood and Elizabeth Wilmshurst (the one official who resigned), who both said, in terms, that they had advised Jack that the war was illegal and that he had discounted their advice, saying it was too dogmatic. Perhaps Jack isn't going to come so well out of this after all.

Wednesday, 27 January

The first person I came across this morning was Ken Purchase, steam coming out of his ears. 'Have you seen this report on inequality?' A government-sponsored commission had reported that Britain was as class-ridden and unequal today as it had been in 1997. 'What have we been doing all these years?'

'Holding back the tide,' I ventured.

'The pivotal moment was when Peter Mandelson said we were utterly relaxed about people getting filthy rich.'

Maybe, but I simply don't buy the line that it has all been a waste of time. The minimum wage, tax credits, all those new schools (17 in Sunderland) have surely made an impact. To be sure, we have succeeded in raising the floor below which no one should be allowed to fall. The problem is all those bankers, hedge-funders, FTSE fat cats, corporate lawyers and Premier League footballers who we've allowed to run riot at the other end of the social scale.

This evening, at a reception in Kensington Palace, the following tantalising exchange with a Cabinet minister of my acquaintance, regarding Geoff Hoon's failed coup attempt.

'A misjudgement,' said I.

'No. He was betrayed.'

'You mean he was expecting a senior member of the Cabinet to join him?'

'Yes.'

'A vague assurance or a promise?'

'A promise.'

'Who?'

'Ah, that will have to wait for my memoirs.'

He added, 'When it's all over, the big question will be how Gordon ever got there in the first place.'

Thursday, 28 January

A call from the chief executive of Shop Direct (formerly Littlewoods), a mail order company, to say that he is proposing to close his Sunderland operation with the loss of 900 jobs, almost all women, many the only breadwinners. The cause is said to be internet shopping, though the company is looking to 'outsource' some of the work to home-workers. So once again our 'redundancy task force' rolls into action. A well-rehearsed routine. Coles's Cranes, Dewhirst, Pyrex, Vaux Brewery – one by one the dominoes have fallen. In fairness the picture is not entirely gloomy. The call centres at Doxford business park are looking to recruit another 200 employees and Nissan announced today that it was taking back 400 workers laid off last year. We are still light years away from where we were in the eighties.

Today's *Guardian* contains the following headline: 'Fox the most trusted US news channel, poll says'. God bless America.

Friday, 29 January

To the Church of St Peter and Paul in Ilford for Uncle Peter's funeral, the last member of Mum's immediate family. A much-loved, self-effacing, technophobe, poet and local historian. An Essex man to the end, except that his was not the Essex of bling, brutalist new towns and vulgar hacienda with gold-topped railings. His was the Essex of unspoiled villages, country lanes and ancient churches – which still exist for those who know where to look. The church was packed, even though Peter had outlived most of his contemporaries. I herewith reproduce, from the order of service, one of his poems in order that some record may exist of the work of this talented man, unrecognised outside his own small circle:

To Beauchamp Church in Winter Time

Could I, of all that's dead and past,
One treasured hour renew at last
Down Essex lanes, content, I'd stride,
With you, my laughing love, beside,
And take the Abbess Road and climb
To Beauchamp Church in winter time.

Through silvered fields by frozen brook,
Near haunts of redwing, thrush and rook,
We'd vault the ditch where ways divide

By stricken elm and coppice side,
Turning at cottage wall to see
The little amelanchier tree,
One faded golden leaf to show
That summer stayed not long ago;
And so the Beauchamp's ghostly height,
Then home before the winter's night.

I've heard men say, as say they will,
Time makes all sweetness sweeter still.
No less, could I one hour renew,
I'd walk the frosty lanes with you,
And take the Abbess Road and climb
To Beauchamp Church in winter time.

Peter Foley 1923–2010

Meanwhile The Man, taut, tense, unrepentant, made his long-awaited appearance before the Iraq inquiry, smuggled in through a back entrance to avoid the baying mob outside. Visibly nervous to begin with, he soon got into his stride and before long, helped by some long-winded questioning, dominated the proceedings, conceding nothing save the occasional tactical error. And yet he had a strangely haunted look. As if, deep down, he knows (as he surely does) that Iraq will cast a malign spell over him for the rest of his life – and beyond into infinity.

Saturday, 30 January

Sunderland

To town in search of new shoes. Pacing up and down outside the station, a man with shoulder-length grey curly hair topped by a straw trilby. Piled high behind, all his worldly goods in two wheeled cases and an array of leather bags. He is smartly dressed and looks for all the world like someone who, after long absence, has just alighted from a train and is waiting for a lift home. Except that he isn't. He is here every day, rain or shine (today, snow), always with his vast baggage, which he moves around the town in shifts. Who is he? Where does he live? He seems too well dressed to be derelict and yet no one seems to know anything about him. The other day I had my assistant, Michael, ring the homeless hostel, but the manager couldn't help. I guess he may be one of those poor souls who once, until something went badly wrong, causing a switch to flip, knew a better life.

Wednesday, 3 February

The Tories appear to be wobbling over their plans for the economy. Shadow Chancellor George Osborne laid out his plans yesterday with a press conference at the British Museum, but he was remarkably light on detail. Gone is all that scary talk of 'a decade of austerity', coupled with accusations of government cowardice for failing to announce an immediate programme of slash and burn. Now Boy George speaks only of 'making a start' and promises that the first year's cuts will not be 'particularly extensive'. What has come over him? Can it be that the Tories have noticed that the Great British Public might not be all that grateful were they to collapse the economy in the name of fiscal rectitude? Witness a slight narrowing in the polls in the last few days, leading to speculation about the prospect of a hung parliament. Nothing to get too excited about, but in these desperate times we must clutch at any straw.

Thursday, 4 February

To the Grimond Room in Portcullis House for an emergency meeting of the Reform Committee to discuss how to respond to the growing evidence that the government is in the process of reneging on promises to concede a modicum of power to the backbenches. After almost three months of shilly-shallying Harriet announced that our proposals will be debated on Monday, 22 February, upon return from the mid-term recess, on a one-line whip, which ensures a low turnout and no vote. What's more, the motion will be put to the House as series of unamendable Orders, requiring only a single Member to object for it to be blocked. It couldn't be more blatant. Yet again the forces of inertia appear to have triumphed. Yet again lofty statements of intent appear to be no more than empty gimmicks. We decided to summon Harriet to explain, with the cameras switched on, but I doubt she is the principal culprit. Gordon and the whips have their fingerprints all over this.

Headline in tonight's *Standard*: 'CHEATING MPs IN £1 MILLION PAYBACK DAY – 350 found guilty of milking expenses'. Actually, despite the hysteria, Sir Thomas Legg's final report turned out not to be the rigorous analysis we were promised. No fewer than 44 of our number – myself included – have had all or part of his findings overturned on appeal. And the inquiry cost marginally more than Sir Thomas managed to reclaim. Not that any of this cuts much ice with the punters. So far as most people are concerned we are all crooks to be despised and vilified. In most of our free press the very act of appeal is treated as evidence of criminality.

Friday, 5 February

The Director of Public Prosecutions has announced charges against three MPs – David Chaytor, Jim Devine and Elliot Morley – all Labour, and one peer, Lord Hanningfield, a Tory. It is rumoured that they are being advised to plead not guilty on the grounds that their actions are covered by parliamentary privilege, which, if true, is disgraceful and will bring even more discredit upon our wretched profession.

Monday, 8 February

This morning an unscrupulous, disgraceful attempt by Cameron to implicate Gordon in the suggestion that parliamentary privilege may be used to rescue the members accused of fiddling their expenses. This resulted in a statement from the Speaker reminding everyone that the case is *sub judice* and that the suspects are entitled to a fair trial. At this evening's meeting of the parliamentary party, the Chief Whip, Nick Brown, solemnly announced the 'administrative suspension' of the three alleged offenders, taking care to emphasise that they were entitled to a fair trial. I feel sorry for them, especially Elliot Morley, who looks a broken man. Goodness knows how he got into this mess.

At lunch in the cafeteria I came across Bernard Donoughue, who offered his assessment of David Cameron: 'A marketing man, no good on policy. My Tory friends say that he starts to unravel in adversity; he's fine while he's winning, but as the polls narrow he doesn't know what to do. A good general for a short campaign, but no good in a long campaign. That's the case for a June election.'

Bernard agrees that that Gordon made the right decisions during the financial crisis. 'And the Tories made the wrong ones. That's the one thing we've got going for us. We should say it over and over again, even though it bores the public silly, until it gets through.'

Tuesday, 9 February

Today's *Times* leads with a poll suggesting that 70 per cent of those interviewed have bought the Tory line that we are living in a broken society and that 40 per cent would like to emigrate – many, no doubt, to a country where there were fewer 'foreigners'. Most people are better off than they have ever been, healthier, wealthier, and they can expect to live longer than their parents. And yet, it seems, they are nostalgic for the days of mass unemployment and inner city riots. What a race of pessimists we have become. Is it all the fault of us poor, despised, inadequate politicians or might it have anything to do with (a) the weather and (b) the tabloid virus?

This afternoon, a visit to Speaker Bercow in his grand office overlooking the river, to canvass my suggestion that I be allowed a valedictory speech. He was enthusiastic and promised to do what he can to find a slot before the curtain falls.

A brief exchange with the Defence Secretary, Bob Ainsworth, re Norine MacDonald's plan to grow opium under licence for medicinal purposes in Afghanistan. A plan which, hitherto, has been dismissed by all the experts as wholly impractical. To my amazement Bob remarked that she was 'spot on'. He added, 'The political classes are so gutless. We even reclassified cannabis. Do we deserve to govern?'

Wednesday, 10 February

Harriet, along with her Tory and Lib Dem shadows (George Young and David Heath), duly appeared before the Reform Committee this morning. Much of the heat had gone out of the event, given that we have now been assured that a proper vote will, after all, be permitted.

Lunch with Keith Hill in the cafeteria. He reported that our far-sighted whips had recently been overheard discussing membership of a future Shadow Cabinet. Evidence, if any were needed, that we have given up the ghost.

Thursday, 11 February

The lovely Denise Robertson, TV agony aunt, novelist, first lady of Wearside, was on the train this evening. 'I've never been so depressed,' she said apropos the political situation. 'I feel as though I've seen the best and everything else is downhill.' In passing she remarked that today's politicians were minnows compared to those of yesteryear. Francois Gordon, with whom I stayed last night, said the same. I beg to differ. Blair and Brown for all their faults are no minnows. Jack Straw would have been a significant figure in any post-war Cabinet. Likewise Margaret Beckett, Peter Mandelson, John Reid or Clare Short. To be sure Bevin was a giant. In retrospect we can see that Attlee was, too, although it may not have seemed so at the time. Bevan, for all his undoubted brilliance, had a monstrous ego, which helped to destroy the '50–51 government and usher in 13 years of Tory rule. Herbert Morrison was always plotting. They were all, in their way, big men, but perhaps they just seem bigger because they are further away and, of course, they never had to live in the glare of a 24-hour media or submit to the demands of the Freedom of Information Act.

Friday, 12 February

Sunderland

Solved, the mystery of the sad man who lingers with his considerable baggage by the railway station. An item in my *Echo* column last night brought in a dozen or more calls. His name is Ernie Roll. He lived with his mother in one of the multi-storey blocks in the town centre. When she died he lost the tenancy and has lived rough ever since.

Apparently, he washes daily in the toilets at the Park Lane metro and spends his nights in the doorway of one of the university buildings. Lord knows how he has survived the winter or how he manages to look so smart. He is said to be a proud, difficult – and on occasions aggressive – man, resisting all offers of help. One of those who rang in had known him since they were at primary school together 57 years ago and said that, even as a child, Ernie was a loner. The consensus seems to be that he is beyond help.

Monday, 15 February

Sunderland

Through our letter box comes a no-expense-spared brochure from our Tory candidate, a brash, handsome young man called Lee Martin. Each leaflet is individually addressed. Clearly some serious money is being spent. He has a good, positive campaign slogan, 'Ambitious for Sunderland', and promises (improbably) to ensure that the city is 'at the heart of the next Conservative government'. He also promises a better NHS, better schools, more affordable homes – and all at less cost, if you believe the item headed 'Scrap Labour's National Insurance Rise', which, on close inspection, promises to do no such thing. On the back, pictures of three upright citizens, including, to my surprise, a bright young woman who recently did a week's work experience in my office, into whose mouth the following words have been inserted: 'It's my generation that has been lumbered with paying off Gordon Brown's debt.' Truly, they have no shame.

Thursday, 18 February

To the University of Hull, my *alma mater*, to see Professor Norton and colleagues, who want me to do a series of 'master classes' for their politics students. I arrived early, walked up Beverley Road to the university and whiled away the best part of an hour exploring the campus, which, at first glance, seems remarkably unchanged. The number of students has increased fivefold but they look remarkably similar to those of 40 years ago, except maybe a tad more respectable. I have to pinch myself to realise that not one of them was born when I first set foot here; most indeed were not born when I was first elected to Parliament. Truly, I am a dinosaur.

Friday, 19 February

This morning's *Times*, which is becoming increasingly excitable, leads with the news that a 'record' slump in tax receipts has resulted unusually in a January deficit instead of the expected surplus. Much wild talk that our deficit will soon exceed that of Greece, which, as everyone knows, is a basket case. The implication being that a panic needs to be organised in good time for the election. A sentiment encouraged by a letter in the *Sunday Times* of five days ago signed by 20 or so leading economists, including that foolish peer Megned Desai, demanding an immediate programme of slash and burn. Happily, however, today's *FT* contains letters signed by three times as many economists, including Nobel Prize-winner Joseph Stiglitz, supporting the government's cautious approach. All of which only goes to prove the old adage that, laid end to end, the world's economists would circle the globe and still not reach a conclusion. Even so, no escaping the fact that we live in dangerous times. One false move could bring the house down.

Saturday, 20 February

Awoke to hear Douglas Alexander being cross-examined by John Humphrys re Labour's election strategy. Humphrys at his sneering worst, pressing Douglas to say that he really loathed Gordon, pretending that the global meltdown was all Gordon's fault, resolutely refusing to engage on the big issues. If it were me I'd have been tempted to take the piss ('Sounds like you've been overdosing again on the *Daily Mail* this morning, John'; 'Oh, John, you really must get out more ...'). Instead Douglas, mild-mannered and professional as ever, kept his cool and ploughed resolutely on with his brief, managing to land only one small blow ('Are you suggesting that the Prime Minister is responsible for the Mississippi mortgage crisis?').

Sunday, 21 February

A huge new onslaught. Today's *Observer* is running extracts from the new Andrew Rawnsley book, replete with dark tales of tantrums, paranoia and bullying on the part of our beloved leader. All the more damaging because this cannot be dismissed as the ravings of the Tory tabloids. On the contrary, these latest charges come from left of centre and appear to be impeccably sourced. By midday the bulletins are running interviews with a woman from an outfit called the National Bullying Helpline saying she has received three or four calls from Downing Street staff seeking advice. So intense is the firestorm that one can't help feeling sorry for Gordon. How can he, how can anyone, hope to survive this relentless bombardment? What a joyless business government has become.

An outing with Emma to Howick, ostensibly to see the snowdrops. By the time we got there they were submerged in pristine snow, but we managed a pleasant stroll through the grounds and down the Long Walk, even as the snow fell.

Monday, 22 February

To London through a frozen landscape, said to be the coldest winter for more than 30 years. This afternoon, the long-awaited debate on the Wright Committee reforms. Harriet, on behalf of the government, was emollient, conceding everything except the most significant of our recommendations – a proper business committee. Likewise, George Young, who is – if anything – more amenable to reform, despite his proximity to power. The trouble is, as we all know, behind them in the shadows lurk the whips, who, one strongly suspects, remain set in their ways. As if to prove the point Hilary Armstrong, the ghost of chief whips past, sat chuntering throughout, intervening occasionally to indicate her implacable opposition. There is to be a vote next week. With any luck we should win the right to choose who shall sit on the select committees, but the great prize – control of the timetable – is likely to elude us.

Tuesday, 23 February

Miraculously the 'Gordon is a bully' story seems to be imploding. Gus O'Donnell, the Cabinet Secretary, has denied, in terms that appear to be categorical, that he has ever had cause to have words with Gordon about his behaviour. So far, at least, there is no sign of the Number 10 employees who are supposed to have called the anti-bullying hotline and some tabloids have turned their fire on the sole source for the allegation – Christine Pratt – who herself appears to have form in this area. Most improbably of all, today's *Mail* carries a full-page article, illustrated by pictures of Elizabeth I, Lyndon Johnson, Margaret Thatcher and Winston Churchill, under the heading 'Bullies make the best leaders'. On another page Ms Pratt is dismissed as 'the high priest-ess of victimhood'. By nightfall the worst seemed to be over. Or at least it would have been, but for some uncharactistically incautious remarks by Alistair Darling to the effect that 'the forces of hell' had been unleashed upon him in the summer of 2008 after he had pre-dicted – accurately, as it turned out – that the economy was facing the worst downturn for 60 years. He even went so far as to identify one of the culprits, Damian McBride, who was, until his downfall, one of Gordon's closest henchpersons.

To Simpson's-in-the-Strand for an 'Oldie' literary lunch, where I found myself sitting next to Tony Benn, who, incredibly, will be 85 in a few weeks' time, frail but in much better shape than when our paths last crossed. The audience were prosperous Middle Englanders of a certain age. Predominantly *Mail* and *Telegraph* readers, I suspect, who would have run a mile from the Benn of old, but when he rose to speak he soon had them eating out of the palm of his hand.

Wednesday, 24 February

Happily the Gordon story has died a death, the tabloids being largely preoccupied with the break-up of Cheryl and Ashley Cole's marriage. Gordon easily saw off Cameron at PMQs. It is even reported that the Tory lead is narrowing, apparently on the grounds that public are beginning to notice that they have nothing sensible to say on the economy.

Lunch with Bruce Grocott in the Adjournment. We discussed who might inherit the throne when the inevitable happens. Bruce remarked that it was a sign of the times that three of the main contenders – Balls and the two Milibands – had identical career paths. Bright young researchers, parachuted into safe seats and, within a couple of years, wafted into the Cabinet. Little or no experience of the real world. 'At least,' he added, 'the Milibands have been brought up in a household where politics was taken seriously.'

Saturday, 27 February

A magnificent piece by Roy Hattersley, in response to the Rawnsley book, in the current *New Statesman*. 'There is no correlation between equitable temperament and statesmanship. Nor is the ability to run the country related to any of the other superficial virtues that are now regarded as essential to political success. That claim is not made in defence of the Prime Minister. It is a declaration of support for a higher view of politics than the fashionable notion that what matters in a party leader is a winning smile, the ability to counterfeit interest in pop music and a willingness to weep in public. Judged against these criteria, neither William Gladstone nor Clement Attlee would have risen above the rank of parliamentary secretary.'

He goes on, 'It may be naive to believe that, in an age of reality television, politics should still provide something more noble than the parliamentary equivalent of mud-wrestling. But unless politicians return to the conflict of ideas, democracy itself will be devalued, and the Andrew Rawnsleys of this world will make their money by suggesting that election should be decided by which party leader the voters would most like to see evicted from the Westminster edition of *I'm a celebrity … Get me out of here.*'

He concludes with a plea for 'a return to the politics of ideas'. It pains me to say so, since Hattersley has excoriated everything I have ever done, but we could do with a few more politicians of his weight in the upper reaches.

Monday, 1 March

Lunch in the cafeteria with Keith Hill. I put it to him that, were we to awake on 7 May and find that Gordon were still prime minister, even we, Labour loyalists as we are, would feel a certain gloom. He did not disagree. As Keith once remarked, Gordon's style of government is joyless.

One other little snippet: after years of prevarication and obfuscation, Lord Ashcroft, the Tories' mega-donor, has been outed as a Non-Dom.

Tuesday, 2 March

On an upper corridor, I came across the former *Sun* editor David Yelland. 'Are you Chris Mullin?' he inquired.

I reluctantly conceded that I might be.

He said, 'When I read your book about the Birmingham bombings I went to Kelvin Mackenzie and said, "We should be campaigning on this", but he told me to f-off.' A bad move on Kelvin's part since the case eventually cost the *Sun* more than a million in libel damages. But I would have missed out on all those wonderful *Sun* headlines that now adorn the wall of my study: 'LOONY MP BACKS BOMB GANG', 'Mr ODIOUS' etc.

Wednesday, 3 March

Much excitement re Ashcroft. Harriet, who stood in for Gordon at PMQs, bashed Hague all around the chamber on the subject, provoking much bawling and shouting from our side. Not a very edifying spectacle, but where Ashcroft is concerned the Tories are vulnerable; after all, he is probably the largest donor in British political history.

Thursday, 4 March

Lunch with Sir Peter Jennings, a former Serjeant at Arms, in the magnificent, if somewhat fading, ducal mansion on Charles Street, Mayfair, that nowadays houses the English Speaking Union. Then back to the House, where we chalked up a small victory for the forces of enlightenment and progress by voting more or less *nem con* to elect select committee members by secret ballot, hopefully putting an end to the present ludicrous situation where the executive decides to whom it shall account. The proposed Business Committee also went through, though it is a pale shadow of what is needed – even so there was a last-minute conspiracy by the two front benches to water it down still further which was easily seen off. Despite repeated assurances that the votes were free, one or two of the whips could be seen offering last-minute guidance to payroll voters. I witnessed an amusing exchange with Ed Balls, who having voted with the reformers was ordered by a whip into the opposite lobby to cancel his vote, only to hastily evacuate when Martin Salter warned him that, if he persisted, he risked ridicule in tomorrow's newspapers. None of this will make a huge difference, but after months of wrangling we have succeeded in inflicting a fleabite on the body politic. Afterwards, Mark Fisher, Evan Harris, David Howarth, Martin Salter and I repaired to the Pugin Room, where our leader, the esteemed Tony Wright, bought us tea and scones by way of celebration.

The media are awash with tributes to Michael Foot, who has died, aged 96.

Sunday, 7 March
Sunderland
State of emergency re Bruce, again, who has been gone for two days. I worry that she may not survive the freezing nights.

Monday, 8 March
As I was departing for London this morning, a faint, barely audible miaow, but from where? I searched our garden and that of our neighbours, to no avail, before realising that the sound appeared to emanate from the derelict basement next door. I duly alerted Ngoc and raced for the train. Half an hour later, Ngoc reported that she had managed to effect entry and there was Bruce, none the worse for her ordeal.

House of Commons

This evening's meeting of the parliamentary party was given over to tributes to Michael Foot. Gordon Brown and Neil Kinnock led the way. Kinnock, in turn irreverent, moving, hilarious, was rewarded with a well-deserved standing ovation.

After the ten o'clock division, the Tory Chief Whip, Patrick McLoughlin, invited me to his office for a glass of wine. Patrick is an unusual Tory. The son of a Derbyshire miner, he worked six years in the pits before being elected in 1986. Working-class Tories are usually the most rabid, but Patrick is the opposite: decent, straight, personable. Like just about everyone I meet, he wants to know why I am going and whether I might be reincarnated in the Lords and suggests a farewell dinner before I depart. I hope I am not going soft, but it is one of the great strengths of our democracy that one can be friends with one's political opponents. After all, we are not actually trying to kill each other.

Tuesday, 9 March

Lunch with A Friend in High Places, who reports that Gordon's behaviour is much improved of late and that the Rawnsley stories about incidents – some of which my friend has witnessed – while generally true, are exaggerated. She thinks that Sarah has been a huge influence for good. The Man still calls in occasionally, though there is some nervousness about his considerable commercial interests. Sir Ronald Cohen has taken over from Lord Levy as Israel's principal lobbyist. 'I can almost set my watch by the time that elapses between the Israeli Ambassador being informed that we intend to vote against them at the UN and a call from Ronnie Cohen demanding an urgent appointment.'

My friend says among the problems that an incoming administration, of whichever party, needs to deal with are the constant short-termism that arises from having to pander to our 24-hour media, who must be fed three times a day, and the endless demands of the military top brass, who are becoming increasingly brazen and shameless in their lobbying and leaking. They need to be told to make choices, instead of demanding more of everything. Re the media, she says, we could make a start by banishing Sky and its rolling news bulletins from ministerial offices. True, now I come to think of it, Sky is on permanently, in every corner of government, even the Downing Street war room. A constant diet of so-called 'breaking news', much of it fatuous, read by self-important anchor persons, endlessly distracting, demanding instant responses. No wonder no one can concentrate for more than a sound bite. We need a much more arm's-length approach. Number 10 should stop taking Lobby journalists to summits and leave the reporting, instead, to local correspondents, who are more likely to have an interest in the issues under discussion. Witness the mess that Lobby play-acting made of Gordon's last two trips to the US.

This evening, to the Empire, Leicester Square, for the UK premier of Paul Greengrass's new film, *The Green Zone*.

Wednesday, 10 March

Twenty, maybe 30 days to go, before I turn into a pumpkin. A cruel reminder this afternoon. I rang the Serjeant at Arms' office to check whether I might be allowed on the premises during the Dissolution, given that I am not standing again and the building remains open to the public.

Answer: 'You can only have access to your room if you are escorted by a security officer.'

'But I don't want access to my room. Only to the public areas and the cafeteria.'

'No Members or their staff will be allowed on the premises during the Dissolution.'

'By that time I shall be an ordinary member of the public ...'

'I suppose you could come in if you bought a ticket for a tour ...'

Friday, 12 March
Glasgow

To the Mitchell Library for a panel discussion with Tariq Ali, Tristram Hunt and others about the future of the Left. An audience of 450, mostly of a certain age in search of some old-time religion. I am sure they found me deeply unimpressive. Only one light moment, when Ruth Wishart, who chaired the discussion, asked for a show of hands from those not intending to vote. Only one hand went up.

'Can you tell us why, sir?'

'Because I am Greek.'

Saturday, 13 March
Glasgow

Breakfast with Tariq Ali. Charming, thoughtful, softly spoken, his Trotskyite past long behind him. He fears Obama may turn out to be a one-term president; that, re Afghanistan, defeat is inevitable and that the only way out is to talk to Russia, Iran and Pakistan and then withdraw with as much dignity as we can muster, taking Karzai with us. We discussed whether John Smith would have got us embroiled in Iraq – one of the great 'what ifs' of recent history. Tariq thought not. 'He was a genuine social democrat, with an irreducible core of decency.'

Tariq recalled a heated exchange with Michael Foot, at Oxford in 1965, when everyone was up in arms about Wilson's refusal to condemn the Americans for what they were up to in Vietnam. 'Someone shouted, "Bring him down." I have never forgotten Michael's reply. "What you don't realise is that Harold Wilson is the most left-wing prime minister we will ever have." He was right.'

Two more events: an enjoyable discussion with Alan Clements about political fiction and a session on the diaries. Then a stroll down Sauchiehall Street to see the statue of Donald Dewar, a fairly good likeness, marred by being coloured sickly green. The centre of Glasgow, a mix of partially rejuvenated Georgian and Victorian elegance, interspersed with 1960s brutalism. The city has undergone something of a renaissance during the last decade but, as with Sunderland, one has an impression of fragility. A few years of Tory government and it could soon unravel.

Monday, 15 March
House of Commons

Arrived to be greeted by the shocking news that Ashok Kumar, my neighbour on Upper Corridor South, is dead, aged 53. He was right as rain when I saw him last Thursday.

This evening, at a thinly attended meeting of the parliamentary party, Jim Sheridan demanded to know why ministers were interfering in the strike by BA cabin crew – both Andrew Adonis and Gordon denounced the strikers over the weekend. 'How have we got ourselves into this situation?' asked Ken Purchase, pointing out that there had been two ballots, the last of which came out 80 per cent in favour of strike action. 'We should either be keeping shtum or back the workers.'

Harriet Harman responded that keeping quiet wasn't an option, but she did not attempt to defend the intemperate tone of the weekend's pronouncements.

Wednesday, 17 March

A historic moment. At PMQs today Gordon admitted a mistake. An event for which there is no precedent. For months he has been insisting, contrary to assertions by the military, that spending on defence increased in real terms every year since we were elected. Today, he conceded that that wasn't quite the case and that in four of our 13 years defence spending had indeed decreased in real terms. In truth, none of this detracts from his general point that the military, despite their constant complaints, have not done badly on our watch, but it does put us on the back foot.

Meanwhile the Tories are doing their utmost to embroil us in the strike by BA cabin crews, making much of the fact that Unite, the strikers' union, is Labour's biggest donor. Posters have appeared depicting a rear view of Gordon, his hands stuffed with union money – vengeance for the trouble we have caused them re Ashcroft. To complicate matters Gordon's former henchperson, Charlie Whelan, the source of many previous embarrassments, has resurfaced, as political officer of Unite. Cameron made much of it at today's Questions – and by most reckoning came out on top.

This evening to Westminster Hall, to hear the Parliament choir sing Mozart's Requiem.

Thursday, 18 March

To the Oxford and Cambridge Club in Pall Mall to deliver yet another book talk. Gradually, courtesy of the diaries, I am working my way along Pall Mall, up St James's and into Mayfair – via the Institute of Directors, the Athenaeum, the Carlton Club, Whites, the D Group and the English Speaking Union. Among those present, Sir Brian Cubbon, a former permanent secretary at the Home Office. Who, I inquired, was the most impressive minister he had served? Without hesitation, he nominated Willie Whitelaw as both the most effective and the most affable. Also present, a mysterious man with an unusually thick crop of combed-back grey hair and a permatan that suggested that he spent much of the year in sunnier climes, who, upon inquiry, disclosed that he once worked for MI5, but declined to elaborate.

Friday, 19 March

To Stockton to speak for Dari Taylor. About 125 people turned out for dinner at a local hotel. Several had been at Ashok Kumar's memorial this afternoon and reported that the church was packed with crowds ten-deep lining the pavement outside, which suggests that we politicians are not quite as despised as popular myth would have it. Or at least that the public are capable of distinguishing between the good, the bad and the indifferent – and Ashok was very definitely one of the good guys.

Saturday, 20 March

As I type this, a huge cheer from the direction of the Stadium of Light, more than a mile away. Ten minutes later Ngoc reports that our benighted football team have just beaten Birmingham 3–1, thereby lifting us clear of the relegation zone. Ha'way the lads!

Sunday, 21 March

Big new sleaze crisis brewing. The evening bulletins contain clips of interviews secretly recorded for Channel Four's *Dispatches* programme with Steve Byers, Patricia Hewitt and Geoff Hoon offering to sell their services as lobbyists for fees of up to £5,000 a day. Steve is heard to say, 'I'm like a sort of cab for hire.' Lord save us.

Monday, 22 March

Byers, Hewitt and Hoon are all over this morning's papers. All we need, just as the polls were narrowing. People are referring to this as the moment New Labour finally expired. This afternoon Harriet made a statement denying Steve's claim – since retracted – that he had successfully leaned on the Transport Secretary on behalf of one of the private railway companies – and she promised a register of lobbyists. The Tories are cock-a-hoop. Outrage at this evening's meeting of the parliamentary party, coupled with demands that heads should roll. Chief Whip Nick Brown attempted in vain to hold the line, saying that he would decide what action to take after consulting the parliamentary committee on Wednesday, but two hours later he issued a statement saying that he had withdrawn the whip from all three of the miscreants. I later came across Geoff Hoon at a party in Speaker's House, as jovial and buoyant as ever. A man not easily embarrassed.

Tuesday, 23 March

Paddy Ashdown was on the bus. He predicts a Tory majority of ten, leading perhaps to a realignment of the Left, of which he and The Man once dreamed.

Wednesday, 24 March

The Budget. Alistair at his most statesmanlike, making no secret of the rocky road ahead, but studious of 'efficiency savings'. Some good news – the deficit is £11 billion less than previously expected, but still a whopping, unsustainable £167 billion. Some nice touches: a doubling of the stamp duty exemption for first-time buyers to be paid for by an increase in the duty on houses worth over a million, an increase in the tax threshold for those aged 75-plus and the announcement – to much cheering and waving of order papers on our side – of a disclosure agreement with three tax havens, one of them Belize, the domicile of Tory deputy chairman Lord Ashcroft, whose tax arrangements continue to excite interest.

Thursday, 25 March

An email from David Banks to say that Daphne Park has died. 'I sat with her for an hour and a half last week and we talked fondly of you.'

Tonight I delivered my last speech in Parliament. The Speaker, who has been kind to me throughout, presided. Harriet Harman responded for the government. About 30 colleagues turned out, including a number of Tory grandees – Patrick Cormack, Malcolm Rifkind, Nicholas Soames, Nick Winterton and George Young. I spoke for 15 minutes from a carefully prepared text. A tour of the horizon, ending (voice trembling with emotion): 'Mr Speaker, these are the last words I shall speak in this place.' Afterwards Harriet embraced me and everyone came and shook hands. Robert Rogers, one of the senior clerks, said he would cut the speech out of tomorrow's *Hansard* and keep it. A sad moment. I came within a whisker of breaking down.

Later, I tapped out a short addendum to the *Guardian*'s obituary of Daphne. She led one of the most remarkable lives of anyone I have known, with the possible exception of Wilf Burchett, who was very definitely on the opposite side of the barricades.

Friday, 26 March

My valedictory led this morning's *Yesterday in Parliament* and the *Guardian* has published 1,000 words culled from the speech.

To Sunderland on an early train. Alistair has rather spoiled the effect of his Budget by appearing to agree with an assertion by the BBC's Nick Robinson that even if Labour wins, we can expect cuts in public spending 'deeper and tougher' than those of Margaret Thatcher. However, today's *Guardian* publishes a table headed 'Who has benefited from Labour?' produced by the Institute of Fiscal Studies. It demonstrates beyond peradventure that 13 years of Labour government have produced a substantial redistribution of wealth. The least prosperous 20 per cent of the population are said to be 12–13 per cent better off while the 20 per cent best off have lost out by between 3 and 5 per cent. Overall 60 per cent of the population are said to be better off, which knocks firmly on the head the nonsense from some quarters that the poor – or even most of the middle class – have got poorer on our watch. Interestingly, the *Telegraph* leads with a mendacious story based on the same report which it manages to spin as '10m families have lost out in Labour's tax changes'. The story below contains the following delicious sentence: 'The report by the IFS discloses that, despite years of Labour declarations of support for the middle classes, its policies have consistently favoured the poor ...' Amen.

Monday, 29 March

'Tories to block National Insurance rise,' declares the headline in this morning's *Telegraph*. That's another £5bn they have to find from somewhere. Where on earth are they going to get it? My guess is that, once elected on a platform of tax cuts, they will immediately push up VAT. Exactly as in '79. One can't be too cynical about these guys.

Alan Milburn was on the tube from King's Cross. Despite all the talk of a hung parliament, he predicts a small Tory majority. Alan also reckons that Gordon will cling on to the leadership, unless there is a complete meltdown.

This evening, dinner with the Tory Chief Whip, Patrick McLoughlin; he too predicts a small overall majority for the Tories.

Tuesday, 30 March

A two-page handwritten note from Mr Speaker Bercow: 'Your speech on Thursday was one of the most moving and powerful I have heard over the last 13 years … At heart I am a romantic and it brought tears to my eyes.'

At lunch in the cafeteria Dennis Skinner berated me for giving up. He dismissed out of hand my suggestion that I wasn't much use any more, but when I said that my wife was the casting vote, she wants to work and it is her turn, we have a 14-year-old daughter and someone has to stay home, he accepted that as a reasonable explanation. Which only goes to prove that Dennis, in his later years, has mellowed.

Friday, 2 April

Oh dear, more trouble. A group of big businessmen have signed a letter to the *Telegraph*, castigating government plans to increase employer National Insurance contributions and praising Tory promises to reverse the increase. Never mind that more than half of them have connections to the Tory party (seven are known to be donors), they have struck a hammer blow at our economic credibility and the media have piled in behind them. To compound our woes, a poll in today's *Guardian* suggests our support has slipped back below 30 per cent and the Tories are again on the rise. A meltdown cannot be ruled out.

A leader in today's *Times*, listing me as one of a handful of departing MPs who will be missed. '*A View From the Foothills* is his eloquent answer to those who believe that all politicians are in it for themselves.'

Tuesday, 6 April

To Westminster with My Two Best Friends. We set out early from Burnham Market, where we have been staying with Liz, stopping en route at Chelmsford to place carnations on Granny's grave.

As expected, the election is to be on 6 May. Gordon went to the Palace this morning. Within the hour the BBC were running vox pops with The Disillusioned: 'I shan't be voting', 'A plague on all of them' etc. No one asks the obvious question: 'Did you vote last time? Or the time before?' By and large one suspects The Disillusioned are mostly the same people who fail to put out their waste bins on the appointed day, allow their dogs to foul the pavement, take no interest in their children's education and so on. No matter, they are allowed to proclaim their disillusion, unchallenged – the Great Expenses Meltdown providing yet another excuse for indolence. Meanwhile a tented media village has sprung up on College Green, where the pundits will spend the next six weeks talking to each other in front of an empty parliament. By the time it's all over the nation will be bored witless. Much talk of a hung parliament, but most of the evidence points to a Tory majority. I suspect most of the pundits think that too. They just keep blathering about a hung parliament to give themselves something to talk about.

Wednesday, 7 April

My last PMQs. Cameron on a high, cheered on by his own side, reading out a long charge list to which Gordon, instead of meeting him head on, responded with a long string of facts. 'Poor Gordon,' Emma remarked afterwards. 'He was proper slaughtered.'

'Bosses step up war on Labour' is the splash headline in tonight's *Standard* over a story that another 30 FTSE fat cats have piled in behind the 20-odd who came out against the proposed increase in National Insurance.

Thursday, 8 April

The last day. To Westminster with Sarah and Emma. A dozen or so 'Vote Conservative' posters on billboards have appeared overnight in gardens along Kennington Road. They have one thing in common: without exception every house sporting a billboard is worth at least £1 million.

At the House we climbed 334 steps to the top of Big Ben (something I have never done before). Lunch on the terrace in bright sunshine followed by a tour of Speaker's House. As we were being shown out down the grand staircase we came across Speaker Bercow and his wife, Sally, who chatted pleasantly for 15 minutes, after which he signed a copy of the guidebook for each of the girls and one for Ngoc and posed for a photo with us on the doorstep.

Everywhere we go people, Members and officials alike, coming up to shake hands, say how much I'll be missed etc. It's been like this all week, giving rise to a hollow feeling inside. No matter, the die is cast.

At just after five the House prorogued and we all – or those of us still on the premises – processed to the Lords to hear the Queen's commissioners, swathed in ermine, with much doffing of caps, give her consent to an agreed list of Bills. Then back to the Commons for the last time, where The Departing lined up to shake hands with the Speaker and a line of clerks behind the Speaker's chair. Then, with the girls, to the Tea Room, where we said goodbye to Noeleen and her staff and posed for photographs in front of the fireplace at the Tory end. All very out of order, but no one complained.

Several hours clearing out my room, 68 Upper Corridor South. Finally, in the cool of evening for a last drink on the terrace. Then we climbed into the car and drove away.

Friday, 9 April

Up at five and on the road by six, the roof box crammed with office papers and other detritus which I cannot yet bring myself to dispose of. The headline in today's *Telegraph* reads: 'Tory win best for economy say top bankers'. Only the lunatics who now run the *Telegraph* could fail to see the irony.

Saturday, 10 April

The President of Poland has been killed in an air crash in Russia, en route to commemorate the slaughter at Katyn.

Sunday, 11 April

Sunderland

Out canvassing in Plains Farm with Julie Elliot, my likely successor. Canvassing is not as it was in my day, when we knocked on every door. These days it is done from a telephone bank and entered into some great computer program. All we are doing is filling in the gaps. As a result, it is difficult to get a feel, but I didn't sense much overt hostility.

Our national campaign grows increasingly inept. The latest folly – a leaflet accusing the Tories of wanting to increase waiting times for suspected cancer patients. They have neatly turned the tables by alleging (falsely) that we have targeted cancer sufferers using confidential NHS files. Nevertheless, the evening bulletins feature people diagnosed with cancer saying how tasteless it all is and who can disagree?

Tuesday, 13 April

Both main parties have now published manifestos. Ours making a desperate bid to recapture the New Labour brand by promising another five years of hyperactivity re the public services, taking over failing schools, hospitals, police forces etc. ... and foolishly promising not to raise income tax. The Tories have come up with a giant new wheeze, 'an invitation to join the government of Britain', which involves local referenda, elected police chiefs, allowing sharp-elbowed parents to set up their own schools and mid-term sackings for errant MPs – a populists' charter, if ever there was. The elephant in the room which no one mentions is VAT. All parties seem to have calculated (and they may be right) that the pampered, mollycoddled British middle classes, not to mention our hysterical media, are simply incapable of coping with a mature discussion about tax.

Wednesday, 14 April

To Oxford with Sarah. Along the A19 through much of North Yorkshire farmers have erected huge hoardings proclaiming, 'Vote for

Change – Vote Conservative'. Elsewhere the Tories are running a mendacious poster campaign depicting an uncharacteristically cheerful mugshot of Gordon with captions such as 'I let 80,000 criminals out early. Let me do it again'; 'I caused record youth unemployment. Vote for me'; 'I doubled the national debt. Vote for me'. Insulting to the intelligence, but will people fall for it? Enough, I fear.

At Oxford, after depositing Sarah at Queen's, I whiled away a pleasant hour with a circuit of the Fellows' Garden at Magdalen, great drifts of blue and white anemones engulfing the daffodils. Then the long drive back to Sunderland, with only my Alan Bennett tapes for company.

Thursday, 15 April

Tonight, the long-awaited leaders' debate. The bland leading the bland. After about 30 minutes I found myself losing consciousness and went upstairs to watch a BBC2 documentary about the men who scratch a living on the huge garbage dump in Lagos. Uplifting, moving, humbling. Not a trace of self-pity. Their dignity, wit, optimism, sense of solidarity and community causing them to soar above their awful circumstances, putting to shame those of us leading what, to the scavengers of Lagos, must be lives of unimaginable comfort, wallowing in our tabloid-induced misery.

Meanwhile in Iceland a volcano has erupted, sending a great cloud of ash into our airspace, grounding all flights until further notice. The silence in the skies is beautiful.

Friday, 16 April

Nick Clegg is widely reckoned to have been the clear winner of last night's debate. Ironic considering that, for all his fluency and utter self-confidence, he is easily the biggest charlatan of the lot. Who would guess, listening to him prattling piously about MPs' expenses, that he was a maximum claimer? Or that six months ago, when it seemed to be the flavour of the hour, he was demanding 'bold and savage cuts' in public spending, a subject on which he is now silent.

Or that this is a man who, according to the needs of the hour, is capable of arguing with equal passion for or against retaining Trident nuclear missiles? From our point of view this is not necessarily bad news. A modest Lib Dem resurgence may be just what we need to dent what, until recently at least, seemed to be the inevitable Tory triumph.

Saturday, 17 April
Sunderland

Much excitement re Nick Clegg's alleged triumph in Thursday's debate. A YouGov poll puts the Lib Dems on 30 per cent, with us on 28 and the Tories down to 33. A flash in the pan or the long-awaited breakthrough? Too early to say. What it does mean is that the Lib Dems' fanciful manifesto will now come under somewhat more rigorous scrutiny than has so far been the case. How, for example, are they proposing to find the several billion needed to raise the tax threshold to £10,000?

Jim Naughtie came to interview me for the *Today* programme and afterwards we had a cup of tea in the garden. He remarked that until now he had been unable to foresee any outcome that did not result in David Cameron ending up as prime minister, but for the first time, one begins to glimpse other possibilities.

Sunday, 18 April

Clegg mania grows steadily more ludicrous. Today a poll suggesting he is the most popular party leader since Winston Churchill. I have been acquainted with each of the last five Liberal or Lib Dem leaders and he is by far the shallowest.

Wednesday, 21 April

Nick Clegg was on a Radio 4 phone-in. I have reluctantly to admit that he was impressive: personable, fluent, on top of his brief. The trouble is that one knows he could argue the Tory or even the Labour cause with equal dexterity.

Thursday, 22 April

The Tory press have launched a huge assault on Nick Clegg: 'Clegg in Nazi slur on Britain,' screams the *Mail*; the *Sun* has a four-page attack, the gist of which is that he's soft on defence and immigration. Nastiest of all, the *Telegraph*, whose three-deck front page headline reads: 'Nick Clegg, the Lib Dem donors and payments into his private account'. On careful reading it turns out that the money was donated to help pay his staff some years ago when he was home affairs spokesman. It all seems to have been properly declared and accounted for. Unwise, perhaps, to run it through his own account, but there is no evidence of impropriety. Naturally, the Tories say that it's nothing to do with them, but you can almost see the strings leading back to the disreputable spinners who lurk in the Tory underworld. If Clegg continues to pose a threat to the Tory revival, he can expect much more of this.

Wednesday, 28 April

To Number 10 to pay a long-overdue social call on Tom Fletcher, my erstwhile private secretary. Eerily quiet, since Gordon and the politicos were campaigning up country. Tom gave me a tour of the parts I have never previously penetrated, upstairs, downstairs, starting with 'The Hub' in what used to be the boardroom of Number 12, where he sits for much of the day within a heartbeat of The Maximum Leader. Gordon sits at the centre of a horseshoe surrounded by key advisers, each in identical black leather chairs, facing identical computer screens. Everyone within earshot. All very modern, clinical and intimate. A wee bit too much so for my liking. Behind, a room overlooking the garden, to which The Leader can retreat when he feels the need and to take important phone calls. The blotter is covered with Gordon's graffiti. 'Still in denial,' reads one. And in a far corner of the garden, just below the Cabinet Office, Sarah's vegetable garden. Sadly, it is unlikely that she will be there long enough to reap the harvest.

Tom speaks highly of Gordon. 'Despite all, I'd work for him again in a flash. He's a person of substance. He wants to make the world a better place. And, yes, you can tease him.'

At intervals around the building, flat screen television sets beaming in, courtesy of Sky, a constant diet of rolling news. Even as we toured, word was coming in of a new disaster. Gordon, in Rochdale, has apparently been overheard labelling as a bigot some harmless lady, a lifelong Labour voter to boot. The drama unfolding minute by excruciating minute. By the time we reached the press office in the basement he had driven to the woman's home to apologise in person. The cameras were focusing on the plastic front door of a modest terraced house, grim-faced Special Branch men keeping the media scrum at bay. 'He's been in there 30 minutes so far,' said someone. Mesmerisingly, mind-numbingly awful. A slow-motion car crash. This, surely, is the point of no return.

Thursday, 29 April
Sunderland

An email from a retired film director arguing that the 'Brown gaffe' story is essentially a Murdoch surveillance coup. 'The sound mixer ought properly to turn the microphone off once the politician/performer has exited the shot. If they don't they are essentially being spied upon. But if conversation is picked up, a professional director or producer will not normally release it nationwide.' Yes, indeed, but this is war and in the current climate any attempt to complain would be laughed out of court.

A call from the *Mail on Sunday*. Would I be interested in writing a piece about 'the curious psychological make-up of Gordon Brown'? I wouldn't actually.

'Can you suggest someone who would?'

'Just about anyone who has served in the Cabinet during the last 13 years, except that I imagine they are otherwise engaged.'

This evening, the third and last of the leaders' debates, which I, taking part in an election event at the University of Newcastle, missed.

Friday, 30 April

The consensus seems to be that Cameron was last night's winner. Gordon is said to have performed well, but sadly no one is listening. The polls indicate that the Tories are pulling away again. Our support is hovering around 25 per cent. Meltdown territory.

A call from the *Daily Mail*. Somehow word has reached them that I am none too keen on Nick Clegg. Would I like to do a 1,200-word knocking job? They are very keen. 'We can ghostwrite it, if necessary.'

Thanks, but no thanks.

Saturday, 1 May

Sunderland

A surprise visit from Our Much Maligned Leader. An 'event' has been hastily arranged at the Glass Centre. By invitation only. All carefully choreographed. A dozen well-scrubbed youngsters arrayed behind the lectern. A battery of cameramen confined to a little pen at the rear. Gordon arrives to rapturous applause. For the first 15 minutes all goes well and then a bearded oaf in his thirties starts bawling. Instantly the cameras home in. We hold our breath, only too well aware that the slightest overreaction will be headline news. Clare Phillipson (height 5' 1"), mother of one of our candidates, makes the first move, gently easing the troublemaker towards the door. She runs a hostel for battered woman and has considerable experience of dealing with out of control males. The miscreant is bundled from the room. The press pack disappear after him and for about 20 minutes he holds court in the corridor, his words receiving far more attention than those of the Prime Minister. Happily, however, he is not a granny with a grievance, just a passing loudmouth who saw a chance to seize his 15 seconds of fame. The evening bulletins make light of the incident.

Sunday, 2 May

This morning, two hours' leafleting in Hill View, a leafy estate of fifties council housing, at least one-third of which is now in private hands, courtesy of the right to buy. Twenty years ago, by this stage in an election campaign, Hill View would have been plastered with Labour posters. Today we came across just two or three. Not that the natives are unfriendly. Several people waved and gave us the thumbs up. Only one man shouted abuse from the comfort of his 4×4. Hard to read the mood. No evidence in Sunderland of a Lib Dem surge. Here the issue is, will they vote or not?

Wednesday, 5 May

A day in the office spent sorting through boxes. Box after box after box. The simplest solution would be to close my eyes, take a deep breath and shred the lot, but buried here are all sorts of gems from campaigns past – miscarriages of justice, Masonic secrecy, gun control etc. The fruits of more than 20 years' work. Each reopened file triggers a memory. Several archives are competing for my paperwork, though goodness knows what use it will be 50 years from now. In deference to the Data Protection Act, we have already shredded thousands of constituency case papers, but I can't bring myself to destroy the rest – and so I must wade through them box by box, file by file. At this rate, it will take months.

The polls are indicating that the Lib Dem surge has receded, putting them just about level pegging with Labour, while the Tories have pulled ahead, i.e., as in 1983, the anti-Tory vote is split exactly down the middle.

Thursday, 6 May

To the count. A wall of cameras, but for the first time in many years I am of no relevance, just an extra on the film set. In Sunderland we count the votes very fast and by midnight all our three seats have declared. Handsome Labour victories all round. We even recaptured several council seats, one a Tory stronghold. Outside our little bubble, however, things are not going too well.

Friday, 7 May

The slaughter is considerable. A list of The Fallen is running in a continuous loop along the bottom of our television screen. Among them,
many good friends and colleagues. Across the Home Counties, the
party of the bankers, hedge-funders and derivative traders is sweeping
all before it.

And yet all is not lost. Not quite. The much-trumpeted Lib Dem
revival, like so many previous ones, has failed to materialise. The
Great British Public have spoken, but it is by no means clear what
they have said.

Saturday, 8 May

A pause while we wait to see who the Lib Dems will appoint to government. Everyone is being nice to them. Cameron talking of 'a big,
open and comprehensive deal'. Gordon, meanwhile, is insisting that
it is his constitutional duty to remain in office until the mist clears.

Monday, 10 May

Gordon announces his resignation. As with his Budgets, however, a
careful reading of the small print reveals that, subject to the mercy of the
Liberal Democrats, he is actually contemplating another five months in
office, until a new Labour leader is elected. Suddenly the political landscape is transformed. Nick Clegg announces that talks with the Tories
are at an end and that he could, after all, work with Labour. Much talk
on our side of 'a coalition of the progressive majority'. The Tories, mightily upset, are talking bitterly of 'a coalition of losers'.

Tuesday, 11 May

'Venal', 'shabby', 'grubby', 'duplicitous', 'shady', 'squalid', 'revolting'.
The Tory press are apoplectic at the thought that the Lib Dems appear
to have been two-timing them. Anonymous briefers are using words
like 'treachery'. On our side, too, no shortage of misgivings. Meanwhile the markets are getting jittery.

By late afternoon it is clear that Nick Clegg is back talking to the Tories again. At which point Gordon threw in the towel. Without further ado he emerged from Number 10, delivered a short, dignified farewell speech and then, joined by Sarah and their two little boys, strode away up Downing Street to the convoy waiting to take him to the Palace. And with that the New Labour era came to an end. Sadly, the little lads are unlikely ever to remember the famous place that was once their home.

As for me, what does the future hold? A couple more volumes of diaries; perhaps a course of lectures to be entitled 'The Rise and Fall of New Labour'; a little light after-dinner speaking. And, if all else fails, I shall grow vegetables.

Goodbye to All That

As you will know, Mr Speaker, it is the custom when we come to this place for a new Member to make a maiden speech. With your indulgence I wonder if I might initiate a new genre: the valedictory speech.

I have been in this place 23 years. I hope that, during that time, I have left the occasional footprint in the sand, but I am under no illusion. Only a handful of those who currently strut these corridors will still be remembered ten or 20 years from now and I do not expect to be among them. Before the waters close over my head I would like to take this opportunity to place on record a few random thoughts that might be of interest to those who come afterwards.

To those who ask where am I coming from, I reply that I am a socialist with a small 's', a liberal with a small 'l', a green with a small 'g' and a Democrat with a capital 'D'.

Although most of us are more prosperous than we have ever been, we live in an age of disillusion and of corrosive cynicism. It is fashionable to believe that all politicians are useless. That nothing works, that everything is bad and getting worse and that all political activity is pointless. I do not accept this.

Despite the catastrophe of Iraq, I sincerely believe that the achievements of the last three Labour governments have been considerable. I have only to look at my own constituency to see the truth of that proposition. With hand on heart I can say with confidence that during these last 13 years the lives and life chances of many of my least prosperous constituents have been immeasurably improved. We have been rather shy about it, but we have redistributed some wealth. The minimum wage, working tax credits, pension credits, huge investment in health, education and public transport have made a considerable impact and I defy anyone to argue otherwise. In my constituency in 1997 there were a significant number of people – security guards, mail order workers, care workers – earning as little as one pound an hour. The waiting time for a hip operation at Sunderland Royal Hospital was up to two years (it is now 18 weeks and falling).

There is a secondary school in my constituency, Sandhill View, at which 15 years ago less than 10 per cent – *I repeat, less than 10 per cent* – of GCSE pupils were achieving five A to Cs. Today Sandhill View has dynamic new management. It has been entirely rebuilt, sharing a library, sports and other facilities with the surrounding community. It covers exactly the same catchment area as the old school and getting on for 80 per cent of pupils obtain five A to C grades. Still room for progress, but a dramatic change on what went before.

Nor do I believe that such changes are confined only to Sunderland.

City centres such as those in Leeds, Manchester, Newcastle – once in near-terminal decline – have been reborn. No doubt there are many reasons why this has happened, but I do believe that it has something to do with the fact that we have had more than a decade of Labour government.

There has been progress, too, in other important areas – the environment, criminal justice, international development and above all Ireland, where peace has been achieved after many years of apparently intractable conflict. And who would have thought that we would live to see the day when a New Labour government took a controlling interest in three major banks with – eventually – Conservative support.

There are social and constitutional reforms which were controversial in their day but which, having been enacted, will endure for ever: the ban on smoking in public places and on cigarette advertising; the requirement that political parties disclose their source of funding; the Freedom of Information Act – painful though it has proved for we humble servants of the people. Whatever the outcome of the election, no one can take those achievements away from the governments of the last 13 years and I note that none of the Opposition parties is intending to do so.

Mr Speaker, I would like now to address the future. Whatever the achievements of the past, we are all well aware that we are as far away as ever from achieving nirvana. Although in some respects my political views have modified over the years, I continue to doubt that there is a long-term future for an economy based on shopping. The frenetic consumerism of recent decades surely contains the seeds of its own destruction. Even more so now that China and India are falling over themselves to make – with knobs on – the same mistakes as we have made. I truly believe that this age of consumerism is only a very temporary period in the history of the human race and that, if we carry on as we are, it will end badly – perhaps within the lifetime of our children and grandchildren. As things stand, we are using up the resources of the planet as if there is no tomorrow and, if we are not careful, there will be no tomorrow.

One way or another, we have to devise lifestyles that are sustainable – and that may well require changes to our way of life that most people have only dimly begun to contemplate. This, Mr Speaker, I regard as the single greatest challenge facing the new generation of political leaders – regardless of which side of the spectrum from which they come.

I think we can all agree that the neo-liberal experiment, which for the last two decades has bewitched politicians on both sides of the divide, is well and truly over. The near meltdown of the global banking system was a wake-up call, if ever there was. Not everyone has got the message, however. Three months ago, at the annual dinner of the Institute of Directors, I was interested to hear the director still chanting the mantra of light-touch regulation and demanding less government intervention in the workings of the market. I thought to myself, 'Lucky there was some big government around when the banks went belly up.'

Nor should we imagine, as we sit tight in fortress Europe, watching other people's catastrophes on our television screens – and perhaps averting our eyes by switching channels – that we will remain indefinitely immune. The world is increasingly a village. What happens in one part has consequences in another. The danger for western Europe is that, if the world beyond our frontiers is allowed to disintegrate – as the oceans rise, the rivers evaporate, the deserts expand and populations multiply – the flow of economic refugees from Africa and Asia will gradually become a tide which will eventually overwhelm our fragile social, economic and political systems. I do not say it will happen, but it must be a possibility that cannot any longer be overlooked. We are deluding ourselves if we imagine this process can be halted by increased repression. In the end it can only be reversed by addressing the root causes and that requires political leaders of courage and vision, willing to face their electorates with home truths and not merely pandering to the basest prejudices.

Here in the United Kingdom our problems are exacerbated by the fact that, for a generation or more, our citizens have been encouraged to believe that they can enjoy European levels of public services and American levels of taxation. Sooner or later choices must be made. Perhaps the moment has come. If we want higher standards in our schools, better hospitals, better pensions, long-term care for the elderly then they will have to be paid for out of taxation. And let us not pretend that such benefits can be paid for merely by taxing the rich. They can't. We, the pampered inhabitants of Middle England, will have to make a larger contribution. By all means crack down on waste and demand value for money, but do not pretend this alone will solve the problem. At the end of the day, there are choices to be made and each choice has consequences which we must face maturely. I keep reading how heavily taxed we are, but I note that the basic rate of income tax today is well below what it was in Mrs Thatcher's day.

Mr Speaker, government needs to become a little less frenetic. The practice of annual reshuffles is massively destabilising and confers enormous power on the civil service. There have been eight secretaries of state for work and pensions in the ten years since that department was invented. Of late we have been getting through Home Secretaries at the rate of almost one a year. Goodness knows how many health and education secretaries we have had. We are on our tenth Europe minister. Our ninth or tenth prisons minister. I was the sixth Africa minister, the current incumbent is the ninth. Mr Speaker, this does not make for good government.

I turn briefly to our 24-hour media. The free flow of information is the life blood of democracy, but I do wonder if we politicians haven't gone too far in trying to ride the tiger. Perhaps future prime ministers should spend a little less time feeding, appeasing, canoodling with tabloid editors and their proprietors, which, anyway, almost always ends in tears.

I refer to another issue which ought to be of concern to all those who care about the condition of our democracy. The funding of politics. We have come some way in recent years in regulating party funding, but it remains an unhappy fact that all the main parties are to a greater or lesser extent dependent upon the favours of rich men. I believe this demeans our politics and it is time it was addressed. The dilemma we face is that we live at a time when the public are less inclined to join political parties. They do not wish to donate and above all they don't want their taxes to fund political parties. BUT – and here is the rub – they all want to live in a democracy. That is the circle that we poor, despised, inadequate politicians have to square. There are no easy solutions, but the one I favour is for every taxpayer to be given a tax-free allowance, up to say £250, which he or she is entitled to donate to the political party of their choice in return for a strict cap on individual donations.

In passing can I say a word about what I regard as one of the most insidious developments in recent years? The growth of outsourcing or agency work. The outsourced are all around us and growing increasingly resentful of their lot. There are two classes of working people in this country. Those fortunate to be employed full-time, entitled to paid holidays, occupational pensions, sickness pay, redundancy pay and all the other hard-won benefits that we used quaintly to associate with the twentieth century. And a class of people who qualify for none of these things. Who can be put down and picked up at will and who are often paid less than others doing the same work. Regrettably the practice of outsourcing is spreading. There is a school of thought that believes this to be desirable. I regard it as a most ominous development, storing up great problems for the future. We talk of lifting families out of poverty, but outsourcing drives people into poverty and insecurity. We are heading remorselessly back towards the nineteenth century. Back to the days of casual work when workers assembled at the shipyard gate and the foreman said, 'I'll have you, you and you, and the rest of you can go home.' I hope that future governments will consider long and hard before pushing more people down this road in the name of the great god efficiency. At the very least, if it cannot be reversed, it needs to be carefully regulated.

Finally, Mr Speaker, a word to the coming generation of politicians. I have one simple message: *Take Parliament seriously*. If we, the elected, do not, then why should anyone else? By all means support the programme on which your party was elected, but we are not automatons. We are not sent here merely to be cheerleaders. Or to get stiff necks looking up at the fount of power. We are sent here to exercise our judgement. To hold ministers to account for the power they hold. That means proper scrutiny. It means insisting that ministers engage seriously with Parliament and that they are open to dialogue. It means, so far as possible, insisting that the government publish legislation in draft so that it might be improved before it is set in stone. And, if you want an easy win, so far as the public are concerned, do away with the 80-day summer recess.

In conclusion, Mr Speaker, there are many people I must thank. The people of the Sunderland South constituency for having allowed me to represent them these last 23 years. Members of the Sunderland South Labour Party for having allowed me to be their candidate through five general elections. Friends and colleagues on all sides of the House for the pleasure of their company. Officials great and small with whom I have worked over the years, both in government and in the House.

Last but not least yourself, Mr Speaker, for doing me the honour of presiding tonight and my Right Hon. Friend the Leader of the House and her distinguished shadow, the Right Hon. member for Hampshire North West, both respected colleagues over many years, for their presence tonight.

Mr Speaker, I depart with mixed feelings. I have heard it said that most MPs stay one parliament too long. I thought it better to go one too early, while people are still asking, 'Why?' rather than, 'When?' There will be withdrawal symptoms. Leaving now is either the best thing I have ever done or the biggest mistake of my life. At this point, I have no idea which. I do know this, however: I count it a privilege to have been born in a democracy and to have served in this place. The great thing about democracy is that, although harsh things are sometimes said, we are not actually trying to kill each other. Differences are ultimately resolved at the ballot box. One side wins, one side loses and the loser lives to fight another day.

Those, Mr Speaker, are the last words I shall speak in this place.

The Blair/Brown government

Tony Blair's Cabinet (Secretaries of State and senior ministers)
May 2005–May 2006

Tony Blair	*Prime Minister*
John Prescott	*Deputy Prime Minister*
Gordon Brown	*Chancellor of the Exchequer*
Charlie Falconer	*Lord Chancellor*
Jack Straw	*Foreign Secretary*
Charles Clarke	*Home Secretary*
Valerie Amos	*Leader of the House of Lords*
Geoff Hoon	*Leader of the House of Commons*
Alan Johnson	*Business, Enterprise and Regulatory Reform*
Ruth Kelly	*Education and Skills*
Tessa Jowell	*Culture, Media and Sport*
John Reid	*Defence and Scotland*
Margaret Beckett	*Environment, Food and Rural Affairs*
Patricia Hewitt	*Health*
Hilary Benn	*International Development*
Peter Hain	*Northern Ireland and Wales*
Alistair Darling	*Transport*
David Blunkett	*Work and Pensions*
John Hutton	*Cabinet Office*
Des Browne	*Chief Secretary to the Treasury*
Hilary Armstrong	*Chief Whip*
Peter Goldsmith	*Attorney General*
Bruce Grocott	*Chief Whip in the House of Lords*

| David Triesman | *Foreign Office (Africa)* |
| Douglas Alexander | *Foreign Office (Europe)* |

Tony Blair's Cabinet (Secretaries of State and senior ministers), May 2006–June 2007

Tony Blair	*Prime Minister*
John Prescott	*Deputy Prime Minister*
Gordon Brown	*Chancellor of the Exchequer*
Charlie Falconer	*Justice Secretary and Lord Chancellor*
Margaret Beckett	*Foreign Secretary*
John Reid	*Home Secretary*
Valerie Amos	*Leader of the House of Lords*
Jack Straw	*Leader of the House of Commons*
Alan Johnson	*Education and Skills*
Ruth Kelly	*Communities and Local Government*
Tessa Jowell	*Culture, Media and Sport*
Des Browne	*Defence*
David Miliband	*Environment, Food and Rural Affairs*
Patricia Hewitt	*Health*
Hilary Benn	*International Development*
Peter Hain	*Northern Ireland and Wales*
Alistair Darling	*Trade and Industry*
Douglas Alexander	*Transport and Secretary of State for Scotland*
John Hutton	*Work and Pensions*
Hilary Armstrong	*Cabinet Office*
Hazel Blears	*Minister without Portfolio*
Stephen Timms	*Chief Secretary to the Treasury*
Jacqui Smith	*Chief Whip*
Geoff Hoon	*Foreign Office (Europe)*
Peter Goldsmith	*Attorney General*
Bruce Grocott	*Chief Whip in House of Lords*
David Triesman	*Foreign Office (Africa)*

Gordon Brown's Cabinet and senior ministers, June 2007–October 2008 (with minor reshuffle in January 2008)

| Gordon Brown | *Prime Minister* |
| Alistair Darling | *Chancellor of the Exchequer* |

David Miliband	*Foreign Secretary*
Jack Straw	*Justice Secretary and Lord Chancellor*
Jacqui Smith	*Home Secretary*
Des Browne	*Defence and Scotland*
Alan Johnson	*Health*
Hilary Benn	*Environment , Food and Rural Affairs*
Douglas Alexander	*International Development*
John Hutton	*Business, Enterprise and Regulatory Reform*
Harriet Harman	*Leader of the House of Commons*
Peter Hain	*Work and Pensions (James Purnell from January 2008) and Wales (Paul Murphy from January 2008)*
Ruth Kelly	*Transport*
Hazel Blears	*Communities and Local Government*
Ed Balls	*Children, Schools and Families*
Ed Miliband	*Cabinet Office*
James Purnell	*Culture, Media and Sport*
Shaun Woodward	*Northern Ireland*
Cathy Ashton	*Leader of the House of Lords*
Andy Burnham	*Chief Secretary to the Treasury (Yvette Cooper from January 2008)*
John Denham	*Innovation, Universities and Skills*
Geoff Hoon	*Chief Whip*
Bruce Grocott	*Chief Whip in the House of Lords (until 2008)*
Patricia Scotland	*Attorney General*
Mark Malloch-Brown	*Foreign Office (Africa, Asia and the UN)*
Yvette Cooper	*Housing and Planning (Caroline Flint from January 2008)*
Tessa Jowell	*Olympics*
Beverley Hughes	*Children, Young People and Families*

Gordon Brown's Cabinet and senior ministers, October 2008– June 2009

Gordon Brown	*Prime Minister*
Harriet Harman	*Deputy Leader of the Labour Party and Leader of the House of Commons*
Alistair Darling	*Chancellor of the Exchequer*

Jack Straw	*Justice Secretary and Lord Chancellor*
David Miliband	*Foreign Secretary*
Jacqui Smith	*Home Secretary*
Peter Mandelson	*Business, Enterprise and Regulatory Reform*
Hazel Blears	*Communities and Local Government*
Ed Balls	*Children, Schools and Families*
Ed Miliband	*Energy and Climate Change*
John Hutton	*Defence*
Hilary Benn	*Environment, Food and Rural Affairs*
Douglas Alexander	*International Development*
Alan Johnson	*Health*
Shaun Woodward	*Northern Ireland*
Jim Murphy	*Scotland*
James Purnell	*Work and Pensions*
Geoff Hoon	*Transport*
Andy Burnham	*Culture, Media and Sport*
John Denham	*Innovation, Universities and Skills*
Paul Murphy	*Wales*
Janet Royall	*Leader of the House of Lords*
Yvette Cooper	*Chief Secretary to the Treasury*
Nick Brown	*Chief Whip*
Patricia Scotland	*Attorney General*
Liam Byrne	*Cabinet Office*
Tessa Jowell	*Olympics*
Margaret Beckett	*Housing and Planning*
Tony McNulty	*Employment and Welfare Reform*
Caroline Flint	*Foreign Office (Europe)*
Beverley Hughes	*Children, Young People and Families*
Mark Malloch-Brown	*Foreign Office (Africa, Asia and the UN)*
Paul Drayson	*Science and Innovation*

Gordon Brown's Cabinet and senior ministers, June 2009–May 2010

Gordon Brown	*Prime Minister*
Harriet Harman	*Deputy Leader of the Labour Party and Leader of the House of Commons*

Peter Mandelson	*Business, Innovation and Skills and First Secretary of State*
Alistair Darling	*Chancellor of the Exchequer*
Jack Straw	*Lord Chancellor and Justice Secretary*
David Miliband	*Foreign Secretary*
Alan Johnson	*Home Secretary*
John Denham	*Communities and Local Government*
Ed Balls	*Children, Schools and Families*
Ed Miliband	*Energy and Climate Change*
Tessa Jowell	*Cabinet Office and Olympics*
Bob Ainsworth	*Defence*
Hilary Benn	*Environment, Food and Rural Affairs*
Douglas Alexander	*International Development*
Andy Burnham	*Health*
Shaun Woodward	*Northern Ireland*
Jim Murphy	*Scotland*
Yvette Cooper	*Work and Pensions*
Andrew Adonis	*Transport*
Ben Bradshaw	*Culture, Media and Sport*
Peter Hain	*Wales*
Janet Royall	*Leader of the House of Lords*
Liam Byrne	*Chief Secretary to the Treasury*
Nick Brown	*Chief Whip*
Patricia Scotland	*Attorney General*
Mark Malloch-Brown	*Foreign Office (Africa, Asia and the UN)*
Pat McFadden	*Business, Innovation and Skills*
John Healey	*Housing and Planning*
Jim Knight	*Employment and Welfare Reform*
Paul Drayson	*Defence (procurement) and Science and Innovation*

Illustration credits

The author and publisher would like to extend their thanks for permission to reproduce the photographs in this book: Andrew Wiard 1; Associated Press 11, 15, 16; Parliamentary Recording Unit 12; *Sunderland Echo* 5, 6; Photoshot 2 and with the kind permission of Valerie Hanson, 3. All other photos are author's own.

While every effort has been made to contact copyright-holders of illustrations, the author and publishers would be grateful for information about any illustrations where they have been unable to trace them, and would be glad to make amendments in further editions.

Index